MW01502564

This is number one hundred and thirty-seven
in the second numbered series of the
Miegunyah Volumes
made possible by the
Miegunyah Fund
established by bequests
under the wills of
Sir Russell and Lady Grimwade.

'Miegunyah' was the home of
Mab and Russell Grimwade
from 1911 to 1955.

SHANNON BENNETT'S

NEW YORK

A PERSONAL GUIDE
TO THE CITY'S BEST

SHANNON BENNETT,
SCOTT MURRAY
& FRIENDS

THE
MIEGUNYAH
PRESS

THE MIEGUNYAH PRESS
An imprint of Melbourne University Publishing Limited
187 Grattan Street, Carlton, Victoria 3053, Australia
mup-info@unimelb.edu.au
www.mup.com.au

First published 2011
Text © Shannon Bennett and Scott Murray, 2011
Design and typography © Melbourne University Publishing Limited, 2011

Designed by Trisha Garner
Typesetting by Megan Ellis
Printed in China by Australian Book Connection

National Library of Australia Cataloguing-in-Publication entry
Bennett, Shannon.

Shannon Bennett's New York: a personal guide to the city's best /
Shannon Bennett and Scott Murray.

9780522858051 (hbk.)

Includes index.

Restaurants—New York (State)—New York—Guidebooks.
Cooking, American.
New York (N.Y.)—Guidebooks

647.957471

CONTENTS

|||||||||||||||||||||||||||||||||||||||||||||||||||||||||||||||||||||||||||||||||||||||||||||||||||||||||||||||||||||||||||||||||||||||||

PREFACE

||||||||||||||||||||||||||||||||||||||||||||||||||||||||||||||||||||||||||||||||||||||||||||||||||||||||||||||||||||||||||||||||||||||||||

I have been fortunate to be a regular visitor to Manhattan, mainly because the word 'No' doesn't seem to be in my vocabulary when approached to cook for good causes and help raise money. This is not because I'm a nice person at heart—not by any means—I just have trouble saying 'No' to people's faces. Trust me, I'm working on it.

Out of the hard work and plenty of fun times cooking in some great places—from the Consul General's house, Hudson Hotel and Waldorf=Astoria to the Lincoln Center and the Natural History Museum, where I cooked in the great hall under the huge replica of a blue whale—came the opportunity to co-write this book. I hope it will give you, the diner-traveller-reader, the insight into why I think—sorry, why I know—New York is the most exciting food city outside of Paris.

I find the diversity amazing in New York. While its Chinatown may be similar to many in the world and its nightlife is not as glamorous as in Paris, on the whole New York is more energetic and fun. It is also one of the only cities in the world where there is still big money and which, in many ways, plays on naïveté. The voice of one person can control so many things, good or bad.

The journo who writes about a restaurant in his popular newspaper column rates a place out of five stars. If it is a good rating, the town flocks to the restaurant, and so do the other publications. Most of the other reviewers follow suit in their admiration. Of course, there is always the occasional other who disagrees just for the sake of it.

If it's a bad rating, the town ignores the restaurant. Nowhere else in the world, apart from Melbourne or Sydney, can one reviewer make or break a restaurant. That is why there is such an amazing array of great restaurants in New York, serving at such a high level. Sure, the town has a huge population and all the money that goes with that, but this is a culture that attracts competitiveness. Its energy is incredible and infectious. So are the concepts within the restaurant culture that blend the old with the new, sandwiched between the everyday.

Australians are used to eating the array of different cuisines representative of our multicultural society. This blend of cuisines will one day be classified as 'Australian', and our culture will perhaps be identified through food. What we grow, raise, catch and eat may very soon—let's say in fifty years' time—be the only thing that we can really say defines us as Australians. Have a think about it. Architecture? Climate? Language? What we wear? Our art? A hot dog or a cassoulet? I believe how we prepare and eat and think about food will inform everything else.

We have a lot to proud of in Australia, but we can also learn a lot from New York and where it is today.

So, what does New York mean to me? Woody Allen films, opulent apartments with snobby doormen and The Russian Tea Room. For some reason, this dining space sticks in my mind as the pinnacle of what all grand dining rooms in New York should feel like.

The restaurant of the 1990s was a place called Union Pacific, next to the Elite model agency offices on Broadway. While I was working for Marco Pierre White in the Big Apple, all that people could talk about was how hard it was to get a table at his 200-seater. There was no discussion about the food. In fact, I don't think anybody even knew if the food had a particular theme! It was a lot about just getting a table.

What defines New York to New Yorkers? Pastrami on rye, hot dogs from street vendors, seafood bars at train stations? Great Italian food served in a fine-dining environment: is that the old New York?

Recently, with the increased focus on the 'celebrity chef' and the Top 50 Restaurants awards (agree with them or not), the industry has had a huge injection of new energy, leading to a new clientele of restaurant-seekers. New York has been the biggest beneficiary of this. It has revitalized the names of such greats as Jean-Georges Vongerichten, Dan Barber, Daniel Boulud, Mario Batali and Tom Colicchio, and, of course, made new names out of David Chang, Wylie Dufresne, Alex Stupak, Scott Conant, Missy Robbins and Australian Shaun Hergatt.

This is what takes me back to New York again and again. The reason I find it the most exciting food city outside of France is not because of its history but because it is making history. Dining at Per Se is like dining at a three-star in no other city. The big problem with some brilliant restaurants around the world is that they could be anywhere in the world. What I want to know when I eat a meal in a restaurant is where I'm eating, to feel and live the moment knowing I'm in a specific place, and that it's real, that I am eating something that is an expression of the city.

What makes Per Se so quintessentially New York is that it is so hard to get into, the chef, Thomas Keller, uses great regional ingredients mixed with the world's best (such as Alba truffles), and the restaurant overlooks Columbus Circle and Central Park from an upmarket shopping centre. Only in New York could this combination occur.

All important travel and food books need to be a reference to the past, incorporate the now and predict the future. I want this book to be relevant even when it becomes the past. I hope it will be a book that you can walk along the street with and not be labelled as a tourist with a travel book but as a foodie heading to their next story-filled destination.

Make your way to this monolith of concrete now before New Yorkers realize just how good their food really is. Ignore *The New York Times* and its rating system—they were wrong to crucify Ducasse and they know it—and go to taste and savour, and stay in some of the best boutique accommodation on the planet.

Shannon Bennett

A WORD FROM SCOTT

|||||||||||||||||||||||||||||||||||||||||||||||||||||||||||||||||||||||||||||||||||||||||||||||||||||||||||||||||||||||||||||||||||||||||||||||||||||||||||||

Shannon and I are great mates, who travel together whenever we can, admiring different lands and delighting in the foods they produce. We both have a healthy passion for three-star restaurants, which is why France has long held a special place in our hearts. We equally love Italy, and spend even more time together there, but its food has so far not seduced us in the same way French food does.

Shannon Bennett's Paris came out of our shared experiences in the City of Light, and its warm reception meant the happy opportunity for us to do more books. The unanimous next choice: New York.

Shannon has been to New York several times recently, and I more than fifteen, though mostly some time ago. As the Paris book reveals, we both believe a visit to a great restaurant twenty years ago can say as much about it as a visit just yesterday, but we both felt it was important to revisit New York to challenge previously held wisdoms while discovering new ones.

Shannon is a profoundly busy man and arranging to have a coffee with him can take weeks of strategizing and careful planning. Arranging an overseas trip together is ... well, in the lap of the gods.

Of course, Shannon may not be that busy; perhaps he has just worked out how much of his life he wants to share with me! Apart from being appalled by my near-certifiable dislike of Chardonnay and unshakeable fondness for Grenache and the simpler wines of Southern Rhône, Shannon also thinks I am the world's grumpiest food critic. (I am actually not a critic, but a filmmaker and writer; visiting great restaurants is simply a great passion.)

Despite any reservations about my company, and the memory of my firmly standing up for our rights at La Maison de Marc Veyrat still biting deep, Shannon feels a key part of our writing these books is that we travel together, whenever possible.

Sadly, this proved too difficult in New York. I guess Shannon was sad about that, though he never said. So, while I went again in May 2010, Shannon met up with friends Adam and Harry there a month later.

Usually, my critical toughness doesn't bother Shannon too much, but he is convinced I went to New York in May 2010 in a state of even-greater-than-usual grumpiness and he feels I should alert readers to this fact, so that they can take any preventative medicine they have to hand.

The story begins when Shannon and I went to Istanbul in September 2009 for a concert tour by David Helfgott. The tour translator turned out to be a very charming young lady, and she and I became good friends.

Better yet, we became gourmet companions. I have rarely met anyone who so loves going to restaurants, who expresses such unbridled joy at a tasty or well-plated dish. (Sadly, my gorgeous wife does not get the same joy from three-star restaurant experiences. Hotels are a different matter.)

Anyway, my Istanbul friend's dream had always been to go to New York (she was in love with an alternative singer there) and, as she is an excellent photographer, Shannon and I decided she should take photos for the book. She would also be great company as we ate our way through more than twenty restaurants and stayed in ten or so different hotels.

Alas, this young woman fell in love with an American living in Istanbul the week before going to New York and I was left to face New York's finest alone.

I don't think this made any difference to my appreciating what New York has to offer. After all, the first three restaurants I went to were SushiAnn, The Modern and Benoit, and I loved them all. And on the fifth day I went to SHO Shaun Hergatt, one of the great restaurant experiences of my life.

But, if on reading my contributions you agree with Shannon that I am a grump, I do apologize. Truly, I am very nice to cats, fascinating women and anyone with access to a good bottle of Vacqueyras.

FRIENDS WITH OPINIONS

Shannon would like to thank all his friends who contributed their thoughts to this book:

PATRICIA AMAD
CEO, The Present Company (Melbourne), daughter of famed chef Abla Amad (Abla's) and owner of the best handbags I have ever seen

HARRY AZIDIS
Harry the Hairdresser and legendary man about Melbourne. Visited Vue de monde in its first week and when cutting Scott's hair a week later demanded Scott eat there

ANTOINETTE BRUNO
CEO and Editor-in-Chief, *starchefs.com* (New York). Mother figure to all the great American chefs

MELANIE DUNEA
Photographer (New York) and creator of the well-known book, *My Last Supper*, and its sequel. Knows more about New York restaurants than the restaurants themselves

ADAM GARRISSON
Property investor (Melbourne). I am still trying to figure out where he gets his clothes

SHARLEE GIBB
Program Manager, Melbourne Food and Wine Festival

PATRICK GORMAN
National Sales Manager of Visy Logistics (Melbourne). School friend, and a mentor to Curtis Stone

PAULA GORMAN
Puts up with Paddy and I'm not sure why

ANDY Y HATA
Senior Sommelier, Vue de monde (Melbourne)

GILLIAN HELFGOTT
Wife and manager of David Helfgott; hates being called 'Jillian'

MARVIN HOLDER
Front of House, Vue de monde (Melbourne), and best player on the VdM soccer team. Needs to be tested for steroids

LARRY KARDISH
Senior Curator, Department of Film, MoMA (New York)

BRYAN LLOYD
General Manager, Operations, Vue de monde (Melbourne). Sleeps in his suit

LUKE MANGAN
Restaurateur (Sydney, Melbourne, Tokyo, P&O Cruises, Singapore). A good mate from Melbourne who has finally opened a restaurant here after gracing the rest of the world (including Danish royalty) with his presence

EDDIE AND CARLA MCGUIRE
Still waiting

SIMON MEADMORE
CEO, The Pancake ~~Queen~~ Parlour

COREY MITCHELL
Advertising executive and bourbon-lover (Brooklyn)

MATT MORAN
Owner-chef, ARIA (Sydney and Brisbane), and Harry the Hairdresser's least successful client

NICK ORD
President, Miele Inc. US (New York)

NEIL PERRY
Chef-director, Rockpool Group (Sydney). Will cut off his ponytail for $1000 donated in cash to the Starlight Foundation

TOBIE PUTTOCK
Chef (Melbourne). Am still waiting to catch up for a coffee

SUSI RAJAH
Novelist and yoga entrepreneur (Brooklyn). Has inspired Scott to take up yoga (so he says)

ADRIAN RICHARDSON
Owner-chef, La Luna Bistro (Melbourne). After two drinks he looks a lot like a young(er, good-looking version of) Mario Batali

FRED SCHEPISI
Aspiring film director and acclaimed grape grower (Mornington Peninsula)

ANNA SCHWARTZ
Gallerist (Melbourne and Sydney). The best mother-in-law in the world

JEREMY SINGER
woodsbagot.com (North America). Designing Rialto Plaza

ABBEY SMART
Marketing consultant, Get Smart with Marketing (Adelaide and New York)

CR SERGE THOMANN
Photographer and 'I still can't believe it' Councillor (City of Port Phillip)

FRANÇOISE VILLENEUVE
starchefs.com (New York)

MADELEINE WEST
Actor and writer (Melbourne). Have no idea why she puts up with me. The only person in the world who adds sweetened condensed milk to meatloaf

MATTHEW WILKINSON
Co-owner, Pope Joan (Melbourne). Went to hell and back working for me in his early days

MICHAEL WRIGHT
Managing Director, Moreland Bus Company (Melbourne). Have known him since I was twelve, so nothing else I can say

RAÚL MORENO YAGÜE
Former sommelier, Vue de monde, now food and wine consultant and Sommelier at Comida Bebe. I am still trying to work out what he is saying, but I love him anyway

Plus, special thanks to:
Anna Augustine and Alison Humphries (they'll never have to pay for one of my books again); Tim White (Books for Cooks); Dean Cambray (for the recipe photographs); and Eugenie Baulch.

A NOTE ABOUT VENUE DETAILS

The name of a restaurant (which may have countless variations in guidebooks) is given as it appears on the restaurant website or the signage at the front door.

The prices of set menus and à la carte meals (three courses, unless otherwise indicated, not including wine) are based on recent visits, the restaurant's website and the latest guides. Be warned, however: this is not an accurate science, due to regular changes to menus and seasonal ingredients. A mountain of black truffle, Maine lobster or Californian caviar will also cause the cost to vary!

All the details (addresses, phone numbers, etc.) were believed to be correct as of October 2010, but some may have changed since. Many restaurants in New York sadly have short lives. And, just as we went to press, new editions of the Michelin and Zagat guides to New York came out. We scrambled to include all the rating changes; apologies for anything we missed.

Words highlighted in burgundy throughout the text indicate that a fuller description can be found elsewhere in this book; see Index.

As with restaurants, the hotels names are given as per their websites or the plaque by the entrance. Room prices are taken from the respective hotel websites (choosing a peak-rate date of 15 September 2010 as the standard) and, sometimes, guidebooks (which usually give rates well under the rack rates shown on a hotel website).

All prices are in US dollars.

A NOTE ABOUT SPELLINGS & STYLE

Americans tend to spell a little differently compared to the rest of the English-speaking world. As this is a book about New York, all the menu spellings (for example, chili, rather than chilli) are preserved as per the menus.

Some words have variant spellings: Oscetra, Osetra and Ossetra caviar. A restaurant's menu preference is used.

Place names, such as Time Warner Center, take the official form.

Each restaurant entry includes the name of the chef or chefs, where known. Usually, it is the name of the person who creates the dishes and menu (such as restaurateur Jean-Georges Vongerichten), and is not necessarily (but often is) the person who actually cooks.

In the Paris book, Les Halles and Le Bernardin would be listed alphabetically in the Hs and Bs respectively. But Americans always take into account the Le and Les, so both restaurants are listed here in the Ls.

FINE DINING
THE BEST OF NEW YORK

Fine dining is very difficult to categorize. It can mean any number of things to different people and cultures, from the classical and expensive to the spontaneous and inventive.

Some of what follows is detailed in the Paris book, so feel free to skip at will.

WHAT TO LOOK FOR

Tablecloths should be ironed, with no creases, and be placed on an underlay. The napkins should be linen, alongside silver or artisan-made cutlery. Show plates are then used to enhance the room and give each setting a purpose when it is vacant. Water glasses should be stemmed or styled. The table centrepiece can be anything from a piece of driftwood with the chef's name engraved on it to a Rembrandt Bugatti sculpture. The tables should be spaced appropriately. That normally means no more than ten to twenty-two tables and a maximum of seventy covers. All staff must be appropriately dressed and their roles identifiable. There should be a ratio of at least one staff member to every two guests.

The wine list—of a minimum 450 different bins or labels—should be managed by a team of fully qualified sommeliers. Different wine varieties need different and appropriate glassware, which should be finely made. There should be aperitif and digestive lists.

In a top-class kitchen, everything is made on the premises. As soon as a food is brought in from somewhere else, it becomes generic. Bought puff pastry is an obvious example of laziness. Bread is another: it should have the personality of the proprietor, not that of a commercial baker. It should be a freshly baked artisan product with a choice of several types. If the chef does not want to serve bread, then he or she needs something similar with which to start the meal.

Excellent quality butter must be served at room temperature, with a choice of salted or non-salted butter (upon request).

The dishes should use the finest ingredients and be carefully crafted by a well-trained team of chefs (a minimum of ten). Ingredients that one would not find in standard supermarkets or providores should be highlighted, such as caviar and truffles, aged cheeses, line-caught fish and free-range meats. Pastries and desserts should be of the highest wow factor.

If a restaurant serves food that you know the average home cook could make just as well, then it should not describe itself as a fine-dining establishment. But be careful before making that sort of judgement, as a dish may seem simple but require much effort behind the scenes; many a great chef strives to create dishes that are served simply but are cooked to perfection.

Coffee and tea should always be served with handmade chocolates and/or *petit fours*.

FINE DINING TIPS

Here are a few ideas on how to choose the perfect fine-dining experience in New York.

Selecting a Restaurant

You will either keep visiting the places you know and love, or you will be brave and try new ones. You don't do this by walking down a street and taking a chance. You may get lucky, but the odds aren't good. Anyway, a fine-dining restaurant is usually booked out weeks in advance.

It is far better to plan ahead where you would like to go for your special meals. You can talk to friends, visit restaurant discussion websites or read any of the cornucopia of guidebooks on sale.

USING A GUIDEBOOK

There are two principal guidebooks to food in New York: the annual *Michelin New York City Restaurants* and *Zagat New York City Restaurants*.

Others you might like to consult are the city guides of *Hg2*, *Wallpaper**, *Time Out*, *Lonely Planet* (Encounter series) and *Top Ten* (probably the best pocket guide to all the sights).

There are also daily and weekly publications such as *The New York Times*, which I have already slated, and, much better, *New York* magazine, where Adam Platt writes some very interesting pieces. The annual *New York* issue on Restaurants of the Year is a must.

Michelin For more than a hundred years, Michelin has reigned supreme in France and Europe. Only recently did it decide to tackle the United States, with guides to New York City (the first in 2006) and San Francisco and the Napa Valley (2007).

Both are printed in English and, unlike the France guide where every entry has only a short description, each restaurant in New York gets half a page or, if accorded one or more Michelin stars, a whole page with a photograph.

Michelin pioneered the star rating (technically, they are rosettes but almost no one uses that term). The three categories are explained by Michelin as follows:

★★★ Exceptional cuisine, worth a special journey.
(One always eats extremely well here, sometimes superbly.)

★★ Excellent cooking, worth a detour.

★ A very good restaurant in its category.

Bib Gourmand indicates an establishment offering good quality cuisine at reasonable prices.

The matter of taking a detour isn't an issue in New York; what is important is the relative merits of the fine-dining restaurants on offer.

Everyone has their own point of view, but there is a fair degree of agreement on the truly great fine-dining experiences of New York. However, there will always be a debate about whether a two-star restaurant deserves three, or whether a three-star has faded slightly and ought to be downgraded.

Zagat Zagat is in many ways the opposite of Michelin. The restaurants listed in Michelin are judged and written about by nameless experts, usually based on one visit per year, but more frequently if the restaurant is of high international standing.

Zagat has no reviewers other than those people who decide to write in with their opinions and ratings out of 30. These ratings cover Food, Décor and Service, but, if someone tells you Per Se has a rating of 28/30, they mean the food.

Many applaud the democratic and non-élitist stance of Zagat, but it has its drawbacks, just like Michelin.

Michelin or Zagat? The answer to which guide is better is easily settled: use both.

The 2011 Michelin lists five three-star restaurants in New York: Daniel, Jean Georges, Le Bernardin, Masa and Per Se. There are ten two-stars: Alto, Chef's Table at Brooklyn Fare, Corton, Gilt, Gordon Ramsay at The London, Kajitsu, Marea, Momofuku Ko, Picholine and Soto.

The 2011 Zagat gives two restaurants 29/30 for food (Sushi Sasabune and Le Bernadin) and eight 28/30 (Per Se, Daniel, Jean Georges, Sushi Yasuda, La Grenouille, Annisa, Gramercy Tavern and Eleven Madison Park).

I have eaten at four of the five restaurants to which Michelin gives three stars, and Scott at three of them. I would only have given the ultimate accolade to Le Bernardin, and also possibly to a restaurant Michelin gives just two stars, Corton.

I think Michelin has somewhat dropped the ball here and doesn't fully understand or appreciate New York dining. It does a brilliant job in France, but in New York I am not convinced.

Not that Zagat is any more accurate. There are too many inconsistencies, with pizza parlours and basic burger joints scoring higher than restaurants run by the brightest chefs in the city. There is also an obvious overrating of everything Japanese. Very few of the sushi restaurants Scott and I visited deserve what Zagat gives them.

So, while both guides are fascinating and essential, both are flawed.

USING THE INTERNET
There are several websites that are great fun to read (though, sadly, the number has been dropping of late). These sites can be a great guide, especially the ones where reviewers spend a thousand words or more on a meal. These reviews also tend to be illustrated with photographs of the different courses. However, as the camera of choice is usually a low-pixel mobile phone, the images can make even the greatest dishes look unappetizing.

Beware, though, what you read on the Internet. There is no guarantee a site has any critical standards that it is trying to live up to.

Some sites that are worth looking up are:

noraleah.com
dailycandy.com/new-york/food-drink
menupages.com
nymag.com/restaurants
newyork.timeout.com
gastroville.com—world food but a great site
andyhayler.com—especially good for young chefs

tripadvisor.com—has some great reviews and rankings, but it is a little hard to use as the opening page lists restaurants by popularity. What you need to do is sort them in order of their rating (out of 5) to see what readers consider the best restaurants in New York

Booking a restaurant
Essentially, you have two choices. One is to ring. You usually can only start doing this exactly one month before the day you wish to visit. Be prepared to ring repeatedly.

The alternative is to book via *opentable.com*, which is used by most restaurants. It is brilliant in that it gives you instant confirmation of available space.

One trick: if you become a member of OpenTable—this is advisable, as it makes the process easier—you cannot make two different restaurant bookings at the same time under the same name. OpenTable will block the second booking, which is just as well as it stops you cancelling one at the last moment and making life tough for restaurateurs like me!

Dealing with difficult waiters

The chance of getting a difficult waiter in a fine-dining restaurant these days is fairly remote. New Yorkers have realized that they need residents and tourists alike, and that they should always be charming to both.

On recent visits, I found the wait staff to be fabulous in just about every restaurant I visited. The best of them are better than any wait staff you will find elsewhere in the world. They are less formal than in, say, France. They don't do things with the same elegance and skill, but their friendliness more than makes up for it.

If you do find a difficult waiter, just relax. Don't let anyone ruin your lunch or dinner. You have travelled thousands of miles to be there; enjoy what there is to enjoy and forget the rest.

À la carte or menu?

I love selecting one of the dégustation menus. It makes everything so much more relaxed. I am happy to walk into any restaurant in the world and tell the chef to cook me whatever he or she likes. I always trust the chef more than an à la carte menu. The chef knows what is particularly good at the time, and what is a little tired and should be deleted from the à la carte menu.

SHANNON'S FIVE MOST EXCITING NEW YORK RESTAURANTS

1. Corton (Paul Liebrandt)
2. Le Bernardin (Eric Ripert)
3. Per Se (Thomas Keller)
4. The Spotted Pig (April Bloomfield)
5. Masa (Masa Takayama)

Restaurants usually offer one or more set menus. Choose the number of courses you feel like, or the one with the dishes that most inspire you. If you want to swap a course from one menu to another, just ask. I have never had a refusal. Just remember that most restaurants these days insist on everyone at the table having the same menu, though they will replace a dish or two for a diner with specific dietary requirements.

Seasonality of produce: what to choose

Rather than study up on what is in season in Upstate New York or the United States in general, at fine-dining restaurants simply put your trust in the chef to be using what is fresh that day at the markets. New Yorkers generally remain committed to using seasonal ingredients, and often organic, so you don't need to worry.

Wine

DEALING WITH A HUGE WINE LIST

Don't. Unless you are a true wine connoisseur, forget about trying to wade through a hundred pages of wines and vintages you have never heard of or tasted. Call over the sommelier.

The other problem with a big wine list, which people don't tend to talk about, is that it removes at least one person from the conversation for up to 15 minutes. That puts a real dampener on the start of a nice meal.

Most New York restaurants, however, list many of their wines on their websites. Download the list and study it at your leisure in the comfort of the your own home; that way, you will arrive prepared. But I still think it is better to ask the sommelier.

FOOD AND WINE MATCHING

Many restaurants now offer a flight of wines to match a dégustation menu. The obvious first advantage of this, when with a group of people, is that everyone knows from the start what the total cost will be. It lessens the chance of someone ordering a wine out of the budget range of other guests.

I also prefer food and wine matches because it makes the restaurant experience so much more relaxing. The chef and sommelier work out these pairings together; they may have spent months perfecting them. How can you hope to compete with that when handed a heavy wine list, not yet knowing how the food will taste?

REGIONAL VERSUS BIG-NAME WINES

Scott and I talk about this all the time. Scott loves regional wines whereas, by preference, I go for the great wines of the world. In New York, you have access to great and rare wines you won't easily find anywhere else. The prices aren't cheap, but you only live once.

SHOULD I ONLY DRINK AMERICAN WINE IN NEW YORK?

The curious thing about most restaurants in New York is that they tend to preference wines from France, Italy and Spain over their own American wines. It is very hard to get American wine by the glass, and if you do find one it could cost $30 a glass or more. Why they don't showcase American wines is a complete mystery, other than the fact that on good wine lists they tend to be very expensive.

It is uncommon to find a bottle of American wine for under $150. A quality $60 Rioja or Châteauneuf-du-Pape can suddenly look very appealing.

As to whether wines from outside America can complement the food, of course they can. But when faced with the greatest collection of American wines in the world, why would you want to drink anything else?

COOKBOOKS BY MASTER NEW YORK CHEFS

Chronological list of recipe books by great New York chefs. The date is of the first American edition.

1. *Charlie Trotter's* (Charlie Trotter, 1994)
2. *The Lutèce Cookbook* (André Soltner, 1995)
3. *Great American Food* (Charlie Palmer, 1996)
4. *The Babbo Cookbook* (Mario Batali, 2002)
5. *Craft of Cooking: Notes and Recipes from a Restaurant Kitchen* (Tom Colicchio, 2003)
6. *Scott Conant's New Italian Cooking* (Scott Conant, 2005)
7. *Asian Flavors of Jean-Georges: Featuring More than 175 Recipes from Spice Market, Vong and 66* (Jean-Georges Vongerichten, 2007)
8. *Ad Hoc at Home* (Thomas Keller, 2009)
9. *The Frankies Spuntino Kitchen Companion & Cooking Manual* (Frank Falcinelli, Frank Castronovo and Peter Meehan, 2010)

WINES TO DRINK IN NEW YORK

As recommended by Raúl Moreno Yagüe

When choosing wines from the United States, one must first browse for specific varietals, then seek out specific regions. After that, look for producers and, finally, vintages.

CALIFORNIA

Because it is a wide region covering most of the west coast of the United States and influenced by the Pacific Ocean, many different styles of wine are produced here. Those to look for specifically are Chardonnay, Pinot Noir, Cabernet Sauvignon and Zinfandel.

CHARDONNAY

NAPA VALLEY/SONOMA VALLEY
Recent vintages to seek: 2007, 2005 and 2004
Producers of note: Kistler, Patz & Hall, Failla, Hansel

....

CENTRAL COAST
Vintages: 2007, 2005 and 2004
Producers: Talley, Foley, Edna Valley, Ridge, Bernardus

PINOT NOIR

SONOMA VALLEY/RUSSIAN RIVER VALLEY
Vintages: 2005, 2003 and 2002
Producers: Williams Selyem, Littorai, Patz & Hall, Kosta Browne, Merry Edwards

....

CENTRAL COAST (SANTA LUCIA HIGLANDS/SANTA RITA HILLS)
Vintages: 2007, 2005 and 2004
Producers: Roar, Pisoni, Sea Smoke, Talley, Fiddlehead

CABERNET SAUVIGNON

Vintages: 2007, 2005 and 2002
Producers: Caymus, Silver Oak, Revana, Ladera, Shafer

ZINFANDEL

Vintages: 2007, 2003 and 2001
Producers: Ridge, Unti, Turley, Carlisle, Four Vines

....

WASHINGTON STATE

Most of the vineyards are in the eastern part of Washington State, where they benefit from rain, constant temperatures and more sunlight hours than California. This ensures manageable growing conditions and favours later-ripening grapes, such as Cabernet Sauvignon, Merlot and Syrah.

The main regions to seek out are Columbia Valley, Walla Walla and Lake Chelan, and the best vintages are 2007, 2005 and 2004.

CABERNET AND MERLOT

Producers: Leonetti, Quilceda Creek

SYRAH

Producers: Betz, Buty, Cayuse, Dusted Valley

....

OREGON

The main grape-growing region in Oregon is the Willamette Valley, which is heavily influenced by the cooling effect of the Eola winds. These winds, in conjunction with the northern enclosure, favour the growing of aromatic varietals such as Pinot Gris, Pinot Blanc, Chardonnay and Pinot Noir. The wines tend to be more structured than those from California.

PINOT GRIS/PINOT BLANC
Vintages: 2008, 2007 and 2006
Producers: Elk Cove, Evesham Wood, Evening Land

CHARDONNAY
Vintages: 2008, 2007 and 2006
Producers: Domaine Serene, Domaine Drouhin, Evening Land, Argyle

PINOT NOIR
Vintages: 2008, 2006 & 2002
Producers: Antica Terra, Domaine Serene, Evesham Wood, Ponzi, Penner-Ash

NEW MEXICO

This is one of the oldest wine-producing regions in the United States and has quite a variable climate. This allows it to produce many different styles of wines, from sparkling and aromatic whites and reds to full-bodied red wines.

Recent vintages to seek are 2007, 2005 and 2004, produced by Gruet, Black Mesa, and St. Clair.

NEW YORK STATE

The third-largest grape-growing region in the United States, New York State is, like New Mexico, one of the oldest producers in the country. There are two main regions: Finger Lakes and Hudson Valley, where you should consider producers before varietals or vintages.

FINGER LAKES
Vintages: 2008, 2007 and 2006
Red Tail Ridge: Riesling
Damiani: Cabernet Sauvignon and Riesling
Dr. Frank: Riesling
Fox Run: Riesling
Lucas: Chardonnay and Riesling

HUDSON VALLEY
Vintages: 2008, 2007 and 2006
Millbrook: Chardonnay, Pinot Noir and Cabernet Franc
Rivendell: Cabernet Franc & Chardonnay
Alison Wines: Cabernet Franc

ACCOMMODATION

HOTELS

The Ratings

Anyone who has travelled to New York will have probably been slightly confused by the star ratings of hotels. This is because the ratings given by the major guidebooks don't necessarily correspond with those used on websites or by the hotels themselves. So, this book has taken a consensus approach.

Choosing the Perfect Hotel

Here are some tricks on how to choose the perfect hotel in New York.

DECIDE WHAT YOU WANT

First, you must ask yourself if you want to stay in five-star luxury near Central Park or tuck yourself away in the romantic atmosphere of a boutique hotel in TriBeCa. In one sense it doesn't matter, because the underground and taxis can easily and swiftly get you anywhere. But why waste time on transport if you can walk? And there are fewer better or safer cities to walk in than New York.

Then, you must decide whether you are a three-, four- or five-star person. If you are unsure, go for a four-star. It will have more than enough luxury and generally none of the stiff formality of some five-star establishments.

DO YOUR RESEARCH

Always go to the hotel's website and check all the photographs. Try and work out how large a room actually is, and don't be fooled by obvious photographic tricks such as the use of wide-angle lenses.

See if the rest of the hotel has what you want: a restaurant, a breakfast room, a private garden or courtyard, public rooms where you can relax and meet friends, a swimming pool and so on. Most important, check what Internet services it provides

(Wi-Fi, LAN) and at what cost. I was furious recently to discover that almost all top hotels charge $15 or more per day for these services. It should be free!

Then go to a commercial booking site, such as venere.com or booking.com, to check their photographs, ratings and reviews. Finally, visit *tripadvisor.com* to read the reviews there (but don't be put off by the terrible photographs taken by guests; they could make The Plaza look like a slum).

Unless you know the travel agent from heaven, you should do this research yourself. An agent is not going to study photos on the Internet to make sure a room is exactly what you want; they won't know if the bright pink wallpaper will thrill or depress you.

Of course, the simplest approach is to just take the advice in this book!

BOOKING

First check the prices on the hotel website. Note also if breakfast is included or an extra charge: this can make a huge difference, especially for two people. You must be careful not to reject a hotel with free breakfast as too expensive and choose one without that in the end will actually cost more.

Then go to booking.com and all the other commercial sites to see if you can get a better price. In New York, you won't find a cheaper rate as often as you do in most other cities, such as Paris.

SHANNON'S TOP FIVE NEW YORK HOTELS

These are my fantasy hotels—where I go for a once-in-a-lifetime experience, for one or two nights, rather than where I stay every time I am in New York. They embody everything New York is about.

1. The Greenwich Hotel (TriBeCa)
2. The Surrey (Upper East Side)
3. The Bowery Hotel (East Village)
4. The Standard (Meatpacking District)
5. Crosby Street Hotel (SoHo)

The main advantage of booking through a hotel as opposed to a commercial site is that you are dealing with the very people who will be looking after you when you are a guest. A request for a room at the back, or a bath instead of a shower, is more likely to be met. You also get a reply about a request from a hotel site; you don't from most booking sites.

Many rack rates will at some stage be discounted, either by the hotel or on an Internet booking site. Remain vigilant.

And have fun choosing!

APARTMENTS

Apartments are the perfect way to spend an extended time in New York, especially with a family. They are also worth considering for a short stay, especially for those who will be dazzled by the food produce on sale and wish to rush back to a kitchen and cook up a feast. There is no doubt that even a moderately talented cook can eat brilliantly in New York after spending just a few minutes at the stove. This is especially true of the prepared food available from a range of stores, from the famous delis and produce-rich markets to the simplest corner store.

Apartments can be much cheaper than a hotel, but you have to make sure making beds and doing housework isn't going to spoil your fun. Of course, several apartment firms can supply maids and cooks.

A group of people can also share a travel experience without being confined to hotel rooms and hampered by the absence of a private communal area.

THE COUNTIES OF NEW YORK STATE

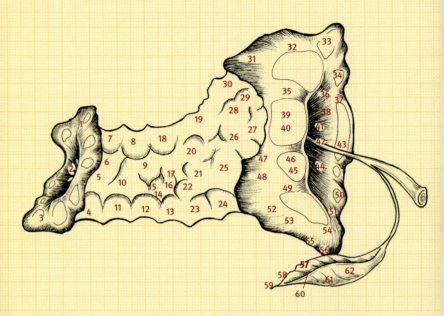

1	Niagara	17	Cayuga	33	Clinton	49	Ulster
2	Erie	18	Wayne	34	Essex	50	Dutchess
3	Chautauqua	19	Oswego	35	Hamilton	51	Putnam
4	Cattaraugus	20	Onondaga	36	Warren	52	Sullivan
5	Wyoming	21	Cortland	37	Washington	53	Orange
6	Genesee	22	Tompkins	38	Saratoga	54	Westchester
7	Orleans	23	Tioga	39	Fulton	55	Rockland
8	Monroe	24	Broome	40	Montgomery	56	Bronx
9	Ontario	25	Chenango	41	Schenectady	57	**New York**
10	Livingston	26	Madison	42	Albany	58	Kings
11	Allegany	27	Herkimer	43	Rensselaer	59	Richmond
12	Steuben	28	Oneida	44	Columbia	60	Queens
13	Chemung	29	Lewis	45	Greene	61	Nassau
14	Schuyler	30	Jefferson	46	Sohoharie	62	Suffolk
15	Yates	31	St Lawrence	47	Otsego		
16	Seneca	32	Franklin	48	Delaware		

Drawing by Madeleine West

DISTRICTS OF MANHATTAN

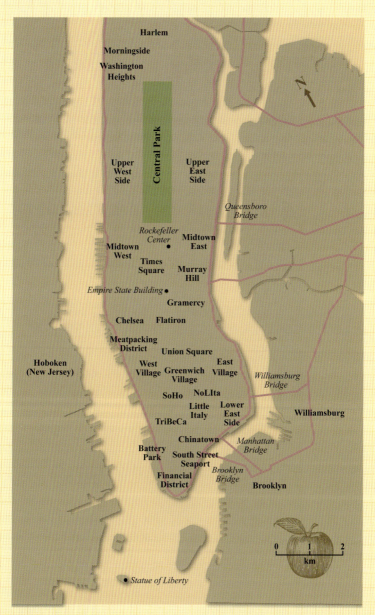

Harlem

Morningside

Washington
Heights

Central Park

Upper
West
Side

Upper
East
Side

Queensboro
Bridge

Rockefeller
Center

Midtown
East

Midtown
West

Times
Square

Murray
Hill

Empire State Building

Gramercy

Chelsea

Flatiron

Meatpacking
District

Union Square

Hoboken
(New Jersey)

West
Village

Greenwich
Village

East
Village

Williamsburg
Bridge

SoHo

NoLIta

Little
Italy

Lower
East
Side

Williamsburg

TriBeCa

Chinatown

Manhattan
Bridge

Battery
Park

South Street
Seaport

Financial
District

Brooklyn
Bridge

Brooklyn

Statue of Liberty

0   1   2
km

DOWNTOWN

BATTERY PARK, FINANCIAL DISTRICT & SOUTH STREET SEAPORT ⌧ TRIBECA ⌧ CHINATOWN & LITTLE ITALY ⌧ SOHO & NOLITA ⌧ LOWER EAST SIDE ⌧ GREENWICH VILLAGE, WEST VILLAGE & MEATPACKING DISTRICT ⌧ EAST VILLAGE

BATTERY PARK, FINANCIAL DISTRICT & SOUTH STREET SEAPORT

FINE DINING

Australian chef Shaun Hergatt proudly flies the flag for fine dining in the southern reaches of Manhattan. His is the only restaurant in this district with a Michelin star or better. Hergatt, who has worked for The Ritz-Carlton group, follows in the fine tradition of many Antipodean chefs by infusing French food with Asian spices. A Spiced Double Duck Consommé with a Chicken Raviolo wrapped with Black truffle and Spring Onion is a typical dish. The restaurant, on the second floor of The Setai, New York (a luxurious condominium), is striking with its Asian-inspired décor, subtle lighting and luxurious feel. Hergatt is now such a major force in The Setai group's plans that there is press speculation that he may be increasingly absent from his eponymous restaurant, leaving the cooking to his Chef du Cuisine Fabien Beaufour (formerly of Eleven Madison Park). No matter who is at the stoves, **SHO Shaun Hergatt** is a major addition to the Manhattan dining scene and won *Esquire* magazine's Best New Restaurant of 2009.

SHO SHAUN HERGATT
Contemporary
Chef: Shaun Hergatt
The Setai, New York
40 Broad Street (between Beaver Street and Exchange Place)
(1 212) 809 3993
shoshaunhergatt.com
Michelin: ★
Zagat: 26/30
Menu: $30 (lunch)/$69

SCOTT: SHO Shaun Hergatt is a stunning restaurant. You know you are in for a special occasion when you exit the Setai's lift on the second floor and see the quality of the decoration that envelops you.

You then walk down a long alleyway between two glass wine cellars with their stunning arrays of wine on show, the golden glow of the Château Rieussecs temptingly radiant. The large restaurant area, divided in two, has a surprisingly gentle light level, embracing and kind on the eyes. At the far end is a floor-to-ceiling glass wall looking in on the immaculate stainless-steel kitchen. You can see everything.

The Chef de Cuisine, Fabien Beaufour, came out to introduce himself in chef Shaun Hergatt's absence. (Hergatt was in Qatar.) Beaufour asked what I would like to eat and I told him I would like him to choose. 'I am excited', he replied most charmingly.

First up were four *amuses bouche* (or canapés as the Americans call them). There was a Ramp-Foam Panna Cotta with Pickled Red Capsicum, a Goat's Cheese Terrine in a Savoury Tuille, a Gravalax of Salmon on a Potato Cake, and a Chicken Bonbon with Green Apple. I wasn't sure about the chicken bonbon, but the rest were stunning and exactly what *amuses bouche* should be: thrilling at first mouthful and designed to get one excited about what is to follow.

The wine waiter was extremely charming and we settled on a Casa Marin Sauvignon Blanc 2007 from Chile and a 2005 Domaine Le Pallières Gigondas, which is now owned by Le Vieux Télégraphe and American wine importer Kermit Lynch.

The perfectly cooked bread rolls (like tiny baguettes) were presented with both normal butter and a divine black-truffle butter.

The first appetizer (a gift) was Smoked Sturgeon with American Caviar and a White Asparagus Velouté. Perfect. Then came a Seafood Niçoise made up of lobster, sea urchin, pickled baby sardines, tiny octopus, tiny green beans and potatoes, and a lobster foam. At first taste, the ingredients seemed a little disparate, unfocused, but as I ate it began to blend into a far more harmonious whole. Like Michel Bras' legendary *Gargouillou des jeunes légumes relevé de grains germées et d'herbes champêtres*, it changed with each mouthful, becoming increasingly magnificent, which every great dish should.

Next came one of the finest dishes of my life: Lynnhaven Goat Ricotta Agnolotti, with Lemon Confit and Spring Sage. The pasta was a little stiff, and folded into the shape of a tiny stuffed envelope, but, as soon as I started to eat it, I realized the pasta was texturally perfect to offset the creaminess of the goat's cheese. The lemon confit was extraordinary, adding sweetness and tang. Covering it all was a wildly generous spread of thinly sliced white truffle. This was a flawless dish.

SCOTT'S FIVE FAVOURITE NEW YORK RESTAURANTS

1. SHO Shaun Hergatt (Shaun Hergatt)
2. Benoit (Alain Ducasse)
3. Le Bernardin (Eric Ripert)
4. The Four Seasons (Fabio Trabocchi)
5. Lexington Candy Shop

Even better (how is this possible?) was the Colorado Lamb, Sous Vide Lamb Belly, with Fermented Garlic and Riberry Jus. This is the best lamb dish I have tasted, even more sumptuous than Yannick Alléno's Lamb with Orange Flower Blossom at Le Meurice in Paris. Forget *agneau de pré-salé* from the salt marshes of Normandie, Colorado lamb reigns supreme—at least in the hands of Shaun Hergatt's kitchen. And riberries go better with lamb than rosemary, which is saying a lot. They are native to Australia, related to cranberries, and the sommelier told me Hergatt was so happy when a huge box of riberries arrived the week before that all the staff have been ribbing him ever since.

The fermented (black) garlic was a brilliant touch, as were the two contrasting textures of lamb loin and belly.

As I still had some Gigondas left, the sommelier suggested I have some cheese. Four arrived, all perfect: Brillat-Savarin, a Chèvre covered in ash and rosemary, a Comté and a Cheddar from Vermont. When I said to the sommelier that the Brillat was so much better than those available in Australia, he told me he was happy to hear this as French customers tend to complain that it tastes so much better in France. A discussion about the cruelty of banning raw-milk cheese followed.

The dessert comprised various citrus fruits sitting (from memory) on a plank of blancmange. It was delicious, a perfect and light end to a wonderful meal.

Michelin rarely gets things wrong (especially in France), but giving only one star to SHO Shaun Hergatt is outrageous. It easily deserves two, if not more, and is leaving more highly rated New York restaurants such as Jean Georges and Daniel in its wake.

RESTAURANTS, STEAKHOUSES, BISTROS, CAFÉS

BOBBY VAN'S STEAKHOUSE

Steakhouse
25 Broad Street
(at Exchange Place)
(1 212) 344 8463
bobbyvans.com
Zagat: 22/30
À la carte: $45–68 (Grill);
$66–88 (Steakhouse)

A traditional Steakhouse (and separate Grill) in a landmark 1898 building, opposite SHO Shaun Hergatt and just down Broad Street from the Stock Exchange. It has the atmosphere of a Texan-style gentlemen's club with wood panelling and chandeliers, and (downstairs in the Grill) a sensational illuminated wall of liquor bottles behind the bar. The steaks are USDA Prime and 28-day dry-aged. There are four other **Bobby Van's** across the city (Park Avenue, East 45th Street, West 50th Street, East 54th Street), as well as one on Long Island.

BRIDGE CAFÉ

Creative American
Chef: Joseph A Kunst
279 Water Street
(at Dover Street)
(1 212) 227 3344
bridgecafenyc.com
Zagat: 22/30
À la carte: $38–52

Claiming a heritage of nearly 220 years, the **Bridge Café** is a Manhattan institution. Set next to the Brooklyn Bridge, 150 metres from the tourist bustle at South Street Seaport, it specializes in creative American comfort food in a warm and embracing atmosphere—rather like an upstate café in a small hippy village. It is most famous for its Corn and Red Onion Fritters, but why not try the Sautéed Crab Cakes or the Basil and Parmesan Crusted Chicken with Early Harvest Tomato Beurre Blanc, Caramelized Shallot Mashed Potatoes and Roasted Carrots? There is a wide selection of beers and fine American wines honouring its tradition as a tavern.

THE CAPITAL GRILLE

Steakhouse and grill
120 Broadway (on Nassau
Street at Pine Street)
(1 212) 374 1811
thecapitalgrille.com
Zagat: 24/30
À la carte: $46–105

This elegant steakhouse is a bastion of WASP powerbrokers. It looks so patrician that you get the feeling you will need to present your shares portfolio for approval at reception before they will let you in. The staff have clearly been chosen to please the eye, as has the discrete decoration, with paintings of the 'great' men of Wall Street hanging on the walls. The food ranges from Bone-in Kona Crusted Dry Aged Sirloin with Caramelized Shallot Butter to Cedar Planked Salmon with Tomato Fennel Relish. The wine list is truly impressive, with 350 different offerings (United States, France, Italy, Germany and South America) and more than 5000 bottles.

Though no longer a favourite of cutting-edge food guides, **Delmonico's** is an American icon, the place where spirited New Yorkers dashed off for fun in countless Hollywood movies. Founded in 1837, it is the birthplace of Eggs Benedict, Lobster Newburg and Baked Alaska. The sumptuous interior and quality table settings still make a night out at Delmonico's feel truly special.

DELMONICO'S
American
Chef: William Oliva
56 Beaver Street
(at South William Street)
(1 212) 509 1144
delmonicosny.com
Zagat: 23/30
À la carte: $56–147

This traditional Italian restaurant has a stunning setting in Battery Place, across from The Ritz-Carlton Hotel, with sweeping (and sometimes windswept) views across lawns to the sea and then, magically, the Statue of Liberty. The panorama is so breathtaking you may fail to concentrate fully on the seafood pasta, fresh crustaceans and classic entrées, such as the Grilled Veal Chop with Red Onion or the *Pollo limone*.

GIGINO AT WAGNER PARK
Italian
Chef: Luigi Celentano
20 Battery Place
(in Wagner Park)
(1 212) 528 2228
gigino-wagnerpark.com
Zagat: 21/30
Menu: $25 (lunch)/
$28 (dinner)
À la carte: $40–75

HARRY'S CAFÉ • STEAK

Steakhouse
1 Hanover Square (between
Pearl and Stone Streets)
(1 212) 785 9200
harrysnyc.com
Zagat: 23/30
À la carte: $65–100

New Yorkers debate forever whether it is better to dry- or wet-age beef, just as they argue over which is the best local steakhouse. Many argue Lower Manhattan's true star is **Harry's Café • Steak** on Hanover Square (at the end of Stone Street). The Café offers simple fare, so serious eaters tend to head to Steak, where the steaks are dry aged for twenty-eight days. The setting is classic American steakhouse with a touch of private club.

LES HALLES

Brasserie
15 John Street (between
Broadway and Nassau Street)
(1 212) 285 8585
leshalles.net
Zagat: 20/30
À la carte: $34–56

Les Halles is writer and television celebrity Anthony Bourdain's take on a French brasserie. Apart from *Moules*, *Frites* and *Brandade de Morue* (Cod with mashed potato and salad), there is a *Gâteau de crabe à la Maximilien* (Crab cake with cilantro, peppers and lemon) and a *Côte de bœuf* for two. Bourdain no longer cooks here, but you can take consolation in a wine list that ranges from a 2007 Jean-Luc Colombo Côtes de Rhone 'Les Abeilles' (Scott's pick, $35) to a 2004 Guigal Côte-Rôtie 'La Turque' (Shannon's, $650). There is a second Les Halles at 411 Park Avenue South in Murray Hill.

MARKJOSEPH STEAKHOUSE

Steakhouse
261 Water Street (between
Peck Slip and Dover Street)
(1 212) 277 0020
markjosephsteakhouse.com
Zagat: 24/30
À la carte: $52–104

Near South Street Seaport, and just a few steps from Bridge Café, **MarkJoseph** is a classic American steakhouse, with restrained lighting, white tablecloths and wooden bistro chairs. You begin with Sizzling Canadian Bacon (you have to live among New Yorkers to understand their passion for all smoked pork products) or Baked Clams before heading on to USDA Prime Dry Aged Porterhouse (for two or more) and Sirloin Steak (for one). There's grilled fish and lobster as well, but you come here for the meat.

NEBRASKA STEAKHOUSE & LOUNGE

Steakhouse
15 Stone Street (between
Whitehall and Broad Streets)
(1 212) 952 0620
nebraskasteakhousenyc.com
Zagat: 21/30
À la carte: $42–103

As famous for its packed Lounge bar as much as its animal protein, the **Nebraska Steakhouse** proves that the moneyed men and women of Manhattan's Financial District like grilled beef. How many fine steakhouses can you fit in so small an area? At least the Nebraska goes an extra mile, offering Roasted Lemon Chicken and *Linguini al pescatore*.

Australian Shaun Hergatt may reign supreme in Lower Manhattan with his eponymous restaurant, but New Zealander Eric Lind is making sure the Kiwis are not forgotten at this Seaport Antipodean love-in. The best produce (green-lip mussels, venison, lamb) is flown in from New Zealand, along with the local wine, including delicious Central Otago pinot noirs, and Steinlager beer. Lind serves comfort pub food that will make any Aussie or Kiwi feel a little nostalgic.

NELSON BLUE
New Zealand
Chef: Eric Lind
233–235 Front Street
(at Peck Slip)
(1 212) 346 9090
nelsonblue.com
Zagat: 18/30
À la carte: $28–42

On the touristy but still fun and atmospheric Stone Street, this Scandinavian restaurant specializes in mouth-watering comfort food such as Swedish Meatballs with Lingonberries or Duck with Braised Red Cabbage, Carrot Ginger Mash and a Cloudberry Reduction. It is all extremely reasonable in price. (There are two other locations: 283 West 12th Street in West Village and Scandinavia House at 58 Park Avenue.)

SMÖRGÅS CHEF
Scandinavian
53 Stone Street (between Pearl Street and Hanover Square)
(1 212) 422 3500
smorgaschef.com
Zagat: 19/30
Menu: $29
À la carte: $34–45

One goes here for the burgers, which range from quarter- and half-pound Kobe Beef and Sirloin to Veggie and Turkey. There are also organic sandwiches, sweet-potato fries, roast chicken, fruit salads and baked muffins.

ZAITZEFF
Organic diner and burgers
72 Nassau Street (between John and Fulton Streets)
(1 212) 571 7272
zaitzeffnyc.com
Zagat: 20/30
À la carte: $9–25

BARS

ANOTHER ROOM
Bar
249 West Broadway
(1 212) 226 1418
no website
5 p.m.–3 a.m.

BIN NO. 220
Wine bar
220 Front Street
(1 212) 374 9463
binno220.com
4 p.m.–midnight

RISE
Hotel bar
The Ritz-Carlton New York, Battery Park
220 Front Street
(1 212) 344 0800
ritzcarlton.com
Noon–1 a.m.

ULYSSES
Pub
95 Pearl Street
(1 212) 482 0400
11 a.m.–3.30 a.m.

LUXURY HOTELS

MILLENIUM HILTON
55 Church Street (between
Dey and Fulton Streets)
(1 212) 693 2001
newyorkmillenium.hilton.com
Rating: 4★
Rooms: 471
Suites: 98
Hotel rates: $430–530

This is a pleasant Hilton, with tasteful furnishings, spacious rooms and stunning harbour views through the floor-to-ceiling windows. A restrained tower of steel and dark glass, the Hilton faces the square where the Twin Towers once stood and new edifices are now slowly rising. Inside, the standard King rooms are Scandinavian in their sparseness, with the King Deluxe more resplendent; either should make you feel comfortably at home. Hilton is proud of its beds and linen, even if the 250 thread count is dwarfed by those of other hotels (should you worry about such things). Whatever they lack in trendiness, Hilton hotels work, because they have all the comforts and technology you need without the deficiencies of some boutique addresses.

SHANNON: I hate Hiltons. I'm sorry, but staying here was like pulling my teeth out with a wrench. There is nothing wrong with the place, it's just a Hilton, that's all. The rooms are decorated as though IKEA decided to let Kevin Rudd come up with a limited edition design: bloody boring, with corners you keep knocking into. Then there's Wi-Fi you have to pay for and breakfast where the fruit comes from the same people who supply all the airlines. Can someone please answer this: why do all cheap buffets and business-class airlines offer green melon? No one likes it—in fact, everybody hates it—so, please! It's up there with out-of-season strawberries.

Staying here strikes a very sombre note, though. Peer out your generous window and you look straight into Ground Zero. It's a poignant reminder that we should stop whining about green melon.

If budget is an issue and you get a great deal, stay here and spend the money you save on food elsewhere in the great streets off Broadway, which is just a stone's throw from the right-hand-side door. Be wary of the trappings that go with being in a tourist area, such as petty crime and cheap souvenirs.

If you are travelling to the Big Apple for the first time with the girl you one day want to marry, don't stay here.

The Ritz-Carlton is the only five-star hotel in Lower Manhattan. With views over the harbour and the Statue of Liberty or the city, the rooms have the quality one expects from one of the world's premier hotel brands. The standard rooms are a large 39 square metres and are beautifully if unostentatiously furnished, with outstanding beds (is there ultimately anything more important in a hotel room?), a separate shower and marble bath (all hotels should have them) and fluffy bathrobes (ditto). There is even a tripod telescope should you be facing the water. The service throughout the hotel is what you expect from Ritz-Carlton. There is also a spa and fitness centre, but no pool. And don't worry if you can't book a harbour view, be happy with the sparkling city lights of Downtown Manhattan. The Museum of Jewish Heritage is also across the road. The only negatives are the blandness of the hotel's exterior and that it sits in an isolated and sometimes desolate part of Battery Park, separated from Downtown life by some rather busy streets.

THE RITZ-CARLTON NEW YORK, BATTERY PARK
2 West Street
(at Battery Place)
(1 212) 344 0800
ritzcarlton.com
Rating: 5★+
Rooms: 259
Suites: 39
Hotel rates: $495–695

THE STATEN ISLAND FERRY

Just like in the movie *Working Girl*, people really do commute from Staten Island to Lower Manhattan and vice versa. The ferry ride is the perfect way to see New York from the water and get an up-close view of the Statue of Liberty without the long waits. I recommend getting on board one hour before sunset, buying a beer at the concession stand and standing at the back of the boat to see Manhattan disappear for the 25-minute ride. Upon arrival, everyone must exit the boat and then get right back on for the return trip. Be sure to run to the front of the boat; you won't want to miss the views. The best part? It's free.

Melanie Dunea

OTHER HOTELS

GILD HALL

15 Gold Street
(enter on Platt Street)
(1 212) 232 7700
thompsonhotels.com
Rating: 3★
Rooms: 126
Hotel rates: $430–480

The Thompson Group has done more than most to revitalize the boutique-hotel scene in Manhattan. **Gild Hall** is perhaps the least well known of the Thompson establishments (see 60 Thompson, Smyth and Thompson LES), but it is a small gem in its own way. Like all the group's hotels, it attracts the young and well cashed, but this time (no doubt in sympathy with its near–Wall Street locale) it has the atmosphere of a gentleman's club rather than the modern design statements of its hotels in TriBeCa and Lower East Side. The small entrance is inviting, the public rooms plush and the guest rooms masculinely decorated (huge brown leather headboards, tartan throw-rugs on the foot of the king beds, high ceilings with brass chandeliers and marble bathrooms). The Library Bar is all dark wood and leather, with (quite oddly, but it works) a dining table and red velvet chairs placed in the middle. Gild Hall is the sort of place *Playboy* would have waxed lyrical about in the late 1960s.

THE WALL STREET INN

9 South William Street
(between Weaver and
Broad Streets)
(1 212) 747 1500
thewallstreetinn.com
Rating: 3★
Rooms: 46
Hotel rates: $350–390

This tasteful period-style hotel occupies two heritage-listed buildings (dated 1895 and 1920) on a cobbled lane dating from the seventeenth century. The homely feel comes from excellent reproduction furniture, a quiet ambience and the kind of high ceilings only old hotels and period buildings can provide. There are two levels of guestroom comfort (Superior and Deluxe), both featuring marble baths and ironing boards (always a blessing). The public areas are rather like a private home's nooks and crannies: small, elegant and comfortable.

SCOTT: This is a gorgeous boutique hotel, well located on the historic and sinuous South William Street. The entrance is inviting, with the tiny but charming breakfast room in front and a spacious (and little-used) lounge area to your left. The lifts are dramatic, with immaculately engraved mirrors and beautifully patterned linen insets bordered with dark wooden frames. Not all the rooms are huge, but they are cosy in the nicest way. Everything is immaculate: the carpet, the cherry-wood bedheads, the bathroom (one of the best kept of any I saw on a recent trip to New York), the beautiful and comfortable armchairs. The air conditioning is a little noisy (where isn't it?), but this is basically a hotel without flaws and an abundance of charm. It is also far more romantic than most.

Across the road is the famous Delmonico's, if you want to step back in time, but there is also a French-Scandinavian crêperie a few doors away (with an inviting wine store in between) and a very atmospheric Irish pub, Dubliners. SHO Shaun Hergatt and Bobby Van's Steakhouse are a few steps away. But perhaps most enticing of all is the room service. The meals come from Smörgås Chef Restaurant, in Stone Street at the back of the hotel, which becomes an open-air eating area in warm weather for myriad restaurants.

TIPPING

New York has great service, but you pay for it. Don't forget 20 percent is the norm for all meals in way of a gratuity or tip. Some argue it is 20 per cent of the total before taxes are added, but you would need to be brave to try that on.

Here's what a knowledgeable New Yorker, Francoise Villeneuve of *starchefs.com*, suggests:

I'd say when porters get your bag or help you to the car or hail a taxi from a hotel, a small tip of $1 per bag for example is in order. I wouldn't tip for a mineral water. If you were to order a seltzer or something for which they don't charge, I'd say you should still leave a tip of $1 for their trouble.

At restaurants, 20 percent is standard.

PUMPKIN SOUP

Simple things are often the most revered, so I'm not going to feed you a line that this is something soothing my mother used to make, or that it brings back floods of memories that make me weep. It's just a simple soup that can be a satisfying ameal. Don't add cream or butter—make it special with great fresh bread.

Americans claim the pumpkin as their own, but it is very hard to find on menus other than with a load of sugar added to it in a pie or sponge.

If using butternut pumpkins (these are not preferred), do not add more than 250 ml of stock during the first stage of cooking as they have a high water content.

Oh, and another thing: if you happen to have a spare black or white truffle lying around during the season, add at the table by shaving very generously.

1 tablespoon of duck fat	Over a medium heat and using a heavy-based saucepan, add the duck fat and onions. Cook and stir for 1 minute to remove the astringency from the onions.
1 brown onion, peeled and diced	
3 cloves garlic, crushed	
1 kg pumpkin, peeled and diced	Add the garlic and the pumpkin. Cook for 2–3 minutes, ensuring the pumpkin does not stick to the base of the pan.
1 L of chicken stock (or 1 Knorr stock cube dissolved in 1 L of water), or just enough to cover the pumpkin	Add the stock and bring to the boil on high heat. Once on the boil, reduce the heat and simmer for 40 minutes or until the pumpkin is tender.
sea salt to taste	Using either a hand-held or bench-top blender, process the pumpkin and stock carefully. Blend until smooth. Add sea salt until satisfied.
	Serve as suggested.

SERVING SUGGESTIONS

Optional garnish of 6 tablespoons of fromage frais with 1 tablespoon of thinly sliced chives folded through.

Another option is to micro-plane fresh black or white truffle over the top of each bowl of soup, and serve immediately with warm baguette.

Serves 4

TRIBECA

IN THE WAY OF MANHATTAN
CRYPTOGRAMS,
TriBeCa (OR Tribeca)
IS SHORT FOR
TRIANGLE BELOW
CANAL STREET

FINE DINING

American-born but of French ancestry, David Bouley is one of New York's finest chefs. Some consider his one-star **Bouley** the equal of Manhattan's top three-star restaurants. It is certainly no less sumptuous in its setting, an Italianate space in what feels like the basement of a *castello*, gloriously appointed with beautiful linens, candelabras and plush armchairs. The food aims for the heights, a luxurious journey through Asian-influenced French classicism: Chilled Kumamoto Oysters with Oscetra Caviar, Homemade Radish Pickle, Thinly Sliced Live Sea Scallops and Parsley Juice, or the Long Island Duckling with a Balinese Pepper Crust, White Truffle Honey, Fresh Fava Beans, Japanese Sweet Kabu Turnips and a Ginger, Lemon Thyme and Lemon Verbena Sauce. It's not the sort of food you whip up at home in five minutes. And at $125 for a six-course meal, it is a relative steal.

Bouley once oversaw a number of fine restaurants in Manhattan, including Secession, Danube, Bouley Bakery and Bouley Market. But after being greatly affected by the attack on the Twin Towers—it not only forced the closure of Danube and Bakery, but Bouley set up Green Tarp to feed relief workers around the clock for four years—the master chef has announced he will now concentrate on his namesake Bouley restaurant and his catering business.

BOULEY

Contemporary
Chef: David Bouley
163 Duane Street
(at Hudson Street)
(1 212) 964 2525
davidbouley.com
Michelin: ★
Zagat: 27/30
Menu: $36/48 (lunch)/
$125 (dinner; 6 courses)/
$250 (chef's menu;
7 courses)
À la carte: $62–77

CORTON

Contemporary
Chef: Paul Liebrandt
239 West Broadway (between
Walker and White Streets)
(1 212) 219 2777
cortonnyc.com
Michelin: ★★
Zagat: 26/30
Menu: $85/$145 (7 courses)

Michelin believes there are five three-star and ten two-star restaurants in New York. Of the two-stars, the one with the most buzz and persistent claims that it deserves the highest accolade is **Corton**. The space that was the famed Montrachet for twenty years (and where David Bouley made his name) is now the domain of restaurateurs Drew Nieporent and Paul Liebrandt. Chef Liebrandt honed his skills under Marco Pierre White in London, Raymond Blanc at Le Manor Aux Quat' Saisons in Oxford and Pierre Gagnaire in Paris. In New York, he was chef at Bouley Bakery, Atlas and Gilt. But Corton is the truest expression of his belief in casual but refined fine dining, French traditionalism with modern touches and techniques.

Liebrandt's three-course prix fixe may begin with a Pheasant Egg with White Asparagus, Octopus, Yuzu and Marcona Almond or 'From the Garden', Liebrandt's take on Michel Bras' famous *Gargouillou des jeunes légumes relevé de grains germées et d'herbes champêtres*. Liebrandt uses at least twenty different vegetables, all separately and differently cooked. While his food is not as out-there as, say, Wylie Dufresne's at wd~50, one can see in Liebrandt's pairing of shrimp and rabbit, rhubarb and beef, egg and octopus that he is a chef exploring new taste and textural sensations. And unlike most starred Manhattan restaurants that churn through multiple seatings at lunch and dinner, Corton is only open at night. This is a serious temple to modern food.

SHANNON: I'm gob-smacked. Strolling through the large entryway, you immediately walk into the main dining area and into the world of Drew Nieporent and Paul Liebrandt's Corton. Finally, a New York restaurant that respects the values of Michelin and GaultMillau with its well-spaced table layout.

The creators of this great restaurant came together when Paul was sacked from his position as chef of the well-known Gilt, owned by the Sultan of Brunei. Paul had done a lot to establish Gilt's good reputation. His dismissal was due to a so-called abuse of his duties: running the kitchen on an 80 percent food cost. It also came at the same time as a senior management member was charged with embezzling $30 million of The New York Palace hotel's revenue over a lengthy period of time. Let's just say that Paul seemed pretty unlucky. But luck seems to bring fortune to those who earn it, and his luck turned around when the legendary Drew Nieporent offered him a partnership and quite possibly his last chance to make it in the Big Apple as a great chef.

My party of three was seated at a beautiful, large, oval-shaped table laden with white linen. What a great idea to have such a unique shape. To my astonishment, the dining room was only three-quarters full. The menu was divided into a three-course choice à la carte for $85 or a tasting menu of nearly all the à la carte dishes at around $125.

We chose the à la carte option. All of us were given a little *amuse bouche* taster of cucumber jelly and a foam concoction that was served in shot glasses. It looked pretty, but was the only item of the night that was pretty underwhelming.

My first course of Foie Gras with Chamomile and Beetroot was a piece of artwork, not only to the eyes but also to the palate. It was so well put together that I treasured every mouthful of this small, ball-shaped foie gras terrine covered in the thinnest layer of beetroot jelly and served with a house-made brioche and berry-infused butter.

Adam had a dish that looked even better than mine. It was simply titled A Taste of Spring: at least twelve varieties of vegetables and fruits in different forms, all plated within an imaginary circular frame on an almost new, shiny white circular plate.

We were all now having a great night and the staff were excellent, except the sommelier was not really identifiable. I think it would have been great if she were in a classic uniform. The wine list, despite being all French, was a real encyclopædia of the great wines. It's the only thing that may attract the big-gun New Yorkers from Uptown. Wines by the glass were limited, but matched the cuisine well.

Main courses were even better. I chose Black Bass with Spinach Cannelloni and Spiced Coconut Sauce. Each dish came with small 'sides', one of which was a little cylinder of locally grown potato, hollowed out and filled with delicately cooked cuttlefish served in a miniature silver fry pan. The other side dish was a classic mini Herb-Rolled Salmon Ballontine sitting on a disc of Squid-Ink Brioche.

Adam beat me by a whisker for the best dish with a stunningly plated Maine Lobster Tail resting on a potato wafer that sat on a bed of *lentilles du Puy*. Artistically placed on the rim of the bowl was a roulade of the trimmings of lobster, bound in a mousse with some fragrant herbs, and a piece of the claw. A sauce of kaffir lime was spooned over the dish at the table. To the side, a small serve of lobster tortellini rested in a cloudy broth of the shells. This was really thoughtful food, reminiscent of Pierre Gagnaire in Paris but a little more classically inspired. This guy can cook.

Desserts were really precise and well thought through. I had the 'Gold Bar' with coffee and passion fruit.

To finish, with tea and coffee, three Perspex trays were placed on the table that contained macarons, and hand-dipped and moulded chocolates. I didn't ask what brand of chocolate they were using, but it was so smooth and balanced that I would swear it was either Amedi or Valrhona.

This restaurant is a must and I will take the responsibility and full force of any abuse if you do not like the food at this up-and-coming TriBeCa eatery.

A good tip is to arrive thirty minutes early. If you are into unique vintage clothes, there is a great store next to the restaurant stocking some fascinating local designers.

ANTOINETTE: Corton might be the one high-concept restaurant I'll go to again and again, even after so many tastings and so much travel around the country. I tasted Paul Liebrandt's food ten years ago at Atlas and then again at Gilt, and I knew Paul was one of the most exciting young chefs in America. But at Corton he seems to have finally come into his own. Liebrandt's quiet reserve has ever so gently tempered his conceptual, creative cuisine into something with as much elegance and sophistication as I've seen anywhere. Liebrandt maintains an avant garde approach to food on a backbone of integrity. His outlook is devoted to the principles of spontaneity and diversity, and his menu, which is freely cross-cultural but never unfocused, engages the diner's mind and palate.

MATT: We had the dégustation menu, which was fantastic. Great food. The room I'm not that keen on. The food is more modern, but not so out-there as some other restaurants. It is sort of deconstructed and put together at the table. The sauces are separate.

ADAM: Chef Paul Liebrandt has created a modern French menu where the flavours are very exact and clean. This was one of the best dinners I had in New York and a great experience. The dining room had a simple elegance and the service was attentive and professional.

A large bare-brick space, with bare wooden tables and black-wood chairs, this is an inviting and lively restaurant. Some call the atmosphere 'farmhouse chic'. Chef Marc Forgione's food is brash and lively, modern American with French, Italian, Japanese and other Asian techniques and flavours. (Forgione trained under Kazuto Matsusaka and Michel Guérard, among others.) You can see the world-mix in everything on the short but satisfying menu.

MARC FORGIONE
American
Chef: Marc Forgione
134 Reade Street
(between Greenwich and Hudson Streets)
(1 212) 941 9401
marcforgione.com
Michelin: ★
Zagat: 24/30
Menu: $39 (Sunday brunch)
À la carte: $47–61

Americans are obsessed with 'omakase', where you tell the sushi chef you want to go with whatever he wants to serve you … until you say stop. This can mean a bill ranging from $100 (**Sushi Azabu**) to $400 (Masa). A cheap sushi snack it isn't, but you won't leave hungry.

The highest-rated Japanese restaurant in TriBeCa, Sushi Azabu is in the basement of The Greenwich Grill (hence the confusing website address). But it is none the lesser for it. This sushi is Edo-mae style (sushi rice, diluted vinegar and grated wasabi). There is a detailed menu, but most customers go for the chef's omakase, with all the fish flown fresh from Japan (Toro, Tairagai, Uni). You can also have nigiri, sashimi and simmered nimono dishes. Pair them with sake or shochu.

SUSHI AZABU
428 Greenwich Street
(at Laight Street)
(1 212) 274 0428
greenwichgrill.com
Michelin: ★
Zagat: 25/30
À la carte: $100+ (omakase)

RESTAURANTS, STEAKHOUSES, BISTROS, CAFÉS

BLAUE GANS
Austrian
Chef: Kurt Gutenbrunner
139 Duane Street
(between Church Street and
West Broadway)
(1 212) 571 8880
wallse.com
Michelin: ★
Zagat: 22/30
À la carte: $40–61

Manhattan has three acclaimed Austrian restaurants—**Blaue Gans** in TriBeCa, Wallsé in Greenwich Village and Café Sabarsky on the Upper East Side—all owned by chef Kurt Gutenbrunner.

Formerly Le Zinc, Blaue Gans is a fun and relatively light take on classic Austrian cooking, from Jäger and Wiener schnitzels (pork or beef) to four different sausages (Weißwurst, Bratwurst, Currywurst, Käsekrainer) and 'Blaue Gans Classics' such as Pork Szegendiner Goulash with Parsley Potatoes, and Wild Coast Halibut with Artichokes and Basil Sauce. The wine list specializes in wines from Austria's Wachau Valley, which is just fine as its Grüner Veltliners and Rieslings are among the world's best. Try the Urgestein Grüner from FX Pichler.

BUBBY'S
American
120 Hudson Street
(at North Moore Street)
(1 212) 219 0666
bubbys.com
Zagat: 18/30
À la carte: $33–44

Bubby's Pie Company runs a catering arm and two restaurants, **Bubby's** in TriBeCa and Dumbo in Brooklyn. But it serves far more than just pies. You can start with a BBQ Pulled Pork Slider and move on to Soft Shell Crab with Brown Butter, Parsley, Fried Capers and Sautéed Spinach.

MELANIE: A local diner with a very American neighbourhood vibe, Bubby's is always packed on the weekends. Super child-friendly, they park your stroller, give you a highchair and have a shelf of toys for the kids to play with. The time to go is definitely brunch. They excel at breakfast food like waffles and pancakes. No matter what time you go, you must try the milkshakes. They are so thick I swear you could turn them upside down and nothing would drip out. Yum. While you are waiting for a table and devouring the delicious hot biscuits they bring you, go downstairs and take a photo in the photo booth; it's a great souvenir.

The hugely popular **The Harrison** specializes in comfort food: from Gilled Pork Chop with 'Hoppin John' Black Eyed Peas and Crispy Pancetta to New York Cheesecake with Honeyed Pistachios and Vanilla Cherries. The atmospheric wood-panelled and mirrored dining area is irresistible, even when warm weather might wish to entice you to try the large outdoor seating area. Owner Jimmy Bradley (The Red Cat in Chelsea) has the magic touch.

THE HARRISON

American
Chefs: Jimmy Bradley,
Amanda Freitag
355 Greenwich Street
(at Harrison Street)
(1 212) 274 9310
theharrison.com
Zagat: 24/30
À la carte: $42–72

MELANIE: Walking into The Harrison, I am always reminded of summers in The Hamptons on Long Island. The dining room has such a relaxed vibe, even though it is a white-tablecloth kind of restaurant. Sitting outside has its bonus as you can see the whole of TriBeCa bustling by. If it's on the menu, try the English-Cut Lamp Chop with Rosemary, Baby Carrots, Anchovy and Fennel; it's delicious. The Skillet Calf's Liver with Bacon Braised Mustard Greens, Confit Shallots and Mustard Sauce is tasty and tender, though I wish there were more shallots. Do not skip the potatoes. I don't care what sort of carb-free diet you are on, the Potato Purée is exquisite and the Duck-Fat Fries thin, crunchy and addictive, especially if you dip them in the mayonnaise. The Oat Ice Cream Brownie Sandwich with Sazerac Caramel and Pecans is really extraordinary. I wish they would do it 'to go'.

LOCANDA VERDE

Italian
Chef: Andrew Carmellini
The Greenwich Hotel
377 Greenwich Street
(at North Moore Street)
(1 212) 925 3797
locandaverdenyc.com
Zagat: 24/30
À la carte: $65–80

Chef Andrew Carmellini made his name at A Voce, particularly for his dish of Sheep's Milk Ricotta with Sea Salt and Herbs. Carmellini was enticed over to The Greenwich Hotel, where he has made **Locanda Verde** one of the area's culinary hot spots. The menu is classic Italian, Carmellini specializing in small plates of antipasti that are so much part of Italian cooking in its homeland. The pasta ranges from the traditional to the more unusual and southern (Goat Cheese Agnolotti with Burro Fuso, Lemon and Sundried Calabrian Peppers). The Fire-Roasted Garlic Chicken for Two is the sort of trattoria cooking one often dreams of but is hard to find. The setting is spectacular, with wooden tables and metal bistro chairs, the walls stacked with wine. It is the perfect movie set for a romantic Italian adventure. It is also the perfect place for breakfast; order the ricotta.

TOBIE: Oftentimes I'll go to a restaurant because it's popular and, as a chef, I must check it out to see what all the fuss is about. Usually, it's difficult to live up to the hype, but Locanda Verde, an Italian taverna, totally exceeded my expectations. I could eat here every day.

Locanda Verde is big and airy and, at 6 p.m. on a Wednesday night, totally crammed with people. The menu is incredibly authentic thanks to head chef Andrew Carmellini, who I hear signed an exclusive seven-year contract with the partners who own the restaurant (one of whom is Robert De Niro), and pastry chef Karen DeMasco, whose dessert menu is a veritable taste-bud teaser. The food here is not flashy and you won't find a foam or a smear in sight. What you will find are simple, beautifully cooked dishes.

We began with Steak Tartara Piedmontese with White Truffles and Quail's Egg, and Burrata with Peperonata Agrodolce, Dandelion and Almonds. For main course, I had Veal Agnolotti with English Peas and Smoked Pancetta, which was one of the best things that has ever disappeared into my belly, and my wife had Trofie with Basil Pesto, Gaeta Olives and Parmigiano Reggiano. It was all so yummy we hardly talked over dinner; we were so busy concentrating on eating and making 'mmmm' sounds.

After all that, we felt full but decided we could possibly fit in a little chocolate ice cream, if not one of the richer desserts. I would go back for that ice cream alone. It was rich, creamy and made of premium chocolate, possibly Valrhona. My wife and I fought each other for every mouthful.

The service was really sharp and friendly without being intrusive. Our waiter had excellent wine knowledge and we trusted him to pick the wine to match our meals, which he did perfectly. This is my kind of place, and I will be back with bells on.

NEIL: Locanda Verde in TriBeCa has a terrific chef, Andrew Carmellini, who is doing some beautiful Italian food, along with a good small wine list and a smaller reserve list of heavy-hitting Italians at great prices. We had some crostini of Blue Crab and Fava Bean, followed by Asparagus and Soft Cooked Egg Salad, *Trippe alla parmigiana* and a cracking burrata and eggplant salad—and that was just for starters. To follow we had a yummy Meatball Slider and two wonderful pasta dishes—one a Trofie with the Classic Pesto and the other a Rigatoni with Lamb Bolognaise, Ricotta and Mint, another great dish. The pasta was cooked to the moment. Fire-Roasted Garlic Chicken followed and we were rubbing our tummies. Add to this the option to eat at the bar close to Aussie bartender Naren Young, who always seems to end up behind the stick at places with outstanding food. This is the perfect place to settle into an empire state of mind!

MATT: Great fresh pasta.

....

This is a stunning den of iniquity, exotic food and libation. The menu has Portuguese (Manila clams with choriço and leeks) and Chinese (black bean and chilli) dishes, along with a drinks and wine list that will keep everyone happy. There is even a fine tea selection, as every half-decent restaurant should have. The décor—a serpentine bar facing a dazzling wall of bottles, basic wooden bistro chairs and glasses, marble tables, posters and objets d'art (including rather spooky dolls)—reminds one of Macao's shady past. With its *Casablanca*-dim lighting, this is an unforgettable place.

MACAO

Macanese-Chinese
311 Church Street
(between Lispenard and
Walker Streets)
(1 212) 431 8750
macaonyc.com
Zagat: 18/30
À la carte: $31–45

....

SHANNON'S FAVOURITE NEW YORK TREATS

BURGERS

See main text for restaurant details.

If you are looking for a great burger, there's Shake Shack—provided you can be bothered lining up in Madison Park. It has been in a lot of recent films. The day I went to eat there, a *CSI* episode was being filmed. Prices are cheap; a burger is only $6.

Corner Bistro in West Village is also in the running: great burgers with a large menu and a very busy place. I loved the fries here and I also recommend it for a late nightspot.

Nicolas, the general manager of Per Se and The French Laundry, says this is his favourite place in New York for a burger and beer late at night after service.

Minetta Tavern also has a large number of fans.

Back Forty in East Village around 10th Street has the best grass-fed burger in town. Many like this because it does not have as much fat as a grain-fed burger. This is also the place for a great range of cocktails.

Matsugen, another star in Jean-Georges Vongerichten's firmament, is many things. Some go to this elegant shared-table restaurant for the seiro soba noodles, which are served either cold (as with Toro Grated Yam) or hot (Ebi Tempura Giant Prawn). Others prefer the sushi or the sashimi (omakase is popular). Apart from a wide range of Japanese appetizers, there is also grilled Sirloin Steak, Kurobuta Braised Pork Belly and Black Cod with Miso. There really is a world of Japanese specialities on offer, priced accordingly.

MATSUGEN
Japanese
Chef: Jean-Georges
Vongerichten
241 Church Street
(at Leonard Street)
(1 212) 952 0202
jean-georges.com
Zagat: 23/30
Menu: $26 (lunch)/
$38 (dinner)
À la carte: $45–100

FRED: Stunning Japanese from Jean-Georges Vongerichten.

. . . .

This breathtaking place is bold, stylish and sensuous—or totally over the top—depending on your taste. Certainly, the carved ice sculpture of Buddha sitting in the middle of a pond strewn with rose petals, under a huge temple bell with its insides painted red and inscribed, is a jaw-dropping sight. But it doesn't stop there: the food is just as dramatic, be it a tiny fish skewered and sitting over a smoking block of wood, thinly sliced Kobe beef sizzling on a hot river stone, or rice cracker–coated flash-fried asparagus standing in a row like Tuscan pines. (There is also a more discreet Midtown Megu at 845 United Nations Plaza.)

MEGU
Japanese
62 Thomas Street
(between Church Street and
West Broadway)
(1 212) 964 7777
megurestaurants.com
Zagat: 24/30
Menu: $125
(omakase dinner)
À la carte: $45–111

. . . .

NOBU

Japanese-Peruvian
Chef: Nobu Matsuhia
105 Hudson Street
(between Franklin and
North Moore Streets)
(1 212) 219 0500
noburestaurants.com
Zagat: 26/30
À la carte: $36–100

So much has been written about **Nobu** in the world press that there is little left to say. This is the first of the worldwide chain, opened in 1994 by Drew Nieporent (of the Myriad Restaurant Group) and chef Nobu Matsuhia, with partners Robert De Niro, Meir Teper and Richard Notar. A famous and fabulous fusion of Japanese cooking and South American cuisine (Peruvian, Argentinean), it pioneered such classic dishes as Yellowtail with Jalapeno, and Black Cod with Miso. David Rockwell's interior, evoking the Japanese country-side, is surprisingly restful, despite the ever-present buzz. Michelin originally gave it one star, but has since taken it away as Nobu restaurants began to take over the world. However, there are those who find it just as irresistible today as nearly twenty years ago.

MATT: If you are going to go to a Nobu anywhere in the world, the one you should probably go to is in New York. Have all the classic Nobu dishes.

....

NOBU NEXT DOOR

Japanese-Peruvian
Chef: Nobu Matsuhia
105 Hudson Street
(between Franklin and
North Moore Streets)
(1 212) 334 4445
noburestaurants.com
Zagat: 26/30
À la carte: $36–100

Originally a 1998 extension of Nobu, **Nobu Next Door** quickly proved to be independent of spirit and became its own place. The menu mirrors Nobu's, but has a no-reservations policy, which means you have a fighting chance of getting in. Instead of the Japanese countryside décor of its big sister, designer David Rockwell has gone for the seaside, with seaweed blan-kets and fishing nets.

....

THE ODEON

Brasserie
145 West Broadway
(between Duane and
Thomas Streets)
(1 212) 233 0507
theodeonrestaurant.com
Zagat: 20/30
À la carte: $45–60

The Odeon is a much-loved and -visited brasserie, with classic French-American food served in a beautiful Art Déco setting. There is a dark-wood bar, wood panelling and de rigueur globe lights. You can begin with a Mixed Green Salad or Steak Tartare before trying the Pan-Roasted Arctic Char with Fava Beans, Baby Zucchini, Hen of the Wood Mushrooms and Sorrel Sauce.

....

A no-reservations restaurant and bar from Employees Only partner Matt Abramcyk.

SMITH & MILLS
American
71 North Moore Street
(between Greenwich and Hudson Streets)
smithandmills.com
À la carte: $28–51

Terroir is a wine bar–restaurant favoured by top chefs after they finish work. The house speciality is charcuterie, but there is a sizeable range of small plates (Bruschetta with Whipped Lardo; Baccalà Balls) and more substantial entrées (Double Loin Steak of Colorado Lamb). There is a second Terroir in East Village at 413 East 12th Street.

TERROIR TRIBECA
Italian
24 Harrison Street
(between Greenwich and Hudson Streets)
(1 212) 625 9463
wineisterroir.com
Zagat: 24/30
À la carte: $26–48

NEIL: Terroir is a new set of wine bars. We visited the one in TriBeCa. Fab wines by the glass and bottles from all over the world, with terrific advice from part-owner and sommelier Paul Grieco. A nice food program of snacks, cheese, charcuterie, fried stuff, salads and the self-proclaimed best panini in New York makes this a great place to drop in for a quick drink, a snack and glass of wine, or even a full meal.

Robert De Niro tends to get all the publicity, but **Tribeca Grill** is another of Drew Nieporent's Myriad Restaurant Group (along with Corton, the three Manhattan Nobus and Centrico), with which De Niro is in partnership. Located on two floors of the Tribeca Film Center, Tribeca Grill opened in 1990 and has been a hit ever since. It has long been a film-world hangout, but the other arts are well represented, too. The food is reasonably priced and reassuringly yummy, ranging from Sautéed Jumbo Lump Crabcake and Poached Maine Lobster to a Grilled Berkshire Pork Chop with a Cassoulet of Spring Beans. If you still need a reason to go, it has more than 300 different Châteauneuf-du-Papes, the world's largest selection. And that is just a fraction of the wines that are on offer.
RECOMMENDED: NICK, FRED

TRIBECA GRILL
American
Chef: Stephen Lewandowski
375 Greenwich Street
(at Franklin Street)
(1 212) 941 3900
myriadrestaurantgroup.com
Zagat: 22/30
À la carte: $43–83

WOLFGANG'S STEAKHOUSE

Steakhouse
409 Greenwich Street
(between Beach and
Hubert Streets)
(1 212) 925 0350
wolfgangssteakhouse.net
Zagat: 25/30
À la carte: $60–100

Wolfgang Zweiner was headwaiter at Brooklyn's legendary Peter Luger Steakhouse before branching out on his own. His flagship restaurant, **Wolfgang's**, is on Park Avenue, but he has this sibling in TriBeCa (as well as another on 54th Street, and in Waikiki and Beverly Hills). You come here for USDA Prime Dry Aged Porterhouse. It is served for two, three or four (meaning solitary diners have to either eat a lot of meat or settle for filet, sirloin or rib eye). Don't forget the creamed spinach. Like all good steakhouses, there is grilled fish and lobster. The dining room is an elegant long room with a highly decorated curved ceiling, white tablecloths, wooden chairs and a polished floor.

BARS

BRANDY LIBRARY

Bar
25 North Moore Street
(1 212) 226 5545
brandylibrary.com
5 p.m.–1 a.m. (Sun–Wed),
4 p.m.–2 a.m. (Thurs),
4 p.m.–4 a.m. (Fri–Sat)

M1-5

Bar
52 Walker Street
(1 212) 965 1701
m1-5.com
4 p.m.–4 a.m.

LUXURY HOTELS

|||||||||||||||||||||||||||||||||||||||||||||||||||||||||||||||||||||||||||||||||||||||||||||||||||||||||||||||||||||||||||||||||||||

Though not in Greenwich but TriBeCa (it is named after the street it resides on, not the area), **The Greenwich Hotel** is one of the most publicized hotels in New York. With Robert De Niro as one of the owners, it has been featured in countless travel articles and fashion photo shoots, largely because it epitomizes Downtown chic—at a price. The highlight may well be the interior swimming pool, lit by Japanese lanterns. There is also a Japanese spa, Shibui, which almost every upmarket hotel seems to need these days. The hotel's restaurant, Locanda Verde, is one of the finest Italian establishments in Manhattan.

THE GREENWICH HOTEL

377 Greenwich Street (at Hudson and Franklin Streets)
(1 212) 941 8900
thegreenwichhotel.com
Rating: 4★
Rooms: 75
Suites: 13
Hotel rates: $495–725

SHANNON: Okay! Have found it—the hotel that best sums up New York. It doesn't have amazing city views, nor does it have the quintessential doorman, nor is it in the bustle of Midtown or the opulence of the Upper East Side. In fact, it's in TriBeCa. This area reminds me of an historic theme park, with cobblestone streets and great old-fashioned shopfronts behind which are stores of passion and content. Take the Johnson Trading Gallery at 490 Greenwich Street: it represents a handful of artists who make installation-type furniture and fixtures.

The Greenwich Hotel's creators—Ira Drukier, Richard Born of BD Hotels and Robert De Niro—have created a residence rather than a hotel. The artworks that adorn the hotel's first floor are by De Niro's late father. The love of art and a connection to a story—and I'm a true believer that everything we love in life we love because it has a story to tell—give this first floor a private-club feel.

I recommend the room I stayed in: 403. It has a great little balcony (and there are not a lot of them) overlooking the back courtyard. I showed the missus my room on Skype and she said, 'It looks like you are in Venice', as I pointed the camera from the laptop out towards the open French doors onto the balcony. She was right: it does have that industrial yet uniquely romantic feel. I wished she were with me, especially when I rummaged through the free (with the exception of alcoholic drinks) minibar and the complimentary snack basket that seemed to include every nostalgic American candy. There was a jar of candy sweets, including butternut cups, discreetly placed on a stunning 'like it's been there for a hundred years' armchair with little bite-size packets of different favourites.

The oversized television actually seemed out of place here. I simply didn't want to watch television. The balcony was my TV.

The Japanese spa is well worth visiting. Massages are not cheap, but the gym and pool are down there, so I checked it out. The pool is one of the only indoor pools featured in lists of the Best Boutique Hotels and that alone made me choose this hotel. The gym is huge and empty all the time I am in-house.

The hotel is full of wonderful surprises at every turn, especially once you realize the effort that has gone into the sustainability and craftsmanship of the fit-out, with almost every material being reclaimed.

Locanda Verde, the hotel's Italian restaurant, was created by a team of people, including the hotel owners, who wanted a neighbourhood eatery that spilled out onto the street and was embraced by the locals. I think that has been achieved. The breakfast menu is limited, but has all you need, with an Italian twist and great Illy coffee. Friends Melanie and Nigel, who live very close by and know their restaurants, really recommend it, so it is worth checking out for dinner if staying close by. You might even be lucky enough to see the great man himself hidden behind a cap sipping espresso at the coffee bar, as I did the morning I happened by.

The Greenwich is all that a great hotel can be, and that is a home away from home. The only issue I had was having to check out of such a wonderful experience!

....

SMYTH

85 West Broadway
(at Warren Street)
(1 212) 587 7000
thompsonhotels.com
Rating: 4★
Rooms: 96
Suites: 4
Hotel rates: $499–650

The Thompson Hotels' entry in the TriBeCa market is the **Smyth**, a bold challenger to The Greenwich Hotel and the Tribeca Grand as the area's premier hotel. Newly built, it makes an impressive sight on the corner of West Broadway and Chambers Street. The bedrooms are well sized (the smallest, the Queen Superior, is 28 square metres), with blonde-wood headboards, Scandinavian-style chairs and footstools, and designer wood panelling. The marble bathrooms have translucent glass showers (but not peek-a-boo as is increasingly common these days), while the rooms have plasma screens and Dean & Deluca–stacked minibars. There are two hotel bars: the Lobby, with its studded green leather sofas, modernist Brazilian chairs and fabric walls, and the Cellar Cocktail Lounge.

....

The luxury hotel pioneer of the 'Triangle Below Canal', the **Tribeca Grand** opened in 2000. It has long reigned supreme, even if now challenged by The Greenwich Hotel (2008) and Smyth (2009). Certainly neither of those recent upstarts has a lobby to equal the spectacular space at the Grand, which intentionally evokes the Prairie style of Frank Lloyd Wright. The rooms are serene and comfortable, but whether the eclectic selection of furniture and objects is to everyone's taste is another matter. However, it is certainly oddly homely. Few who stay here will dream of staying anywhere else when Downtown. The Church Lounge caters for breakfast, lunch and dinner, priding itself on its signature cocktails, some of which it invented (Tartini, The Perfect Ten).

TRIBECA GRAND
2 Sixth Avenue
(1 212) 519 6600
tribecagrand.com
Rating: 4★
Rooms: 196
Suites: 7
Hotel rates: $401–605

OTHER HOTELS

New York has surprisingly few bearable budget-priced hotels. One good exception is the **Cosmopolitan**, in the south-west corner of lively TriBeCa, and close to Chinatown and Little Italy. The cutest room may well be the cheapest: a mini-loft with the double bed up the stairs, though there are no arm-chairs. So, if crashing somewhere other than on a bed is a must, get a double room with sofa for $10 more. There is no room service (with so many cafés and delis in Manhattan, this is hardly a problem; Le Pain Quotidien is just steps away), but there is free Wi-Fi and satellite television. The lobby is welcoming and, while the hotel's design is hardly award-winning, this is a pleasant hotel in the heart of bohemian Manhattan at a great price.

COSMOPOLITAN
95 West Broadway
(at Chambers Street)
(1 212) 566 1900
cosmohotel.com
Rating: 2★
Rooms: 125
Hotel rates: $195–235

One of the trendiest hotels in TriBeCa is the **Duane Street Hotel**. It is featured in many guidebooks and rightly so. It has such boutique requirements as plasma televisions and glass-encased showers with rain shower heads. Close to a proposed stay, you may find rates on the Internet are less than those quoted here.

DUANE STREET HOTEL
130 Duane Street
(between West Broadway and Church Street)
(1 212) 964 4600
duanestreethotel.com
Rating: 3★
Rooms: 45
Hotel rates: $340–399

HARRY IN TRIBECA

See main text for restaurant details.

For fancy dining, my friend Donald recommended that I 'absolutely must without question make a reservation at Corton'. Donald has some very good tips, but I was a little hesitant about following up on all of them—he also suggested I try a sleazy gay bar nearby in East Village called The Cock (where The Hole used to be).

Shannon and Scott had heard good things about Corton, and so it was on the list and booked. I was with Adam, and as usual we were running late to meet Shannon.

On the way I stopped while Adam continued on. I had gotten distracted by J Crew. It looks like a converted bar, but this was an Aladdin's Cave of cool nautical gear, vintage watches and casual sports jackets and shoes. It was all very masculine. I bought up big time.

I tried to blend in with the two Italian male-model customers who were also admiring the vintage stripy-banded Omega watch I was holding. When I was told the price, I nodded and slowly put down the watch, saying in my best Aussie-Italian accent, 'Si, si, bello.' Still, I got carried away. Three shopping bags later—no, four; I did buy those beautifully hand-sewn Quoddy boat shoes—I stumbled into Corton, ready to meet my mates as if it were a blokey *Sex and the City* moment, shopping bags and all. Oh no, everyone was well suited up. I should have bought that chequered jacket in the window.

The cool waitress, sporting a number-one clipper haircut, suit and designer glasses, noticed my bags, smiled and squealed, 'Ooh, you've just been to the J Crew flagship store!' I immediately felt relaxed. I think the lads were impressed and hopefully forgave my lateness. It was only later I read on the website that Corton's staff uniforms are also by J Crew.

Corton is the place to take someone for a special dinner. The room has minimalist design features that work really well. It is a combination of subtle, modern French–Japanese design elements, soothing, with vine-like branches embossed onto a feature wall. The award-winning designer-architect is Stephanie Goto, who is also the design brain behind a number of other fine New York eateries, including Monkey Bar, Morimoto and Buddakan.

This eye for design is what the food is all about and, I have to say, it was by far the best meal experience I had in New York. The food presentation was like an intricate display of food architecture. If you could describe the season 'spring' in a dish, then Adam's meal looked the part. Each vegetable was arranged and displayed on the plate as if it were the most precious jewel. The meals were incredible. I commented to Shannon that this kind of dedication reminded me of his food.

Before we finished, four tiers of delicious chocolates and sugared jelly cubes were put before us. The chef, Paul Liebrandt, came out to greet us warmly. He knew who Shannon was and had a staff member who had worked at Vue de monde—funny what a global world it is these days. He also asked about his friend Gordon Ramsay and how he was going with Maze in Melbourne.

Feeling content, we went for a warm summer-night walk and opted for an evening cocktail at Smith & Mills instead, which we had spotted one morning. Adam ditched Shannon and myself for a 'kind of date', which was fair enough as we both had partners back home whom we were starting to miss.

Across the road, all you see is an old wooden stable door with no signage at all. This place doesn't need it. Step inside and it is like a film set from Jean-Pierre Jeunet and Marc Caro's *Delicatessen*: rusty metal, lead-light windows, a classic zinc bar, plush bench lounges and industrial bar stools. It had the feel of an old French workingman's bar, but very stylish and hip. This was my kind of place.

We ordered two old-fashioned cocktails. My martini came in a rustic, stemmed glass as thick as a jam jar. There was an olive plonked into it. No toothpick here; you had to fish for it. The martini was good—I liked the elegant roughness of it all.

Towards the end of the evening, I went to the bathroom, which is made from an old vintage elevator and quite amazing. I got back and Shannon had already paid for the drinks.

As we left, he said he was a little amazed that a small group had turned up and just took over my vacant seat, even though he told them it was taken. But remembering a similar experience at Fette Sau in Brooklyn, I just said, 'Don't worry mate, this is New York.'

SHANNON'S NEW YORK RECIPES

WARM CHOCOLATE MOUSSE

This is the simplest recipe I know. Serve it with fresh seasonal fruit. I have included two versions below: the dinner-party version that uses crème anglaise (French custard sauce for those of you who support Collingwood!) and the healthy kids' version that can be knocked up in less than five minutes with a couple of egg whites instead of the crème anglaise. Make sure to use great-quality couverture chocolate.

Why include this recipe in a book about New York? Well, because it's simple and exciting. It makes you feel king of the kitchen without the ego, makes you feel good just like the city does, and it also reminds me texturally of those great deli sundaes—just like mock whipped cream but only better.

The best chocolate brands for the job are Valrhona, Amedei from Tuscany and Weiss. All these brands are available in good-quality providores.

250 ml crème anglaise (or pasteurized egg whites)

250 g dark couverture chocolate, between 65 and 70 percent bitterness, melted

1 cream whip gun

2 CO_2 charge bulbs

Ensure the crème anglaise is warm. Combine the crème anglaise (or egg whites) and melted chocolate together with a whisk until smooth and shiny.

Add the mixture to the cream whip gun. Charge it twice and attach the appropriate nozzle, such as a fluted one. Shake vigorously and gently squeeze the mousse into serving dishes. Keep warm in a bain-marie until ready to serve. The mousse will hold in a warm place for 2 hours.

Serve warm with poached pears or fresh berries or, if feeling decadent, warm chocolate cake.

Serves 4

CHINATOWN
& LITTLE ITALY

RESTAURANTS, STEAKHOUSES, BISTROS, CAFÉS

Little Italy does not have the dangerous zing it once had. Mafia dons just don't get whacked at dinner like they used to. However, it is still worth venturing there for an Italian experience, and a good one is **Da Nico Ristorante**. The inside is as plain as plain can be, but the sun-dappled outdoor eating area is a winner. The food is home-style cooking, from *Vitello Marsala* to *Osso buco Milanese*, and very affordable pizzas (*Margherita* for $10, *Quatro stagioni* for $12). Accompany it with a Nero d'Avola from Sicily or, if you are feeling flush, a Sassicaia Tenuta San Guido. You could have an American or Australian red, but why?

DA NICO RISTORANTE
Italian
164 Mullberry Street
(between Broome and
Grand Streets)
(1 212) 343 1212
danicoristorante.com
Zagat: 22/30
À la carte: $38–75

As the name implies, this is a temple to dim sum with some twenty-five varieties, all cooked to order. A Dim Sum Platter (ten pieces) costs just $12. Other Chinese dishes are available, from fluffy seafood rice to roast chicken with fried garlic stems and strips of salt-baked pork. The downstairs area is preferable with its tiled floor, metal chairs, round tables and white linen. Upstairs is a riot of red wallpaper and white plastic chairs—not that the flow of steaming buns and dumplings will give you time to notice. **Dim Sum Go Go** was opened by Colette Rossant, the French-born author of *The World in My Kitchen*, *Return to Paris* and *Madeleines in Manhattan*.

DIM SUM GO GO
Chinese
5 East Broadway
(at Chatham Square)
(1 212) 732 0797
no website
Michelin: Bib Gourmand
Zagat: 20/30
À la carte: $20–45

About the cheapest way to eat fresh seafood in New York is to visit **Fuleen Seafood**. There are the obligatory (and always dispiriting) fish tanks at the front and a rather bland interior, but people come from afar for the Dungeness crab cooked in the incendiary Harbour style. You can inspect your fish before it is cooked and, if you prefer something other than seafood, the Peking Duck is well regarded. There is a lunchtime special at a mere $5.50.

FULEEN SEAFOOD
Chinese
11 Division Street (between
Bowery and Market Street)
(1 212) 941 6888
no website
Zagat: 22/30
À la carte: $5.50–55

GOLDEN UNICORN

Chinese
18 East Broadway
(between Catherine
and Market Streets)
(1 212) 941 0911
goldenunicornrestaurant.com
Michelin: Bib Gourmand
Zagat: 21/30
Menu: $14 (lunch)/
$23 (dinner)/$45 (banquet)
À la carte: $15–45

Promoted as Chinatown's first upscale Cantonese restaurant, **Golden Unicorn** opened in 1989 and has been in New York restaurant guides ever since. They are not kidding about the golden in the name: gold is everywhere throughout the interior, with the odd splash of red providing an additional wow factor. The restaurant is not only famous for its dim sum but for the challenge of attracting a trolley-waiter's attention to get some. You could take the easy option and order Deep Fried Seafood Roll or Baked Lobster with Supreme Sauce from the menu. There is a three-course $14 prix fixe that rockets to an outrageous $23 at dinner, but has more courses. How is this possible?

GREAT N.Y. NOODLETOWN

Chinese
28 Bowery (at Bayard Street)
(1 212) 349 0923
no website
Michelin: Bib Gourmand
Zagat: 22/30
À la carte: $16–28

One of the most celebrated Cantonese restaurants in Chinatown, **Great N.Y. Noodletown** is a basic space, not unlike a million simple Chinese restaurants across the globe. But it has a long menu, cheap prices, is usually packed and has a long stream of people wanting to 'take out' the roast duck and pork.

SCOTT: This is beloved by many guides and my New York–based friends Susi and Corey, especially for the Lo Mein noodles and the Baby Pig on Rice. Susi had adored David Chang's version of Noodletown's Lo Mein at Momofuku Noodle Bar and went in search of the original version. She decided it wasn't quite as good as Chang's, but good enough at a fraction of the price to make her fall in love with the place. And for so simple a dish, it certainly was delicious.

The rest of food Susi and I had, though, was mediocre. The famed baby pig seemed to have grown well into its teenage years and was overcooked and dry, the accompanying rice gluggy. A separate order of baby pea shoots revealed they were not baby in any way and rather tough. Susi was shocked.

Still, this is an authentic Chinatown restaurant that too many people adore for me to write it off after just one lunchtime visit.

Il Cortile is Zagat's equal-highest-rated Italian restaurant in Little Italy, along with Angelo's, Il Palazzo and Pellegrino's. Chef Michael DeGeorgio specializes in Italian Mediterranean cuisine. His most popular dishes include *Gamberi fritte 'Cortile'*, *farfalette con pollo, asparagi e speck* and *Pollo rollatine 'Val d'Aosta'* (chicken stuffed with mushrooms, prosciutto, mozzarella and onions in a light Marsala sauce). There is a simpler and cheaper 'Power Lunch' menu for about $32. The restaurant has several dining rooms, all decorated in the Mediterranean style, but most regulars head for the Garden Room, which is actually a courtyard ('il cortile') with a glass ceiling and a striking display of fresh vegetables and produce on a table in the centre.

IL CORTILE
Italian
Chef: Michael DeGeorgio
125 Mulberry Street
(between Canal and
Hester Streets)
(1 212) 226 6060
ilcortile.com
Zagat: 23/30
Menu: $32 (lunch)
À la carte: $46–74

. . . .

Il Palazzo is best known for its melt-in-the-mouth potato gnocchi, *Linguini Sinatra* (with shrimp, clams, lobster, mussels, mushrooms and pine nuts in a red clam sauce) and *Pollo ai carciofi* (chicken breast with artichokes and tomato).

IL PALAZZO
Italian
151 Mulberry Street
(between Grand and
Hester Streets)
(1 212) 343 7000
no website
Zagat: 23/30
À la carte: $52–74

. . . .

One of the best cheap eateries in the city.

NHA TRANG 2
Vietnamese
87 Baxter Street (between
Bayard and Walker Streets)
(1 212) 233 5948
no website
Zagat: 22/30
À la carte: $18–30

MELANIE: Nha Trang 2 is on Baxter Street in Chinatown and not to be confused with the original one on Centre Street. Walk down the steps into the restaurant and the vibe transports you to Vietnam. This is not a fancy or expensive place, it's just damn good. The service is friendly but brusque, the menus straightforward—some even have photos of the food. My favourite dish is the Rice Vermicelli Summer Rolls with Shrimp; they are amazing. The Shredded Green Papaya Salad is delicious and you can never go wrong with the Chicken with Vegetable in Curry Sauce. The crowd is diverse and, if you look hard, there will probably be a famous chef having a good time.

. . . .

NYONYA

Malaysian
199 Grand Street (between
Mulberry and Mott Streets)
(1 212) 334 3669
no website
Michelin: Bib Gourmand
Zagat: 21/30
Menu: $6.50 (lunch)
À la carte: $17–32

This unpretentious Malaysian restaurant, named after the Chinese women who were obliged to marry Malaysians for political and cultural objectives, is one of the pioneering spice invaders of Little Italy. It has a large menu, ranging from lunch specials for $6.50 and more than twenty appetizers (Squid with Chinese Watercress; Poh Piah) to myriad noodle and noodle-in-soup dishes, and casseroles (Curry Fish Head; Jumbo Shrimp in Assam).

PEKING DUCK HOUSE

Chinese
28 Mott Street (between
Chatham Square and
Pell Street)
(1 212) 227 1810
pekingduckhousenyc.com
Zagat: 23/30
Menu: $27.50 (Peking Duck
dinner)/$32.50 (special
house dinner)
À la carte: $23–38

The first choice for many New Yorkers for classic Peking Duck is this always-packed restaurant on Mott Street. And why not, at the very reasonable $27.50 per person (for four or more), with a choice of two entrées? There is a full menu of other traditional dishes and a Midtown branch at 236 East 53rd Street.

RED EGG

Chinese
202 Centre Street (between
Hester and Grand Streets)
(1 212) 966 1123
redeggnyc.com
Michelin: Bib Gourmand
Zagat: 21/30
À la carte: $15–30

There now seem to be more quality Chinese restaurants in Little Italy than there are south of Canal Street in Chinatown. **Red Egg**, with its *Sex and the City* décor, is one. Newly opened, it has quickly become a favourite site for dim sum. And if the trolley cart doesn't appeal, there is classic Cantonese cuisine and what Michelin calls 'Latin-Cantonese Fusion', with appetizers like *Chicharrón de pollo* (chicken nuggets with salsa de ají) and *Choros a la chalaca* (mussels topped with tomatoes, onion, corn and hot pepper). Traditionalists may prefer the Steamed Dungeness Crab or the Garlic Jumbo Shrimp. The Peking Duck Sliders (carved duck with green onion and hoisin sauce on a bun) sound irresistible.

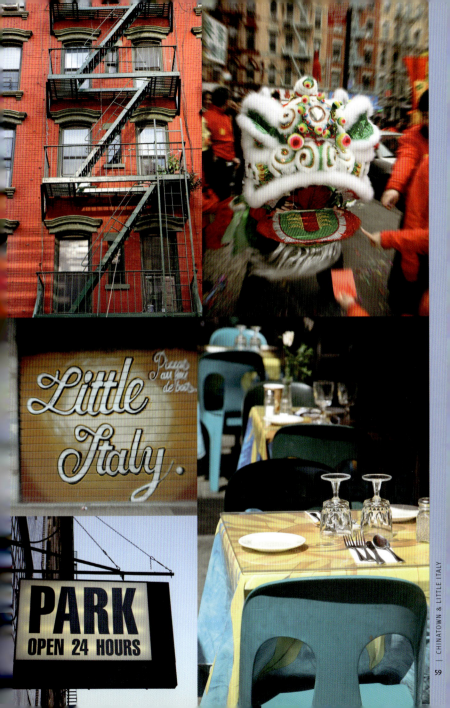

HOTEL

SOHOTEL

341 Broome Street
(at Bowery)
(1 212) 226 1482
sohotel-ny.com
Rating: 2★
Rooms: 100
Hotel rates: $199–269

You don't go to Chinatown or Little Italy for a good hotel (Michelin skips the area altogether), the sole exception being **SoHotel,** which should be in SoHo but isn't. Claiming to be the oldest continuously running hotel in Manhattan (under many names and guises), the hotel's website firmly places the hotel in the history of The Bowery, even though technically it's in Little Italy. (Manhattan can be confusing this way.) Certainly it is just a few steps from the historic thoroughfare, and the hotel has lived through many dark and turbulent times. Only recently with the gentrification of the area has the term 'The Bowery' lost its connotations of skid row and poverty-fuelled depression (though you still see pockets of it here and there). The SoHotel's rooms are rather stark, with exposed brickwork, polished floorboards and little else on view except the beds. Avoid the Standard rooms, which are too small for a couple, even if they have a plasma television and Italian bath amenities. Start with the Deluxe and move upwards.

SHANNON'S FAVOURITE NEW YORK TREATS

CHOCOLATE

Most of these chocolate shops have multiple addresses across New York; only one has been listed.

CHOCOLATE MICHEL CLUIZEL

584 Fifth Avenue (between West 47th and 48th Streets)
(1 646) 415 9126
chocolatemichelcluizel.com

Small, pleasant store, with the world's most bizarre espresso machine (the results, though noisy, are good), a wide range of Cluizel's beautiful French chocolates and a small array of very fine cakes (go for the Opéra).

GODIVA CHOCOLATIER

52 West 50th Street (between Sixth and Fifth Avenues)
(1 212) 399 1875
godiva.com

There are many Godiva stores across Manhattan. It used to be said that the store on Fifth Avenue (now closed) was the only one to sell the original Belgium Godiva chocolates, every other store selling American-made Godiva. Does it matter? If you like the chocolate, provenance is probably irrelevant.

JACQUES TORRES CHOCOLATE

66 Water Street, Brooklyn (between Old Dock and Main Streets)
(1 718) 875 9772
mrchocolate.com

LA MAISON DU CHOCOLAT

63 Wall Street (between Hanover and Pearl Streets)
(1 212) 952 1123
lamaisonduchocolat.com

New York outpost of the famous Parisian chocolatier (and maker of very rich macarons).

LI-LAC CHOCOLATES

213 50th Street, Brooklyn (between Second Avenue and Gowanus Expressway)
(1 718) 567 9500
li-lacchocolates.com

MARIEBELL NEW YORK

484 Broome Street (between West Broadway and Wooster Street)
(1 212) 925 6999
mariebelle.com

MARTINE'S CHOCOLATES

1000 Third Avenue (at East 60th Street)
(1 212) 705 2347
Also at 400 East 82nd Street.

VOSGES HAUT CHOCOLAT

1100 Madison Avenue (between East 82nd and 83rd Streets)
(1 212) 717 2929
vosgeschocolate.com

SHANNON'S NEW YORK RECIPES

WAGYU BURGERS

Nowhere do they make a better burger than on the north-east coast of the USA. The smoky juiciness of a blend of grass-fed and grain-fed beef, intertwined with the simple ingredients of onions, mustard, great Heinz ketchup and thinly sliced mild American cheese, all sandwiched within a semi-sweet soft bun, cuts all other attempts to shreds. Yet separately these ingredients can be nondescript, even terrible.

The worst meal of my childhood—and every fortnight!—was meatloaf. I always wondered why Mum couldn't just get over it and slice the bloody thing, throw it on a char-grill with some sliced onions, sandwich it in a soft bun, and throw away the over-cooked broccoli.

God, how the world goes around. One thing Australia does better in the mince department is Wagyu. The fat from this Japanese breed has a very low melting point, perfect for medium burgers, and, because the cattle are grain-fed, the fat contains a lot of flavour. Wagyu beef is available in all good butcher shops, but don't panic if you cannot source any. Just get some good grass-fed beef and add a little duck fat when binding the mince.

600 g Wagyu mince

2 tablespoons of chopped parsley

½ brown onion, finely minced or chopped

2 tablespoons of Dijon or American white mustard

3 g sea salt

3 g black pepper

4 sweet burger buns

1 tablespoon of cultured butter

1 tablespoon of extra virgin olive oil

4 slices of aged Cheddar cheese

4 grilled bacon rashers

4 teaspoons of mayonnaise

4 teaspoons of sauce bois boudran (see separate recipe)

4 generous handfuls of thinly sliced iceberg lettuce

Combine the mince, parsley, onion, mustard, salt and black pepper together in a mixing bowl. Portion into 4 equal amounts and roll into balls, then gently press each ball to form a patty. Rest the patties in the fridge for at least 30 minutes before using.

Preheat a char-grill or broiler. Cut the burger buns in half. Place onto the char-grill and heat for 20 seconds. Butter the rolls.

Season the burger patties and brush with a little olive oil. Place onto the very hot grill and cook for 90 seconds. Turn and cook for a further 60 seconds. This will deliver a medium-rare burger. Remove and rest the patties.

Assemble the burgers in order of listed ingredients, with one slice of cheese, one bacon rasher, 1 teaspoon each of mayonnaise and sauce bois boudran and one handful of lettuce to each burger and serve.

Serves 4

SAUCE BOIS BOUDRAN

200 ml tomato ketchup

3 teaspoons Dijon mustard

1½ tablespoons finely chopped shallots

½ teaspoon Tabasco sauce

3 teaspoons Worcestershire sauce

300 ml extra virgin olive oil

1 tablespoon sherry vinegar

2 teaspoons chopped chives

2 teaspoons chopped tarragon

Combine the ketchup, mustard, shallots, Tabasco, Worcestershire, olive oil, sherry vinegar, chives and tarragon in a bowl, and stir.

SOHO & NOLITA

SoHo (OR Soho) MEANS
'SOUTH OF HOUSTON STREET'
AND NoLIta (OR Nolita) MEANS
'NORTH OF LITTLE ITALY'

FINE DINING

'Australasian fusion' doesn't necessarily mean an Aussie or Kiwi chef. Brad Farmerie hails from Pittsburgh, but was trained in London at Le Cordon Bleu and under Peter Gordon at SoHo's The Sugar Club. Travel then took him through the Middle East, North Africa and South-East Asia, and from that emerged a personal form of modern world cooking. Not only does his menu feature Carrot and Cardamom Soup with Aleppo Marshmallow, Cilantro Oil and Toasted Pumpkin Seeds, there is Pan Seared Tasmanian Sea Trout on a Salad of Fennel, Green Apple and Pistachio, with Preserved Lemon Yoghurt and Fennel Pollen. You can sense and taste the world in those dishes. RECOMMENDED: FRED

PUBLIC
Australasian fusion
Chef: Brad Farmerie
210 Elizabeth Street
(between Prince and
Spring Streets)
(1 212) 343 7011
public-nyc.com
Michelin: ★
Zagat: 24/30
Menu: $50 (Sunday dinner)
À la carte: $40–65

RESTAURANTS, STEAKHOUSES, BISTROS, CAFÉS

Once a garage and now a lively restaurant with antiques for sale, **Antique Garage Restaurant** specializes in light Turkish fare (kebaps, eggplant salads, grilled spiced meatballs), though influences from other Mediterranean cuisines are easy to pick. At night, candles turn this into a romantic couples hot spot.

ANTIQUE GARAGE RESTAURANT
Turkish
Chef: Utku Cinel
41 Mercer Street (between
Broome and Grand Streets)
(1 212) 219 1019
antiquegaragesoho.com
À la carte: $25–35

One of the highest-rated seafood restaurants in New York, **Aquagrill** offers fresh fish simply cooked and a wide range of the finest oysters and crustaceans. The most famous dish is probably Grilled Atlantic Salmon with a Falafel Crust, Tomatoes and Lemon Coriander Vinaigrette. The most complicated dish is the Truffle-Crusted Casco Bay Cod with Wild Mushroom Ravioli, Roasted Hen of the Wood Mushrooms and Creamed Spinach in a Truffle Mushroom Sauce. (Hen of the Wood mushrooms are everywhere in New York.) Caviar will cost you an extra $95–155 an ounce depending on whether you prefer American or Russian.

AQUAGRILL
Seafood
Chef: Jeremy Marshall
210 Spring Street
(at Sixth Avenue)
(1 212) 274 0505
aquagrill.com
Zagat: 26/30
À la carte: $39–61

AURORA

Italian
510 Broome Street
(between Thomson Street
and West Broadway)
(1 212) 334 9020
auroraristorante.com
Michelin: Bib Gourmand
Zagat: 24/30
À la carte: $35–70

In an atmospheric room of exposed brick walls and wooden tables and chairs, you will find classic Italian food, ranging from *la burrata* (creamy pulled cow-milk cheese from Puglia with beef-steak tomatoes, arugula and pesto) to *il Branzino* (grilled Mediterranean Branzino with rainbow chard and rosemary potatoes). It is the sister restaurant of Aurora in Brooklyn and Emporio in SoHo.

. . . .

BALTHAZAR

French
Chefs: Riad Nasr,
Lee Hanson
80 Spring Street
(between Broadway and
Crosby Street)
(1 212) 965 1414
balthazarny.com
Zagat: 23/30
À la carte: $37–65

One of the most famous restaurant openings in Manhattan history was **Balthazar**'s in 1997. Overnight, Keith McNally's French bistro seemed to be featured in every travel magazine and be part of every glamorous photo shoot on the planet. Yes, it looks spectacularly good (a zinc bar always helps), with more Parisian feel than many Left Bank haunts. As for the food, people keep waiting for it to slip from its opening highs, but all agree it hasn't. The range is wide, from a Fresh Morel Risotto with Green Asparagus and Spring Garlic (although if morels are fresh in autumn, how can they be paired with spring garlic?) to Steak au Poivre with Pommes Frites. The dessert list offers not only the obligatory *Tart Tatin* but also a (startlingly non-French) Pavlova. Balthazar is open from breakfast till late and there is a bakery next door. You really have no excuse for not going. RECOMMENDED: LUKE

SHANNON: A very smart enterprise that is always crowded from early in the morning until late at night. The bakery is also very crowded and not worth entering on a quick visit to New York, given the long wait. The dining room is loud and energetic with a great Parisian-themed bistro fit-out.

The menu is made up of traditional French dishes, mixed with American items the local clientele obviously demand, such as warm sandwiches and very large salads that are not at all French. I have certainly never eaten braised short ribs in Paris!

Simply go for the atmosphere and the Whole Roast Free-Range Chicken, if it is still on the menu, or the half lobster. The shellfish here is excellent, especially the oysters.

I prefer Pastis (which McNally opened in 1999), but I do like the area where Balthazar is located. The action along here is always fun, with some cool clothes shops, good hotels, great little cafés and a great mix of people.

Service is very good and the atmosphere on a Sunday at brunch time is unbeatable. Their Eggs Meurette is a very accurate interpretation, with the farm-fresh, free-range eggs poached in red wine and served with bacon and caramelized onions, and a garnish of flat-leaf parsley. It is great.

It is almost directly opposite the Crosby Street Hotel.

ADAM: On my first night in New York after travelling straight from Australia, I checked into the Crosby Street Hotel with my daughter, Charlotte. (It was her first visit to New York and *the* city that she had most wanted to go to in the world.) Within one hour, we were sitting at a great table in Balthazar, a perfect way to start a visit to New York. I ate Seared Organic Salmon 'Petit Pois à la Française'. We shared a Warm Goat Cheese and Caramelized Onion Tart as a 'starter', then Charlotte ordered a Hamburger and we shared Profiteroles with Vanilla Ice Cream and Chocolate Sauce.

An elderly businessman sitting at the table next to us was reading a book while eating his 'special' steak (no pommes frites, as he described it to us), passing occasional comments and pleasant smiles. The food was predictable but very good, the environment fabulous.

MATT: Balthazar is probably my favourite bistro in New York. I always go there when I am in town. The vibe is great and you always see someone famous. It is always pumping. I think they do close to a thousand covers a day. Just drop in there, casually, and have a meal.

SHARLEE: You can't go to New York without a visit to the iconic Balthazar. It's a wonderful, bustling, French-style bistro that is always packed with beautiful people— and the food is great, too! Find yourself a perch at the bar and enjoy a Lillet Blanc and oysters. For we Aussie girls, remember to take your handbag to the toilet to tip the bathroom attendant.

SERGE: A chic French brasserie in the heart of fashionable SoHo. The converted leather wholesaler's warehouse teams with New York's cool-and-corporate crowd, who dine on traditional bistro fare combined with an expansive and affordable wine list.

FRED: For breakfast and lunch, and after shopping.

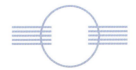

BLUE RIBBON

Contemporary
97 Sullivan Street (between
Prince and Spring Streets)
(1 212) 274 0404
blueribbonrestaurants.com
Zagat: 25/30
À la carte: $34–202

Blue Ribbon is the flagship of Bruce and Eric Bromberg's culinary empire, a classic brasserie with an American twist. The food is as straightforward as it sounds: Pigeon with Toasted Barley, Sweet Potato and Apple; Skate with Potatoes, Bacon and Shrimp; Foie Gras Terrine. And just in case you forget you are in New York, there is Matzoh Ball Soup and Wor Matzoh for two. There is also the almost obligatory raw bar, with oysters, crab, clams and so on. It is one of the best in Manhattan and part of the reason why this late-night haunt (it closes at 4 a.m.) is so popular with off-duty chefs.

Blue Ribbon was such a hit that there are now eight, ranging from Blue Ribbon Sushi to various bakeries and a café in the Brooklyn Bowl.

BLUE RIBBON SUSHI

Japanese
Chef: Toshi Ueki
119 Sullivan Street
(between Prince and
Spring Streets)
(1 212) 343 0404
blueribbonrestaurants.com
Zagat: 26/30
Menu: $75 (omakase)/
$150 (special platter)
À la carte: $33–83

One of the highest-rated sushi restaurants in New York, **Blue Ribbon Sushi** has an astonishing array of *zensai* (appetizers), including Sake Kazu Zuke (broiled Salmon cured with miso and sake lees) and Kanpachi Usuzukuri (thinly sliced Amberjack with yuzu pepper). There are seven soups, countless vegetable and special rolls, and a range of sushi and sashimi platters. Omakase is very reasonable by New York standards at $75. Apart from a large selection of cold sake, the restaurant has a small but intriguing wine list, including whites from the Loire, Spain and Uruguay, and unusual reds from Germany, the United States, Italy and so on. It is almost unfair Manhattan has so many great sushi restaurants, and this is a gem.

ADAM: A whole series of hand rolls of really good quality. It has a cute basement environment with lots of wood. Recommended.

MATT: One of the best places for sushi in New York. What you tend to do in New York is have sushi for lunch and then go out for a big meal at dinner.

A hip hang-out on one of the hippest streets in New York. (There is an offshoot in The Jane hotel.)

CAFÉ GITANE
French-Moroccan
242 Mott Street
(at Prince Street)
(1 212) 334 9552
no website
Zagat: 20/30
À la carte: $25–35

TOBIE: Café Gitane is a NoLIta institution, serving simple French-Moroccan fare for breakfast, lunch and dinner. We stumbled upon it on our first morning in New York, just in time for a late Monday breakfast, so it was very quiet compared to the weekends, when lines can stretch down the street and waitresses supposedly become harried.

On this sunny summer morning, the blue outdoor settings and stripy umbrellas were fresh and inviting, and we happily settled down outside with a *pain au chocolat*, toasted panini and jam, and strong black coffee. This was all simple fare but lovely, and made all the more delicious by the setting and the incredible amount of good-looking people walking by. It was a glorious introduction to New York City.

Lunch and dinner options include Gorgonzola with Walnuts and Honey served with slices of fresh baguette, Baked Pasta with Prosciutto, and Moroccan Couscous with Merguez Sausages. It all looks yummy and is quite inexpensive. The service was friendly and efficient, though we were there at a quiet time of day. Café Gitane accepts cash only.

ED'S LOBSTER BAR

Seafood
Chef: Ed McFarland
222 Lafayette Street
(between Kenmare and
Spring Streets)
(1 212) 343 3236
lobsterbarnyc.com
Michelin: Bib Gourmand
Zagat: 23/30
À la carte: $23–46

Does any Manhattan restaurant have a more enticing name? Come here for a Lobster Roll with Fries and Ed's Pickles or the even-more-famous Lobster Galette with Crème Fraîche. Then there are the more traditional pleasures of Fried Ipswich Clams or New England Clam Chowder. A lot of dishes are listed at 'market price', so the total bill can build.

ANTOINETTE: You're in New York City. How likely is it you'll find a lobster roll this good? But I did, and I keep going back for it, again and again, because it's good enough to rival anything I've had in New England. Huge chunks of sweet, tender Maine lobster practically spill out of a chewy roll, and just enough mayo gives it a perfect touch of tang and creaminess. Sure, you can find butter-poached lobster with caviar and gold leaf in a lot more city restaurants, but you won't find a lobster roll like this. One bite and I'm transported to Cape Cod, without any of the traffic.

SCOTT: Sitting at the bar—something I usually hate, but here there are chairs, not stools—is a joy. This tiny bit of Nantucket is a divine oasis on bustling, dirty Lafayette Street. Everything seems at peace.

I ask for the Lobster Galette, but bizarrely it is not served at lunch. So, I have a Lobster Salad instead. The tail flesh is fine, but the claw is way overcooked (an American preference). The lettuce and tomato are just okay. A 2008 Honig Sauvignon Blanc from the Napa helps.

I probably should have had the Linguini with Clams, which looks great, whereas the Lobster Ravioli is the richest-looking dish I have ever seen, totally drowned in sauce. (Americans do not follow the Italian lead of keeping the pasta sauce to a bare minimum.) Still, the couple eating it, both regulars and at least eighty years of age, are looking incredibly happy and healthy. Most people at the tables deeper into the tiny restaurant are eating an entire lobster each. They are large enough to feed a family.

What I ate was average, but I love the feel of the place and will happily return. If you are staying at the Crosby Street Hotel, consider it your local.

In an industrial space with a dramatic steel-and-glass roof, this simple but spirited Italian restaurant uses organic produce wherever possible. The food ranges from the traditional (Ricotta Agnolotti) to the American-influenced (Crystal Valley Farm Organic Chicken Under a Brick, with Fresh Cranberry Beans, Applewood Bacon and Charred Broccoli Rabe). The pizzas are just as intriguing.

EMPORIO

Italian
231 Mott Street (between Prince and Spring Streets)
(1 212) 966 1234
emporiony.com
Michelin: Bib Gourmand
Zagat: 21/30
À la carte: $34–65

This simple and attractive French bistro (with red geraniums in pots outside its red-framed windows) has remarkably low prices. The $25 dinner menu served between 6 p.m. and 7.30 p.m. is a steal. There are Crispy Sweetbreads with Portabello Confit and Caramelized Leeks or Honey-Lime Glazed Duck Breast with Green Leaf Lettuce, Shiitake Mushrooms and Truffle Sauce. Wine is available by the carafe and half-carafe, along with well-priced bottled wine. For a true Left Bank experience outside Paris, **Jean Claude** is hard to beat.

JEAN CLAUDE RESTAURANT

French
137 Sullivan Street (between Houston and Prince Streets)
(1 212) 475 9232
jeanclauderestaurant.com
Michelin: Bib Gourmand
Zagat: 23/30
Menu: $25
À la carte: $30–45

L'ECOLE

French
462 Broadway
(at Grand Street)
(1 212) 219 3300
frenchculinary.com
Zagat: 24/30
Menu: $28 (lunch)/
$35 (dinner; 4 courses)/
$42 (5 courses)

The dining room of the French Culinary Institute, this is where the students cook for you—and very well, given its 24/30 rating in Zagat. It is food that strives to be modern but is grounded in classic French technique, with appetizers including Braised Pork Belly and Clams in Puff Pastry. The fish can range from Trout to Striped Bass. The four- and five-course dinner menus are exceptional value. It is also a beautiful, light-filled space, so you are not short-changed on décor or ambience.

LOMBARDI'S

Pizza
32 Spring Street (between
Mott and Mulberry Streets)
(1 212) 941 7994
firstpizza.com
Zagat: 23/30
À la carte: $15–40

More than a hundred years old, **Lombardi's** is a national treasure. America's first pizzeria, it sold pizza according to what you could afford (two cents for a slice this big, three cents that big ...). It became even more of an icon after World War II and continued to shine until 1984, when it closed. Re-opened ten years later in a different locale, Lombardi's has managed to impress clients with its pizzas even more than with its history. Proudly cooked in a 'coal oven', the pizzas are as you create them. The restaurant has bare brick walls and gingham tablecloths. What more could you want?

SERGE: Founded by Italian immigrants in 1905, Lombardi's has turned the simple calzone into an art form, and is renowned for its Clam Pizza.

LURE FISHBAR

Seafood
Chef: Josh Capon
142 Mercer Street
(at Prince Street)
(1 212) 431 7676
lurefishbar.tumblr.com
Zagat: 23/30
À la carte: $33–89

Lure is a stylish raw bar and seafood restaurant from John McDonald and Josh Pickard (of Chinatown Brasserie and Casa Lever). The oysters range from Blue Point (Long Island) to Beau Soleil (New Brunswick) and Kumamoto (Washington), the crustacean, sushi and sashimi selections are large, the entrées traditional (Steamed Branzino with Oyster Mushrooms, Scallions, Ponzu and Cilantro). Designed to look as though you are dining on a private yacht, with porthole windows, it is a fun and bustling place.

Jean-Georges Vongerichten's ever-expanding culinary empire ranges across many styles of cooking and several districts of Manhattan. (There were fifteen restaurants by late 2010.) In the basement of the trendy Hotel (The Mercer), Vongerichten's **Mercer Kitchen** is at the centre of contemporary cuisine in SoHo. That doesn't mean it's complex, because a lot of the best cooking in New York is simplicity itself. There's a Tuna Spring Roll with Soybean Paste, and a Roast Chicken with French Beans, Baby Carrots and Mashed Potato. RECOMMENDED: FRED

MERCER KITCHEN
Contemporary
Chef: Jean-Georges
Vongerichten
99 Prince Street
(at Mercer Street)
(1 212) 966 5454
jean-georges.com
Zagat: 22/30
Menu: $26 (lunch)/
$38 (dinner)
À la carte: $40–70

ADAM: A great place to watch people, and the food is good, too.

. . . .

This candle-lit, bare-brick restaurant is a romantic hang-out for starry-eyed couples. It is also considered to have the best and purest Italian food in NoLIta. You can start with an *Insalata puntarella con acciuga* (Chickory salad with anchovies) before an *Orecchiette con crime di rape* (Orecchiette with rape cream) or the classic *Bistecca alla Fiorentina*. The wood-fired pizzas are always in demand, from the *Margherita D.O.C.* to the *Pizza bianca con mortadella*. The wine list is Italian, from the Alto Adige to Campania and Sardinia. If the budget allows, try the Argiolas Turriga 2000. RECOMMENDED: FRED

PEASANT
Italian
Chef: Frank DeCarlo
194 Elizabeth Street
(between Prince and
Spring Streets)
(1 212) 965 9511
peasantnyc.com
Zagat: 24/30
À la carte: $29–52

ADAM: Some of the best simple Italian food I have tasted. They have a wood-fired oven, which they also use for many dishes other than pizza. The Skate I had was simply wood-fired. Prior to that I ate an Italian Tuna salad with beans and cucumber. The desserts were excellent.

. . . .

RAOUL'S

French
180 Prince Street
(between Sullivan and
Thompson Streets)
(1 212) 966 3518
raouls.com
Zagat: 23/30
À la carte: $38–76

Atmosphere, atmosphere, atmosphere. Open now for more than thirty years, the brainchild of two impoverished brothers from Alsace, **Raoul's** is one of the most iconic bistros in New York (and even starred in Martin Scorsese's *The Departed*). The paintings placed thickly on the walls (one a very sensuous nude), the dim lighting and leather banquettes, wooden tables and chairs make this a magical place to visit. The food is said to be classic French, but clearly borrows just as much from Italy and America: Sunchoke Soup with Peekytoe Crab, Asparagus and Citrus Oil; Lake Okeechobee Frog Legs with Green Garlic Risotto and Watercress. Like all good French restaurants in New York, the profiteroles come stuffed with vanilla ice cream (not hideous patisserie cream or custard!) and masses of hot chocolate sauce.

SHORTY'S.32

American
Chef: Josh 'Shorty' Eden
199 Prince Street
(between MacDougal and
Sullivan Streets)
(1 212) 375 8275
shortys32.com
Zagat: 21/30
À la carte: $46–76

The mission statement says it all: 'reasonably priced, seasonal food in an inviting environment'.

ANTOINETTE: Go for the McShorty burger—I promise you'll love it—but stay for the rest of the menu. Chef Josh 'Shorty' Eden is a chef's chef, the kind of guy you want to have feed you after a long night of service, whether you're tucking into a burger or the off-menu-but-doggedly-adored McShorty at brunch. Eden is a New Yorker born and bred, and his neighbourhood restaurant is the end result of more than a decade of working his way through the ranks of some of the city's best kitchens, with twelve years alone under Jean-Georges Vongerichten. Finally in his own place, in his hometown, Eden is serving bold, frills-free comfort food that's ultra-crave-worthy, any time of the day or night.

There are only five tables in this Greek grocery store, but if you are lucky you'll find space to try the salads and meze, the roast chicken, Greek sandwiches, savoury pastries and daily specials. Greek beers and wines, which can be incredibly good but often hard to find, are also available. (There is also Snack Taverna at 63 Bedford Street in West Village.)

SNACK
Greek
105 Thompson Street
(between Spring and
Prince Streets)
(1 212) 925 1040
Zagat: 22/30
À la carte: $8–25

Soups, salads and sandwiches ... and cookies. There are ten stores across New York, including at 60 East 8th Street (Greenwich Village), 555 Fifth Avenue (Midtown East) and 397 Greenwich Street (TriBeCa). RECOMMENDED: MELANIE

'WICHCRAFT
Café
568 Broadway
(between Prince and West
Houston Streets)
(1 212) 780 0577
wichcraftnyc.com
Zagat: 20/30
Menu: $1–10

BARS

EAR INN
Bar
326 Spring Street
(1 212) 226 9060
11.30 a.m.–4.00 a.m.

EIGHT MILE CREEK
Bar
240 Mullberry Street
(1 212) 431 4635
eightmilecreek.com
4 p.m.–4.a.m. (Mon–Fri),
11 a.m.–4 a.m. (Sat–Sun)

MERCBAR
Bar
380 Lafayette Street
(1 212) 966 2727
5 p.m.–2 a.m. (Sun–Tues),
5 p.m.–4 a.m. (Wed–Sat)

N
Bar
33 Crosby Street
(1 212) 219 8856
Noon–2 a.m. (Sun),
11.30 a.m.–2 a.m. (Mon–Thurs),
11.30 a.m.–4 a.m. (Fri–Sat)

PEGU CLUB
Bar
77 West Houston Street
(1 212) 473 7348
5 p.m.–2 a.m.

TOAD HALL
Bar
57 Grand Street
(1 212) 431 8145
Noon–2 a.m.

XICALA
Bar
151 Elizabeth Street
(1 212) 219 0599
5 p.m.–2 a.m.

ZINC BAR
Bar
90 West Houston Street
(1 212) 477 8337
6 p.m.–3 a.m. (Mon, Fri–Sat),
6 p.m.–2.30 a.m. (Tues–
Thurs, Sun)

SHANNON'S FAVOURITE NEW YORK TREATS

HOT DOGS

CRIF DOGS
113 Saint Marks Place (between
First Avenue and Avenue A)
(1 212) 614 2728
crifdogs.com

The most famous hot dogs in New
York, by far. The website lists fifteen,
but the owners keep asking top
chefs to invent new ones, including
Paul Liebrandt from Corton. His dog
includes squares of pan-fried foie
gras and a julienne of truffles. For
$25, it's a bargain.

   Crif Dogs also does burgers and
fries, shakes and beers. PDT is out
the back.

LUXURY HOTELS

||||||||||||||||||||||||||||||||||||||||||||||||||||||||||||||||||||||||||||||||||||||||||||||||||||||||||||||||||||||||||||||||||||||||||||||||||||||||

This new SoHo establishment from Firmdale Hotels (and thus a proud sister to London's Charlotte Street Hotel) is a dramatic design statement, with eye-catching use of colour (or lack thereof) in the spacious bedrooms, each individually designed by Firmdale's Kit Kemp. The rooms are filled with light from the factory-like floor-to-ceiling paned windows. The views yell freedom and air, even if they are not the most beautiful and dramatic in Manhattan. The Crosby Bar, overlooking a verdant garden, makes the hotel's boldest statement, with brightly coloured, dangling light-shades and striped couches pressed back to back. (It is a tight squeeze getting through to a drinking spot.) Breakfast is served here as well as afternoon tea, which is kindly made available all day. The hotel entrance has a film-set feel, which ties in with the Sunday Night Film Club in the hotel's state-of-the-art cinema. One can enjoy a three-course meal and movie ($50) or a drink, bar snack and flick ($25). RECOMMENDED: FRED

CROSBY STREET HOTEL
79 Crosby Street (between Spring and Prince Streets)
(1 212) 226 6400
firmdale.com
Rating: 5★
Rooms: 86 (including suites)
Hotel rates: $495–650

SHANNON: My guests and friends at Vue de monde will think this hotel was designed and built for them. It's because of the attention to detail. Kit Kemp, the hotel operator and designer, together with husband Tim, finds solutions to the annoying things that a lot of hotels just seem to accept as standard and give up on. For instance, the minibar has a glass door and is built in at waist height. It is also filled with gourmet treats from places like Dean & Deluca, such as vitamin supplements, big buckets of gummy bears and really drinkable wines. There is toothpaste in the bathrooms, organic apples by the bed, every satellite channel known to couch potatoes and, of course, free Internet. Also supplied is a bottle of Sleep Well aromatherapy spray as part of the nightly turn-down service.

The downstairs cinema runs themed dinners and is a seriously full-on movie theatre. The gym is great and so are the three or four meeting rooms, as well as a beautiful dining room and bar that leads out on to Lafayette Street. There's a wonderful courtyard that would make my designer buddy Joost seriously jealous.

The location is another important detail: sandwiched between Broadway, Spring and Lafayette Streets, the hotel is surrounded by a million things to do, including cool shopping and eating. Balthazar is opposite.

The art collection here is undoubtedly the best of all the Firmdale Hotels. Modern and eclectic, every piece seems to have been hung with the décor in mind. Kit's style is the type you want to photograph, then get straight home on the next plane and demand the missus get cracking on DIY, before being dramatically brought back to reality—well, in my case, anyway!

Seriously, this is what hotels should be: statements. They should be like the signature dish of a famous chef. You should be able to read the personality of the owner in the space.

This hotel wins hands down.

ADAM: The palette of rich colours and patterns are Kit Kemp's trademark, and it works well. The rooms are a generous size, well laid out and with great attention to detail. Fittings are all high quality. Some may find the interior design a little busy, but it all seems to hang together. The art is mainly by London dealer Rebecca Hoswell.

The service is generally very good and not too formal. The concierge was excellent. Breakfast was very good, but the service there was inconsistent. Try the drawing room with its honour-system bar.

It's strange that they only have one laptop for guests to use, and it comes complete with a flat battery that needs to stay connected to the electricity in order to function.

....

HOTEL (THE MERCER)

147 Mercer Street
(at Prince Street)
(1 212) 966 6061
mercerhotel.com
Rating: 4★+
Rooms: 67
Suites: 8
Hotel rates: $595–820

One of the classic modern boutique hotels of New York, **Hotel (The Mercer)** was opened in 2001 by André Balazs of Chateau Marmont (Los Angeles) fame. The building is Romanesque Revival in striking orange-red brick. It sits in the best and most fashionable part of SoHo. Designed by Parisian Christian Liaigre, the bedrooms have bare brick walls, polished wooden floors and white beds, offset by the odd chair or sofa in a plain pastel. It is cool, elegant and relaxed, a striking riposte to the tizziness of many traditional Manhattan hotels. The lobby, with its wall of books, is inviting. One of the hotel's most unique assets is Mercer Kitchen, run by Jean-Georges Vongerichten. After all, where else does a hotel's 24-hour room service come from a three-star chef's kitchen?

FRED: Restaurant downstairs and a great bar. It's nice to sit in the lobby for tea.

....

Jason Pomeranc's Thompson Hotels group goes from strength to strength, now with five properties in New York (and four across the rest of America). Like Hotel (The Mercer), **60 Thompson** employed a French designer, Jane-Michel Frank, to achieve the typically American SoHo look and feel. The floors are polished wood, with folding wooden-paned doors to separate the living and sleeping areas in the suites. The walls are white, with colour provided by headboards and furniture in neutral colours like grey or beige. It is calm and restful. The rooms are spacious, starting at 28 square metres. The twelfth-floor Thom Bar (guests and VIPs only) is a must, with its 360-degree views of the city. Snacks come from the in-house Thai restaurant, Kittichai.

60 THOMPSON

60 Thompson Street
(between Broome and
Spring Streets)
(1 212) 431 0400
60thompson.com
Rating: 4★
Rooms: 85
Suites: 13
Hotel rates: $500–600

MATT: Stayed here a couple of times. Quite groovy in its own right. New York is famous for boutique hotels and this is definitely one of the best.

FRED: Nice place to sit outdoors for breakfast and a good lunch.

. . . .

This large hotel by SoHo standards has a very European feel. The lobby could be in Paris, Cannes or on the Lido in Venice. Other areas are pure SoHo, with dramatically exposed brick; best is the steel-and-glass-bottle staircase. Sister hotel to the Tribeca Grand, the **Soho Grand** is a beautiful place to reside, designer William Sofield having created a luxurious retreat in Downtown Manhattan. Though comfortable and relaxing, the rooms are less striking than the rest of the hotel, with wooden and leather chairs one doesn't feel like sitting in for too long, and IKEA-like bedside tables. The rooms are also a little small: a Grand King, for example, is just 23 square metres. However, if you feel a pressing need to play volleyball in your room, there are two Loft Suites starting at 125 square metres, at a mere $4500+ a night. It's where you stay if your film is a big hit at Robert De Niro's Tribeca Film Festival.

SOHO GRAND HOTEL

310 West Broadway
(between Canal and
Grand Streets)
(1 212) 965 3000
sohogrand.com
Rating: 4★
Rooms: 361
Suites: 2
Hotel rates: $400–575

MATT: It's been there for ages and has a great bar—if you can get in. I have been taken there a few times and felt very, very special, as if I had a lot of money!

. . . .

TRUMP SOHO

246 Spring Street
(between Varick Street and
Avenue of the Americas)
(1 212) 842 4500
trumpsohohotel.com
Rating: 5★
Rooms: 391
Suites: 2
Hotel rates: $600–660

The new contender in SoHo's hotel market, though looking as if placed there by an alien spaceship, is the glass-tower **Trump Soho**. With floor-to-ceiling windows offering stunning views over the city, this is a Midtown Manhattan high-rise experience in the heart of Downtown bohemia. With huge brown leather headboards (a recent New York obsession), the rooms are beautifully appointed and plush. There is an outdoor pool on the Bar d'Eau deck, a truly impressive pillared lobby, a spa and all the necessary accoutrements of a luxury hotel (such as the now de rigueur library, this one stacked with Taschen books). It also doesn't have the excessive use of tacky gold that bedevils some of Donald Trump's other glitzy palaces. This is restrained, a bit like a gentleman's club. It is a major addition to the Manhattan hotel scene, if you can forgive a 46-storey tower in so low-rise and discreet a neighbourhood.

ADAM'S SHOPPING

My daughter and I spent a couple of days exploring SoHo. Among the standouts were:

PALUMBO LIMITED

63 Crosby Street (between Broome and Spring Streets)
(1 212) 734 7630
palumbogallery.com

Really nice (though not cheap) twentieth-century classic furniture and objects. (The main store is at 972 Lexington Avenue.)

BDDW

5 Crosby Street (between Howard and Grand streets)
(1 212) 625 1230
bddw.com

Run by Philadelphia-based Tyler Hays, BDDW is a great, airy, open warehouse space, white-painted with clean lines. Hays' handmade furniture is modern American, matching simple angles and contemporary design with natural materials (hand-rubbed oils, wood, stone, metals, fabrics). Most pieces are fairly simple but evocative of quality and thought: chairs, beds, tables, carpets, some paintings. Pieces are sometimes manufactured to order in Brooklyn. Look out for his collection of old American industrial equipment. When I was there, there was a wonderful loom dating from the 1880s.

MICHELLE VARIAN

35 Crosby Street (between Grand and Broome Streets)
(1 212) 226 1076
michelevarian.com

Reasonably priced decorative home accessories.

TED MEUHLING

27 Howard Street (between Broadway and Lafayette Street)
(1 212) 431 3825
tedmeuhling.com

Interesting jewellery and design objects. Not only are Muehling's designs featured, so are those by designers such as Gabriella Kiss, Lynn Nakamura and Axel Russmeyer.

TASCHEN AMERICAN LLC

107 Greene Street (between Spring and Prince Streets)
(1 212) 226 2212
taschen.com

Great collection of virtually every book Taschen has published, including limited editions.

SATURDAY SURF NYC

31 Crosby Street (between
Grand and Broome Streets)
(1 212) 966 7873
saturdaysnyc.com

Cool shop, recently opened.
Good coffee. Surfboards
and skateboards.

JACK SPADE

56 Greene Street
(at Broome Street)
(1 212) 625 1820
jackspade.com

Men's clothes. Jack is the husband of Kate Spade. Popular and
reasonably priced.

MOSS

150 Greene Street (between Prince
and West Houston Streets)
(1 212) 204 7100
mossonline.com

Really interesting furniture and
lighting, and some collector's
objects (plates, cutlery, etc.).
If you like industrial design, this
store is worth a look. Many items
are fairly pricey, but some are
reasonable and most are unique.

KIDROBOT

118 Prince Street (between
Wooster and Greene Streets)
(1 212) 966 6688
kidbrot.com

Cute Japanese-inspired store with
toys, art toys, clothing and more.

KING OF GREENE STREET

72 Greene Street (between
Broome and Spring Streets)
(1 212) 302 5470
kingofgreenestreet.com

Clothing and accessories.
Nice small café in the shop.

PRADA BROADWAY

575 Broadway (between Prince
and West Houston Streets)
(1 212) 334 8888

PAUL SMITH INC

142 Greene Street (between
Prince and West Houston Streets)
(1 212) 254 3530
paulsmith.co.uk

COSTUME NATIONAL

108 Wooster Street (between
Spring and Prince Streets)
(1 212) 431 1530

Iconic Milan-based men's and
women's fashion.

MARTIN MARGIELA

801 Greenwich Street (between
West 12th and Jane Streets)
(1 212) 989 7612

Plus ...

TOM FORD

845 Madison Avenue (between
East 70th and East 71st Streets)
(1 212) 359 0300
tomford.com

Far from cheap, but an experience.

BERGDORF GOODMAN

754 Fifth Avenue (at West 58th Street)

(1 212) 753 7300

bergdorfgoodman.com

There are also lots of cool boutiques in the Meatpacking District and the Lower East Side.

Adam Garrison

SHANNON'S NEW YORK RECIPES

TUNA MELTS

This is always the staple of a great deli. Good tinned Tuna is crucial. Don't skimp on quality; pay the extra couple of dollars. Also, don't break up the Tuna too finely when combining with the mayonnaise. Simple and fulfilling, Tuna Melts make great bite-size appetizers for a cocktail party or are simple to serve for lunch with a rocket salad.

The first time I ate a Tuna Melt was not a great experience. It was in the Port Authority Building, New York; I was twelve and waiting by myself for a transfer to Newark Airport. The béchamel really put me off, which is why I do not add this unnecessary sauce to the dish.

8 slices of olive and rye bread

2 tablespoons of cultured butter

425 g of Serrats or Sirena Tuna

2 shallots, finely chopped

6 cornichons, finely chopped

6 tablespoons of mayonnaise

2 tablespoons of finely chopped parsley

juice of ½ a lemon

6 boiled eggs (cooked for 8 minutes in boiling water, cooled then sliced)

8 thin slices of Swiss cheese

sea salt and black pepper for seasoning

Toast the bread and butter on both sides. Keep warm and preheat the grill.

Place the drained Tuna into a mixing bowl and add shallots, cornichons, mayonnaise and parsley. Season well and add a little lemon juice.

Spread the Tuna mix onto the bread in an even layer. Add the egg and season once again. Place the slices of cheese evenly over the top of the egg and put under the grill to lightly melt the cheese. Place the other slice of bread on top. Cut in half and serve.

Serves 4

LOWER
EAST SIDE

FINE DINING

|||||||||||||||||||||||||||||||||||||||||||||||||||||||||||||||||||||||||||||||||||||||||||||||||||||||||||||||||||||||||||||||||||||||||||||||||||||||||||||||||||||||||||||||||||||||||||||||||

Wylie Dufresne is at the forefront of molecular gastronomy in the United States. Happily embracing every tag from '*enfant térrible*' to 'mad professor', Dufresne has developed a cult following for his out-there combinations of flavours and textures. Pickled Beef Tongue with Fried Mayonnaise and Carrot-Coconut Sunnyside-Up? Inspired by El Bulli's Ferran Adrià, Dufresne made his name as sous chef at Jean Georges, before opening his own restaurant, **wd~50**, in 2003. It has been full ever since.

WD~50
Eclectic
Chef: Wylie Dufresne
50 Clinton Street
(between Rivington and
Stanton Streets)
(1 212) 477 2900
wd-50.com
Michelin: ★
Zagat: 25/30
Menu: $140 (12 courses)
À la carte: $48–67

SHANNON: Wylie Dufresne has made a huge impact on the New York dining scene with his radical approach to dining. When his Pickled Beef Tongue and Fried Mayonnaise creation popped up in *New York* magazine, we thought, 'This dish has been created by a real talent'. I think that staying in the same venue has stunted Wylie as a chef in terms of profile, but it has not hampered his restaurant, wd~50. I have eaten here twice, once à la carte and once the menu. I much preferred the à la carte, which has great balance and is perfect for a three-course meal.

I found the wines by the glass really intriguing, but if I'm going to be critical I don't think there is a need to serve Australian wines by the glass. I mean, sure, serve and list some great iconic Aussie stuff and then a few out of left-field, but America has such an interesting and growing reputation for wine that there is much to explore on its own doorstep.

It's a shame this place does not open for Sunday lunch; in fact, it's only open for five dinners, Wednesday to Saturday. The cuisine here is not for the faint-hearted. It is bold, creative and combines sentimental theatre with common American cultural favourites, such as in the Smoked Salmon Bagel, which I loved. The cream cheese was served crispy and the Salmon was served as the bagel. I also had a Foie Gras Cereal, which was fun.

Desserts are a must with a menu from renowned chef Alex Stupak. This guy was the original head pastry chef at Alinea in Chicago, so it's definitely an insult not to have his Sicilian Pistachio Cake with Meyer Lemon and Honey Dew Ice Cream. This was a sensation, with modern creativity but a classic basis. The texture of the cake was so light, yet full of nutty and rich flavour.

I recommend this place for a number of reasons, but mostly because it's different, and with an open kitchen it has a great atmosphere. I couldn't wait for Scott to eat here. I just knew he would hate it!

SCOTT: With a sense of both expectation and apprehension, I ventured through the hell of the Lower East Side, a rusting slum dotted with designer shops and eerie tattoo parlours. The poorer suburbs of Moscow look better than this.

wd~50 is half bar and half restaurant, a dark and tightly packed space. The tables are chunky wood with 1950s-style finely woven mats, basic glassware (it gets better if you order a $500 bottle of wine) and cheap cutlery. It is odd that such cut-rent table settings are used in a restaurant where the dégustation menu is $140, not including taxes and service.

Most of the waiters have very thick accents (Jamaican?) and I couldn't catch what the *amuse bouche* was, but it looked like a post-modern mini bagel (frozen cream cheese?) on a powder that tasted like—and had the texture of—sawdust. Was this the dish Shannon liked so much? Far better was the sesame bread, which was incredibly thin and crisp, and well dotted with sesame seeds. It crunched beautifully, but had little taste.

My appetizer was a Shrimp Cannelloni with Cranberry, Daikon and Mint, but it was not cannelloni at all; it was more like an Asian rice-paper roll. It had shrimp and shrimp paste, and various other unidentified ingredients. On the plate was a mint essence that tasted like toothpaste and Daikon radish of very watery texture and flavour. It was not thrilling in any way, and really needed the 2007 Copain 'Tous Ensemble' Pinot Noir from Willamette, Oregon, to help it down.

Next was a gift offering: Egg Ravioli. This was much better. The cube of egg was a brilliant technical achievement, looking like a well-cooked omelette on the outside but deliciously runny inside. But it tasted just like under-seasoned everyday egg.

My entrée was Duck Breast with Apple, Cheddar and Kimchee Cous Cous. It came in a deep earthenware bowl, which made reaching in and cutting up the duck breast very tricky indeed. It was perfectly cooked, moist and tender, but again close to flavourless. The cous cous was bland, the broth pleasant but unmemorable.

The pre-dessert was a Lychee Sorbet with Lemongrass Foam, with pistachio hidden underneath. Plus celery. Yes, celery. Whatever possessed pastry chef Alex Stupak to add celery is anyone's guess. No matter what you do to celery, it still tastes like celery and it is not a taste, or a texture, that sits well in a soft dessert. As for the foam, it had absolutely no taste and the sorbet did not recall lychees in any way.

My main dessert then arrived with, yes, more lemongrass foam. What was this restaurant thinking? You never repeat a key ingredient in adjacent dishes unless you have some powerful culinary story to relate. Apart from the foam, there was a lemongrass mousse, which was piped onto the plate like a slithering snake of toothpaste, plus an ice cream of something or other (I couldn't tell) and a crunchy macaron-type pastry. Such as it was, it was the night's highlight.

Thank heavens I didn't have the dégustation menu, where each of the twelve courses would constitute a main serving anywhere else in the world. It beggars belief how diners get through it. Yet the Japanese couple next to me were delighted with everything they were given—as was everyone else I could see or hear. I had the feeling I was the only one in wd~50 who was not ecstatic at being in this laboratory of culinary experimentation.

RESTAURANTS, STEAKHOUSES, BISTROS, CAFÉS

ÁPIZZ

Italian
217 Eldridge Street
(at Stanton Street)
(1 212) 253 9199
apizz.com
Michelin: Bib Gourmand
Zagat: 24/30
À la carte: $39–61

ápizz (pronounced ah-BEETS) advertises itself as 'one room, one oven'; the main photo on its website is of a large wood-fired oven, suggesting this is just a pizza parlour. Yes, there are a couple of pizzas on the primi menu (*Margherita* and *Bianca*), but most of the food is classical Italian, from *insaladas* and *Fungi con polenta* to *Lasagna cighiale* (wild boar) and *Pesce arrosto* (de-boned wood-roasted whole fish with rosemary, thyme, lemon and an arugula and tomato salad). The 166-entry wine list has plenty of fine Italian bottlings, though it can tend to the populist, offering the Stella & Mosca Cannonau from Sardegna rather than, say, the finer Arigolas.

BONDI ROAD

Australian
153 Rivington Street
(between Suffolk and
Clinton Streets)
(1 212) 253 5311
bondiroad.com
Zagat: 17/30
À la carte: $20–39

Known for its 'surfer-dude décor' and hard-drinking customers, **Bondi Road** celebrates Australian food and beer (and its national soccer team, whenever it is playing somewhere in the world). There are Mussels with Cooper's Beer, Bondi Shrimp Pasta and that sadly ignored classic, Steak Diane. The Daily Catch is a mere $10, leaving plenty of spare cash for drinking a Sex on Bondi Beach or a Coolangatta Gold. (Sister restaurants are The Sunburnt Cow in East Village and The Sunburnt Calf on the Upper West Side.)

CONGEE VILLAGE

Chinese
100 Allen Street
(between Broome and
Delancey Streets)
(1 212) 941 1818
congeevillagerestaurants.com
Michelin: Bib Gourmand
Zagat: 21/30
À la carte: $21–100

Congee Village does not limit itself to thirty different and affordable rice porridges (lobster for a generous $6.75); there are more than 250 (mostly Cantonese) dishes on its menu. It has proved so successful with Lower East Side customers that a nearby Congee Bowery was opened in 2007.

Calling this an 'Anglo-Asian restaurant' may sound like a marketing ploy until you explore the menu, which reveals itself to be full of cross-cultural delights. Chinese Five-Spiced Foie Gras with Pickled Plums and Mizuna sounds like the work of a trendy French chef, but look further to the Butternut Squash Curry with Grilled Flatbread and Snake Bean Salad, or the Singapore-Style Lobster, Chili Baked in the Shell. **Double Crown** is the creation of Brad Farmerie (from the one-star Public). Next door is Madame Geneva, an affiliated bar that does many interesting things with gin.

DOUBLE CROWN
Anglo-Asian
Chef: Brad Farmerie
316 Bowery
(at Bleecker Street)
(1 212) 254 0350
doublecrown-nyc.com
Zagat: 20/30
Menu: $35 (Sunday Nonya dinner)
À la carte: $34–58

FRED: Go for weekend brunch and make your own Bloody Marys. Then visit the popular New Museum of Contemporary Art.

This revival of a rustic American colonial tavern is recommended by just about everyone you talk to about New York restaurants. Hidden in a Lower East Side alley, in the hunting-lodge surroundings you can sample Grilled Sardines with Fennel, Treviso, Citrus and Crushed Olives, or Goffle Road Farm Oven-Roasted Chicken. You can eat ($26) and drink well here on a budget ($35 for a Domaine de la Petite Mairie Bourgueil) or splurge.

FREEMANS
American
Freeman Alley (between Bowery and Chrystie Street; off Rivington Street)
(1 212) 420 0012
freemansrestaurant.com
Zagat: 21/30
À la carte: $26–60

ADAM: Hidden little restaurant on Freeman Alley in the Lower East Side. Delicious, but no reservations.

Ninety-four (and counting) flavours of ice cream, from Acacia Honey to Wasabi, and fifty sorbets from Apple (Fuji) to Watermelon. RECOMMENDED: MELANIE

IL LABORATORIO DEL GELATO
Ice cream and sorbets
95 Orchard Street (between Allen and Orchard Streets)
(1 212) 343 9922
laboratoriodelgelato.com

KATZ'S DELICATESSEN
205 East Houston Street
(at Ludlow Street)
(1 212) 254 2246
katzdeli.com
Zagat: 24/30
À la carte: $11–30

Founded in 1888 by a Russian immigrant, **Katz's** proclaims itself as New York's oldest and finest delicatessen. It is a vast space, with an endless counter but almost nothing behind it except hundreds of plastic bags of sliced rye bread and containers. This is much more a café than a deli, where you can sit down for Matzo Ball Soup, Knishes (potato, broccoli or sweet), Knoblewurst or Knockwurst, a Double Cheeseburger and New York Cheesecake. Just don't say, 'I'll have what she's having'.

MATT: Katz's is a famous deli. You know, *When Harry Met Sally* .... You can't go to New York without experiencing a deli.

SCOTT: When you enter Katz's, the first thing you notice is a sign warning you that if you lose your ticket and don't present it to the cashier on your way out you will be levied with a minimum fine of $50. A man sitting by a turnstile then hands you that precious ticket. It is covered with numbers: 390, 890, etc. What they have to do with ordering food will remain a lifelong mystery.

You take this ticket to a counter that looks at least 20 metres long. I handed over mine and ordered the #1 Breakfast, which consists of orange juice, coffee, toast, chips and eggs (however you like). Katz's famous beef sausage is an extra. I was handed the orange juice and told by the guy that he would call out when the hot stuff was ready. My coffee, apparently, had to be obtained from another guy further along counter. Then, I learnt, it was back up to the far end to order my chips.

Anyone who has ever spent time in the former Soviet Union will recognize what's happening here. The fact you have to visit four or five or more people to complete a simple transaction is one of the Soviet Union's least-appreciated gifts to the planet.

I then stared at the vast and empty space—at 9 a.m., I was the only diner there—looking for a place to sit. There was a row of tables along the wall, below hundreds of photos of famous visitors to the deli. A sign warned 'Waiter service only'. The whole time I was there, I never saw a waiter. I resisted the opportunity to sit underneath the sign proclaiming that this was where they shot the famous scene in *When Harry Met Sally* .... The table next to it would do.

As I awaited my hot food, I noticed another sign suggesting 'Send a Salami to Your Boy in the Army!' It is a wartime classic and apparently one reason people come here. If you feel so inspired, you can send a salami via the deli's website.

Finally, my name was called out, and I collected my eggs and sausage. The eggs were supposed to be scrambled but were fried and beyond dry. I had to add copious tomato sauce to help get them down. The toast toppled distressingly in the hand, the coffee was nearly flavourless and the sausage was not made from the finest cuts of meat.

The most exciting moment was when I couldn't find my entry ticket and panicked about the $50 fine. It was stuck to the bottom of the plate of eggs. I left wondering why this place was so iconic, so high on so many peoples' Bucket Lists. Maybe you have to go at lunch to understand it better.

....

Restaurateur Keith McNally can do no wrong—except alienate critics with his sometimes less-than-calm response to their comments. Everything McNally does works, from Balthazar and Pastis to The Odeon and Minetta Tavern. His Lower East Side star is **Schiller's Liquor Bar**, an industrial-design masterpiece that fits in brilliantly with the image the Lower East Side has of itself as the coolest place in Manhattan. It is open for breakfast (though not until 11 a.m.) and finishes late, with people packing in for the wild cocktails (Schiller's seems proudest of The Delancey) and simple comfort food (Cheeseburger, Grilled Chicken Palliard, *Moules frites*). RECOMMENDED: FRED

SCHILLER'S LIQUOR BAR

European
131 Rivington Street
(at Norfolk Street)
(1 212) 260 4555
schillersny.com
Zagat: 19/30
Menu: $16 (lunch)
À la carte: $42–58

....

BARS

|||||||||||||||||||||||||||||||||||||||||||||||||||||||||||||||||||||||||||||||||||||||||||||||||||||||||||||||||||||||||

THE BACK ROOM
Bar
102 Norfolk Street
(1 212) 228 5098
7.30 p.m.–4 a.m.

There is a main room and the famous back room, where legend has it you must be a friend of the owners to get in.

PAULA AND PATRICK: With the façade of a toy store, this speakeasy bar is not easy to find. Walk down the left-hand side of the main room and you'll be greeted by a security guard who will escort you into the back bar. It is a good idea to get there early as it does fill up quickly. The beers are wrapped in paper bags and all other drinks are served in teacups. Quite a novelty, but it certainly takes you back to the days of prohibition. The décor is from the 1930s, which truly fits the genre.

. . . .

MILK & HONEY
134 Eldridge Street
(between Broome and
Delancey Streets)
(1 212) 625 3397
Until 4 a.m.

This hard-to-find gem is the original post-Prohibition New York speakeasy and is invitation only.

. . . .

ARLENE'S GROCERY
Bar
95 Stanton Street
(1 212) 995 1652
6 p.m.–4 a.m. (Mon–Sat)

BOB
Bar
235 Eldridge Street
(1 212) 529 1807
7.30 p.m.–4 a.m. (Tues–Sun)

BOTANICA
Bar
47 East Houston
(1 212) 343 7251
5 p.m.–4 a.m. (Mon–Fri),
6 p.m.–4 a.m. (Sat–Sun)

CLANDESTINO
Bar
35 Canal Street
(1 212) 475 5505
4 p.m.–4 a.m.

EAST SIDE COMPANY BAR
Bar
49 Essex Street
(1 212) 614 7408
7 p.m.–4 a.m. (Mon–Sat)

HAPPY ENDING
Bar
302 Broome Street
(1 212) 334 9676
10 p.m.–4 a.m. (Tues),
7 p.m.–4 a.m. (Wed–Sat)

MADAME GENEVA
Bar
4 Bleecker Street
(1 212) 254 0350
6 p.m.–4 a.m. (Mon–Sun)

MAGICIAN
Bar
118 Rivington
(1 212) 673 7851
7 p.m.–4 a.m.

NURSE BETTIE
Bar
106 Norfolk Street
(1 212) 614 7408
6 p.m.–2 a.m. (Sun–Tues),
6 p.m.–4 a.m. (Wed–Sat)

SWEET & LOWDOWN	WHISKEY WARD	WHITE STAR
Wine bar	Bar	Bar
123 Allen Street	121 Essex Street	21 Essex Street
(1 212) 228 7746	(1 212) 477 2988	(1 212) 995 5464
6 p.m.–2 a.m.	5 p.m.–4 a.m.	6 p.m.–3 a.m.

LUXURY HOTELS

Of the new glass-towered boutique hotels, **The Hotel on Rivington** is arguably the gem. The high-level rooms are dazzling in the amount of floor-to-ceiling glass. Whereas most hotels can give you only one of four outer walls, the Rivington offers more. That is because it is a new, freestanding all-glass 21-storey extravaganza, which cleverly uses its irregular outside shape to maximum views in many directions. The interior design is minimalist—nothing must obstruct the eye's journey to the outside—and subtly Scandinavian. There are high-tech features everywhere, but you may not notice them. The marble floor of the bathroom is heated, but best of all are the Swedish beds, which adjust to body weight and temperature. Some rooms have steam showers and/or two-person Japanese soaking tubs. Spa services are available in your room. The lobby and lounge are restricted to guests and their friends, which is a policy many hotels would do well to adopt to avoid 'train-station' bustle. Recently awarded Hotel of the Year by *The Times* of London, the Rivington is one of the world's hottest new hotels.

THE HOTEL ON RIVINGTON
107 Rivington Street (between Ludlow and Essex Streets)
(1 212) 475 2600
hotelonrivington.com
Rating: 4★+
Rooms: 89
Suites: 21
Hotel rates: $375–479

ADAM: The Lower East Side is a fabulous area to explore and The Hotel on Rivington is a good place to do that from. The service is attentive, and the contemporary space is enjoyable under the influence of Marcel Wanders (although his touches seem to be distorted by other interior concepts). I was given a fabulous room that had more than 10 square metres of floor-to-ceiling windows overlooking what seemed like the whole of Manhattan. In addition, there was a second bedroom with four double bunk beds, each with a television. It was an amazing experience to leave the curtains open and be woken by the sunrise over New York. The Lower East Side is full of interesting shops, bars, and places to eat.

THOMPSON LES

190 Allen Street
(between Stanton and
East Houston Streets)
(1 212) 460 5300
thompsonhotels.com
Rating: 4★
Rooms: 141
Hotel rates: $399–499

The **Thompson LES** is an eighteen-storey boutique hotel that has had almost every travel reporter reaching for the word 'gorgeous'. It is a bold design statement, the lobby and sitting room saying it all: dark-grey slate tiles, golden walls, vertical columns of bulbs of blown glass containing hidden lights, glass-sided black leather chairs and massive black leather couches. It is gritty, industrial, raw, decadent and luxurious. The restaurant Shang (acclaimed Chinese chef Susar Lee's first American venture) is a riot of orange and gold, with more black leather. Unusually for New York, there is a swimming pool, set on a cute terrace with orange designer chairs and lounges. At the bottom of the pool is a reproduction of Andy Warhol's face, the area being occasionally used for open-air screenings of an artistic bent. The large bedrooms are designer glam, with illuminated light-box headboards by Lee Friedlander, low-rise beds, black floors and cement ceilings, with the odd splash of beige and white. The floor-to-ceiling windows have diaphanous golden curtains. There are five cool places to drink, with Above Allen glowing from its seventh-storey perch.

SCOTT: From personal experience, if you are male and tell a male Manhattan sommelier or maître d' that you are staying at the Thompson LES there is a good chance you will be asked out on a date. This, after all, is a hotel with a male-masturbation kit ($39) in the minibar but nothing for females. Everything is beautifully done, with quality finishes and clever touches. Jason Pomeranc of Thompson Hotels is a very savvy hotelier, with a Steve Jobs–like finger on the pulse, and the desire and ability to do a job properly. (Thompson hotels don't quickly go tatty like some other trendy places.)

My room was a corner one, affording vast views through the floor-to-ceiling windows of East Village to the north and Lower East Side to the east. Not being a fan of the Lower East Side (it is a district I doubt I will ever revisit, though most of my friends think it is one of the coolest areas around), the views, while dramatic, are not as inspiring as those from the Helmsley Park Lane or Cooper Square.

If you love the LES, then go for this or The Hotel on Rivington as a great glass-tower hotel experience. The Thompson is a faultless hotel, even if finding the pool could be made a little easier. This is a quality, cutting-edge place to stay.

OTHER HOTELS

More subdued than some Downtown designer statements, the **East Houston Hotel** is a discretely modern and stylish boutique hotel. The bedrooms aren't large (don't aim lower than the East Houston rooms with their king-size beds), but they are nicely, if a tad austerely, appointed. The technical specs are well up to standard, with plasma screens (though televisions attached directly to a wall always have a slightly budget-hotel feel), iPod docking stations and digital telephones with speakers. The bathrooms have Bvlgari amenities. (Hotels always boldly advertise what's in the line-up of bottles in the bathroom, but does anybody ever choose a hotel because of the brand of shampoo?) This hotel is excellent value, perfectly located within easy walking distance of Chinatown, Little Italy, SoHo and East Village, let alone the Lower East Side.

EAST HOUSTON HOTEL

151 East Houston Street
(at Eldridge Street)
(1 212) 777 0012
hoteleasthouston.com
Rating: 3★
Rooms: 40
Hotel rates: $279–319

This boutique hotel has affordable one- and two-bedroom suites. The smaller ones share a kitchen with an adjoining suite, but the large suites (sleeping four) have private kitchens. These are large, well-appointed apartments, with the benefits of being part of a hotel, including housekeeping and a business centre.

OFF SOHO SUITES HOTEL

11 Rivington Street
(between Bowery and Chrystie Street)
(1 212) 979 9808
offsoho.com
Rating: 2★
Rooms: 38
Hotel rates: $199–299

MUSSEL CHOWDER—THE 10-MINUTE WAY

Mussels and soup are like Bradman and cricket. This isn't actually a chowder, but I called it that just so I could include the recipe in the book. I would describe chowder as a complete meal in a bowl.

Mussels are now available live in vacuum-sealed bags, and are very good either from the Port Lincoln region in South Australia or anywhere in Tasmania. By the way, the orange-coloured mussels are the females.

40 large mussels, de-bearded
1 tablespoon of extra virgin olive oil or enough to coat the base of the pot
½ bottle of old white wine
1 carrot, finely diced
1 stick of celery, finely diced
1 onion, finely diced
200 g picked broad beans, blanched and shelled
2 cloves of garlic, finely crushed
1 tablespoon French tarragon, finely chopped
1 tablespoon finely chopped parsley
100 g cultured butter
½ lemon
sea salt and black pepper to taste

Thoroughly wash the mussels under very cold running water. Preheat a heavy-based large saucepan or casserole pot with a fitted lid.

Add olive oil and the mussels, and put the lid on. After the initial burst of noise and heat has dissipated, add the white wine, all of the vegetables and the garlic.

Cook on very high heat for 1 minute. Add the herbs and butter. Boil for 1 minute and add the herbs. Adjust the seasoning with lemon juice, salt and black pepper, and serve in generous bowls with lots of hot corn bread.

The mussels in this recipe can be replaced by any type of shellfish.

Serves 4

GREENWICH VILLAGE, WEST VILLAGE & MEAT-PACKING DISTRICT

FINE DINING

||||||||||||||||||||||||||||||||||||||||||||||||||||||||||||||||||||||||||||||||||||||||||||||||||||||||||||||||||||||||||||||||||

A fire nearly wiped out **Annisa** in 2008, but it has bounced back to become an entrancing fine-dining location in a very pretty part of the West Village. Owner-chef Anita Lo and co-owner and sommelier Jennifer Scism have created a very delicate space (a 'jewel box' some have said), with delicate Asian-French-American fusion food, such as Grilled Halibut with Glazed Radishes, Mustard Greens and Bacon Miso Sauce. The extensive wine list features wine from female winemakers.

ANNISA
Contemporary
Chef: Anita Lo
13 Barrow Street (between Seventh Avenue South and West 4th Street)
(1 212) 741 6699
annisarestaurant.com
Michelin: ★
Zagat: 28/30
Menu: $75 (5 courses)/ $75 (7 courses)
À la carte: $47–55

- -

A lot of people say this is their favourite restaurant in New York, and not just for its organic farm-to-table approach. The restaurant not only proclaims 'Know thy farmer'; the website also gives you details on all the key producers, which includes the family farm, Blue Hill, in Massachusetts. The wine list shows an equal passion for the artisanal.

This Greenwich restaurant opened in a basement speakeasy in 2000 and has been acclaimed ever since, deftly but simply cooking the freshest farm produce. This Morning's Farm Egg is just that, with sweet corn, fava beans, lardo and new potatoes, while Berkshire Pig comes with braised and grilled radicchio, pistachios and smoked cherries. (There is also a Blue Hill at Stone Barns restaurant and café in upstate New York.)

BLUE HILL
American
Chef: Dan Barber
75 Washington Place (between Sixth Avenue and Washington Square West)
(1 212) 539 1776
bluehillfarm.com
Michelin: ★
Zagat: 27/30
À la carte: $56–64

SHANNON: Dan Barber runs this urban bistro like a fine diner: white tablecloths, well-informed staff and a very good sommelier with a fine list. The venue itself is in the basement of small residential terrace-style building, with a small bar that is always packed. Eating by yourself is a common thing to do here. Most tables are positioned close together, adding to the electric feel, but this may annoy some.

Jen Lorden is the general manager and her knowledge is outstanding on what Blue Hill is all about, which is knowing where each ingredient has come from.

It all starts with a 45-minute drive upstate from Manhattan to a restaurant called Blue Hill at Stone Barns. This restaurant is closer to fine dining than its Manhattan sister, and a jacket and tie are recommended. There is also a café where children

are most welcome, and there is plenty to see on the neighbouring 180+ acres, where everything from lamb, pork and dairy to heirloom vegetables are raised or produced. Local and surrounding farms also have their produce sold at the barn and used in the restaurant's dishes. There is no real menu at Stone Barns, just a list of seasonal ingredients that will be used in your meal. This list changes daily. Everybody who has been to Stone Barns highly recommends it as a great day trip.

Meanwhile, back in Manhattan, **Blue Hill** was pumping when we went there on a Sunday night. We sat down and the chef decided to send us a selection of smaller versions of dishes on the à la carte menu. Watching a lot of the food go out, I saw very well presented but large portions of food. Everybody that night started with fresh lettuces and vegetables, simply presented on fine nails protruding from a polished piece of wood. Each nail held an individual vegetable, such as a radish. Everything looked really nice and fresh. Other small eats on the night included Paté with a Crispy Chocolate Wafer—very intriguing and surprisingly good. My favourite, though, was a Crushed Pea Burger served in a bite-sized brioche bun.

The main dishes ranged from a stunning bowl of vegetables presented in the style of Michel Bras to meat dishes like Roast Duck simply done and washed down with a Sonoma County Pinot Noir that the wine team had blended themselves. Desserts were a highlight, in particular the Strawberry Cannelloni that came with the most intense baby strawberries and fromage blanc, married with a streak of some sort of acidulation.

This meal was so simple yet so complicated. I had had no real expectations for this restaurant other than what I knew about Dan Barber's passion for the land, and how caring for nature provides great ingredients for our plates. It went beyond expectations, but I don't wish to raise your hopes of finding the best meal in the world here. You will probably have one of the happiest, though.

FRED: Great. The Aussie maître d', Franco, is wonderful.

SHARLEE: This was my first introduction to chef Dan Barber's fiercely seasonal food. Make sure you introduce yourself to Franco.

ADAM: A wonderful experience. The produce was beautifully fresh and delicately executed. The staff had a detailed knowledge of all aspects of the produce from how it was grown through to its preparation.

GOTHAM BAR AND GRILL

Contemporary
Chef: Alfred Portale
12 East 12th Street
(between Fifth Avenue and
University Place)
(1 212) 620 4020
gothambarandgrill.com
Michelin: ★
Zagat: 27/30
Menu: $31 (lunch)
À la carte: $70–85

Open for more than twenty-five years, the **Gotham Bar and Grill** has long been the shining star of Greenwich restaurants. A few snipe here and there that it's New American cuisine isn't quite as cutting edge as it used to be (Curry Spiced Muscovy Duck Breast, Miso Marinated Black Cod), but it remains a top destination for tourists and New Yorkers alike. It is a radiant, light-filled space.

MATT: This restaurant has been open for a long time: same owners, same chef, still cutting edge. The restaurant has been full for lunch and dinner all that time, so they must be doing something right.

MINETTA TAVERN RESTAURANT & BAR

Gastropub
113 MacDougal Street
(at Minetta Lane)
(1 212) 475 3850
minettatavernny.com
Michelin: ★
Zagat: 24/30
À la carte: $40–88

Keith McNally is one of the two or three most discussed restaurateurs in New York, with an uncanny ability to nail the dining zeitgeist. His roll call of restaurants is legendary, but the place people are talking about most today is the **Minetta Tavern Restaurant & Bar**, which McNally opened with partners Lee Hanson and Riad Nasr in 2009. The restaurant is far older than that, having begun in 1937. If you are lucky enough to get in, you can admire its tiny, packed and truly fun bar while waiting to be seated in the equally packed dining rooms (a small one next to the bar and a larger inner sanctum at the back). Given the way Americans like to be seen, the front part is probably the preferred locale. No matter, the design is a winner, with white pressed-metal ceilings, clubby banquettes where you may just be able to move your arms while eating, and a mural ringing the room above framed photographs. The buzz is infectious.

SCOTT: That Minetta Tavern is one of the hottest restaurants in New York is obvious the moment you arrive. As soon as you open the heavy wooden front door, even at an early 6 p.m., you are confronted by a seething mass of very happy people squashed into a tiny bar. In the distance, one can tell that all the tables are packed, with some diners already moving onto desserts.

My childhood friend Lisa, who lives in the glorious village of Nyack upstate on the Hudson River, was caught in traffic coming down and I told the receptionist I was the first of our party of two to arrive. Feigning great despair, she told me to come back when 'all your party is together' and then she would see what she could do. It didn't inspire hope.

When Lisa did arrive, thirty minutes late, the receptionist again looked exhausted by the grief I was causing her, and told us to sit at the bar 'where there is the full menu', an offer I did not respond to. Forty minutes later (the Hendricks gin and tonic was way too weak), we got very lucky—maybe it had been Lisa loudly proclaiming, 'But he has flown all the way from Australia to be here'—and were ushered to our tiny table.

The bustle around us was like a scene in a Hollywood movie where half of Broadway is celebrating after the annual Tony Awards or some such event. The place was incredibly noisy and enormous fun. If you don't feel happy to be alive in Minetta Tavern, then there is no hope for you.

Certainly it is the atmosphere you should go for, not the food, which looks great on the menu but can be pretty dull in reality. Pleasant green asparagus was served on goat's cheese with peanuts (the nuts actually worked surprisingly well), but the special of Guinea Hen Terrine was dreary. My Minetta Burger with Cheddar and Caramelized Onions ($16) was okay, miles better than Shake Shack's but still short of The Spotted Pig's. I should have had the $26 Black Label Burger or the $45 Bone-In New York Strip, which looked fabulous. Lisa's Pan Fried Deep Sea Bass was slightly overcooked and was good rather than great.

We skipped on dessert, but greatly enjoyed a Syrah-Grenache 'Cuvée des terrasses' from the Northern Languedoc. It is a little-known area, but produces wines Shannon and I greatly enjoyed at Michel Bras and the Grand Hotel Auguy in Laguiole a couple of years ago.

The best approach with Minetta Tavern is to gather a group together and book way ahead, then go with no expectations about the food and simply have a great night out in Manhattan. Just be prepared to wait at the bar (many of those without a table when we arrived were still waiting when we left) and don't punch the bartender when you hand him $40 for your $28 drinks and he asks, 'Do you want change?'

TOBIE: When Minetta Tavern first opened in Greenwich Village, it was frequented by the likes of Ernest Hemingway and Dylan Thomas. It was later taken over by Keith McNally and partners, and has the same charm as his other establishments (Pastis, Balthazar).

You enter the dining room through thick red velvet curtains, and the restaurant itself is classic with black-and-white tiled flooring, and red leather booths and banquettes. It has been described as 'Parisian steakhouse meets classic New York tavern' and that pretty much sums it up.

The food is pretty good. Not the best French cuisine I've tasted, but not bad either. We shared a Mesclun Salad with Warm Goat Cheese to start and for main course I had Filet Mignon au Roquefort and Pomme Frites, and Georgia had Grilled Dorade with Braised Artichokes, Spring Onions and Salsa Verde.

Our friendly and efficient waitress approached us three-quarters of the way into our main and offered us the option of pre-ordering soufflé, as they take twenty minutes to cook. This is something rarely undertaken these days and we duly ordered the Chocolate Soufflé for Two, which was fantastic.

The thing we least liked about Minetta Tavern is that the tables for two are small and so close together my neighbour was closer to me than my wife. Reservations can be made by phone or in person one month ahead.

ADAM: Full of atmosphere and character, Minetta Tavern has one of the best burgers in New York. But go for the Black Label, which is a selection of prime dry-aged beef cuts with caramelized onions and pommes frites.

Perry Street may well be the most beautiful in the West Village, and is home to Carrie Bradshaw (Sarah Jessica Parker) of *Sex and the City*. It is also, at its western end, the location of Jean-Georges Vongerichten's **Perry Street**. It is situated on the ground floor of a Richard Meier glass apartment tower (original residents include Calvin Klein and Nicole Kidman), overlooking the Hudson River, with chaotic West Street in between. Like all of Vongerichten's restaurants, there are spectacularly good lunch and dinner prix fixe menus on offer, meaning just about anyone can afford to eat here if they wish. And with Pan Roasted Black Sea Bass with Meyer Lemon Sauce, Portabello Fries and Couscous on the menu, why not? But if you don't like the food (and Michelin just took away its one star), just remember where you are. Look around and decide if Richard Meier is as great an architect as they say.
RECOMMENDED: FRED

PERRY STREET
Contemporary
Owner: Jean-Georges
Vongerichten
176 Perry Street
(at West Street)
(1 212) 352 1900
jean-georges.com
Zagat: 25/30
Menu: $26 (lunch)/
$28 (dinner)
À la carte: $37–75

....

Soto is generally agreed to be the finest sushi restaurant in Greenwich, though not yet challenging the more famous Midtown ones. One goes here for the raw fish sashimi and sushi, with the $45 raw omakase a steal by New York standards.

SOTO
Japanese
Chef: Sotohiro Kosugi
357 Sixth Avenue (between
West 4th Street and
Washington Place)
(1 212) 414 3088
no website
Michelin: ★★
Zagat: 27/30
Menu: $45 (raw omakase)
À la carte: $45–120

ANTOINETTE: Unless they seriously do their homework, a tourist could easily overlook Soto and opt for one of the glitzier, louder Japanese restaurants in the city. But I've eaten Japanese cuisine in this town for years, and Soto is worth seeking out. It's a small, unassuming restaurant that seats only forty-two people in an interior that can come across as austerely simple. But the blonde wood, a few delicate patterns and clean geometric decorative touches are all that's needed to accent chef Sotohiro Kosugi's cuisine.

Kosugi's sushi has introduced jaded New York diners (who can get halfway-decent sushi at almost any hour, and in most neighbourhoods) to fish and cuts they knew nothing about. But what really distinguishes Kosugi and his namesake restaurant is his love of—and extraordinary expertise with—uni. Like any chef who's tasted and fallen in love with it, Kosugi knows that pure uni—a lush, creamy pillow of rich ocean purity—is sublime enough to serve sashimi-style. But he also treats it to a variety of whimsical preparations, such as in his 'Bird's Nest from the Sea', which combines fresh uni with squid and julienne nori in the shape of a bird's nest, topped with fresh quail egg yolk. If you haven't ever tried uni, try it at Soto. And if you have tried uni, well, you're likely a regular.

....

THE SPOTTED PIG

Gastropub
Chef: April Bloomfield
314 West 11th Street
(at Greenwich Street)
(1 212) 620 0393
thespottedpig.com
Michelin: ★
Zagat: 23/30
À la carte: $21–50
(lunch)/$40–65

April Bloomfield's gastropub is a delightfully quirky place, a very pretty corner building covered in creeper, with an almost missable entrance and enchanted but tiny interior. There's a bar to the left and a row of tiny tables to the right, with some banquettes at the back. The feel is more Upstate New York than Manhattan, and delightfully so. Even if the food weren't good, you would love it here. But the food is what made **The Spotted Pig** famous (and earned it a Michelin star). Lunch is simpler than dinner, so to really test the place you should come at night for, say, the Braised Rabbit with Fennel and Ramps. (Ramps, like hazelnuts and fiddlehead ferns, are huge in New York.) Fortunately, Bloomfield's legendary Sheep's Milk Ricotta Gnudi with Basil Pesto is always available.

SHANNON: Crowded and atmospheric, The Spotted Pig will either embrace you or spit you out bitter, pissed off and hungry—literally!

I am so anticipating a negative response from Scott on this one; he will hate it, I know. Some cute 19-year-old waitress will tell him it's a two-hour wait for dinner and that will be it. He will sit silent on one glass of wine for two hours, then hate every morsel. In fact, I haven't felt so much excitement about someone else eating out since Scott told me he was going to eat at wd~50. It's like making my missus watch highlights of every Arsenal game from last season by herself in a locked room.

My experience was with friend and Vue's former head chef, Ryan Clift. We had a great time. We walked in on a jammed Friday from the cold and wet outside. We were told there were no bookings. The place seemed busy, but not with a lot of diners, just a lot of drinkers. We thought, 'Okay!' We were told there'd be a 45-minute wait, so I said, 'Fine, we can have a couple of beers at the bar'.

As we watched the hoards of drinkers come and go, and forty-five minutes become ninety, I became a little curious as to why at least twenty tables turned over before we finally, after two hours, got seated. I asked why it had taken so long and was given the

Gen Y answer: 'We're just so flat out with regulars'. This made me miffed. I knew all those diners before us had put their name down after me, but it came down to whom you know.

I hate that; it's a form of élitism. I'm not an egotist. I'm not famous. I'm just a regular nice guy who loves food and spends his life working with it, someone who is going to spend a lot of money in a restaurant. They can't judge whether I'm wealthy or successful. In fact, they know nothing about me. Yet I'm judged to be number twenty on a waitlist by some 19-year-old girl who thinks I'm just a boring old fart because I haven't had a shave in three days and look tired. That's because I've just worked fifty-five hours in the past three days! This food better be bloody good.

And it was. We started with great oysters, served natural and really well sourced. I've said it before and I'll say it again: there are some great native oysters coming out of the Atlantic waters of Northern America and Canada. Nice and lean, not fatty and milky as we are told by the frauds who farm the Pacific variety in Australia.

Next, I had the Skate Grenobloise. Whenever I am in the northern hemisphere and within 10 kilometres of the coast, I order Skate Wing. It has a much more delicate texture than the rubbish found in southern waters. The distance between each muscle is so much finer and the texture is just so much more pleasing to the eye and the palate. This dish was finished with burnt butter, chopped lemon segments, finely chopped parsley and Lilliput capers. Garnished with sautéed spinach and fondant potato, it was a great success. Ryan had a good piece of venison with a fruity currant-flavoured jus and *pommes paille*, which is a type of crispy shoestring potato.

We both finished with a Crème Brulée, simple and executed really well. This was all washed down with a very nice 2000 Burgundy Village made by Louis Latour. It was midnight by the time we finished and the place was still pumping. I don't hold grudges, just questions.

SCOTT: The Spotted Pig is a delightful reminder of the days of Woodstock, a gorgeous, funky hang-out with a romantic hippie feel. The small restaurant and bar looks out through creeper onto a tree-lined street, as if in a New England town. The room itself has a gorgeous pressed-metal ceiling and exposed pipes, a rustic feel that is beautifully done. Downstairs (I never realized there was also an upstairs), it only seats twenty odd at tiny tables with banquettes at the back.

I went for lunch and the menu was far simpler than I had been led to expect: a Grilled Cheese Sandwich, Chargrilled Burger, Smoked Haddock Chowder with Homemade Crackers, etc. The specials were Basil Marinated Baby Mozzarella with Prosciutto, and a Wild Nettle Pesto Bruschetta.

I decided on the Chargrilled Burger with Roquefort Cheese (another of those lovely American food tautologies, like Tuna fish and Andouille sausage), served medium-rare with a tangle of Shoestrings (i.e., fries). It was such a relief to eat a decent hamburger after the horrors of **Shake Shack** the day before. But, again, the bun, cutely detailed with heavy grill marks, was soft, doughy and way too sweet. But why complain? Americans invented the hamburger and they like their buns this way.

The meat patty was flawlessly cooked and had a mild flavour, with none of the dodgy meatiness many American burgers have. The Roquefort, though, was the masterstroke, a salty and tangy sensation. But that was it—no lettuce, tomato, pickles or anything else—which makes it a delicious but truly monotonous eating experience. The shoestring fries were perfect, however, thin, crisp and not at all fatty. With it, I had a 2007 Pinot Noir from Willamette, Oregon. As usual with Oregon pinots, it was fine but not life-altering.

For dessert, I opted (though I wasn't hungry; I was indulging only for the sake of the reader) for the Rhubarb Tart, served with a single dollop of cream. While some may feel the almond pastry overwhelms the fruit, it was delicious. The espresso was strong and Italian in style.

So, despite all Shannon's fears about me sitting there in misery after being put down by a 19-year-old girl (life is full of such risks), this was a highly pleasurable lunch, served by a charming and skilled waiter from England. It was a joy to sit inside this small, cute and privileged space. And all the guests looked very happy, except for the old New Yorkers beside me who waited forty-five minutes for their Grilled Cheese Sandwich. But they loved it so much they forgave The Spotted Pig everything.

The only mystery is why Michelin gives this one star. It is a casual café with good honest food. Nothing more.

TOBIE: April Bloomfield has had an amazing career. She worked at several Michelin-starred restaurants in Europe before a four-year stint at The River Café, London. She was scouted as the head chef for The Spotted Pig by Mario Batali, working for Alice Waters at Chez Panisse in Berkeley until The Spotted Pig was up and running.

The gastropub is a pretty little building (Jay-Z is the landlord), covered in creeper and adorned with pots of wild flowers and herbs. Inside is dark and cosy, with a multitude of pig-themed ornaments. The staff are friendly and cool, sporting customized Spotted Pig t-shirts that are available for purchase at the bar.

The bar serves quality British beer (by the pint) and the wine list is good, though not cheap. The Spotted Pig serves seasonal British and Italian fare, using fresh local ingredients when possible. My wife and I shared a deliciously simple Eggplant and

Squash Bruschetta, followed by Smoked Haddock Chowder with Homemade Crackers, and Sheep's Milk Ricotta Gnudi with Basil Pesto, which was best gnudi I have ever tasted.

I had a great time here, though be warned: The Spotted Pig is very popular and they don't take bookings. My tip is to pop in around 4 o'clock and put your name on the list for the first sitting, then either have a drink at the bar or stroll down Bleecker Street to splurge at the likes of Marc by Marc Jacobs, James Perse, Ralph Lauren and Lulu Guinness. Try not to fill up on cupcakes at the famous Magnolia Bakery on the way.

SHARLEE: Four words: Sheep's Milk Ricotta Gnudi. It melts in the mouth and is absolutely amazing. Be there at 5.30 p.m. to put your name down for a table as this place is busy, busy, busy. Save room for the Banoffee Pie. It was so good we ordered another.

....

One of the prettiest restaurants in New York; its masses of vased flowers and pot plants delight both guests and passers-by. But you'll need to book ahead to enjoy the modern Austro-European food of restaurateur Kurt Gutenbruner (Blaue Gans, Café Sabarsky). He has a fondness for white asparagus and other seasonal vegetable specials, but diners will be equally delighted with his Spring Rack of Lamb with Local Beans and Young Carrots or, more traditional, Weiner Schnitzel with Potato-Cucumber Salad and Lingonberries. The cheeses are all Austrian, like the desserts: Marillenknödel and Röster with Walnut Coulis or Mozartkugel with a Pistachio Parfait and Chocolate Streusel. RECOMMENDED: FRED

WALLSÉ
Austrian
Chef: Kurt Gutenbrunner
344 West 11th Street
(at Washington Street)
(1 212) 352 2300
wallse.com
Michelin: ★
Zagat: 26/30
Menu: $75 (4 courses)/
$98 (6 courses)
À la carte: $40–66

....

57 NOVELS SET IN NEW YORK, PLUS A TRILOGY, A NOVELLA AND A SHORT STORY

A chronological list; only one work per author.

1. *A History of New York from the Beginning of the World to the End of the Dutch Dynasty* (Washington Irving, 1809)

2. *Ragged Dick, or Street Life in New York with the Boot-Blacks* (Horatio Alger Jr, 1868)

3. *Washington Square* (Henry James, 1881)

4. *The Age of Innocence* (Edith Wharton, 1920)

5. *The Great Gatsby* (F Scott Fitzgerald, 1925)

6. *Call it Sleep* (Henry Roth, 1934)

7. *The Thin Man* (Dashiell Hammett, 1934)

8. *My Sister Eileen* (Ruth McKenney, 1938)

9. 'The Girls in their Summer Dresses' (short story, Irwin Shaw, 1939)

10. *A Tree Grows in Brooklyn* (Betty Smith, 1943)

11. *The Fountainhead* (Ayn Rand, 1943)

12. *The Big Clock* (Kenneth Fearing, 1946)

13. *Trois Chambres à Manhattan* (Three Bedrooms in Manhattan, Georges Simenon, 1946)

14. *I, the Jury* (Mickey Spillane, 1947)

15. *The Victim* (Saul Bellow, 1947)

16. *East Side, West Side* (Marcia Davenport, 1947)

17. *The Catcher in the Rye* (JD Salinger, 1951)

18. *Invisible Man* (Ralph Ellison, 1952)

19. *Marjorie Morningstar* (Herman Wouk, 1955)

20. *Breakfast at Tiffany's* (novella, Truman Capote, 1958)

20. *Another Country* (James Baldwin, 1962)

21. *Portrait in Brownstone* (Louis Auchincloss, 1962)

22. *The Group* (Mary McCarthy, 1963)

23. *The Bell Jar* (Sylvia Plath, 1963)

24. *Last Exit to Brooklyn* (Hubert Selby Jr, 1964)

25. *Rosemary's Baby* (Ira Levin, 1967)

26. *The Chosen* (Chaim Potok, 1967)

28. *The Godfather* (Mario Puzo, 1969)

29. *Desperate Characters* (Paula Fox, 1970)

30. *The Taking of Pelham One Two Three* (Morton Freedgood, 1973)

31. *A Fairy Tale of New York* (JP Donleavy, 1973)

32. *Looking for Mr. Goodbar* (Judith Rossner, 1975)

33. *Sophie's Choice* (William Styron, 1979)

34. *Endless Love* (Scott Spencer, 1979)

35. *Dancing in the Dark* (Janet Hobhouse, 1983)

36. *Zoë* (Dirk Wittenborn, 1983)

37. *Bright Lights, Big City* (Jay McInerney, 1984)

38. *Money* (Martin Amis, 1984)

39. *Low Tide* (Fernanda Eberstadt, 1985)

40. *New York Trilogy* (Paul Auster, 1985–86)

41. *The Bonfire of the Vanities* (Tom Wolfe, 1987)

42. *American Psycho* (Bret Easton Ellis, 1991)

43. *Bad News* (Edward St Aubyn, 1992)

44. *Fearless* (Rafael Yglesias, 1993)

45. *Nude Men* (Amanda Filapacchi, 1993)

46. *Sex and the City* (Candace Bushnell, 1996)

47. *Underworld* (Don DeLillo, 1997)

48. *No Lease on Life* (Lynne Tillman, 1998)

49. *Music for Torching* (AM Homes, (1999)

50. *The Amazing Adventures of Kavalier & Clay* (Michael Chabon, 2000)

51. *The Corrections* (Jonathan Franzen, 2001)

52. *Beautiful Bodies* (Laura Cunningham, 2002)

53. *The Fortress of Solitude* (Jonathan Lethem, 2004)

54. *Beautiful Lies* (Lisa Unger, 2006)

55. *The Emperor's Children* (Claire Messud, 2006)

56. *Mergers & Acquisitions* (Dana Vachon, 2007)

57. *Exit Ghost* (Philip Roth, 2007)

58. *Lush Life* (Richard Price, 2008)

59. *The Song is You* (Arthur Phillips, 2009)

60. *The Privileges* (Jonathan Dee, 2009)

RESTAURANTS, STEAKHOUSES, BISTROS, CAFÉS

ALTA

Tapas
Chef: Harrison Mosher
64 West 10th Street
(between Sixth and
Fifth Avenues)
(1 212) 505 7777
altarestaurant.com
Zagat: 24/30
Menu: $420
('The Whole Shebang!')
À la carte: $27–43

Chef Harrison Mosher's revisiting of traditional tapas plates has seen him called a visionary and the pioneer of 'anti-tapas'. Whatever you wish to call his lusciously outrageous concoctions (Fingerling Potato Saltimbocca with Fresh Sage, Prosciutto di Parma and Lemon Truffle Sour Cream), **Alta** is an always-packed West Village treat.

SERGE: One of New York's finest tapas bars, it has refined a moribund, culinary theme into something spectacular. Some of the finest red and white sangria you'll taste outside of Madrid.

An icon of Mario Batali's ever-widening empire, **Babbo** specializes in the food of Puglia. You can see it in the Goat Cheese Tortelloni with Dried Orange and Wild Fennel Pollen, and 'Guancia ripiena', a homemade sausage wrapped in pork fat and roasted, then served with an eggplant caponata and broccoli-rabe pesto. Babbo opened in 1998 and won the James Beard New Restaurant Award; its star has not dimmed since. It has a stunning Italian-American wine list that starts at $30 for an Aquileia Refosco and rises to the 1985 Sassicaia at $4750 a magnum. RECOMMENDED: LUKE, FRED

BABBO

Italian
Chef: Mario Batali
110 Waverly Place
(between Sixth Avenue and Washington Square West)
(1 212) 777 0303
babbonyc.com
Zagat: 27/30
Menu: $69 (Pasta tasting menu)/$75 (Traditional tasting menu)
À la carte: $47–100

TOBIE: Mario Batali is, in my opinion, the godfather of Italian cooking in America. He believes 'Food is best when left to its own simple beauty', which is certainly my ethos in the kitchen. He forged his skills working under culinary great Marco Pierre White. Batali now has twelve restaurants throughout America; however, Babbo, the flagship in Greenwich Village, is considered to be his best, where everyone wants to go, and this is certainly proved when attempting to make a reservation! Bookings can be made one month from the date and only via telephone or in person. Yet, one month in advance I was only able to make either a 5.30 p.m. or an 11 p.m. booking.

I have been a huge fan of Batali's for many years and this visit was going to be my first at one of his restaurants. Like a child going to Disneyland, my expectations were high—maybe a little too high. I'd wanted to eat at Babbo for years!

The downstairs dining room is grand, with wooden floorboards and massive floral arrangements, but the feeling is welcoming, warm and cosy, the room bathed in a soft golden light. At 5.30 in the afternoon on a sunny summer's day, it felt like night-time.

The menu is regional Italian food cooked with a twist. With the best local ingredients, the kitchen does a great job maintaining the authenticity of regional Italian cuisine. Salumi, guanciale, lardo, coppa and soppressata are all made in-house, which excites me.

We started with two pasta specials, a simple and delicious Pappardelle with Porcini Mushrooms and Ravioli with Goose Liver Filling in a Balsamic Broth. They were both delicious and the portion sizes quite large. For secondi, we had *Brasato al barolo* (braised beef with porcini) and Spicy Two Minute Calamari, Sicilian Lifeguard Style. The portions were huge. The wine list is excellent, 100 percent Italian and very extensive, while still catering for those without money to burn.

Overall, we thoroughly enjoyed Babbo and I would love to go back at a decent dinner time so I am hungry enough to sample more of the beautiful dishes on offer.

MATT: Babbo is the best Italian restaurant I have eaten in anywhere in the world. Tony Zagat made the booking for us and we had the best table and the most amazing experience.

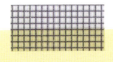

LUKE MANGAN'S NEW YORK

My favourite five restaurants:

1. Babbo
2. Gramercy Tavern (front bar)
3. Balthazar
4. Pastis
5. Casa Mono

Luke Mangan
Restaurateur

BILL'S BAR & BURGER
American
22 Ninth Avenue
(at West 13th Street)
(1 212) 414 3003
billsbarandburger.com
Zagat: 20/30
À la carte: $6.50–20

This burger bar is as famous for its clientele (from 6-foot models to seriously tattooed bikies) as its produce. The Classic Burger is a mere $6.50, with a toasted bun, with pickles, tomato and lettuce on the side. But why not go for the Fat Cat with added caramelized onion and American cheese? Fries are extra, but the brave should go for Disco Fries, which are smothered with gravy and melted cheese. If that doesn't make you feel slightly queasy, try the Peanut Butter Banana Fluff Shake.

Bistro de la Gare is a partnership between chefs Maryann Terillo and Elisa Sarno, who first met in 1987 at the West Village restaurant, Café de la Gare. When that closed in 1991, both succeeded in all manner of separate culinary endeavours and so decided to reunite in a new venture called Bistro de la Gare. It serves seasonal Mediterranean (French and Italian) fare. RECOMMENDED: LARRY

BISTRO DE LA GARE
Mediterranean
Chefs: Maryann Terillo,
Elisa Sarno
626 Hudson Street
(at Jane Street)
(1 212) 242 4420
bistrodelagarenyc.com
À la carte: $36–60

Essentially a sushi hang-out, noted for its cool crowd and pretty staff, **Bond Street** also has a wide range of traditional Japanese dishes. It is considered by many to be in the top twenty 'omakase' restaurants in Manhattan. RECOMMENDED: FRED

BOND STREET
Japanese
6 Bond Street (between
Broadway and
Lafayette Street)
(1 212) 777 2500
no website
Zagat: 25/30
Menu: $80–120 (omakase)
À la carte: $48–72

A childhood in the American south-west instilled in chef David Schuttenberg a passion for the flavours and textures of Mexican food. Apart from Tacos (pork belly with a tamarin-arbol glaze) and Huaraches, there are some serious specialities, including the restaurant's namesake Cabrito, which is goat rubbed with sour orange, garlic and chilli, then slow roasted and served chopped up with salsa borracha and warm flour tortillas.

CABRITO
Mexican
Chef: David Schuttenberg
50 Carmine Street
(between Bedford and
Bleecker Streets)
(1 212) 929 5050
cabritonyc.com
Zagat: 17/30
À la carte: $30–50

CAFÉ CLUNY

American-French
284 West 12th Street
(at West 4th Street)
(1 212) 255 6900
cafecluny.com
Zagat: 21/30
A la carte: $33–51

Sister restaurant of The Odeon and Café Luxembourg, this is a successful cross between a French brasserie and an American diner. RECOMMENDED: LARRY

....

CAFÉ GITANE @ THE JANE

French-Moroccan
113 Jane Street
(near West Street)
(1 212) 255 4113
thejanenyc.com
Zagat: 20/30
À la carte: $25–35

Café Gitane is the in-house café of The Jane, everybody's favourite 'haute flophouse'. (The original Café Gitane remains in SoHo.)

HARRY: While staying at The Jane, I would start my morning or evening here with a drink of sorts. It has a very nice *Casablanca* feel, with the ceiling fans and a stuffed alligator on the wall. Great fun service.

....

CHINATOWN BRASSERIE

Chinese
Chef: Joe Ng
380 Lafayette Street
(at Great Jones Street)
(1 212) 533 7000
chinatownbrasserie.com
Zagat: 22/30
À la carte: $30–65

Opened by Josh Pickard and John McDonald (Lure and Casa Lever), this is a very stylish place to eat the best of Chinese cuisine. Don't be fooled by the name: the restaurant is in NoHo, not Chinatown.

PATRICIA: I love the **Chinatown Brasserie**! I first heard about it when my brother Mark returned home after having run the New York Marathon and told me I had to go there when I was next in New York. I put it on my list of places to eat and did exactly that. I was with a friend from New York, Joseé Parys, and we ate virtually the entire menu.

The moment I set foot in this restaurant, my imagination was abuzz, and I knew I was in for an experience both culinary and cultural. The interior is spacious, grand and quite dramatic, with its black-lacquered furniture, exotic silk curtains and drapery, old black-and-white photographs around the walls and stunning red lanterns. I felt as though I had stepped back in time to Shanghai of the 1920s and '30s, or at least onto the set of *Stowaway*, a movie from 1936 with Shirley Temple playing a Chinese orphan. Sounds silly, I know, but it's true.

The Chinatown Brasserie is renowned for its dim sum, especially its dumplings, which can be had at any time of the day. They are fresh, clean, flavoursome and delicate—so delicate that Joseé and I tried to guess every single ingredient that went into them. You can have the traditional-style dim sum such as Pork and Chive Dumplings or Vegetable Spring Rolls, but be adventurous, too, and try modern specialties like Crispy Taro Root Shrimp, Dumplings with Sweet Soy Bean and Chanterelle Mushrooms, or a Smoked Salmon and Mango Roll. I got goose bumps every time I bit into something new.

I can also remember sharing Vegetable and Pine-Nut Wraps, a plate of Crispy Skin Chicken Wings cooked in a sweet chilli sauce with lemongrass, some sensational Peking Duck, fish steamed with white asparagus and ginger, and an assortment of other dishes with names too long to list. This is one Chinese restaurant where I wanted to taste everything on the menu. Luckily, Joseé was with me. I was ordering so much food she made sure every dish that came to our table was also 'to go'.

THE CORNELIA STREET CAFÉ

American-French
29 Cornelia Street
(between Bleecker and
West 4th Streets)
(1 212) 989 9319
corneliastreetcafe.com
Zagat: 19/30
Menu: $25 (2 courses and
house wine)
À la carte: $28–46

The Cornelia Street Café is a cabaret, art gallery and café rolled into one. It is open for breakfast, lunch and dinner seven days a week, with brunch on Sundays.

SERGE: Good spot for brunch and to feel like you're in a New York film. The street is straight out of a movie, and the café is classic New York: okay food made better by a good setting. It is a great spot to kill an afternoon.

CORNER BISTRO

American
331 West 4th Street
(at Jane Street)
(1 212) 242 9502
cornerbistrony.com
Zagat: 22/30
À la carte: $7–15

Legendary burgers and BLTs, 'seen it all before' staff and great beers on tap. No cards.

EN JAPANESE BRASSERIE

Japanese
435 Hudson Street
(at Leroy Street)
(1 212) 647 9196
enjb.com
Zagat: 24/30
Menu: $65/$90
(Hiwawari/chef's osusume;
both 7 courses)
À la carte: $35–73

Martha Stewart's favourite Japanese restaurant in New York is unusual in that it strives to remove all foreign influences from its cooking, aiming to provide an eating experience identical to that available in Japan. In spring, for example, it has a month-long Cherry Blossom Festival, where blossom features in—or as decoration on—every dish.

ADAM: Highly recommended. The décor of this izakaya restaurant is very well executed. The service was excellent, and the menu and ingredients were very good. If you are there around May, have the nine-course Sakura Kaiseki (Cherry Blossom dégustation), which I enjoyed immensely.

Highlights were the Sawara and Yuba Shabu Shabu, thinly sliced spring fish and vegetables served with a cherry-leaf dashi for light cooking and a sakura ponzu dipping sauce; the Sakura Dofu, which is a silken cherry-blossom tofu; and the grilled sakura-infused takenoko (young bamboo shoot).

....

Fatty Crab is principally inspired by Malaysian cooking, but also by neighbouring Asian cuisines. It adopts a very casual approach to dining, preferring to think of itself as a 'joint' rather than a restaurant. Its specialties include Chili Crab with White Toast, Singapore Black Pepper Bouchot Mussels, and Creekstone Short Rib Redang Braised with Kaffir Lime, Coconut and Chili. The flavours are bold. (There is a second Fatty Crab at 2170 Broadway on the Upper West Side.)

FATTY CRAB
Malaysian
643 Hudson Street
(between Gansevoort and
Horatio Streets)
(1 212) 352 3590
fattycrab.com
Michelin: Bib Gourmand
Zagat: 20/30
À la carte: $28–57

....

Eggs any style, burgers, salads and Michigan sandwiches (such as a Tuna Melt with Cheddar, plum tomato and Bermuda onion). Serious coffee. And cookies! RECOMMENDED: MELANIE

THE GREY DOG'S COFFEE
Café
90 University Place
(between East 11th and
12th Streets)
(1 212) 414 4739
thegreydog.com
Zagat: 22/30
À la carte: $5–12

....

IL BUCO

Italian
Chef: Ignacio Mattos
47 Bond Street (between
Lafayette Street and
Bowery)
(1 212) 533 1932
ilbuco.com
Zagat: 26/30
À la carte: $37–51

Film actors often supplement their incomes with stints as waiters, but few filmmakers start restaurants to add to their creative challenges. However, that is what independent director Donna Lennard did. It is therefore only fitting her restaurant is often frequented by one of Australia's finest filmmakers, Fred Schepisi. The chef, Ignacio Mattos, is actually Uruguayan, but his food is distinctively Mediterranean. The wine list is considered one of the most outstanding in the world by *Wine Spectator*, a notoriously tough judge.
RECOMMENDED: FRED

. . . .

JACK'S STIR BREW COFFEE

Café
138 West 10th Street
(between Waverly Place and
Greenwich Avenue)
(1 212) 929 0821
jacksstirbrew.com
À la carte: $7–15

At Jack's, the coffee is organic and fair trade. There are also premium teas. To hold off hunger pains, there are Vegan Organic Kosher Scones, Aunt Rosie's Chocolate Chip Cookies, H&H bagels, and fresh-baked muffins and croissants.

SERGE: Brilliant staff who take real pride in preparing your morning brew. It has some of the best coffee in Manhattan. Try the Mad Max to jump-start the heart or the Green Hornet for those who prefer tea.

. . . .

JOE'S

Café
141 Waverly Place
(near Gay Street)
(1 212) 924 6750
joetheartofcoffee.com
À la carte: $5–12

Coffee and Anne Sedaris cupcakes. There are four **Joe's** across Manhattan.

SERGE: Best coffee and service in the West Village. They know their coffee and enjoy working there. Makes a difference.

. . . .

Manhattan's answer to a typical Roman trattoria (hard to find even in Rome), **Lupa Osteria Romana** opened in 1999 and has been hugely popular ever since. Owners Jason Denton, Mario Batali and Joseph Bastianich set out to not only capture the cuisine of Rome, but the spirit. The light touch can be seen in the dishes (Ricotta Gnocchi with Sausage and Fennel; Skate with Artichokes alla Guida) and an Italian wine list that is wide-ranging and wonderfully affordable (such as eight fine Sicilian reds for $42 or less). RECOMMENDED: FRED

LUPA OSTERIA ROMANA

Italian
Chef: Mark Ladner
170 Thompson Street
(between West Houston
and Bleecker Streets)
(1 212) 982 5089
luparestaurant.com
Michelin: Bib Gourmand
Zagat: 25/30
À la carte: $37–58

SHARLEE: I have been to Lupa four times and it is without doubt my favourite little neighbourhood Italian place. It has amazing Italian artisan meats and cheeses, handmade pastas and wines. On my last visit, it was Christmas Eve with a twist—Feast of the Seven Fishes—with dishes like *Zimono de ceci e polpo*, *Baccalà ravioli* and *Turbot al cartoccio* being our favourites.

SERGE: All-round great food.

Simple, classic pizza-and-pasta restaurant (albeit with fine cured meats, seafood and cheese) from restaurateurs Mario Batali and Joseph Bastianich. Dan Dohan oversees the in-house meats, Meredith Kurtzman the desserts and Bastianich the wine.

OTTO ENOTECA PIZZERIA

Italian
1 Fifth Avenue (enter on
East 8th Street between
Fifth Avenue and
University Place)
(1 212) 995 9559
ottopizzeria.com
Zagat: 22/30
À la carte: $21–35

SHANNON: Mario Batali's pizza restaurant is a little gem not far from wd~50. I was really feeling the effects of eating two big dinners in two days, so I decided to go to MoMA for a look around and had a great afternoon. What did I really need after that? Well, catching up with the rest of the Vue de monde team, who were taking the Sunday off with a pizza and carafe of good American Sangiovese.

For those of you whom like me cannot do Michelin every night, **Otto Enoteca Pizzeria** comes highly recommended. But be warned that our taxi driver could not find 1 Fifth Avenue. It was a quiet night on the streets and there wasn't a lot of activity out the front of the restaurant, which really disguises what you find inside very well. I love the building that houses Otto. It is an Art Déco period place that has been turned into apartments.

The pizzas are not all that are good here, but the salads, seafood and pasta are great. Start with a cold meat platter that is sliced to order with some olives and marinated anchovies. Order some salads to come with the pasta and pizza. As this is not the normal order of service in America (they tend to eat salads at the start), make sure you make yourself very clear.

Ice creams are very classic in presentation and fit perfectly with an espresso to finish what was the cheapest meal I had in New York. Without a doubt, it is a really rewarding place to visit.

The atmosphere is what you would call 'awesome'. The front room is a holding room, bar and take-out area, and then there are two main rooms at the back, all decked out in a theme I'd imagine is what an Italian restaurant would have looked like in the 1960s on a Hollywood movie set. I mean that in a good way.

MATT: Otto, another Mario Batali place, has probably the best pizzas in New York.

Arguably the design masterpiece of the Keith McNally restaurants, **Pastis** sits in a lonely part of the still-to-be-fully-developed area of the Meatpacking District. The location almost has the feel of a deserted country town, Pastis commanding a corner and overlooking wide and relatively quiet streets. There are so few people on the sidewalks you may wonder if there is actually anyone inside the restaurant. There is, for Pastis has been a hit since it opened and all claim it was instrumental in the trendification of the area (after taking over the building from Florent). Pastis is pure French bistro, with Onion Soup Gratinée, Oysters, Steak Tartare and *Moules frites au Pernod*. There is a daily Plat du Jour. RECOMMENDED: LUKE, FRED

PASTIS

French
Chef: Pascal Le Seac'h
9 Ninth Avenue (at
Little West 12th Street)
(1 212) 929 4844
pastisny.com
Zagat: 21/30
À la carte: $40–60

SHANNON: When your biggest complaint about a place is that you cannot get over how busy it is and finding a table is an issue, then it's not really a complaint. Pastis has a great location and is a huge space. It is very different from the type of eatery it's trying to replicate, but it works for many reasons. Its big sister, Balthazar, has a very French feel from a completely different era. Pastis has unique tiles, a zinc bar top and a very large bar area that has a good beer focus. The second room is mostly large shared tables that work very well. It's the kind of place I use to meet friends who live in New York, or I go alone and sit at the bar where the staff are more than happy to recommend and talk about anything and everything, including what oysters are on the menu and their favourite wines by the glass. Breakfasts are very good and include slightly American items such as eggs with hollandaise, but they also do good pastries, coffee and omelettes. At night, I prefer to come for good oysters, a glass of nice French white and a simple dessert.

New York needed Pastis like Pastis needs New York.

BRYAN: Pastis is a French bistro in the classic New York style, and is packed all night. If you don't have a booking, be prepared to wait.

It is actually a fascinating restaurant to watch operate. I arrived at 7 p.m.—it was a 45-minute wait for a table—and left at 10.15 p.m. It has a great buzz and people are waiting everywhere: at the bar, between tables and outside. The room is run by two staff who know whom everyone is and where they are on the list. To watch it all unfold is probably more interesting than the actual meal itself, which is standard bistro food, executed well.

Pastis represents a wonderful opportunity to get lost for a few hours—as if you need that in New York.

MATT: Pastis is my favourite breakfast place in New York. Just love it. It is really cool. Groovy. You sit on the pavement as people walk past. Great baked eggs.

ADAM: An enjoyable place for lunch or breakfast with lots of character. Similar to Balthazar. Try and get a table close to the street.

....

SCARPETTA

Italian
Chef: Scott Conant
355 West 14th Street
(between Ninth and
Eighth Avenues)
(1 212) 691 0555
scarpettanyc.com
Zagat: 26/30
À la carte: $48–69

Scott Conant is one of the most famous Italian chefs in Manhattan. He is a star judge on television's *Chopped* and now runs, among others, **Scarpetta** on the northern border of the Meatpacking District (which some guides wrongly place in Chelsea). Since it opened, it has been abuzz and the Conant phenomenon shows no sign of abating, largely because the man can cook.

SCOTT: Anyone who eats at Scarpetta is likely to come to the conclusion Conant could open a serious Michelin-starred restaurant if he wanted to, but simpler Italian cooking is clearly what he is all about. Though the food here has just a hint of the mass-produced, it is often remarkable and never less than fine.

The night before, the kindly sommelier at SHO Shaun Hergatt had promised to ring a mate at Scarpetta and make sure I was looked after, given the tragedy of my Per Se non-visit (which I was retelling to all who would listen). To his word, he had rung and my arrival was greeted with an enthusiasm you would think was reserved for rock royalty. It also meant I got extra courses and extra large serves.

To celebrate it having been two years since Scarpetta opened, Conant was offering a three-course menu that included three complimentary glasses of wine for $50. That was impossible to resist.

First up was a basket of breads: ciabatta roll, foccacia, stromboli (with cheese) and an Italian version of pain de campagne whose name I didn't catch. They were served with olive oil, roasted eggplant and a firm ricotta. All were delicious. The first wine was a glass of a not-bad Prosecco. It is a cliché to say Prosecco has improved immeasurably over the past decade, but it is undeniably true.

The real courses began with Creamy Polenta and a Fricassee of Truffled Mushrooms. The polenta was divine and almost like soup, with none of the grittiness of a similar attempt at The Modern. The mushrooms were yummy but surprisingly under-salted. Conant stands almost alone in New York for not adding a lot of salt.

Along with it came a gift serve of Braised Short Ribs of Beef, Faro and Vegetable Risotto. The ribs melted in the mouth and didn't taste at all fatty. The risotto was pleasant, but the dish was really about the ribs. Both courses were paired with a delicious 2007 Sauvignon from Abbazia di Novacella in Alto Adige.

Then came Short Rib Agnolotti with Hazelnuts, Brown Butter and Horseradish. As with the hazelnuts and the soft shell crab at The Modern, I just didn't get it. They didn't meld in any way with the agnolotti or the sauce. Conant talks all the time on *Chopped* about how everything in a dish must blend into a unified whole, but they didn't here. But maybe hazelnuts are a New York thing that Antipodean foreigners just don't get. The agnolotti, though, were delicious.

Having seen the fish options from the prix-fixe menu arrive at other tables (Halibut, Black Cod), I was left hoping my serve would be just as petite. But no, the restaurant had kindly decided I should have the whole thing: Lard-Wrapped Halibut, with Morels, Asparagus and Smoked Potatoes. The fish was astonishingly good, flawlessly cooked, from-the-sea fresh, moist and delicious. You don't get better fish in the three-star Le Bernardin. The morels were a bit bland, but the asparagus and potatoes were fine. Overall, it was a very, very good dish. And it was paired perfectly with a Cabernet from Campagnia.

Not that I had room, but a chocolate cake followed, served with an unidentified ice cream. The cake was as moist as a coulant but without a separate runny centre. It was stunningly rich with chocolate taste.

So, what of Scarpetta? It was a shock to find it was as bustling as a canteen, rather than a calmer and more luxurious place, given all the reviews. Conant can obviously cook anything, at any level. He offers quality at a price that is almost impossible to comprehend.

This is a wonderful restaurant when you want a fun night out, but book ahead. It is packed—so tightly packed, in fact, that you will get to know some of your fellow diners intimately. But that's part of the fun. The couple next to me revealed that they had hoped the food would be terrible because they don't like Conant as a judge on *Chopped*; they said he was too grumpy. Sadly for them, they had adored his food and his restaurant. They then discussed their many New York restaurant experiences (they live in Long Island but go out in Manhattan a lot). Their favourites: Eleven Madison

Park and Corton. Their favourite steakhouse: Wolfgang's. The restaurant they most wanted to visit due to fabulous word of mouth: SHO Shaun Hergatt. Worst restaurants (hands down): Minetta Tavern, Union Square Café.

....

SNACK TAVERNA
Greek
63 Bedford Street
(at Morton Street)
(1 212) 929 3499
no website
Zagat: 22/30
À la carte: $10–53

Sister restaurant to the five-table Snack in SoHo, **Snack Taverna** is huge in comparison, catering to more than fifty customers. The food is traditionally Greek. The wine list has a greater selection of Hellenic treasures than Snack, but they are equally affordable.

....

SPICE MARKET
South-East Asian
Chefs: Jean-Georges
Vongerichten, Anthony Ricco
403 West 13th Street
(at Ninth Avenue)
(1 212) 675 2322
spicemarketnewyork.com
Zagat: 23/30
Menu: $48
À la carte: $36–63

One of Jean-Georges Vongerichten's many takes on Asian street cooking is the widely successful **Spice Market** in the Meatpacking District. Many Vongerichten fans think it is his best restaurant. You can start with Black Pepper Shrimp with Sun-Dried Pineapple or Fragrant Mushroom Egg Rolls and move on to Nonya Seafood Laksa with Gulf Shrimp and Scallop or Char-Grilled Chicken with Kumquat Lemongrass Dressing. The interior has an Indonesian feel, freely interpreted with a sense of fun. RECOMMENDED: FRED

SHANNON: This amazing restaurant and bar encapsulates everything that New York is in a restaurant. Jean-Georges Vongerichten once again is the creator of the concept, which has now been commissioned by W Hotels to be the flagship in several new W Hotels being rolled out around the world. But there is nothing like the original, as they say! And this original is set in a very large warehouse in the Meatpacking District. The atmosphere is electric and infectious. On every occasion, I have just popped in with the intended purpose of a quick dinner, but ended up having a relaxed and enjoyable night that flowed into being a late one.

Open seven days, use this place as it was intended. If it's not a Friday or Saturday night, don't book. Just decide on the night—most probably after a big Michelin dinner the night before—and turn up without expectations. If you plan it and expect a big exciting dining experience, you will go away disappointed.

The space is made up of two main levels, with an entry bar that is large and spacious, and has been designed sympathetically for single diners and large groups without alienating either. Be warned, though, this place is noisy. The décor is a cross between Balinese and Indian.

Duck is something done very well here, mainly in some form of a curry; so is the whole steamed fish. I love the lobster steamed with ginger. Make sure you sit downstairs for dinner, as it's a lot more favourable noise- and service-wise. The cocktails are good and so are the wines by the glass; they are not by any means extensive, but the list is well chosen.

The whole experience is very well priced. At $70 per person including tip, you will get a nice two-hour dinner.

....

THE STANDARD GRILL

American
Chef: Dan Silverman
The Standard
848 Washington Street
(between Little West 12th
and 13th Streets)
(1 212) 645 4100
thestandardgrill.com
Zagat: 21/30
À la carte: $39–71

The Standard Grill has made many New Restaurants of the Year lists for its elegant steakhouse vibe. There are studded-leather banquettes, tablecloths, a few red retro chairs and loads of paned windows. At night, when it is invariably packed (even hotel guests need to book well ahead), it has the feel of a private—and very lively—club.

ADRIAN: Here is a place for everyone. Located in the heaving, way-too-cool Meatpacking District, this place shines, with brand-new everything and sharp, good-looking staff. The place is clean and crisp, a bit like the whitewashed *Desperate Housewives*.

The food is simple, fast and fresh; it has to be. This is a place designed to make money and it does. The Standard Grill heaves day and night; I visited three times and could not believe how busy it was. If you're having brunch on the weekend, book or be prepared to wait. New Yorkers love to brunch and they congregate most where the food is good and the crowd is chic. There are plenty of New York City's good-looking here. I'm told only the best of the bridge-and-tunnel people (those who don't live on Manhattan) come here.

A warning to coffee lovers: you won't get great coffee here. You are better off with caffeine tablets. Believe me: avoid the temptation.

The space is the All-American diner, with red leather banquettes, lots of wood and red-and-white check tablecloths. At the back is a kitchen, with shiny stainless steel and plenty of hands on deck. There are about eight seats along a big wooden bar that look straight into the kitchen; it is great for those wanting to watch the machine in action.

At night, after the dinner service, the lights are dimmed, the music turned up and the place heaves with thirty-somethings. It becomes a bar nightclub with standard American fare given an Italian twist. Great burgers ($13), with the fries hot and crisp arriving in stainless steel cups. There is creamy polenta, with broccoli-rabe sausage and fried egg. Freshly shucked oysters are $17 per dozen. There is a cheese-and-meat board to snack on while waiting for friends. The Bloody Bull is a Bloody Mary with beef bullion. I had a few of those.

While not cutting edge by any means, this is a great place to be: good food, great service and a genuine NYC buzz.

ADAM: An unforgettable experience—unforgettable for some of the rudest, most disorganized service I have ever encountered. I cannot comment on the food because my daughter Charlotte and I walked out after fifteen minutes. We didn't even get to the table.

This is one of the trendiest restaurants in New York, and one of the hardest to get into, due to its ownership by *Vanity Fair* editor and man very much about town, Graydon Carter. Not many people are kind about the food, though. Since it is run rather like a private club, with Carter often dining with friends at his usual banquette, and very small, the chances of your getting in are so remote that you needn't worry. The Macaroni and Cheese is $55, but it has truffles, the scent of which also flavours the chips accompanying the $13 Waverley Burger. If you want to go where it is important to be seen, this is it. Good luck.

WAVERLY INN & GARDEN
American
16 Bank Street
(at Waverly Place)
(1 917) 828 1154
no website
Zagat: 20/30
À la carte: $31–80

FRED: Very trendy.

. . . .

Burgers, sandwiches, grilled trout and chocolate chip cookies in a small neighbourhood restaurant. It has been such a hit that there are other **Westville**s in Chelsea (246 West 18th Street) and East Village (173 Avenue A).

WESTVILLE
Eclectic American
210 West 10th Street
(between Bleecker and
West 4th Streets)
(1 212) 741 7971
westvillenyc.com
Zagat: 22/30
À la carte: $21–34

SERGE: Comfort food for the weary traveller. You may as well have 'Mom' in the kitchen, with a classic menu that includes American staples such as buttered beans, collard greens and authentic hamburgers.

. . . .

SHANNON'S FAVOURITE NEW YORK TREATS

COCKTAILS

In the city that never sleeps, what better way to spend your evening than at one of the world's best cocktail bars. New York is where the art of the cocktail has been perfected and some of the world's finest bartenders continue to inspire and lead the way.

The following are just a few of my favourite cocktails crafted in New York and where to find them, compiled with the help of Thiago Vieira dos Santos.

EARL GREY MARTEANI

The infused Earl Grey MarTEAni is the star at Audrey Saunders' bar, Pegu Club, a South-East Asian–inspired gin palace. Pegu Club's name pays tribute to a British colonial officers' club in Burma. Saunders' mentor is the master mixologist Dale DeGroff.

1 oz fresh lemon juice

½ oz simple syrup (2:1 sugar-to-water ratio)

1½ oz Earl Grey tea–infused Tanqueray gin (see recipe at right)

1 egg white

lemon twist

Measure all the ingredients into a mixing glass. Add ice, and shake hard to a 10-second count. Strain into a chilled martini glass, and garnish with a lemon twist.

EARL GREY TEA–INFUSED TANQUERAY GIN

1 750 ml bottle of Tanqueray gin (for its flavour and high proof)

4 tablespoons loose, Earl Grey tea

Measure tea into bottle. Cap and put into boiling water for 30 minutes. Let sit at room temperature for 2 hours. Strain through a fine sieve or coffee filter into a bowl. Rinse out bottle to remove loose tea leaves and pour infusion back into clean bottle. It will store indefinitely refrigerated.

FINAL WARD

Skilled bartenders in New York love to 'twist' classic cocktails while respecting the original. Phil Ward from Death & Co executes the twist on a classic really well, going so far as to improve the drink from its original, the Last Word. Swapping gin for rye whisky, the Final Ward is fresh and complex with flavours deepened by the spicy elements of the rye.

¾ oz rye whisky

¾ oz Green Chartreuse

¾ oz Maraschino

¾ oz lemon juice

Shake all ingredients with ice and strain into a cocktail glass.

PENICILLIN

The Penicillin is an amazing, spicy variation of the Whisky Sour. A classic combination with a modern twist, the flavours work together in a natural harmony. The natural honey flavours occurring in the whisky are enhanced by the addition of the honey and ginger syrup, while the ginger adds a spicy element that reinvents the original as a modern classic. It is a refreshing drink with warm flavours.

Created by Sam Ross, Penicillin can be found at bars all around the world and is the drink credited with giving Ross and Milk & Honey recognition on the world stage.

2 oz Scotch whisky

¼ oz Laphroaig (single-malt Islay Scotch)

¾ oz fresh lemon juice

¾ oz honey water (1:1 honey to water ratio)

a dash of ginger juice or grated ginger

1 egg white

Combine ingredients and shake with ice. Strain over ice.

BENTON'S OLD FASHIONED

This is a perfect example of smokiness infused into a drink to deepen its flavour. PDT uses a traditional, much-loved breakfast flavour combination to create a smoky twist on the classic Old Fashioned. At PDT, the drink is served with a giant ice cube, which, unlike a traditional ice cube or crushed ice, works to keep the drink cold without over-diluting it.

1½ oz bacon-infused bourbon (see recipe below)

¼ oz maple syrup

2 dashes Angostura bitters

twist of orange

In a mixing glass, stir 1½ oz bacon-infused bourbon, maple syrup and bitters with ice. Strain into chilled rocks glass filled with ice. Garnish with orange twist.

BACON-INFUSED BOURBON

3 or 4 slices bacon, or enough to render 1 ounce of fat (PDT uses Benton's, but any extra-smoky variety will do)

1 750 ml bottle of bourbon

Cook bacon in pan and reserve rendered fat. When bacon fat has cooled a bit, pour off one ounce from pan.

Pour bourbon into a non-porous container. Strain the bacon fat into the container and infuse for 4–6 hours at room temperature. Place mixture in freezer until all the fat is solidified. With a slotted spoon, remove fat and strain mixture back into bottle.

SHANNON'S FAVOURITE NEW YORK TREATS

MASTER THE ART:
MORE COCKTAIL RECIPES TO TRY AT HOME

CAIPIRINHA (THE BRAZILIAN CLASSIC)

1 whole lime (cut into quarters)

2 teaspoons of sugar

45 ml cachaca (Brazilian sugar-cane spirit)

Muddle the lime with the sugar in a glass tumbler and add the cachaca.

Half-fill the glass with crushed ice, pour in the cachaca mixture and stir from the bottom to the top. Top up with crushed ice and serve.

COPACABANA

45 ml chilli-infused cachaca (see recipe below)

25 ml Monin passion fruit syrup

15 ml fresh lime juice

1 egg white

Mix ingredients, shake with ice and strain into a martini glass. Garnish with a chilli.

CHILLI-INFUSED CACHACA

2 chillies

750 ml cachaca

Remove some of the seeds of the chilli and macerate in the cachaca overnight. Strain through a fine strainer.

CAFÉ VUE SANGRIA

250 ml sweet vermouth

250 ml Amaro Nonino or Montenegro

700 ml red wine

150 ml brown sugar syrup (1:1 sugar to water ratio)

150 ml water

200 ml lemon juice

¼ sliced pineapple garnish

4 mint stokes

1 sliced lemon garnish

1 sliced orange garnish

Mix all the liquid ingredients together. Add all the sliced fruit and the mint and refrigerate for 3 hours. Adjust the citrus if necessary. Add ice and serve. Makes 16 drinks.

SPANISH CONNEXION

30 ml quince and Pedro Ximenez syrup (see recipe at right)

15 ml fresh lemon juice

champagne

In a champagne flute, mix the quince and Pedro Ximenez syrup with the lemon juice. Fill glass with champagne and garnish with a lemon twist.

QUINCE AND PEDRO XIMENEZ SYRUP

Mix 1 part quince paste, 2 parts Pedro
Ximenez Sherry and 1 part simple
syrup (1:1 sugar to water ratio) in
a blender. Strain into a sterilized
bottle; add a dash of vodka to make
it longer lasting.

ICE

Ice is more important than you
think! Choosing the right ice is just
as important as choosing the right
spirit. Once the ice melts, the water
becomes part of your drink. If the
water is poor quality, it will affect the
quality of your drink.

The size or shape of the ice will
determine how long the drink stays
cold and the amount of dilution.
If you have already achieved the
desired dilution when preparing the
drink, you are best to use a big piece
of ice as it will keep the dilution
to a minimum all the way through
the drink.

Crushed ice, good for a refreshing
drink, will cool the drink down
dramatically.

With shaken cocktails, it is
important to pick ice cubes that are
relatively small in size, which will
allow for better dilution.

The size of the ice cubes also
affects how long a carbonated drink
will keep its fizz. Larger cubes will
make the bubbles last longer.

BARS

|||||||||||||||||||||||||||||||||||||||||||||||||||||||||||||||||||||||||||||||||||||||||||||||||||||||||||||||||||||||||

BIERGARTEN
Beer garden
The Standard
848 Washington Street
(between Little West 12th
and 13th Streets)
(1 212) 645 4646
standardhotels.com
4 p.m.–midnight (Mon–
Thurs), 4 p.m.–1 a.m. (Fri),
noon–midnight (Sun)

An outdoor German 'beer hall' under the High Line at The Standard.

PAULA AND PATRICK: Great in summer on a Sunday, but best get there early so that you can get a table, otherwise you might end up sharing with a group of strangers. If you love German beer, pretzels and sausages, you have come to the right place. The wine selection is not impressive, so expect to be drinking beer.

SERGE: Total summer scene.

. . . .

THE BOOM BOOM ROOM @ THE STANDARD
Bar nightclub
The Standard
848 Washington Street
(between Little West 12th
and 13th Streets)
(1 212) 645 4646
standardhotels.com

Promoted as the new Studio 54 (but fortunately with no nude men and snakes), and denounced as the world's most expensive airport lounge, **The Boom Boom Room @ The Standard** is probably the hottest bar in New York.

. . . .

SHANNON: On the top floor of The Standard in the heart of the Meatpacking District is an über-cool bar with views inside and out. Make sure you choose your time to have a drink here because for some for strange reason the bar closes at 8 p.m. and then re-opens at 10.30 p.m. with more of a clubby feel. My friend Harry and I popped in for a drink. Harry likes a Negroni but I can't drink it as it reminds me of cough medicine, so I went for a $21 Rusty Nail instead. It was then that Harry spotted 'Jennifer'. Having no idea who he meant, I discreetly looked over my shoulder and there she was: Jennifer

Aniston. And was that Lisa Kudrow sitting directly behind her? I like to think of that sighting as a mystery.

With two private areas and futuristic fireplaces dangling from the ceiling, I recommend making a booking here in the late afternoon to watch the sun go down.

HARRY: My superstar hairdresser friends Dean and Franco, who work at the famous Cutler Salon in SoHo, recommended I go here. This is an impressive bar with an almost Gatsby, Déco-style fit-out. I went with Shannon for a very nice $20 cocktail. One is usually enough and they are strong. Jennifer Aniston was there, glancing over at us. Starstruck, I tried to whisper to Shannon, but he yelled 'Who's Jennifer?' I panicked and said 'Shush', unsuccessfully trying to be cool. She was still checking us out, but then I began to think maybe she was just wondering what a couple of guys like us were doing in a place like that. A little embarrassed, I gulped the rest of my Negroni and rushed out.

PAUL AND PATRICK: A trendy, secret restaurant that says it serves Serbian food that is pretty basic but delicious. It can be a little hard to find. It is on Hudson Street, but there is no obvious entrance. It's just a green awning with EO written sideways and the window has 'psychic' written in neon, with a lady sitting there pretending to be one. So, walk past her, past the curtains and you are in the place.

EMPLOYEES ONLY
Bar and restaurant
510 Hudson Street
employeesonlynyc.com
(1 212) 242 3021
6 p.m.–4 a.m.

SIMON: This is the tiniest, narrowest bar that is so dark that even with blazing daylight outside the bar it feels like it's 3 a.m. inside. I sat 2 metres from the singer and was in almost total darkness, a dim key-light illuminating what was for me one of the greatest performances I've ever seen. At 6 p.m. a two-drink minimum ensured only the very keen were there, mostly other musicians and friends of the band. One of the coolest places I've been, and you can still make a show by 8 p.m.

ZINC BAR
Bar
82 West 3rd Street
(between Sullivan and
Thompson streets)
(1 212) 477 9462
zincbar.com
6 p.m.–2.30 a.m.

ART BAR
Bar
52 Eighth Avenue
(1 212) 727 0244
4 p.m.–4 a.m.

BAR NEXT DOOR
Bar
129 MacDougal Street
(1 212) 529 5945
6 p.m.–2 a.m. (Sun–Thurs),
6 p.m.–3 a.m. (Fri–Sat)

BLIND TIGER
Bar
281 Bleecker Street
(1 212) 462 4682
4 p.m.–4 a.m.

FAT CATS
Pub
75 Christopher Street
(1 212) 675 6056
2 p.m.–2 a.m. (Mon–Fri),
noon–2 a.m. (Sat–Sun)

LITTLE BRANCH
Bar
20 Seventh Avenue
(1 212) 929 4360
7 p.m.–3 a.m. (Mon–Sat),
9 p.m.–3 a.m. (Sun)

THE OTHER ROOM
Bar
143 Perry Street
(1 212) 645 9758
5 p.m.–2 a.m. (Sun–Tues),
5 p.m.–4 a.m. (Wed–Sat)

THE RUSTY KNOT
Bar
425 West Street
(1 212) 645 5668
Noon–4 a.m.

675 BAR
Bar
675 Hudson Street
(1 212) 699 2400
6 p.m.–4 a.m. (Mon–Sat)

SULLIVAN ROOM
DJ bar
218 Sullivan Street
(1 212) 252 2151
9 p.m.–5 a.m. (Wed–Sat)

24 RABBIT CLUB
Bar
124 MacDougal Street
(1 212) 254 0575
6 p.m.–2 a.m. (Mon–Thurs),
6 p.m.–4 a.m. (Fri–Sat)

VOL DE NUIT BAR (AKA BELGIUM BEER LOUNGE)
Bar
148 W 4th Street
(1 212) 982 3388
4 p.m.–midnight (Mon–Thurs),
4 p.m.–2.30 a.m. (Fri–Sat)

LUXURY HOTELS

The **Gansevoort** is everything a boutique designer hotel should be. The entrance is spectacular, with a 4.3-metre-high revolving glass door. Inside, there are bursts of pastels and shimmering gold throughout the impressive lobby. This is certainly a place you could take anyone to impress them. Rooms start at 24 square metres and are luxuriously decorated, with subtle rather than in-your-face modern design. The featherbeds are covered in 400-thread Egyptian cotton, with goose-down pillows and hypo-allergenic duvets. You are sure to sleep well. The bathrooms are stunningly appointed, with showers that also double as steam rooms and have Cutler Salon amenities. The heated rooftop pool is a stunner (though one could probably do without the multicoloured lighting), the surrounds boasting a 360-degree view over the Hudson River and Manhattan. If you are one of the iPod generation, you can relax because the pool has music pumped underwater for you. The Plunge Bar & Lounge is one of the hottest in New York. The hotel's gastropub, Tanuki Tavern, specializes in izakaya-themed sharing plates, along with a range of rare sakes. You can also indulge at the Exhale Spa, which is far larger and more serious than those found in many hotels. This is one reason the Gansevoort brands itself as a resort rather than a hotel.

GANSEVOORT
18 Ninth Avenue (at West 13th Street)
(1 212) 206 6700
hotelgansevoort.com
Rating: 4★
Rooms: 166
Suites: 21
Hotel rates: $525–605

MATT: Stayed here. Great rooms, a bit bigger than your average New York hotel room. Great rooftop pool and bar, which is still really cool whether summer or winter. It's a great area, great culture.

SOHO HOUSE NEW YORK

20–35 Ninth Avenue
(at West 13th Street)
(1 212) 627 9800
sohohouseny.com
Rating: 4★
Rooms: 24
Hotel rates: not quoted;
email or telephone
enquiries only
Internet: $575–1450

This private members club and hotel was made famous by a guest spot in *Sex and the City*. Non-members may book via *lastminute.com*, and there are other web specials as well. The twenty-four rooms are huge, ranging from 32 square metres to 88. The smallest, the Playpens, have exposed brick walls and ceiling beams, with wooden floors. The walk-in showers have a prison-block feel. These rooms have a converted warehouse approach that doesn't quite meld with the interior decorations. The design starts to come together fully in the Playhouse rooms, which blend white Venetian beds with modern photographic collages stuck straight onto the wall. The bath is a super-cool egg shape, with the benefit of 1.8-metre mirrors positioned behind it so that bath privacy is reduced to zero. You have to be seriously in love to stay here. If you can bear to leave this room, there is the Cowshed Spa, a 44-seat cinema you can book for private screenings, a restful library (not that it has many books), and a restaurant with leather banquettes and Swarovski chandeliers. But perhaps the best reason to venture out is the spectacular rooftop pool and lounge areas (where brunch is served). The views are sensational.

SHANNON: My friend Melanie Dunea, a New York portrait photographer, well known for her book *The Last Supper*, is a member here along with her husband. So, when she asked if we wanted to meet up for a beer at this well-known institution, I jumped at the chance. Located in the Meatpacking District, it blends well into the cool warehouse apartments, galleries and restaurants surrounding it.

SoHo House is everything to its members. The spacious rooms with great one-off pieces of furniture and exposed wood can be booked by non-members on *lastminute. com*, so check a week before you intend to arrive.

The rooftop swimming pool is fantastic, the best swimming pool in New York. Okay, let me rephrase that: the best outdoor swimming pool. The Mandarin Oriental has a great indoor pool overlooking Central Park, which just makes you feel that life is so precious. Both experiences sum up why New York is a living, breathing thing!

There are several places to hang out and have a drink or something to eat inside the hotel. The Restaurant and Bar is on the sixth floor, as is the Games Room, with pool tables and large televisions for watching sports games. On the same floor is the Drawing Room, which is really a great conversation room. A floor below, with very comfortable furniture, is the Library, a cool, quiet space. Then there is the Roof for great summer lunches and relaxed evenings, where the heaters work really well.

The burgers here are great and it's the sort of food I feel like when in this environment. But that said, I saw some great grilled whole Sole that really got me excited go out to a table.

The wine list is extensive, the staff great and very friendly. Prices are cheap with mains in the mid $20s. I really recommend staying here if you want the its 'like a home away from home' feel. The breakfasts, such as the Fried Duck Eggs, are great.

Memberships are relatively easy to get but pricey. The yearly membership cost plus joining fee of $2500 allows you to use the sister clubs in London, such as Shoreditch House. I recently stayed at Dean Street Townhouse, the group's newest property in London's SoHo, and I must say it was fantastic. Keep it in mind.

....

THE STANDARD

848 Washington Street
(at West 13th Street)
(1 212) 645 4646
standardhotels.com
Rating: 4★
Rooms: 337
Hotel rates: $536–895

Though listed by some guides (such as Michelin) as a three-star hotel, **The Standard** is easily a four-star and one of the great trend-setting hotels of New York. Opened by André Balazs of Chateau Marmont fame, it has helped further revitalize the Meatpacking District and has been lauded by every trendy magazine from *Wallpaper** to *Vogue*. Its bar at the top, The Boom Boom Room @ The Standard, is hotter than hot, which just about sums up the whole place. Good luck if you want to get into The Standard Grill, the Biergarten (in warm weather) or the hotel's second bar, The Living Room, on the ground floor. Pedestrians on the restored High Line get uninterrupted views into some of the lower-level guestrooms. This led to a rumour, never proved, that the hotel employed beautiful young things to walk around in a state of undress to create publicity when the hotel first opened.

SCOTT: The Standard is a stunning architectural achievement, straddling the 19-block High Line, which is now being progressively turned into a park. The hotel dominates the Meatpacking District like the Colossus dominated Rhodes. The entrance is dramatic: an opaque yellow revolving door that spins you into a dazzling entrance hall, with a black mirrored ceiling and white side walls that look like massively enlarged Chux Super Wipes. They lead to two reception desks (and two concierges) who treat you as if you have just been granted the keys to a magic kingdom.

The lifts that whisk you upwards are black and shiny, with two video installations that reveal an animated montage of the journey from heaven to hell (or vice versa). You'll wish your room was on a higher floor just so you can watch more of it.

I was on the lowish sixth, a corner room with dramatic views over inland Manhattan (the other side looks at the Hudson from an oblique angle, except for the privileged corner rooms at the western end). The room is miles smaller than what you would expect for $700+ a night, the bed taking up most of the sleeping area, with a small sofa and single leather chair pressed against a white plastic table. The lamp dangling above it is a design classic and the mirror behind does add a sense of space. But it remains a very small room.

The bathroom, though, is bigger, with an open shower with rain shower head and a freestanding white bath designed by Philippe Stark. Like so many trendy fittings these days, it is seriously flawed. The only way to empty the bath is to stay there holding the round tap that minimally raises the plug, otherwise the weight of the water forces it shut. Prepare to abandon ten minutes of your life. Still, sitting in this vast and deep bath looking out over Manhattan is an extraordinary experience.

The minibar inside a 1950s sideboard cabinet is extensively stocked and is only a fraction of the cost of nearly every other minibar in New York. There is also a tiny newsstand with magazines on the wall.

While the view is dramatic, it isn't romantic: the Meatpacking District is low-rise and grungy, a mass of deserted buildings and rusted roofs. In daylight, it is ugly, at night something altogether different, especially if you face the Hotel Gansevoort, which lights up colourfully, a vibrant party scene happening on its roof every night.

The Standard has a famous bar on its top floor, another off the entrance, and two restaurants, The Standard Grill and the Biergarten, the latter an open-to-the-elements space under the High Line that is only open in warmer months.

The clientele at The Standard is young (late twenties and early thirties), all doing well enough to cope with the high tariffs, and to sit around discussing the latest and greatest shopping coups and restaurant discoveries. They are the kind of clients who don't mind that the hotel is located in a loud neighbourhood with music blaring at night from various locales (including The Standard). The windows, which don't open, aren't soundproofed as they should be. Guests also love the fact it is a short walk to one of the trendiest shopping areas in New York. Many fine restaurants reside there as well, such as Scarpetta, Del Posto and Bill's Bar & Burger.

ANNA: Last time I was in New York, to exhibit in The Armory Show, we all stayed at The Standard. It has vertigo-inducing views across the Hudson and of the still-living meatpacking industry on the street below. Mix that with my favourite clothes in the shops around those streets and Pastis, always reliable for any meal of the day on the corner … and it is very good indeed.

At breakfast, you can arrange to see many of the people you want to meet during the day, so the meal can take half the day. Room service is exactly the same food as the restaurant. Best is the Barbequed River Trout, grilled only on the skin side, and delectable.

MATT: The Standard is notorious for people sitting outside in the High Line Park looking in at you as you get changed. It has a fantastic bar on top, but you have to get there early because it is invite-only after 8.30 p.m. A fantastic hotel and probably the grooviest in New York.

ADAM: The rooms are small but with fabulous views. The rooftop Boom Boom Room is an absolute must, even if it is just for the view and spotting the odd celebrity, many of whom act oddly while there, anyway!

OTHER HOTELS

|||||||||||||||||||||||||||||||||||||||||||||||||||||||||||||||||||||||||||||||||||||||||||||||||||||||||||||||||||||||||||||

THE JANE

113 Jane Street
(near West Street)
(1 212) 924 6700
thejanenyc.com
Rating: 2★
Rooms: 200
Hotel rates: $99–250

The Jane is the coolest budget priced hotel in Manhattan, so cool you might want to stay there at twice the price. The smaller-than-miniscule rooms (a staggering 4 square metres for a single-bed or double-bunk room) are like cabins on a ship or train, with absolutely no room to bend over, but cosy and embracing. The designers somehow still managed to find room for a small plasma screen and an iPod dock. The sheet thread count may only be 300, but there's free Wi-Fi, telephone and safe. If you want to splash out at double the price for five times the space, go for a Captain's Cabin, the only rooms with a private bathroom (marble sink, rain shower head). Once the American Seaman's Friend Society Sailors' Home, the building was taken over by Eric Goode and Sean MacPherson of The Bowery and The Maritime fame. The downstairs public rooms are inviting and eclectic, as one would expect. The lobby looks like a gentleman's club until you notice a few bizarre touches here and there. For a drink or basic comfort food (avocado on toast), there is Café Gitane, an offshoot of the one in NoLIta. Bicycles are provided free of charge to check out the neighbourhood and the High Line Park. This is a great cheap hotel, worth a visit despite sitting just metres from the noisy West Side Highway.

WASHINGTON SQUARE HOTEL

103 Waverley Place
(between Sixth Avenue and Washington Square West)
(1 212) 777 9515
washingtonsquarehotel.com
Rating: 3★
Rooms: 100
Hotel rates: $234–370

In the middle of Greenwich Village and next to the park made famous by Henry James (and others), the Washington Square Hotel is a good hotel for the price. As one would hope given the Jamesian connections, it is more old-fashioned than trendy. The rooms are not huge, except for the Deluxe Quad and the Executive King, where the Art Déco pieces can look a little lost. There are bathrobes in all rooms (which is rarer than you might think) and LCD televisions, with Wi-Fi and continental breakfast included. The in-house North Square restaurant has a Jazz Brunch every Sunday. The highlight, though, is the Déco Room, where afternoon tea is served. Bob Dylan and Joan Baez lived here when busking in the park.

ABBEY'S GREENWICH

I used to live on Greenwich Street in West Village, so my favourite haunts are in this part of town. I don't think you can go past the Ginger Crush cocktail at Employees Only, on Hudson Street in the West Village. Or drop into The Spotted Pig around the corner on West 12th Street for the daily lunch special, which normally includes roast meats. Always amazing. And now start the short hike along the High Line with a pit stop at Andre Balazs' The Standard. For the girls, no visit to this part of the neighbourhood is complete without a visit to Darling, a unique little boutique that has a great range of the latest fashions, little black dresses and gorgeous vintage clothes and jewellery.

Abbey Smart
Marketing Consultant

HARRY IN THE MEATPACKING DISTRICT

See main text for restaurant details.

There is something annoyingly creepy yet intriguing about The Jane. It seems to be styled on a combination of the rundown Hotel Earle (from the Coen brothers' film *Barton Fink*) and ship or train sleeping cabins. You are either greeted by an old-fashioned bellhop or the odd long-term resident sitting on the steps, messy-haired and bewhiskered. Or you walk in on someone washing their underpants in the shared bathroom, if you have a single room. The hallway had a strange, lingering cigar-like scent. I was also reminded of that other spooky film, *The Shining*, and hoped I would not have any nightmares.

When I entered my tiny little red room (or should I say 'red rum'?), I immediately felt depressed. It was tiny!

However, The Jane is historically interesting, with some of the survivors of the *Titanic* once billeted there. Earlier it was a seaman's mission, when the area had a bit of a reputation as a transvestite and bohemian hang-out. RuPaul (drag queen and host of *RuPaul's Drag Race*) once stayed here, and there was some cinematic connection with the film *Hedwig and the Angry Inch*. This is all very interesting, but I still got a weird juju vibe from the place.

I can say it was fine for a short stay because it is in a great position and inexpensive at $99 room during peak season (inexpensive by New York City standards). But remember that the rooms are really, really small, and did I mention depressing? I think the larger Captain's Cabin rooms are the way to go.

What is great about this hotel is the amazing bar to the right of the entrance, opposite Café Gitane @ The Jane. It's all very British colonial–looking with excellent cocktails. The bar is complete with its own ballroom and is a real gem. I went there a lot, to avoid my room. Construction was underway for a bar on the roof, facing the Hudson, which should be really good.

From The Jane I would go on early morning jaunts, picking up a coffee from the Chelsea Market and taking a walk along the High Line, a former elevated railway that went right through the city and even some buildings. It is now redeveloped into a beautiful garden walk with great views, lots of sitting areas, and a strange auditorium where you can sit in a hypnotized state and view the traffic of all things.

That is when I saw her, that extreme facelift woman in a black wig. That night I did have nightmares at The Jane. I could not sleep with these floating ghost-like images of facelift faces and large clown-like wigs. The next morning I checked into The Standard.

No more Jane for me, I wanted to do New York City in style. And, dammit, no more hearing about Mr Garrison and Mr Bennett's critiques of their four-star hotels while I was in a miniscule closet of a room. Yes, my meagre budget was about to be blown.

The Standard's lifts show a video loop of a film called *Civilization* by Marco Brambilla, who is a film-based artist. It is quite an amazing experience. It gets dark when you get in, with a matching moody sound score. When you go up, it takes you all the way to Heaven. When you go down, it takes you all the way to Hell. Also great was the incredible view of the Hudson River from my room.

The Standard has a number of nice eateries and bars attached. The Standard Grill does a good breakfast and a simple coffee in a pot. Keep an eye out for the penny-floor fit-out, along with the other interior details. The place seemed to be full of hotel guests, such as the cool dudes from a Japanese rock band with skateboards in hand. I tried to fit in by wearing jeans, but does that count?

Biergarten under the High Line is also impressive. It has a great German beer selection, sausages and giant pretzels, along with two table-tennis tables. Love the concept, but it does get very busy. There is also an old diner opposite if you want to go old-school style.

SHANNON'S NEW YORK RECIPES

PEAR DOUGHNUTS—THE DANISH WAY (ÆBLESKIVER)

A Danish doughnut iron is called an Æbleskiver. A great feeling comes over you once you own an Æbleskiver. You may be surprised by the shape of the doughnuts, which are quite small and round, but please order one of these machines online. They are just like the classic Aussie waffle maker.

The traditional recipe for Æbleskiver does not call for a filling inside the doughnut, but I love to add savoury and sweet to mine. My favourite savoury one is foie gras and truffle, and for sweet you cannot go past a simple spiced-pear purée or your favourite jam.

Why would I include a Danish recipe in a New York food and travel book? Well, that's easy to answer. The Scandinavian influence in New York is growing. Its cuisine is the unsung backbone of Manhattan. There certainly are not as many corner Scandinavian restaurants as Middle Eastern or Asian ones, but the cuisine is very true to the nature of what New Yorkers like to eat, especially cured fish and salads. That is why places like Aquavit are so famous around this part of the world. They even do it better—everyday food experiences, that is—than the places that inspired the original ideas!

2 cups plain flour
pinch of sea salt
½ tablespoon caster sugar
1 teaspoon baking soda/ powder
2 eggs, beaten
1 cup of buttermilk or full cream milk
1 tablespoon extra virgin olive oil
½ cup icing sugar in a sifter
Jam to serve

Preheat a skillet or electric doughnut maker. Mix flour, salt, sugar and baking soda in a bowl using a hand blender. Add the eggs and buttermilk.

Brush the skillet or each hole of the doughnut maker with olive oil. Place one dessertspoon of mixture in each hole so it is three-quarters full (or free-form onto the skillet).

Cook until it starts to become golden and then, while it is still cooking, turn with a small toothpick or skewer so that you get a nice round shape—or until the mixture is cooked through and the outside is golden all over. Do not cook for too long or the doughnuts will become tough.

Sift the icing sugar over the doughnuts, rolling to coat. Serve with jam on the side for dipping.

Serves 4

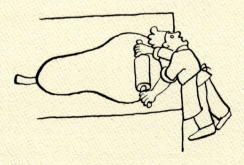

BIG APPLE

EAST
VILLAGE

FINE DINING

Shaped like a tunnel bunker, but glistening all over with gilt and gold, this fabulously trendy restaurant is considered by many (including Adam Platt at *New York* magazine) to be the best Downtown sushi restaurant. Not that it matters: your chances of ever getting a seat here are slim. The owners, Jack and Grace Lamb, have movie-star status in New York.

JEWEL BAKO
Japanese
239 East 5th Street
(between Cooper Square and Second Avenue)
(1 212) 979 1012
no website
Michelin: ★
Zagat: 26/30
Menu: $95 (omakase)
À la carte: $50–76

Kajitsu ('fine day' or 'day of celebration') specializes in Shojin cuisine, which adheres to the principle of not taking life and is strong on seasonal vegetables. To drink, there is a range of sakes (including a pairing menu for $34) and Japanese green tea from Ippodo, which has been making tea in Kyoto for 300 years.

KAJITSU
Japanese vegetarian
Chef: Masato Nishihara
414 East 9th Street
(between First Avenue and Avenue A)
(1 212) 228 4873
kajitsunyc.com
Michelin: ★★
Zagat: 27/30
Menu: $50 ('Kaze':
4 courses)/$70 ('Hana':
8 courses)

ANTOINETTE: Kajitsu is a very special place. There's no other way to say it. From its interior, all grace and minimalism, to its humble and extremely talented young chef, to its arresting, poetic cuisine, Kajitsu is like a Zen retreat, an unlikely find in the colourful, pulsating East Village. But step into the restaurant and you'll feel ensconced in a kind of peace that's unparalleled anywhere else in the city. Chef Masato Nishihara's style is Shojin, a vegetarian cuisine based on the principles of Zen and done kaiseki-style, each dish a meticulous composition to honour the season. Each dish is a harmony built on a poetic structure, with delicate grace notes like flower petals and such whimsical touches as 'treasure pouches', making the dining experience feel more like a succession of extremely thoughtful gifts than a multi-course meal. I come here when I want to quiet my mind, focus my palate and give myself over to the sublime, humble beauty of kaiseki.

KYO YA

Japanese
Chef: Chikara Sono
94 East 7th Street (between
First Avenue and Avenue A)
(1 212) 982 4140
no website
Michelin: ★
Zagat: 26/30
Menu: $120+ (kaiseki)
À la carte: $30–72

Kyo Ya is yet further proof that Asian cooking reigns supreme in the East Village. This subterranean and easy-to-miss kaiseki restaurant specializes in a chef's tasting menu (served with tea) that must be ordered two days ahead. There is an à la carte menu for those lucky enough to be passing and find a free spot. Expect dishes such as Cherry Wood–Smoked Hokkaido Scallop Marinated in White Sesame Oil, and Inaniwa Thin Udon Noodle from Akita, served cold or hot.

MOMOFUKU KO

Contemporary
Chef: David Chang
163 First Avenue
(between East 10th and
11th Streets)
momofuku.com
Michelin: ★★
Zagat: 27/30
Menu: $175 (lunch)/
$125 (dinner)

East Village's most famous restaurant is part of the David Chang phenomenon sweeping Manhattan and the world. It seats only twelve (on backless stools at a bar), so unless you're a personal friend or a Hollywood A-lister, a top Australian chef or have just won the Nobel Peace Prize, your chances of getting in are minimal. (President Obama failed.) Dinner takes two hours and is a set $125, lunch three hours and $50 more.

SHANNON: One week before the desired date that Adam, Harry and I want to eat at Momofuku Ko, my assistant Ali gets up at midnight exactly and heads straight to their website, hoping for the best. Only thirty-six people can eat there every day and the website is the only way to book.

Having arrived in New York, I was sure our booking was for 8.10 p.m., but I thought I'd better have another quick look. Damn, it was for 7.10 p.m. The sheet also said, 'Please call if you will be late and leave a message. If you are more than fifteen minutes late, your seat will be given away and you will be charged a $150 cancellation charge'.

I called Adam and let him know. He was in the barber's chair getting his hair cut. He is paranoid about his hair; he must get it cut every two weeks. He needs to take a leaf out of my book! I told him to stuff his haircut and get over to the restaurant straightaway. It's now 7.10 p.m.

I was Uptown in The Mandarin Oriental, just getting out of the shower. I have never dressed so fast in my entire life. I jumped in a cab and got a text from Adam. He was there already with only half a haircut and in a t-shirt and jeans, but it was Adam and I'm sure the apparel cost him well over a thousand dollars!

I arrived twenty minutes later. I have to thank the taxi driver; he did a great job. At one stage, he even drove over a corner footpath and through a red light. I handed him a $10 tip and he looked as if I had just given him a dirty tissue.

The front entrance to the restaurant was unassuming and so was the inside: just a bar with a kitchen running the length of it. It's tiny. I entered and apologized profusely, and the manager was lovely and seated me with a huge smile. At that stage, I thought I was in for a treat. I had already stuffed up and I was thinking that I owed the restaurant.

Then it changed. It started with the chefs. There was no smiling. All three of them were stone-faced. Now I was thinking, 'What the hell do I owe this restaurant? I'm meant to come here and spend money to have fun, not worry about a mistake I made. How does that work? Okay, I have now forgiven myself'.

On to the food. First, we received some small appetizers. They consisted of a bread-like scone; nothing special, it just tasted like a dense scone. It was followed by a tapioca-type crisp, then two small dishes of a potted square of terrine, and a buttermilk disc with some herbs and a small dot of black purée. It had a really nice aftertaste that was familiar to me but I couldn't pick. I wanted to take a picture on my phone— without a flash, of course—but was refused. What a load of bullshit. Give me a logical reason why I can't, as long as I'm discreet and not affecting fellow diners. If it's so no one copies their food, these guys have some serious ego issues. I started to become a bit ruffled.

At that point, a young chef from California was warming to us. He was a nice guy. But he kept being told off by the older, fatter chef with a funny cap, so he kept quiet for a while.

The first main dish was my favourite. It was a simple poached egg (thermo regulated, I think) with a generous quenelle of caviar. There were small, thin, delicate croutons and, from memory, some nice little herbs. Sorry, I would be able to describe it better if I had been able to take a photo. Anyway, it was a good simple dish that had some nice complexity. Not groundbreaking, but nice.

The next dish was a piece of toasted brioche buttered with bone marrow, then sprinkled with a black onion powder that had very little flavour, and topped with some sweet black purée and wild wood sorrel. It was presented in a bowl and a Gruyère-infused water was then poured into it. The flavour was reminiscent of French onion soup. The wood sorrel lacked the intensity of the wild weed that we get back in Oz.

Other courses consisted of micro-planed (grated) foie gras over lychees and, the only meat course, broiled rib. I had no idea what meat it was, but I have had better broiled rib at Hill Country with Patrick and Melanie. The leek-wrapped rillettes and a daikon and Vietnamese mint pressed terrine were nice and the best part of the dish.

Dessert consisted of a pre-dessert—peach sorbet with some caramelized powder; nice and simple—then a pretzel pannacotta that was scooped out of a takeaway container and served with a caramel-like, burnt butter–flavoured ice cream. We were offered espresso—no infusions—and nothing else. No *petit fours*. And that was it. By this time, another couple was waiting for our table.

My advice is to try the Noodle Bar or one of the other David Chang restaurants. Chang is the new 'it' chef in the world of cooking. I wanted to like this place, but I'm also part of the reason why I didn't enjoy it. It's a neighbourhood restaurant that is priced okay for what it is, but it's not designed for foodie freaks like myself. Readers should not fly twenty-two hours and expect to be blown away by the package, because it is simply not a complete gourmet experience—nor do I think David Chang is aiming to establish it as such.

Ferran Adrià said that Ko's was the most important restaurant opening ever in New York, but I'm sure he regrets the quote for a number of reasons, if he even said it at all. The type of cuisine is not actually defined. Ask the chefs that work there and they actually call it 'no boundaries'.

Ali, I'm very grateful for you getting up at midnight to make the booking for us, but I have never been to a more hyped restaurant in my life. Maybe New York has forgotten the basic rule in hospitality: 'The Customer is King'. Also, Best Restaurants in the World may need to change their marketing and title to the Most Fashionable Restaurants in the World if this is what they wish to promote.

I feel sorry for David Chang and I hope he survives the hype to become a great American chef, but he has a long way to go.

ADAM: I had huge expectations of this restaurant, having dined at David Chang's less formal restaurants in New York, where the food was fabulous. I had also attended the dinner he held at Cumulus Inc in Melbourne, which was an exceptionally memorable evening. In addition, my adrenalin was raised due to a misunderstanding about Shannon's and my reservation time, which according to the rules would mean, if we were late, no seat for purportedly one of the most difficult restaurant to get into in the world. What followed was a disappointment. The front-of-house staff were pleasant and attentive, but in the kitchen there was an underlying feeling that they were just going through the motions of cooking. The passion was not there. This was evident in the food. I hope that this was just a one-off incident, but perhaps not.

RESTAURANTS, STEAKHOUSES, BISTROS, CAFÉS

BACK FORTY

American
190 Avenue B (between
East 11th and East 12th
Streets)
(1 212) 388 1990
backfortynyc.com
Zagat: 22/30
À la carte: $25–49

Another contender for the best burger joint in New York, uses grain-fed beef. But this place does a lot more than burgers, also serving Quinoa-stuffed Japanese Eggplant, Olive Oil Poached Cod and Grilled Catskill Trout. If all that sounds too healthy, have a Basket of Fries with Rosemary Sea Salt and some Beer Battered Onion Rings with Smoked Paprika Mayo. Yum.

DBGB KITCHEN AND BAR

French
Chef: Daniel Boulud
299 Bowery (between
Houston and East 1st
Streets)
(1 212) 933 5300
danielnyc.com
Michelin: Bib Gourmand
Zagat: 22/30
Menu: $24.07 (lunch
weekdays; see Box)
À la carte: $35–62

Another of Daniel Boulud's restaurants, is a stylish 'French brasserie meets American tavern'. Designed by Thomas Scheller, the modern industrial look somehow captures elements of The Bowery's past without being retro. It is a striking space. The Lyonnais-inspired food ranges from *Coq à la bière* (Amish chicken braised in amber lager, with baby turnips, sugar snap peas and spaetzle) to Steak Frites and Sautéed Skate with Carnaroli Risotto, Spring Peas, Black Trumpets and Parmigiano Reggiano. Like all of Boulud's food, it looks extremely pretty on the plate. There is a $14 burger (with a cute uncut pickle on top of the bun) and a three-course lunch special on weekdays for $24.07. There are twenty-two beers on tap.

Just turn left from the front door of The Bowery Hotel on Bowery and you will walk straight into Daniel Boulud's new venture. It is basically an upmarket burger joint. The décor is really my style and I must say I love the wallpaper; in fact, it is the same wallpaper motif I used for my own café brand four years ago. There are some classic French dishes, particularly meat dishes like *Boudin Basque* (spicy blood and pig's head sausage with scallion mashed potato) and *Tunisienne* (lamb and mint merguez with harissa, lemon-braised spinach and chickpeas).

I had The Yankee Burger and loved it; great fries and homemade pickles, all mixed with smart and efficient service. Desserts are very simple and mainly consist of things like Milk Chocolate Mousse and Pecan Brownie Cake, and great sundaes. The wine list is focused on beer and cocktails. The place has a great buzz and is well worth a trip if you are staying Downtown.

DBGB is Daniel's new place. What he has done is actually get everyone from around the world to send in a copper bowl, and they are all hanging from the ceiling, which is fantastic.

If you are anywhere near The Bowery Hotel, this is a perfect spot for lunch.

Another of Jack and Grace Lamb's stylish restaurants (see Jewel Bako), **Degustation** seats just sixteen for its 'Franco Spanish–inspired small plates', otherwise known as tapas. Chef Wesley Genovart is formerly of Perry Street and is a huge fan of molecular gastronomy (*sous vide*, xanthan gum, et al.). He prepares the bite-size snacks right in front of you (Coca Mallorquina with Duck; Seared Foie Gras, Cocoa and Hazelnut Butter), though the delicious taste will probably impress more than the dazzling techniques.

DEGUSTATION WINE & TASTING BAR
Tapas bar
Chef: Wesley Genovart
239 East 5th Street
(between Third and Second Avenues)
(1 212) 979 1012
no website
Zagat: 27/30
Menu: $30
À la carte: $21–40

$24.07

Twice a year, in January–February and June–July, many New York restaurants offer a three-course lunch for $24.07 (and some even a dinner for $35). These Restaurant Week celebrations (which last for much more than a week!) are a fabulous way to experience the best of New York food at a very reasonable price. Restaurateurs treat this promotion seriously, so don't fear a dumbed-down menu for the price.

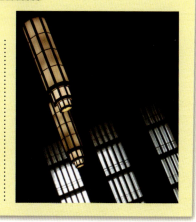

DIRT CANDY

Vegetarian
Chef: Amanda Cohen
430 East 9th Street
(between First Avenue
and Avenue A)
(1 212) 228 7732
dirtcandynyc.com
Michelin: Bib Gourmand
Zagat: 27/30
À la carte: $38–41

The dirt candy of the name are, of course, vegetables. Chef-owner Amanda Cohen not only loves them, she applies her whimsical sense of humour to cooking them. The dishes are listed by their principal ingredient, such as mushroom (Portobello mousse, spring pea flan, pear and fennel compote) or corn (stone-ground grits, corn cream, pickled shiitakes, huitlacoche and tempura poached egg). Note: it is not uncommon for a vegetarian dish to include egg in New York.

ANTOINETTE: Amanda Cohen is an adventurous chef, because she doesn't have any preconceptions of what vegetarianism should be, and she opened her own vegetarian restaurant in a city full of notoriously picky (and let's face it, a little touchy) eaters. Cohen isn't driven by what's healthy; she's oblivious to the crunchy, granola, Zen ideals of your average vegetarian evangelist. She creates her menu at **Dirt Candy** from a chef's perspective, treating her vegetables as if they were protein, entirely deserving of as many rich ingredients and preparations as their carnivorous counterparts. When I think of what Amanda Cohen does best, I think of her Portobello Mousse, a dish that by some magic (or Cohen's skill) tastes more like foie gras than you could possibly imagine. She's a risk-taker and, at Dirt Candy, vegetables have never had it so good.

....

FAUSTINA

Italian
Chef: Scott Conant
The Cooper Square Hotel
25 Cooper Square
(between East 5th
and 6th Streets)
(1 212) 475 3400
thecoopersquarehotel.com
Zagat: 23/30
À la carte: $36–63

Scott Conant (Scarpetta and *Chopped*) has now taken over the restaurant at the fabulous The Cooper Square Hotel. **Faustina** is a beautiful space, part of which is used for breakfast, and with a large outdoor area that is on a side street and fairly well sheltered. Conant is more than a whiz at pasta and Italian food.

SCOTT: Only managed breakfast here (light, fresh and beautiful), but having eaten at Scarpetta there is no reason to doubt that Faustina will make The Cooper Square an even finer place to stay. Conant is a brilliant chef.

....

Ippudo is a Japanese ramen-noodle brasserie, where the noodles are made downstairs behind glass for all to see. You then sit at communal tables to enjoy the ramen dishes. The Shiromaru Hakata Classic uses original tonkotsu noodles, slices of simmered Berkshire pork, kikurage, red pickled ginger, menma, boiled egg, sesame and scallions. If noodles aren't your thing, there is a large array of specials from a Creamy Croquette (of soy milk, crab and soybeans, served with a sweet chilli mayonnaise sauce) to Washu Beef Aburi (lightly grilled and served with ippudo sauce, sautéed Eringi mushrooms and vegetables).

IPPUDO NY
Japanese
65 Fourth Avenue
(between 9th and
10th Streets)
(1 212) 388 0088
ippudo.com/ny
Zagat: 25/30
À la carte: $28–35

Grace and Jack Lamb (Dégustation) do it again, this time with a raw bar (seating eight) and a seafood restaurant (just twenty-four). The Lambs just love small spaces. Not surprisingly, it is always busy and throbbing, especially given the more-than-fair prices.

JACK'S LUXURY OYSTER BAR
Seafood
101 Second Avenue
(at East 6th Street)
(1 212) 979 1012
no website
Zagat: 27/30
Menu: $50 (chef's tasting)
À la carte: $21–40

Kanoyama is a tiny sushi bar with many devoted fans. There are a few entrées (such as Sui Gyoza in a Hot Pot or Black Cod Marinated in Saikyo Miso) for those not in a raw-bar mood.

KANOYAMA
Japanese
175 Second Avenue
(at East 11th Street)
(1 212) 777 5266
kanoyama.com
Zagat: 26/30
Menu: $60 (sushi tasting)/
$65 (sashimi tasting)
À la carte: $30–52

MERCADITO AVENUE B

Mexican
179 Avenue B (between
East 11th and 12th Streets)
(1 212) 529 6490
mercaditorestaurants.com
Zagat: 23/30
À la carte: $41–50

East Village's place for *cebiches*, *tacos* and *platos fuertes*. There is also a Mercadito Cantina a few doors away at 172 Avenue B, and a Mercadito Grove in Midtown West (100 Seventh Avenue).

SERGE: The menu has some of the most traditional Mexican food you'll find in New York, but it bursts with creativity and flair. The guacamole, always a good barometer of Mexican cuisine, is exceptional, while contemporary ingredients reinvigorate the humble taco. Mercadito can become a scene on weekends, so book a corner table and do your own thing.

....

THE MERMAID INN

Seafood
96 Second Avenue
(between East 5th and
6th Streets)
(1 212) 674 5870
themermaidnyc.com
Zagat: 21/30
À la carte: $35–51

Suggesting Americans should eat local fish instead of meat, **The Mermaid Inn** offers a raw bar (Jumbo Lump Crab Cocktail, Chilled Lobster) and daily seafood specials, from Sautéed Skate Wing to a Pan Seared Tuna Burger. At night, with its paned glass windows, low lighting and candles, you could feel as if you have been sent back to colonial times. There is also a Mermaid Inn on the Upper West Side (568 Amsterdam Avenue) and a Mermaid Oyster Bar in Greenwich Village (79 MacDougal Street).

....

MOMOFUKU NOODLE BAR

Asian
Chef: David Chang
171 First Avenue
(between East 10th
and 11th Streets)
momofuku.com
Michelin: Bib Gourmand
Zagat: 24/30
À la carte: $30–60

With simple blonde-wood décor and invigorating food, **Momofuku Noodle Bar** has been full since it opened and is the favourite haunt of many David Chang groupies. Despite its name, its most famous dish is actually the Fried Chicken Dinner, which must be ordered in advance. You get two whole fried chickens, one done in Southern style, the other Korean, with *mu shu* pancakes, bib lettuce, four sauces and seasonal vegetables. If you want to buck the trend, or you arrive unannounced and somehow manage to get in, then you can try Chang's legendary Steamed Pork Buns (see Momofuku Ssäm Bar), the Slow-Roasted Beef Brisket or even some of the namesake noodles. At lunch, try the Fried Oyster Bun.
RECOMMENDED: NICK

....

Momofuku Ssäm Bar is the latest of the Momofuku restaurants from David Chang (after Ko and Noodle Bar). It is an unprepossessing restaurant on a busy corner site, and looks rather like a million modern Asian restaurants the world over. It is always packed and bustling inside, with crowds from all over New York coming for the Steamed Pork Buns with Hoisin, Cucumbers and Scallions. The famed Bo Ssäm ($200) is a whole free-range bone-in pork butt, a dozen oysters, kimchi, rice and lettuce, and is best ordered in advance.

MOMOFUKU SSÄM BAR
Asian
Chef: David Chang
207 Second Avenue
(at East 13th Street)
(1 212) 254 3500
momofuku.com
Michelin: Bib Gourmand
Zagat: 25/30
Menu: $25/$200 (Bo Ssäm)
À la carte: $27–52

NEIL: David Chang's Momofuku Ssäm Bar is in the West Village. He has a couple of places down there and has now opened Ma Pêche Uptown, which is also serving delicious produce-driven food with a Vietnamese flavour. At Ssäm Bar, you will experience Dave Chang's Korean and Japanese food with a few classics thrown in showing other influences. The restaurant is mainly made up of shared tables or bar seating, the staff are in jeans—and some wear hats and lots of tats—and the music is rock. It is really packed and the energy of the crowd and staff is electric. This is a really cool place with great food, knowledgeable staff, a small yet smart wine list and killer cocktails. Try stuff from the raw section: oysters, crab, prawns and hamachi. The famous steamed pork buns and BBQ Rib Sandwich with Red Onion Slaw are crazy good. I wish every time I went to a sporting event I could get those with a cold beer. Heaven!

MATT: Those pork buns are my god. They are a taste sensation. Mario Batali, a friend of mine, took me there.

SHARLEE: You've seen the cookbook, so vegetarians stay away. This is pork city with buns, butts, country hams, bacon and pork fat. Make sure you taste the deliciously fatty pork belly steamed buns. Crazy busy, so go at weird times to avoid the queues.

SCOTT: The whole world seems to crave David Chang's pork buns, but I can't see what the fuss is about: they are fatty, overly sweet and doughy—the Asian equivalent of a hot dog at a football game. Fortunately, there is a lot of great food to be had at Ssäm Bar, if you look.

Apart from the raw bar and a list of country hams, the menu is divided between take-out American-style snacks (the buns, Pork Scrapple) and more serious food (Diver Scallops, Bo Ssäm).

Friend Susi and I started with the snacks ('small plates')—we had to try what was famous—and sat there puzzled and rather disappointed. Apart from the underwhelming pork buns, we had the Pork Scrapple with Fried Egg, and Benton's Bacon and Pear Mostarda, which were yummy (especially the pear mostarda), but hardly yummy enough to make Ssäm Bar a serious destination restaurant.

Then we had a Damascene moment when a stream of unordered dishes poured out from the kitchen (the booking had been made via Shannon's Vue de monde and a penny had generously dropped somewhere). This food, almost without exception, was delicious and explained David Chang's stellar reputation.

The Diver Scallops with XO Sauce, Bok Choy and Black Garlic were stunning. (Why does America have such great scallops? It seems so unfair to all those who live elsewhere.) Equally brilliant were the Fried Baby Artichokes with Pistachio, Sunchokes and Bottarga, and the BBQ Rib Sandwich with Red Onion Slaw.

For dessert, though absolutely full, we had the Thai Iced Tea Parfait, which was an awful pink colour just like Thai Iced Tea (but still not as hideous a pink as the rhubarb 'foam' at Jean Georges), and absolutely delicious. It was served with a fluffy lemon mascarpone and a crunchy and sugary nut trimming. The Grapefruit Cream Pie may have been equally scrummy, but was served too cold to tell.

Chang calls his cooking 'Japanese-influenced American', but call it what you will: this is comfort food worth travelling the length of Manhattan for.

Manhattan has several fine Greek restaurants and this is one of them. The consulting chef is Diane Kochilas, regarded as one of the world's top authorities on Aegean cuisine. The restaurant advertises its food as 'rustic', but the dishes are never lacking in refinement. The *Anginares moussaka* is an artichoke-heart moussaka layered with caramelized onions, herbs and a béchamel sauce made with three Greek cheeses. The *Saganaki tou merakli* is Saganaki cheese not fried but melted in a clay pot, the *Htapothi scharas* grilled marinated octopus with a reduced balsamic sauce and capers. You would want Greek wine to go with this, and that's exactly what they provide on an interesting drinks list.

PYLOS

Greek
Chef: Diane Kochilas
128 East 7th Street
(between First Avenue and Avenue A)
(1 212) 473 0220
pylosrestaurant.com
Zagat: 25/30
À la carte: $37–54

Soba-Ya is packed with New York University students, but why let them have all the fun? This is a lively, homemade noodle restaurant, whether you like your soba or udon noodles cold (with Shrimp, Shiso and Shishito Tempura, or Salmon Roe and Grated Radish) or hot (Kama-Age, Grated Mountain Yam, or Ginseng Root Tempura).

SOBA-YA

Japanese
229 East 9th Street
(between Third and Second Avenues)
(1 212) 533 6966
sobaya-nyc.com
Michelin: Bib Gourmand
Zagat: 24/30
À la carte: $22–42

A restaurant that serves hearty northern Italian fare, that doesn't take bookings or credit cards, and has long lines of expectant diners outside. If you feel like Veal Polpettini in a rich *sugo d'arrosto* (reduced roasted meat broth) or Pappardelle with Asparagus, Peas and Tomatoes, accompanied by a fine Italian wine (the only foreign intrusion is one from Francis Ford Coppola's vineyards in the Napa), then this is your place. And there are daily risottos and entrée specials, Sunday's *Bollito misto* being an obvious favourite.

SUPPER

Italian
156 East 2nd Street
(between Avenues A and B)
(1 212) 477 7600
supperrestaurant.com
Michelin: Bib Gourmand
Zagat: 24/30
À la carte: $37–49

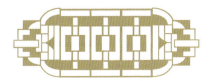

YAKITORI TAISHO

Japanese
5 St Marks Place (between
Third and Second Avenues)
(1 212) 620 0808
yakitoritaisho.com
À la carte: $21–29

Extremely reasonable and authentic yakitori restaurant that has been abuzz since opening in 1993.

ANDY: A real hole-in-the-wall yakitori place that my brother and I always go to when we're out in the city.

YERBA BUENA

Pan-Latin
Chef: Julian Medina
23 Avenue A (at East
2nd Street)
(1 212) 529 2919
ybnyc.com
Zagat: 23/30
À la carte: $46–57

Yerba Buena fuses the Latin flavours of Cuba, Peru, Chile, Brazil, Mexico and Argentina. It's a coolly stylish space (part steakhouse, part Cuban bar and sometime nightclub), with colourful, flavourful food that leaps from the plate. There is a Peruvian Shrimp Soup, Blue Corn Meal-Crusted Calamari with Sweet Plantins, and a Suckling Pig with Yucca Purée. Needless to say there is an extensive (and very reasonable at just $12 each) cocktail list, plus wines from Argentina, Chile and Spain. Sister restaurants are Toloache in Midtown West and another Yerba Buena in West Village.

BARS

DEATH & CO

Bar
433 East 6th Street
(1 212) 388 0882
6 p.m.–midnight

Death & Co, whose name is a reference to a Prohibition-era art movement, is one of the world's top cocktail bars. The hidden speakeasy-style bar was the first proper cocktail bar in Manhattan's East Village. This is a serious bar with some serious accolades.

Out the back of Crif Dogs is PDT, or Please Don't Tell. So, we won't … or, maybe, we just will! RECOMMENDED: NICK

PDT
Cocktail bar
113 St Marks Place
(1 212) 614 0386
6 p.m.–2 a.m. (Mon–Thurs),
6 p.m.–4 a.m. (Fri–Sat)

SHANNON: Well, sorry Jim Meehan, I am about to tell everybody. This is the most fun bar in New York. I honestly thought it had been designed by Melbournian bar tsar Vernon Chalker, of Gin Palace and Madame Brussels' fame, but, no, this is in East Village. Scott is not comfortable around this part of town; in fact, he said the area is a dive. I think he has spent too long at The Carlyle! This part of town is brilliant, young, hip and busy. Yes, it's a bit dingy but I find myself in a real neighbourhood.

Jim Meehan is the man in charge here, and he has been to Melbourne to check out the scene; that's how dedicated he is and what drives his ideas.

Let me paint the picture for you. Crif Dogs is a cool hot-dog shop. Walk in and it's packed with all sorts lining up for creative types of dogs. To the left is a very discreet phone booth. Pick the phone up and it instantly dials a number. A young female voice will answer and ask, 'What you want?' She will not give anything away. You mention you have a booking and I won't give the rest away, but then imagine you wake up and you have stepped into a super-cool, dimly lit old-world bar that is not packed to the rafters; it's just comfortable. No people-watchers here, just aficionados of fine spirits and cocktails.

I got talking to the barman about ice and how important it is to great drinks. He showed me the three different types he had and we exchanged views on how long the best ice should take to make. I said one week (that's how the Japanese make it; it has no oxygen at all and takes a long time to melt, thereby not diluting the spirits). These guys are passionate and it's a great bar well worth the trip. Even Scott would get rid of his cold sweats about the East Village in here!

[**SCOTT:** Actually, mate, I said I hated the Lower East Side, which is to the south. The East Village is just fine.]

ANTOINETTE: I finally went to PDT and it's already made it onto my favourites list. This is a cocktail bar for the initiated and uninitiated alike. Of course there's the little thrill of stepping into the suave interior through … no, I won't tell. PDT is, after all, an exemplar of early New York speakeasies. But beyond the ambience, which is lush and spot on, the real draw of PDT is the menu, and the extremely affable bartenders who oversee it. Unlike some New York bars where you're forced to order at your own peril (and pocketbook), the bartenders at PDT will guide through the menu, which is structured from lighter to heavier drinks, making the often intimidating world of high-end cocktails that much more accessible and fun to explore. And don't miss the beef and pork hot dogs at Crif Dogs next door; my favourites are the Wylie Dog (as in wd~50) and the Chop Tank, a veritable hot-dog symphony with crab dip, Old Bay–seasoned potato chips, and cheese, all atop a bacon-wrapped hot dog.

PAULA AND PATRICK: Make sure you call ahead earlier in the day to make a booking as you will not get in otherwise. Great cocktails, beers and wines, and you can also order food at Crif Dogs next door.

....

BAR VELOCE
Bar
176 Seventh Avenue
(1 212) 629 5300
5 p.m.–3 a.m.

BLACK & WHITE
Bar
86 East 10th Street
(1 212) 253 0246
6 p.m.–4 a.m.

BOWERY WINE COMPANY
Bar
13 East 1st Street
(1 212) 146 0800
bowerywineco.com
5 p.m.–1 a.m. (Mon–Thurs), 5 p.m.–2 a.m. (Fri), noon–2 a.m. (Sat), noon–1 a.m. (Sun)

THE COCK
Gay bar
29 Second Avenue
(1 212) 473 9406
11 p.m.–4 a.m.

D.B.A
Pub
41 First Avenue
(1 212) 475 5097
drinkgoodstuff.com
1 p.m.–4 a.m.

11TH STREET BAR
Bar
510 East 11th Street
(1 212) 777 5415
5 p.m.–midnight

ELSA
Bar
217 East 3rd Street
(1 917) 882 7395
7 p.m.–2 a.m.

HEATHERS
Bar
506 East 13th Street
(1 212) 254 0979
6 p.m.–2 a.m. (Sun–Wed), 4 p.m.–4 a.m. (Thurs–Sat)

INTERNATIONAL BAR
Bar
120 1/2 First Avenue
(1 212) 777 1643
Noon–2.30 a.m. (Mon–Wed, Sun), noon–3.30 a.m. (Thurs–Sat)

IN VINO
Bar
215 East 4th Street
(1 212) 539 1011
invino-ny.com
5 p.m.–11 p.m. (Sun–Thurs), 5 p.m.–midnight (Fri–Sat)

KGB BAR
Bar
2nd floor, 85 East 4th Street
(1 212) 505 3360
5 p.m.–1 a.m.

LOUIS 649
Bar
649 East 9th Street
(1 212) 673 1190
6 p.m.–4 a.m.

NUBULU
Bar, club
62 Avenue C
8 p.m.–4 a.m.

ZUM SCHNEIDER
Bar
107 Avenue C
(1 212) 598 1098
zumschneidr.com
5 p.m.–1 a.m. (Mon–Thurs), 5 p.m.–4 a.m. (Fri–Sat), 1 p.m.–1 a.m. (Sun)

LUXURY HOTELS

The Bowery Hotel has two room sizes apart from suites, the Queen (20 square metres) and King (23 square metres), which are way too small for the price. But they blend the modern (new redbrick mini skyscraper) with the old (it feels like a renovation inside). The dark floorboards are partially covered with oriental rugs, the walls white and the ceiling fan from a W Somerset Maugham novel. The red linear border on the duvet and pillows is a brilliant design (and brand) statement. The one-bedroom suite, with its huge outdoor terrace, spacious living area and inset marble tub, is stunning. The linen tops out at 500 threads, whereas the lesser rooms have to make do with 400. All the rooms have huge windows with memorable city views. The restaurant, Gemma, is highly regarded for its fresh Italian cuisine. But the space is so beautifully designed, from the hanging wicker baskets and the classic bistro chairs and wooden tables to the striking wine cellar and sparkling bar, ordinary food would still taste good here. The hotel is a favourite with movie stars and the Lobby Bar is regarded as attracting only the coolest crowd. Be prepared to fight for your rights. Created by The Maritime's Eric Goode and Sean MacPherson (see also The Jane), this is one of the most sought-after Downtown addresses.

THE BOWERY HOTEL
335 Bowery (between East 2nd and 3rd Streets)
(1 212) 505 9100
theboweryhotel.com
Rating: 4★
Rooms: 135
Suites: 7
Hotel rates: $425–475

SHANNON: I think we need to get one thing straight about New York: it's not cheap. The Bowery Hotel is the perfect example. I love the hotel for its quirkiness and unique, smart décor that makes the hotel feel as if it's been part of the city for longer than its inception in 2007. But would I pay $400+ for a Queen room? This is the most basic option and the rooms aren't big, even if well designed and with lovely charm. Try for a corner room, as they have floor-to-ceiling windows and great bathtubs with skyline views. This is not a five-star hotel. Everything you use you pay for, including umbrellas, gym and mineral water. But I must say that that's not a bad thing; other hotels with higher rack rates charge in a similar fashion. Wi-Fi is free, which I applaud, plus there is a great collection of DVDs—literally four pages of choices, with Woody Allen obviously featuring heavily.

I thoroughly enjoyed the ground-floor lounge. It has a Moroccan feel in style and detail, and very low lighting. The hotel has a young television-and-advertising creative sort of clientele, with no dress code or uptown glamour here, but real atmosphere.

There is a simple outside courtyard; nothing special, but plenty of comfortable seating. Next door there is a fabulous Italian trattoria. I say fabulous because of the décor and the really reasonable prices. Pasta dishes including taxes are $21. The tables spill out onto Bowery and quickly fill at lunchtime with a diverse clientele.

Breakfast didn't start off well. One thing I don't understand in New York is that it seems like every waiter is so set on just doing his or her own job that it's a struggle to even get seated. Here, hotel guests have to walk through the back of the hotel lobby into the back of the restaurant. Not once was I greeted. Then, as I headed for a table in an empty dining room, I was pointed to the front of the room by a fast-paced host. I mean, give me a break. You want a 20 percent tip? The other wait-staff saved the day as I started to watch a pre–World Cup match on my laptop to calm myself down and got talking to one of the senior waiters.

Overall the entire hotel is nice and I like the area, but it has nothing on The Surrey. I wanted to like this place as, contrary to my frustrations, the staff here are really what make this hotel one of the best small boutique hotels in Manhattan.

....

THE COOPER SQUARE HOTEL

25 Cooper Square
(between East 5th
and 6th Streets)
(1 212) 475 5700
thecoopersquarehotel.com
Rating: 4★
Rooms: 139
Suites: 6
Hotel rates: $425–525

This steel-and-glass tower at Astor Place rivals the best of the Thompson Hotels and the not-far-away Hotel on Rivington. It is hardly boutique with 145 rooms, but staying here feels like a personal experience. The entrance is luxuriously reassuring, with an impossibly high ceiling and an enveloping sense of calm space. Off it is a small library that actually has a decent collection of books (unlike the pretend libraries so many hotels have). The restaurant, Faustina, is supervised by Scott Conant of Scarpetta fame. The rooms are large and light-filled, with the corner ones the pick. The amenities are superb, from a signature scent created by Red Flower to a minibar stacked with jewellery (!), Blu-ray players with a selection of rare film titles, and Italian instead of Egyptian linen. RECOMMENDED: FRED

SCOTT: Of the modern hip hotels (like The Standard and 60 Thompson), The Cooper Square is arguably the best. It is a beautiful modern building from the outside, its subtly curved shape reminding one of a yacht at sail. The guestrooms are equally fine. They are large and have floor-to-ceiling windows with stunning views in all directions. The rooms are filled with light and you almost feel as if you are floating in space. The interior design is very clever and smart, without being over the top. The freestanding cupboard, with its irregular doors, is a design and functional delight, with top-of-the-range clothes hangers inside, a separate safe and a brilliant minibar. Standing nearby is a steel ladder, the steps serving as bookshelves. The television is a huge flatscreen with a Blu-ray player. Even the phone is hands-free.

The bathroom is stunning, with a huge shower and beautiful tiling on the walls and floor. Best is a choice of three bathrobes: the traditional long fluffy terry towelling, a black Japanese cotton, and a short and sexy silk number. Couples may get into a fight, though, as there is only one of each. I am sure a phone call would fix it, as the staff here seem delighted to attend to any need.

Yet more touches reveal this to be a top-class hotel, such as envelopes with stamps already attached.

Apart from seriously too-dark lifts (it is hard to read the buttons and the non-vertically challenged have to bend down low to get a decent look), the only flaw, depending on which side of the hotel your room is, is that music can drift up past your window. Otherwise, this is a fabulous new hotel and one of the great stays of New York.

....

TEN INGREDIENTS CURRENTLY FASCINATING NEW YORK CHEFS

1. Yuzu
2. Hazelnuts
3. Passion fruit
4. Kumamoto oysters
5. Wagyu beef
6. Panko crumbs
7. Hen of the Wood mushrooms
8. Ponzu
9. Fiddlehead Ferns
10. Ramps

NICK ORD'S NEW YORK

See main text for restaurant and hotel details.

FINE DINING
ELEVEN MADISON PARK

The most recent restaurant to be awarded four stars by *The New York Times*, Eleven Madison Park is elegant in menu, service and design. Owned by one of New York's most successful and generous restaurateurs, Danny Meyer, Eleven Madison exemplifies all the traits of a great restaurant. The service is knowledgeable and attentive, the room is stunning and the food leaves you speechless. Chef Daniel Humm is cooking in a refined new French style and serves only a prix-fixe menu. He offers a two-course $28 lunch menu that is the best bargain in New York City.

CASUAL DINING
MOMOFUKU NOODLE BAR

The mystique and magic of chef David Chang began at this small East Village noodle bar. Momofuku means 'lucky peach', and you'll certainly feel like one after eating here. It will be a little crowded and a bit noisy but the food is certainly worth braving the din. Considered by many to be his best restaurant, Momofuku Noodle Bar exemplifies what Chang does best: flavour, texture, unexpectedness and attitude. All sourced from local ingredients, sustainable and organic where possible, the menu changes regularly. Go for his little plates of vegetables (in the spring, expect Sugar Snap Peas with Horseradish, Mint and Trout Roe), or the salty Sautéed Bok Choy with Pork Broth, Cipollini and Chili Flakes. Chang offers three kinds of pork buns—I recommend you try them all, as well as noodles both in and out of broth. Dessert comes in the form of delicious soft-serve ice cream, or you can walk a couple of blocks to his Momofuko Milk Bar for his Crack Pie experience.

BEST BAR
PDT

Don't yell at your cab driver. If you've stopped in front of the Crif Dogs hot-dog stand, you are in the right place. PDT is a very small speakeasy bar tucked inside Crif Dogs. You enter through a phone booth, and you need a reservation. Owner and master bartender Jim Meehan has created an intimate and serious bar for people to enjoy cocktails. You need to be on time—fifteen minutes past your reservation and they give away your table—and be respectful of the rules. No talking to other tables, no wandering around. But if you respect the rules, and you should, you will be introduced to a world of cocktails you've never experienced before. Meehan says, 'I mix lesser known, historic spirits with more familiar ingredients to introduce guests to new flavour combinations. My goal is to develop delicious, quaffable drinks that are easy to prepare in my bar, with ingredients that are widely available. If a drink is going to stand the test of time, it needs to have all these characteristics'. PDT only uses fresh, seasonal produce for juices, hand-cracked ice and the finest base spirits.

BEST-KEPT SECRET
TRIBECA GRILL

In the constant search for the new and trendy, we often forget the classic places. The Tribeca Grill was the first restaurant venture in the Robert De Niro empire, which now includes Nobu and Locanda Verde around the corner. A cool, casual outpost of modern American cuisine with an almost constant flow of celebrity guests, the Tribeca Grill serves many of your favourite dishes—crab cakes, lobster salad, short ribs, rack of lamb, New York strip—and is still as exciting today as it was when it was the only restaurant in the neighbourhood. With walls adorned by paintings done by De Niro's late father, the big, airy space with exposed brick walls, colourful banquettes and comfortable tables centres on a massive, handsome mahogany bar that feels like quintessential Downtown New York. It also serves an excellent brunch.

BEST HOTEL
HOTEL (THE MERCER)

The hotel all the celebrities request when on press junkets to New York City, hotelier André Balazs' jewel 75-room property in a landmark Romanesque revival building in the heart of SoHo is considered by many a perfect hotel. *The New York Times* wrote, 'If God is in the details, someone at the Mercer is a true believer'. The Mercer's loft-like rooms and suites all have high ceilings, large windows that open and plenty of natural light. Interior designer Christian Liaigre created soothing modernist interiors emphasizing comfort, and calming, subtle colour palettes. Spacious bathrooms enhance the loft experience, the majority featuring oversized marble bathtubs that fit two people or more. All rooms include complimentary wireless Internet access, sumptuous bedding with 400-thread-count Egyptian cotton sheets, HD televisions and a wide range of amenities. Twenty-four-hour room service is available from The Mercer Kitchen run by celebrity chef Jean-Georges Vongerichten.

Nick Ord
President, Miele Inc., US

SHANNON'S NEW YORK RECIPES

BEET SALAD

This recipe is inspired by what New York has become: a city that cares where its society is heading. Slowly but surely, projects such as the High Line, precincts like TriBeCa and establishments including Blue Hill are making the population embrace the rich cultural history of the city and the great food that only twenty years ago was scoffed at but is now blended with the new.

Out of that comes my inspiration for the following recipe. It's simple but relies on care, love and great ingredients.

When searching for ingredients, Wholefoods Market is one of the world's great supermarket chains. New York has the best of them. There are also a huge number of small grocers dotted around the likes of Chelsea Market.

10 baby beetroots (keep any good leaves from the bunch)

2 large beetroots cut into 2 cm cubes and cooked in 4 parts water with 1 part vinegar (tinned beetroots are also very good and don't require cooking – if using, reserve liquid for dressing)

1 tablespoon thinly sliced cornichons

1 tablespoon baby capers

1 tablespoon finely chopped shallots

1 tablespoon finely chopped chives

sea salt and black pepper

1 grapefruit, juiced

1 lemon, juiced

extra virgin olive oil (equivalent to reduced beet juice – see method below)

4 tablespoons goat's curd

4 red salad radishes, thinly sliced

1 cup of baby beetroot shoots or baby flat-leaf parsley leaves

Cut 8 of the baby beetroot into quarters. Cook the large beetroots in a saucepan until tender. Strain the large beetroot, reserving the juice. Place the juice into a saucepan and add the quartered baby beetroots. (If using tinned beetroots, use the reserved juice from the tin.) Cook until tender and strain, once again reserving the juice.

Slice the remaining 2 baby beetroots very thinly into discs, similar to the radishes, and reserve for plating.

Once all of the beetroots are cooked, place the large beetroot in a bowl. Add the cornichons, capers, shallots, chives, salt and black pepper.

Reduce the remaining beetroot juice by half. Place in a bowl and, using a hand blender, add the grapefruit and lemon juices into the reduced beet juice, then gradually blend in an equal amount of olive oil. If you end up with 100 ml of reduced beet juice, add 100 ml of olive oil. Add salt to taste.

Dress the large chopped beetroot with some of the dressing. Plate either as a shared platter or on individual plates, by liberally placing a large serving-spoon full of the large cooked beetroot on the plate. Spoon or pipe the curd around the beetroot pieces. Place the raw slices of baby beetroot and radishes on top of the curd and large beetroot. The slices of radish will be the focal point, offsetting the colour of beetroot.

Add the baby beetroot shoots or baby flat-leaf parsley leaves before serving.

Serves 4

MIDTOWN

CHELSEA  GRAMERCY, FLATIRON & UNION SQUARE ⊠ MIDTOWN WEST ⊠ MIDTOWN EAST & MURRAY HILL

CHELSEA

FINE DINING

Mario Batali has long been the pre-eminent Italian chef in Manhattan, a brilliant cook, restaurateur and television personality who has juggled his many roles without ever losing his core focus on making diners happy. **Del Posto** is his most elegant flagship, the highest rated of his restaurants in Zagat. But there is a view that Scott Conant (Scarpetta) and Missy Robbins (A Voce) are nipping at his heels. Batali has to keep on his toes to stay ahead and one way to do that is maintain Del Posto as the most revered Italian restaurant in the city. Certainly, it is a dazzling space, casually stylish and throbbing with the sense of a special occasion. Inside, you really could be in a luxury Tuscan trattoria. And it can be equally expensive, if you have the Veal Chop with Asparagus Tricolore and Truffled Tongue Salad for $110 or the Ribeye with Fried Potatoes, Parmigiano Reggiano, Ruchetta and Tomato Raisins for $130. The five-course $95 prix fixe is a good and safe option, but Del Posto is a big-night-out restaurant and probably not best stinted on. And that goes for a wine list from the gods, with prices that can pleasantly surprise ($130 for a 2004 Argiolas Turriga or $145 for the 2005 Mille e Una Notta from Donnafugata). The online wine list will make you swoon and instantly call up for a reservation. Some argue Batali's Babbo has slightly surpassed Del Posto in terms of Italian cooking, but Babbo is a more casual place with less sense of occasion. Del Posto rules supreme on that front.

DEL POSTO

Italian
Chefs: Mario Batali, Lidia Bastianich
85 Tenth Avenue (between West 15th and 16th Streets)
(1 212) 497 8090
delposto.com
Zagat: 26/30
Menu: $95 (5 courses)/$125 (7 courses)
À la carte: $63–176

RESTAURANTS, STEAKHOUSES, BISTROS, CAFÉS

BLOSSOM RESTAURANT

Vegan
187 Ninth Avenue (between West 21st and 22nd Streets)
(1 212) 627 1144
blossomnyc.com
Zagat: 22/30
À la carte: $37–41

If you want to help fund a duck pond and habitat, rather than eat the feathered wonders, then **Blossom** is for you. This is a charming and (at night) romantic restaurant that proves organic vegan cuisine doesn't have to be served in shabby student digs. There are many pasta dishes, but the menu is inventive enough to include Cape Cod Cakes (a blend of hiziki seaweed, tofu, herbs and spices) and Phyllo Roulade (French lentils and root vegetables baked in a phyllo crust with a carrot-cream sauce, caramelized onions and Swiss chard). There is also a Blossom Up Town on the Upper West Side (466 Columbus Avenue) and, just to be fair, a Blossom Bistro on the Upper East Side (1522 First Avenue).

BUDDAKAN

Asian fusion
75 Ninth Avenue
(at West 16th Street)
(1 212) 989 6699
buddakannyc.com
Zagat: 24/30
À la carte: $38–59

This is pure Shangri-La, one of the most dramatic restaurant spaces in the world. The décor is from Hollywood (stunningly done), the cuisine from China.

PAULA AND PATRICK: Hidden behind a brass decorative feature on Ninth Avenue, Buddakan is probably most famous for being where Carrie (Sarah Jessica Parker) has her wedding rehearsal dinner in the first *Sex and the City* movie. Before you sit down to eat, start with a Fate Cocktail in the bar. This drink was originally designed for Kate Winslet's character in *The Reader* and is absolutely delicious. You get the choice to sit on the grand communal table or a private table; both experiences are equally enjoyable. This is definitely a restaurant where you want to share all of the food. I can highly recommend the Edamame Dumplings (their signature dish), Cold Tuna Spring Roll, Crispy Duck Spring Rolls and the Boneless Spare Ribs to start with, followed by Mongolian Lamb Chops, Steamed Red Snapper, Whole Peking Duck and the Sizzling Short Rib.

If you feel you need to walk off all the scrumptious food, make sure you check out the High Line, a park built on a section of a former elevated railroad spanning 2.3 kilometres along the West Side. The views are phenomenal.

MICHAEL: I loved the restaurant Buddakan. I personally thought it was one of the better restaurants I have been to. Great food, but it's the building, the size of the place and atmosphere that make the experience.

Though listed in guides as a pizzeria, **Co.** (pronounced 'company') is a communal space where people come to sample the wide range of artisanal pies. If the Flambé (béchamel, Parmesan, Mozzarella, caramelized onions and lardoons) is too wild, try the Peas & Prosciutto (also with a lot of cheese) or the Rosa (crushed tomato, garlic, fresh oregano and chilli). It is an offshoot of Jim Lahey's Sullivan Street Bakery.

CO.
Pizza and pies
230 Ninth Avenue
(at West 24th Street)
(1 212) 243 1105
co-pane.com
Zagat: 22/30
À la carte: $17–31

COLICCHIO & SONS

American
Chef: Tom Colicchio
85 Tenth Avenue
(at 15th Street)
(1 212) 400 6699
colicchioandsons.com
Zagat: 23/30
Tap Room menu: $25
(lunch)
À la carte: $37–49
Dining Room menu: $135
(dinner; 6 courses)
À la carte: $57–72

In the space that was once Craftsteak comes a new restaurant from restaurateur-chef Tom Colicchio. It is divided into the Tap Room and Dining Room, with separate menus.

NEIL: Colicchio & Sons is another must do. Tom Colicchio is the creator of the Craft brand in the United States, and also the host of *Top Chef*. Could he be any more famous? Well, I don't know, but he is a hell of a guy and a brilliant chef and restaurateur. Craft is well worth a visit as well. That is where his food is driven by ingredients and great cooking, simple food that tastes of itself, full flavoured and perfectly cooked.

At Colicchio & Sons, Tom heads back to the type of food that made him famous at Gramercy Tavern, using ingredients that are just as well sourced but with a lot more layering of flavour and complexity. The result is a great restaurant, open only for dinner seven days a week. It has an impressive choice of fifteen or so starters and almost that many mains. Lots of raw seafood, salads and dishes such as Spice Roasted Lobster with Purple Artichoke that show the great craft of cooking. An extensive fish section containing dishes of Striped Sea Bass and Monkfish, as well as Wild King Salmon, fills out the mains, along with rabbit, duck and chicken, all roasted, and dishes of veal breast and tripe for the more adventurous. Desserts are terrific and the wine list is very good.

The Tap Room attached to the restaurant is open for lunch and dinner and, as the name would suggest, many beers are available to wash down salads, sandwiches and a killer burger, as well as pizza and a few main plates. Easy to drop into for lunch after a hard morning's shopping.

Cookshop's Marc Meyer, Vicki Freeman and Ginger Pierce (from Five Points and Hundred Acres in Greenwich Village) passionately believe in sustainable farming and humanely raised animals. To cook, Meyer prefers the simplicity of a grill (Rabbit Saddle with English Peas), a rotisserie (All Natural Chicken) and wood-burning stone oven (Pig in Porchetta). The wine list is full of gems, from a Rudi Pichler Grüner Veltliner to a Biondi Santi Brunello. Not for people who like a quiet dinner, however. It is regarded as one of the busiest restaurants in Chelsea.

COOKSHOP
American
Chef: Marc Meyer
156 Tenth Avenue
(at West 20th Street)
(1 212) 924 4440
cookshopny.com
Zagat: 22/30
À la carte: $37–69

SHARLEE: Go for brunch and try the Bloody Mary in the bar while you wait for a table. The kitchen focuses on using top-notch produce from independent farmers, with a menu that changes daily.

SERGE: A great new restaurant. Fab ice creams!

da Umberto is an elegant and well-heeled Italian restaurant with Italian food that is classically cooked and presented. The Italian wine list is stunning.

DA UMBERTO CUCINA FLORENTINA
Italian
107 West 17th Street
(between Seventh and Sixth Avenues)
(1 212) 989 0303
no website
Zagat: 25/30
À la carte: $52–69

For a quick tapas, rather than a sit-down meal, **El Quinto Pino** is the hottest spot in Chelsea. It's tiny (just sixteen bar stools), but stand if you must. It is owned by the people behind the acclaimed Tía Pol just around the corner. Try them both.

EL QUINTO PINO
Spanish
401 West 24th Street
(between Tenth and Ninth Avenues)
(1 212) 206 6900
elquintopinonyc.com
Zagat: 21/30
À la carte: $26–44

IN TRANSITION

EMPIRE DINER

American
Formerly at 210 Tenth Avenue
(at West 22nd Street)
empire-diner.com

Since 1976, the **Empire Diner** has been an icon on the corner of Tenth Avenue and 22nd Street in Chelsea.

A glitzily restored Pullman railroad diner, minus the wheels, this 24/7 eatery was as well known for its clientele (all sorts) as for its food (burgers, sandwiches, salads, beer). It has been in more movies than you've had fried onion rings. Sadly, it closed in May 2010, and was still looking to find a new home as this book went to press.

KLEE BRASSERIE

Contemporary
Chef: Daniel Angerer
200 Ninth Avenue
(between West 22nd
and 23rd Streets)
(1 212) 633 8033
kleebrasserie.com
Zagat: 19/30
À la carte: $40–56

Fun bare-brick and blonde-wood brasserie with unusual and innovative takes on many classic dishes. The burger is Muscovy Duck with grilled pickle, pâté spread and chef's mustard, while the Grilled Shrimp and Octopus comes with porcini mushrooms, olive polenta and grilled lemon. The restaurant uses sustainable seafood and there are heartfelt nods to vegan diners.

MORIMOTO

Japanese
Chef: Masaharu Morimoto
88 Tenth Avenue (between
West 15th and 16th Streets)
(1 212) 989 8883
morimotonyc.com
Zagat: 25/30
Menu: $120 (omakase)
À la carte: $55–79

The Japanese star of Chelsea, Masaharu Morimoto's eponymous restaurant is also for many the sexiest, looking more LA than NY with ethereal white curtains strung across the ceiling, billowing down. Any nightclub would be proud of the bar (and super-cool website). Apart from an extensive raw bar, with sushi and sashimi, there is an à la carte menu that would happily grace any East-meets-West restaurant.

Homely American food, ranging from Shrimp Corn Cakes to Lamb T-Bone with Black-Olive Vinaigrette and Potato Mash. Regulars insist on the Parmesan Fries with Aioli. The simple restaurant space is enchanting at night with hanging Moroccan glass lanterns and candle-lit tables.

THE RED CAT
American
227 Tenth Avenue (between West 23rd and 24th Streets)
(1 212) 242 1122
theredcat.com
Zagat: 24/30
À la carte: $40–70

Fans are divided about whether you should come here for the margaritas (nine on offer) or the inexpensive and lively food. The food is as colourful as the bold surroundings.

ROCKING HORSE CAFÉ MEXICANO
Mexican
Chef: Jan Mendelson
182 Eighth Avenue
(at West 19th Street)
(1 212) 463 9511
rockinghorsecafe.com
Zagat: 20/30
À la carte: $30–40

TWO MARKETS

CHELSEA MARKET
75 Ninth Avenue (between West 15th and 16th Streets)
chelseamarket.com

Housed in the former Nabisco factory, there are more than thirty shops and restaurants, with an upstairs studio where the Food Network films a lot of its shows. A definite should-do if you like food.

UNION SQUARE GREENMARKET
33 East 17th Street (between Broadway and Park Avenue South)
(1 212) 555 1212
no website

Around one hundred and fifty producers each week on 2 acres at the north end of the square. Held four days a week, this is a favourite market for chefs such as Danny Meyer and Mario Batali.

TÍA POL

Tapas
205 Tenth Avenue
(between West 22nd
and 23rd Streets)
(1 212) 675 8805
tiapol.com
Zagat: 25/30
À la carte: $15–30

With few Spanish restaurants in New York hitting the culinary heights (it's an odd gap some savvy restaurateur will correct one day), devotees usually make do with tapas, and **Tía Pol** is the star (together with Casa Mono). The tapas span culinary styles across Spain, from Galicia to Andalcía, and the Basque regions to Cataluña. Like its sister restaurant, El Quinto Pino, this is a tiny space, so be prepared to be patient.

202 AT NICOLE FARHI

Contemporary
Chef: Annie Wayte
75 Ninth Avenue
(at West 15th Street)
(1 212) 638 1173
no website
Michelin: Bib Gourmand
Zagat: 19/30
À la carte: $39–49

If you like to eat in a fashion boutique, then try **202 at Nicole Farhi**, which occupies a corner of the Nicole Farhi store on Ninth Avenue. A London-based designer, Farhi has nine clothing stores around the world, with restaurants in two (the other is Nicole's in her Bond Street, London, head-quarters). 202 is all bentwood bistro chairs and wood floors, stylishly dressed mannequins placed just metres away. The food ranges from Warm Goat Cheese Salad with Prosciutto and Toasted Pistachios to English-Style Fish and Chips with Mushy Peas.

BARS

ART BAR
Bar
52 Eighth Street
(1 212) 727 0244
4 p.m.–4 a.m.

ASPEN
Bar
30 West Street
(1 212) 645 5040
aspen-nyc.com
6 p.m.–midnight (Mon–Sat)

AVENUE
Bar
116 Tenth Avenue
(1 212) 337 0054
9 p.m.–4 a.m.

BARRACUDA
Bar
275 West 22nd Street
(1 212) 645 8613
4 p.m.–4 a.m.

BLACK DOOR
Bar
127 West 26th Street
(1 212) 645 0215
4 p.m.–4 a.m.

CHELSEA BREWING COMPANY
Pub
505 West 23rd Street
(1 212) 336 6440
Noon–midnight

THE GATES
Bar
290 Eighth Avenue
(1 212) 206 8646
thegatesnyc.com
5.30 p.m.–4 a.m. (Tues–Sat)

GLASS
Bar
287 Tenth Avenue
(1 212) 904 1580
9 p.m.–4 a.m. (Wed–Sat)

HALF KING
Bar
505 West 23rd Street
(1 212) 462 4300
9 a.m.–4 a.m.

JULIET
Bar
539 West 21st Street
(1 212) 929 2400
11 a.m.–4 a.m. (Sun–Mon),
7 p.m.–4 a.m. (Tues–Sat)

PARK
Bar
118 Tenth Avenue
(1 212) 352 3313
11 a.m.–2 a.m. (Mon–Wed),
11 a.m.–4 a.m. (Thurs–Sun)

TILLMAN'S
Bar
165 West 26th Street
(1 212) 627 8320
5 p.m.–2 a.m. (Mon–Tues),
5 p.m.–4 a.m. (Wed–Sat)

LUXURY HOTELS

EVENTI—A KIMPTON HOTEL

851 Avenue of the Americas
(at West 30th Street)
(1 866) 996 8396
eventihotel.com
Rating: 4★
Rooms: 292
Hotel rates: $439–509

Eventi—A Kimpton Hotel is a large hotel but with the occasional urge to recreate the feel of a boutique hotel. The entrance of this striking skyscraper is similar in shape to that of many a corporate hotel, but it's done up in a funky style (loud burgundy splashes, Warhol-like artwork). The rather masculine rooms are mostly teak wood and grey fabric. They have a club-like atmosphere, large with striking design features, such as a huge white lily attached to a wooden slat wall. The bathrooms are boldly marble, with twin rain showers and fluffy robes. There is a restaurant, business centre, cinema and full-service spa, with spa services also offered in guestrooms (as is the breakfast, an increasingly rare phenomenon). The hotel advertises itself as gay-friendly.

FASHION 26—A WYNDHAM HOTEL

152 West 26th Street
(between Seventh and
Sixth Avenues)
(1 212) 858 5888
f26nyc.com
Rating: 4★
Rooms: 280
Hotel rates: $349–404

This large hotel in the Garment District is a rather uninteresting glass-and-brick tower (it looks like many an impersonal hotel in a thousand cities), but inside it can be impressive. The lobby is certainly bold, with a striking staircase rising to mezzanine level, while dramatic, thick disc lights hang from the high ceiling. You will either gasp in awe or mirth. The bar and restaurant are a bit of a hodgepodge, but some of the rooms are calmly elegant, with clever use of patterned wallpaper and fabrics to set off the blank tones and colours of the rest of the room. The bathrooms are cleanly efficient.

One of the most iconic buildings in the Chelsea district is Albert C Ledner's National Maritime Union, built in 1966. Thirty-nine years later, Eric Goode and Sean MacPherson turned it into **The Maritime**, a very trendy hotel. Its most famous features are the round windows, 5-foot versions of a ship's portholes. They dominate each bedroom, giving it an eccentric and also slightly claustrophobic feel. If only they could have been bigger. But, hey, you are staying in a genuine design classic, which you don't do every day. The cabin-like interiors are cleverly done, with teak panelling and a simple use of colour (the solid bold blue of a folded blanket or hanging curtains) to give life to an otherwise beige world. The chairs and lampshades add nice touches of period patterning to accentuate but not dominate. There are two bars (the Lobby and the striking rooftop Cabanas), plus two restaurants: La Bottega, a rustic trattoria with outdoor terrace, and the rated Japanese Matsuri, specializing in sushi and sake. There is even a nightclub, Hiro.

THE MARITIME
363 West 16th Street
(between Ninth and
Eighth Avenues)
(1 212) 242 4300
themaritimehotel.com
Rating: 4★
Rooms: 121
Suites: 4
Hotel rates: $365

OTHER HOTEL

A genuine boutique hotel amid all the bold claims made by the large hotel chains in Chelsea, **The GEM** has a colourful lobby and colourless rooms (all white except for a red pillow and runner; even the bathroom is all white). The guestrooms aren't huge, but are well designed and comfortable. And there are masses of free amenities, from Wi-Fi to LCD screens, down pillows, Gilchrist & Soames bath products, bottled water and, best of all, proper bathrobes. The hotel sits on a charming tree-lined street in the heart of restaurant-, club- and art gallery–rich Chelsea. (There are other GEM hotels in SoHo, Union Square and Midtown.)

**THE GEM HOTEL—
CHELSEA**
300 West 22nd Street
(between Ninth and
Eighth Avenues)
(1 212) 675 1911
thegemhotel.com
Rating: 3★
Rooms: 81
Hotel rates: $309–429

SHANNON'S FAVOURITE NEW YORK TREATS

BAKERIES

BIRDBATH BAKERY
145 Seventh Avenue
(1 646) 722 6565
buildagreenbakery.com

A totally eco-aware bakery; even the drinking cups are made of corn.

ADAM: Organic bakery, eco-friendly. Built from recycled materials including bench tops made from recycled Brooklyn beer bottles, and LED lighting. Fabulous chocolate chip cookies.

BOUCHON BAKERY
Chef: Thomas Keller
Time Warner Center
10 Columbus Circle
(1 212) 823 9366
bouchonbakery.com
Zagat: 23/30
À la carte: $20–35

This is Thomas (Per Se) Keller's answer to Le Pain Quotidien and Financier Patisserie (and countless others). Not only is there a range of French breads, there is a dazzling selection of pastries and muffins, tarts and chocolate. There are also savoury café dishes, from soups and salads to sandwiches and quiches. There are even treats for your pets.

SHANNON: This is a very simple counter-style café in a shopping centre that a lot of readers probably think I am bonkers to have spent so much time in! But I was curious enough to eat in the Time Warner Center several times. There is no table service at Bouchon Bakery; you order at the counter from a very simple and slightly luxurious menu, and from a lovely array of classic gateâu and pastry items, such as crunchy caramelized choux pastries filled with vanilla cream called 'Paris Brest', macarons and beautiful citrus tarts and chocolate mousse cakes called *gateâux truffe*.

Don't be disappointed when you see that it's an open-top refrigerated counter serving good French café items. It is what it is and I suggest you visit it at least once to see that a great chef like Thomas Keller can serve people who may not even recognize the connection. All the items here are made in-house and are worth trying if you are in the area or you are a chef wanting to know how to diversify successfully.

CITY BAKERY
3 West 18th Street (between Sixth and Fifth Avenues)
(1 212) 366 1414
thecitybakery.com

Savoury and sweet: the cookies are baked fresh every thirty minutes and the hot chocolate is legendary. There are also salads, using seasonal and organic ingredients. Nothing costs more than $10 and there are locally crafted beers as well.

RECOMMENDED: MELANIE

DOUGHNUT PLANT

379 Grand Street (between Essex and Norfolk Streets)
(1 212) 505 3700
doughnutplant.com

Forget Krispy Kreme, this is the real thing. After all, where else can you get a Lavender Flower doughnut? Not only are there yeast doughnuts (Crème Brûlée, Valrhona Chocolate), there are cake doughnuts (Blackout, Vanilla Bean Glaze). Go now.

PAULA AND PATRICK: Unique doughnuts made on site. If you visit on a weekend, you might find yourself lining up with the rest of them around the block. Owner Mark Israel is an eccentric who loves what he does. If you are lucky enough to end up in the bakery, be ready to sample the crème brûlée. Also, the chai tea is delicious.

FINANCIER PATISSERIE

Bakery and café
62 Stone Street (between Mill Lane and Hanover Square)
(1 212) 344 5600
financierpastries.com
À la carte: $6–12

There are six (and counting) **Financier Patisserie** outlets across Manhattan, but the prettiest is on Stone Street,

just behind South William Street. Standing outside, you might feel you are in a backstreet of Paris. Inside, the beautifully crafted cakes and tortes remind one as much of Austria as France. One can take breakfast here (pastries, organic teas, decent coffee) or a more savoury lunch (salads, cold and toasted sandwiches, daily quiches and hot panini). Grab one of the few tables and enjoy.

SCOTT: After a huge meal at SHO Shaun Hergatt the night before, all I could manage here for breakfast was an Apple Galette (perfect pastry and masses of fruit) and a double espresso (not bad). The filled rolls and other savoury offerings looked very good. For what is becoming a large chain restaurant, the atmosphere was good, though my accidentally less than 20 percent tip was not appreciated.

LA BERGAMOTE PATISSERIE

Patisserie
169 Ninth Avenue
(at West 20th Street)
(1 212) 627 9010
labergamotenyc.com
Zagat: 25/30
À la carte: $32–38

This French patisserie also does breakfast, lunch and dinner. The food is more wide-ranging than you might expect, from the usual quiches, tartines and salads to *Poulet aux Herbes de Provence*, with sautéed asparagus, wild mushrooms and potatoes, and *Filet de Sauman Roti*, served on ratatouille with green beans.

LE PAIN QUOTIDIEN
Belgian Bakery
81 West Broadway (at Warren Street)
(1 646) 652 8186
lepainquotidien.com
Zagat: 19/30
À la carte: $23–37

Le Pain Quotidien's founder, Belgian Alain Coumont, trained under Michel Guérard at Eugénie-les-Bains, Georges Blanc (Vonnas) and Joël Robuchon (Paris). But a baker rather than a chef he preferred to be. His approach—to serve organic produce whenever possible and build using recyclable, non-toxic materials—has seen his first shop on rue Antoine Dansaert in Bruxelles (1990) morph into an empire spanning sixteen countries, including twenty-two outlets in Manhattan. The philosophy was, and is, to have a bakery with a large communal table (there are smaller ones as well) and highlighting naturally fermented stone-ground, whole-wheat sourdough breads. Open for breakfast, brunch and lunch, the chain also serves an expansive menu, including salads, sandwiches, tarts (savoury and sweet), quiches and pastries. The coffee is organic and fair trade.

SCOTT: Inside, it is a gorgeous space, with a French-American country style. I sat at a long table seating maybe thirty. I chose a Parfait of Homemade Granola with Low-fat Yoghurt and Fresh Fruit (mostly seasonal berries). It was delicious, as was the double espresso. There was a calm, contented feel to the place, a true refuge from hectic Manhattan outside. Le Pain Quotidien is a huge success because it deserves to be.

MAGNOLIA BAKERY
40 Bleecker Street
(at West 11th Street)
(1 212) 462 2572
magnoliabakery.com

Magnolia Bakery is seemingly every New Yorker's favourite pit stop for cupcakes smothered in thick icing. They are pretty things indeed, and intriguingly flavoured: Caramel Meringue Buttercream with Caramel Drizzle; Pumpkin with Maple Cream Cheese Icing. There are also Icebox Pies: Peanut Butter with Cream Cheese; Banana with Vanilla Pudding and Whipped Cream. (There is another Magnolia Bakery at Grand Central Station.)

marshmallow). To drink, there is Stumptown coffee and Kopparberg Pear Cider. Chang's legendary (and very sweet) Pork Buns are also on the menu here. (There is another Momofuku Milk Bar at 15 West 56th Street.)

SULLIVAN STREET BAKERY

533 West 47th Street (between West 11th and 10th Avenues)
(1 212) 265 5580
sullivanstreetbakery.com

Jim Lahey's naturally leavened bread is as famous as bread gets in America. Lahey also owns the upmarket pizza house, Co.

MOMOFUKU MILK BAR

207 Second Avenue
(at East 13th Street)
(1 212) 254 3500
momofuku.com

Not happy with four restaurants (Momofuku Ko, Noodle Bar, Ssäm Bar and Ma Pêche), David Chang has also opened **Milk Bar**, filled with sweet delights. So, come here for a Composite Cookie made up of—wait for it!—pretzels, potato chips, coffee, oats, butterscotch and chocolate chips. Then there is the Candy Bar Pie (chocolate crust, caramel, peanut butter nougat and pretzels) and Chocolate Malt Cake (malt fudge, malted milk crumbs and charred

GRILLED BEEF SHORT RIB WITH BAY LEAF DRESSING

This recipe comes from Clinton, a chef de partie at Vue de monde. He first introduced me to it during a Friday-night staff meal. Dinner that evening consisted of marinated, char-grilled lamb chops, served with a great potato salad and a simple radicchio salad. Memories came flooding back of my afternoon at Hill Country, the smoky flavours of the meat combining with a simple type of sweet 'n' sour. My version substitutes beef short ribs for the lamb chops.

800 g of short rib, cut into strips with bone attached to each

500 ml Heinz tomato sauce

3 cloves garlic, crushed and blended with ¼ cup of extra virgin olive oil

½ cup minced shallot or onion

500 ml Worcestershire sauce

150 ml plum sauce

200 ml sherry vinegar

10 fresh bay leaves (crushed fine with a mortar and pestle)

2 sprigs of thyme (crushed fine with a mortar and pestle)

sea salt and black pepper

Add all of the ingredients apart from the meat into a saucepan set over a medium heat. Simmer for 30 minutes. The sauce can be prepared well in advance and stored in the fridge.

Once cooled, marinate the beef in 4 tablespoons of the sauce for 1 hour. Season the meat and place onto a hot char-grill. Cook for a minimum of 3 minutes on each side.

Serve some extra marinade as a sauce on the side.

Serves 4

GRAMERCY,
FLATIRON &
UNION SQUARE

FINE DINING

IIIIIIIIIIIIIIIIIIIIIIIIIIIIIIIIIIIIIIIIIIIIIIIIIIIIIIIIIIIIIIIIIIIIIIIIIIIIIIIIIIIIIIIIIIIIIIIIIIIIIIIIIIIIIIIIIIIIIIII

Missy Robbins is one of the most talked-about new chefs in New York, her every move charted in articles read by devoted foodies, her **A Voce** winning several Restaurant of the Year nods.

A VOCE
Italian
Chef: Missy Robbins
41 Madison Avenue
(enter on East 26th Street)
(1 212) 545 8555
avocerestaurant.com
Michelin: ★
Zagat: 24/30
Menu: $29 (lunch)
À la carte: $51–62

SCOTT: A Voce is on the corner of Madison Avenue, opposite the beautiful Madison Square Park, but sadly facing ordinary 26th Street instead. Inside—and it takes very cold weather to make people give up on the outside seating area—is a radiant and rather feminine design statement. The extraordinary dangling sculptures are made from twigs, while the atmosphere and lighting feels warmly embracing. I sat facing inward, which with the weather turning bad was not a bad idea, and was quickly offered a simple menu by one of the many friendly staff. Given the debate over Robbins' newfound culinary prominence, I found it surprising the menu is so constrained.

My first course was *Sgombro*: Roasted Mackerel with Mandarins, Fennel, Capers and Pistachio. It was utterly delicious, light and flavoursome, showing a deft and confident hand.

The friendly waiter had pointed out that the primi could come in half serves, so I opted for a portion of *Strascinati*, an almond-shaped pasta with guinea hen sausage, morel mushrooms and pecorino. Like many a dish employing guinea hen, it started subtly but built into a yummy mouthful. I wish I had been more greedy and ordered a full serve. It certainly trumped by a long way the oomph of the Guinea Hen Terrine served at Minetta Tavern a few days later.

The entrée was Rosemary and Garlic Marinated Chicken with Baby Artichokes, Grilled Lemons and Marjoram. A huge serve, it too was delicious, moist and packed with flavour, the grilled lemons a perfect accompaniment.

To go with both I had a half bottle of Cannonau from Santa Maria, La Palma, 2005, which is a simple and delicious wine from Sardegna. Being a half bottle, it had matured at nearly twice the rate of a standard one and will probably never be better than it was that night. At least, that was my view and that of the charming sommelier, who was astonished by how well it had come up. He called around several staff to smell its bouquet. In top New York restaurants, you often get the feeling you are being judged by the rarity and expense of the wines you order, but here was a bunch of New Yorkers excited by a common, garden-variety Cannonau that was holding its own beautifully.

By this stage, I had befriended Thomas, the charming maître d', who seemed to know every restaurant in New York and had clear and precise views about each of them. I hope this does not get him into any trouble, but his views, kindly offered, seemed absolutely on the mark. We had absolute agreement on the out-of-date classicism of Daniel, the unpretentious brilliance of Benoit, the dazzling eccentricity of wd~50. He had not yet eaten at SHO Shaun Hergatt, but he said all his restaurant mates felt it was the great new restaurant of Manhattan. He was venturing there soon.

When I later ordered dessert, Thomas offered me a complimentary 2009 Moscati d'Asti from Biancospino, La Spinetta, a very pleasant end to the meal. Even better, just before I paid the bill, a little voice told him the wine may have been accidentally added to my bill and he went immediately to check; it had and he removed it as a 'manager's discount'. Every diner has at some stage found a free glass of wine incorrectly added to a bill, so it was nice to know there are people out there who care.

So, what of the fuss about Missy Robbins? Is she the new Italian star of New York, a rival to Scott Conant and Mario Batali? Obviously one cannot tell from one meal alone, but like Conant she is an effortless chef who turns out simple food that shows the mastery of someone who could aim much higher up the starred ladder if she chose to.

Thomas the maître d' was honoured I had included A Voce on a two-week sprint through Manhattan's finest restaurants, but it and Robbins deserve to be part of any fine-dining discussion. I would return with great pleasure tomorrow. (There is a second A Voce in the Time Warner Center at Columbus Circle in Midtown West.)

....

This attractive and fun Spanish restaurant (part owned by Mario Batali) sits on a corner in the Union Square district, open on both sides to the bustling street life. On a perfect summer's evening, this is a sublime place to be, the division between inside and out lost as diners and drinkers take over this very pretty part of Manhattan. It is always lively, as any good tapas bar should be. The menu has all the classics (*Jamón iberíco*, *Bacalao croqetas*, Razor Clams a la Plancha), plus a range of daily specials written on the black glass. The serves are much larger and more expensive ($13–19) than usual. The wine list is a dream, with 600 choices. It has not only won a *Wine Spectator* award, it scored 9.5 out of 10 from the Spanish wine magazine, *Sibaritas*. If you are one of those people with the sneaking suspicion that the Spanish make the best wine in the world, here is where you can put that theory to the happy test. After all, where else could you find twenty-two reds from Bierzo? RECOMMENDED: LUKE

CASA MONO
Spanish
Chef: Andy Nussar
52 Irving Place
(at East 17th Street)
(1 212) 253 2773
casamononyc.com
Michelin: ★
Zagat: 26/30
À la carte: $40–60

ANTOINETTE: Casa Mono is a little Spanish tapas place in Gramercy, easily one of my favourite places in the city. It's my haven from chaos, a quiet respite to luxuriate over a simple plate of food and a glass of wine. The menu balances a focus on single ingredients with complex flavours and rustically simple presentations. After eating a lot of fussy food, there's nothing I like better than going to Casa Mono, and splitting a few quartinos of wine with a friend as we pick over a scattering of small plates. When it's cold out, the dark, rich interior, with tiles glistening in flickering candlelight, feels like a rustic, old-world kitchen; and when it's warm with the doors wide open, you're transported to a something like a Mediterranean café. All in this little corner of noisy New York City.

ADAM: Great Spanish.

ELEVEN MADISON PARK

French
Chef: Daniel Humm
11 Madison Avenue
(at East 24th Street)
(1 212) 889 0905
elevenmadisonpark.com
Michelin: ★
Zagat: 28/30
Menu: $28/
$42 (lunch; 2/3 courses)/
$95 (dinner)/
$135 (5 courses)/
$175 (11 courses)

Though only awarded one star by Michelin, there are those who believe Danny Meyer's **Eleven Madison Park** to be the finest restaurant in New York. Set in the famed MetLife Insurance building opposite Madison Square Park, it has commanding views and an atmosphere of contented elegance. Meyer came to fame with the Union Square Café (and later Gramercy Tavern) and now has a small stable of fine restaurants in that Midtown area. Swiss-born chef Daniel Humm, who has a passion for vertical plating and a sense of dramatic colour and contrast, won the James Bear Award for Best Chef in 2010. RECOMMENDED: NICK

. . . .

SHANNON: Probably the biggest buzz in town right now is this place. The building encasing this grand restaurant is your typical example of a place lacking an identity. The restaurant is very grand, but it sits next to a very ordinary café that makes you feel not that special. However, that is all forgotten when you are presented with a warm smile at the reception and you hear the buzz of the dining room.

The fit-out is more lunch than dinner, a slightly Art Déco feel with pale polished timbers. Overall, the décor is not mind-blowing and, if anything, it's a little dated.

Menus are broken into a three-course à la carte for $95, five courses and eleven courses. I decided to go for the three-course à la carte after landing in New York from London only an hour earlier.

So, is it worth travelling twenty-one hours for a meal that makes you feel like there is no other worry or issue in the world—basically, a food orgasm? I would say yes, but is this the place? No. The ingredients were excellent, but I was confused: classic ideas but with frozen pea lollipops thrown in!

The chef Daniel Humm is a real talent—I don't want to take away from that—but worldwide we are going through a molecular 'Look at me, Mum!' renaissance, and it's misguided. It has no story. I would rather be served a dish inspired by the founding of Manhattan or a recipe the chef's grandmother cooked. Give me something that tells me I'm dining in New York.

Goujons were served as soon as I sat down and they don't get any better. They were followed by a canapé plate. I didn't enjoy the carrot marshmallow served alongside some small and delicate morsels that included a parfait of diced Tuna with a square of some sort of white mousse. They were all very Pierre Gagnaire–like, but I would rather have eaten a carrot picked that day, straight from the garden of someone named Bob or Barry, or anyone who has a story.

Mushrooms with Boneless Sautéed Frogs' Legs, 62-degree Egg and Sabayon was a dish that was too clumsy. It had big, nice flavours, but the portion was far too large, and it looked like an old man wearing a dressing gown when up against Adam's Scallops with Strawberries.

My main course was Milk Fed Pork Chop with Rhubarb. This was very successful and probably the best piece of pork I have ever eaten. The chop was carved from a whole roasted side and perfectly cooked, with a small square of belly baked in the oven or sous vide. This dish made the visit worthwhile. I then ordered Vanilla Soufflé with Passion Fruit Sorbet, which together with the pork was an item on the menu that really stood out. It too was perfectly cooked and the passion fruit paired perfectly with the richness of the vanilla. A great success.

The wine list is very big and has all the great wines from around the world, and a well-thought-out half-bottle list, mainly of European names.

Don't forget this restaurant is for New Yorkers and it caters for their clientele really well. The staff are excellent and I would recommend it, but ignore the hype: it is just a very well-run restaurant with great food.

ADAM: Very good but not as exceptional as I had expected. The Déco room was very impressive and the service excellent, but some of the courses weren't as successful as they should have been.

GRAMERCY TAVERN

Contemporary
Chef: Michael Anthony
42 East 20th Street
(between Broadway and
Park Avenue South)
(1 212) 477 0777
gramercytavern.com
Michelin: ★
Zagat: 28/30
Menu: $55 (lunch)/
$92 (vegetarian dinner)/
$112 (dinner)

Opened in 1994, with rarely a spare seat since, Danny Meyer's **Gramercy Tavern** is a hip version of a colonial American tavern, albeit with elegant white tablecloths and bizarre anachronisms. The wagon-wheel chandelier looks like an escapee from a Texan steakhouse, while Robert Kushner's murals add a spicy burst of colour. Executive chef Michael Anthony arrived here in 2006 after an already stellar career at Manhattan's and Stone Barns' Blue Hill restaurants, following apprenticeship at some of Paris' most acclaimed restaurants (L'Arpège and Astrance). His menu is surprisingly simple given his French background, ranging from Soft Shell Crab with Fingerling Potatoes and Pickled Ramps to Grilled Sturgeon with Buckwheat, Leeks and Fennel. This is far more Blue Hill than L'Arpège, but you can see the latter restaurant's passion for vegetables in Anthony's vegetarian dinner menu—though how he can serve Smoked Pork Broth with English Peas and Garlic Scapes on a vegetarian menu is a mystery. No matter, Gramercy Tavern is the most popular restaurant in the 2010 Zagat guide and only SHO Shaun Hergatt and Aureole get a higher score for food. RECOMMENDED (FRONT BAR): LUKE

SHANNON: Danny Meyer was the first guy I knew of to give up his title of chef and become a restaurateur. He has now become one of the biggest names in America. The Gramercy was the first of his restaurants to place him on the international map. The room is a time capsule of another era in American dining. I'm not sure what brings that statement on, but it's most probably the wood grill and old-fashioned hot cupboard.

The menu is unashamedly American. We originally dropped in on the advice of a hotel concierge who said that they do great burgers, but there wasn't a burger in sight. It had been replaced by a Pulled Pork Sandwich with Coleslaw and Pickled Swiss Chard. But there was great service, with really nice non-alcoholic drinks such as fresh lemonade and iced tea. No bookings are taken for the front bar/bistro (Tavern), so be patient and have a drink at the long bar or try late afternoons. Prices are very reasonable.

ADAM: The space was a disappointment, but the Pulled Pork Sandwich was very enjoyable.

GRAMERCY, FLATIRON & UNION SQUARE

ANTOINETTE'S BLACKBERRY LIST

TEN FAVOURITE NEW YORK DINING DESTINATIONS FROM A PROFESSIONAL EATER

I travel the country (and the world) eating some of the greatest cuisine there is. But when I come home to New York, after eating so much rich and conceptually involved food, I tend to crave simplicity and comfort and a feeling of 'Welcome home, have a bite to eat'. Sure, there are a few upper-echelon restaurants that keep me engaged with the top of fine dining in New York City, but there are as many lesser-known spots that shouldn't be missed.

And so this list has evolved over the years, as I've discovered those places that not only feed me extremely well but transport me somewhere very special. I keep the list on my Blackberry—hence the name—so it's handy when I want to share it with visiting friends and chefs—anyone who wants a taste of the soul of New York dining. My list doesn't represent all of what New York has to offer, and no list could. But it has at its core the essential variety and spirit of New York dining: democratic, big-hearted, ambitious and full of soul.

THE BLACKBERRY LIST
Casa Mono
Shorty's.32
Kajitsu
Ed's Lobster Bar
Raines Law Room
PDT
Dirt Candy
Xie Xie
Corton

Antoinette Bruno
CEO and Editor-in-Chief, *starchefs.com*, New York

RESTAURANTS, STEAKHOUSES, BISTROS, CAFÉS

ABC KITCHEN
Organic
Chef: Jean-Georges
Vongerichten
35 East 18th Street
(between Broadway and
Park Avenue South)
(1 212) 475 5829
abckitchennyc.com
Zagat: 24/30
Menu: $26 (lunch)/
$38 (dinner)
À la carte: $35–67

ABC Kitchen, run by Jean-Georges Vongerichten and Phil Suarez, is committed to fresh, seasonal, organic and sustainable produce. All the fittings in the restaurant come from artisans.

SERGE: As an Alsatian, I have to make note of one of New York's great chefs, Jean-Georges Vongerichten, who is also from Alsace. The range of his restaurants, from Jean Georges, his signature restaurant and the ultimate haute-cuisine experience, to his latest adventure, ABC Kitchen, a kind of hamburger bar, is astonishing.

Like all good steakhouses, **BLT Prime** (dry) ages its own beef. Offering up to twenty different cuts of meat, including Black Angus and USDA Prime, BLT Prime is carnivore heaven. The only issue is that the meat comes on a hot cast-iron pan, which keeps cooking it while you eat. Potato is served in eight different ways, from baked to gratin. And if grilled steak is too stark an option, there are fish and crustaceans to choose from. The BLT in the name stands for Bistro Laurent Tourondel; Tourondel worked under Jacques Maximin, Joël Robuchon and Claude Troigros. There is a range of BLT restaurants, from Steak (Midtown East) to Burger (Greenwich) and Fish (Gramercy).

BLT PRIME
Steakhouse
Chef: Laurent Tourondel
111 East 22nd Street
(between Park
Avenue South and
Lexington Avenue)
(1 212) 995 8500
bltprime.com
Zagat: 25/30
À la carte: $54–93

This all-American BBQ swings with jazz and the sounds of contented diners munching on their Kansas City Spare Ribs, Applewood Smoked Organic Chicken and Pulled Pork Platter.

BLUE SMOKE
BBQ
Chef: Danny Meyer
116 East 27th Street
(between Park
Avenue South and
Lexington Avenue)
(1 212) 447 7733
bluesmoke.com
Michelin: Bib Gourmand
Zagat: 21/30
À la carte: $26–61

SHANNON: I did not end up having time to eat here, but lots of people, including Melanie and her friends, love it. It is owned by the well-known chef-restaurateur Danny Meyer (Eleven Madison Park), and is more upmarket than Hill Country Barbecue.

THE BRESLIN BAR & DINING ROOM

Contemporary
Chef: April Bloomfield
Ace
16 West 29th Street
(between Broadway and
Fifth Avenue)
(1 212) 679 1939
thebreslin.com
Michelin: ★
Zagat: 21/30
Menu: $65 (chef's table)
À la carte: $41–96

Situated in the Ace hotel, **The Breslin Bar & Dining Room** is as hot as New York gets. It's so hard to get in it is probably easier to sample its food by checking into the hotel and ordering room service. Run by the folk at The Spotted Pig, Breslin hits you with its love for porcine products, with pig scratchings handed to you in a paper bag as a gift when you enter. Then, when you get a table, you can get serious with Smoked Belly with Mashed Potatoes or the Stuffed Pig's Foot. Lighter eaters might consider the Spanish Mackerel on the Plancha with Radicchio, Potatoes and Anchovy. The Breslin is open for breakfast, brunch, lunch and dinner.

ADAM: April Bloomfield and Ken Friedman from The Spotted Pig own this English-style restaurant inside the Ace hotel. The menu embraces 'nose-to-tail' cuisine methodologies and offers handmade terrines, sausages and charcuterie. Try the Lamb Burger. Service is mixed, from great to arrogant.

....

CRAFT

American
Chef: Tom Colicchio
43 East 19th Street
(between Broadway and
Park Avenue South)
(1 212) 780 0880
craftrestaurant.com
Zagat: 25/30
À la carte: $51–97

Tom Colicchio was named the James Beard Outstanding Chef of the Year in 2010, a recognition not only of his outstanding career so far, but for the fact his many restaurants are at the forefront of (affordable) American cuisine. Colicchio rose to fame in 1994 with the opening of Gramercy Tavern with partner Danny Meyer. In 2001, he opened Craft and its more casual sibling, Craftbar. The empire has continued to grow, but Craft, New York, remains the proud flagship.

....

Craftbar is a modern interpretation of an all-day diner. The menu ranges from panini (Piquillo Pepper, Mozzarella, Charred Onion, etc.) at $10 to Foie Gras Torchon with Rhubarb Chutney ($19) and Berkshire Pork Three Ways with Baby Turnip and Anson Mills Polenta ($26).

CRAFTBAR
Contemporary
900 Broadway
(at East 19th Street)
(1 212) 461 4300
craftrestaurant.com
Zagat: 23/30
À la carte: $35–54

SHANNON: Great location on Broadway. It's in the sort of spot that you seem to pass every day. I always use Broadway as my navigator, because it splits the heart of New York. I use it to get my bearings and Craftbar is always one of the bearings on Broadway that seems to say, 'You will have to try me one day'.

Tom Colicchio is well known worldwide as the host of *Top Chef*. Craft is also a brand with outlets America-wide, broken down into Craft, Craftbar, Craftsteak and 'wichcraft. Look out for which ones are in your part of New York. Craftbar and 'wichcraft do great hot sandwiches and quick breakfast items; the only issue is the coffee. When will Americans get over quantity and go with quality when it comes to coffee?

Craftbar does a great brunch, which I preferred to my hotel's on my last visit. The brunch made a great weekend breakfast substitute. It's also excellent for a late-night snack with glass of wine following, in my case, cooking dinner for others, after not having eaten since breakfast. It is also a good place to visit in between Michelin-starred dinners. The sandwiches are great, as is the beer list.

Owned by Tocqueville's Marco Moreira and Jo-Ann Makovitzky, **15East** is Gramercy's most acclaimed Japanese restaurant, with people packing in for the omakase (it starts at $55) and the chef's tasting menu. You can eat far more simply and cheaply, should you wish. The fish is flown in fresh from Japan several times a week. Become a regular and discover when. The desserts are unusually bold and inventive for a Japanese restaurant, such as Passion Fruit Pudding with Pineapple Broth, Mango Salad and Coconut-Lime Sorbet.

15EAST
Japanese
Chef: Masato Shimizu
15 East 15th Street
(between Fifth Avenue and Union Square West)
(1 212) 647 0015
15eastrestaurant.com
Zagat: 25/30
Menu: $29 (lunch)/ $120 (chef's tasting)
À la carte: $46–81

HILL COUNTRY BARBECUE • MARKET

BBQ
30 West 26th Street
(between Sixth Avenue
and Broadway)
(1 212) 255 4544
hillcountryny.com
Zagat: 22/30
À la carte: $26–40

If smoked meat isn't the staple diet of New Yorkers, what is? It is found in the trendiest restaurants, as well as in Texan roadhouses like **Hill Country Barbecue**. If you have a hankering for brisket, then you'd better come here. You can have it moist or lean, or maybe you'd prefer Pork Spare Ribs or Beer Can Game Hen, ordered perhaps with a side of Beer Braised Cowboy Pinto Beans or Sweet Potato Bourbon Mash. With so much alcohol in the cooking, you can probably skip the cocktail and wine lists. On Tuesdays, there is a Pit-Smoked Whole Hog.

SHANNON: What can I say? I'm afraid to write this entry! You may lose a lot of respect for me in the following few lines, but, yes, I'm human and guess what? I love this place. It rocks! It took me back to my childhood.

Walk in off the street and expect a short wait in the bar. Choose a night when there is a sports event on and this place will be on steroids. Beer comes in bottles and deals are done for six packs. After downing the aperitif of Budweiser or any number of boutique beers, you are given a passbook. Yes, passbook. This is something really unique. It enables one hungry person to venture to all the little food outlets housed in the basement and on the ground floor. Each counter features different menu items to accompany the real feature: Texas dry-rub BBQ items such as brisket and ribs.

When food is served to you at each outlet, they stamp a page with what you have ordered and you pay at the counter on the way out the door. I found it hard to spend more than $70 including the 20 percent tip. Portions are designed to share and I found it refreshing to have this sort of food in New York. The portions are huge and are served in baskets lined with butcher's paper.

There is live music downstairs, and there is a huge range of beers, spirits and reasonable wines. This place soon becomes a feast.

Few words give more hope to dedicated pizza aficionados than 'thin crust', and that's what you will find here. The pizzas (or pies, as they call them) come as 9 or 16 inches. Try the Homemade Pumpkin Pie for dessert. This a tiny place that also does a lot of take-out.

POSTO THIN CRUST PIZZA
Pizza
310 Second Avenue
(at East 18th Street)
(1 212) 716 1200
postothincrust.com
Zagat: 24/30
À la carte: $20–25

Danny Meyer, the brilliant chef-restaurateur, moved into hamburgers and created a sensation. His first **Shake Shack** was (and still is) in Madison Square Park. Others later opened on the Upper West and East Sides, with still more planned. The burgers are raved about in seemingly every magazine and guide. Apart from hamburgers, there are Flat-Top Dogs and Fries. Desserts and drinks include Frozen Custard, Fresh Squeezed Lemonade (no bubbles) and Concretes ('dense frozen custard mixed at high speed with Shack mixins').

SHAKE SHACK
Burgers and dogs
South-east corner,
Madison Square Park
(near Madison Avenue and
East 23rd Street)
(1 212) 889 6600
shakeshack.com
Zagat: 23/30
À la carte: $10–15

SHANNON: Shake Shack is not far away from The Gramercy Hotel. We tried to check out the famous burger here, but I have never in my life seen a longer queue. The line stretched for 500 metres—all for a $6 burger that many say is the best in Manhattan. I guess I will have to take their word for it.

ADAM: I didn't feel like waiting two hours in a queue.

MELANIE: My daughter Emma and son Jack cheer when we announce a visit to Shake Shack in Madison Square Park. The place is reminiscent of a roadside stand, but in the middle of the park. The wait is always long, but if you are strategic you can go onto the live webcam called the 'shack cam' before your visit to see how long the line is. It is worth the wait. The shack burgers are great and the cheesy fries—well, they are very cheesy. If you are a vegetarian, the Mushroom Burger is really good and leaves you feeling included in the burger experience. Finish it off with a cone of the frozen custard. I think the flavours change all the time.

SCOTT: I went to the Shake Shack on the Upper West Side's Columbus Avenue (opposite the Natural History Museum). The queue was predictably epic and it took forever to get served with only one dedicated dude (the apposite word) taking orders, and then just as long to get the food. Take a book or stream a movie on your phone.

I had the Cheeseburger and, like everyone, I had to laboriously list what Shake Shack deems to be extras: lettuce, tomato and pickles. Seriously, does anybody ever order a bun with just a meat patty and nothing else? Get real, guys! I also ordered chips and fresh-squeezed lemonade.

The burger finally came in a plasticky bag that didn't breathe and ensured the hamburger was so soggy it risked disintegrating by the time I found a space in the packed restaurant to eat it. (Avoid the airless and windowless cellar below; it is even worse than the one at l'Arpège in Paris!)

Maybe the dampness of the burger is an attempt to recreate the famous wet hamburgers available on Taksim Square in Istanbul. Whatever the intent, Shake Shack's minimally toasted bun was disgusting, rather like a pikelet that had been marinated in water. The meat patty was equally unpleasant and gamey, the lettuce nondescript, the cheese flavourless American glug. Only the pickles were first class and the chips (from Yukon Gold potatoes) brilliantly crisp, even if crinkle-cut. The lemonade was bland but tolerable.

Overall, this was the worst burger I have ever eaten—or tried to eat. A cruel person would say they wouldn't feed it to an animal. Shake Shack's hamburger makes you feel that cruel.

....

TOCQUEVILLE
Contemporary
Chef: Marco Moreira
1 East 15th Street
(between Fifth Avenue and
Union Square West)
(1 212) 647 1515
tocquevillerestaurant.com
Zagat: 25/30
Menu: $24.07 (lunch)
À la carte: $53–76

From the team behind 15East also comes **Tocqueville**, which, as the name suggests (think nineteenth-century writer Alexis de Tocqueville), is a French-inspired restaurant. It is a subdued and elegant space with yellow-cream walls, grey high-backed chairs and dazzlingly white tablecloths. The food is prettily plated and showcases contemporary culinary styles. Perhaps because of the connection to 15East, the wine and cocktail list specializes in various sakes, as well as more than 300 top wine labels from around the world.

....

Danny Meyer's **Union Square Café** is one of the most famous restaurants in New York, and a long-time first-choice visit for tourists. It opened in 1985 and has largely been full since, even though there are vague rumblings every few years that standards aren't quite what they were. You go here to relax in the unpretentious bistro surrounds, and the confident and clean cooking of Meyer's chef, Carmen Quagliata. Apart from subtle modern variations on bistro standards, there are 'Weekly Classics', such as Maine Lobster on Monday and Roasted Roman-Style Baby Lamb with Spring Vegetable Scafata and Market Greens on Friday.

UNION SQUARE CAFE
American
Chef: Carmen Quagliata
21 East 16th Street
(between Fifth Avenue and
Union Square West)
(1 212) 243 4020
unionsquarecafe.com
Zagat: 26/30
À la carte: $49–68

BARS

||||||||||||||||||||||||||||||||||||||||||||||||||||||||||||||||||||||||||||||||||||||||||||||||||||||||||||||||||||||||||||||||||||||||||||||||||

ANTOINETTE: This is the ultra-sultry speakeasy I go to after a long day to catch up with friends and luxuriate on one of the velvet couches beneath lush dark curtains. The interior is reminiscent of the 1920s or '30s, comfortably luxurious, dark and dramatic—a speakeasy you can almost melt into. The cocktails are incredible—everyone I bring here is impressed—a combination of classics and modern innovations that range from my favourite, their Negroni, to spirit-forward drinks that are all silk and smoke on the tongue. The bartenders vary from night to night, so you can get a variety of styles in the span of a few days. And they work in a little kitchen, not behind a bar, so you're welcome to stand around and chat with them as they muddle fresh berries and measure out bar spoons of pomegranate molasses. And though most of the city's speakeasies promise to call you back when space opens up, Raines actually does!

RAINES LAW ROOM
Cocktail bar
48 West 17th Street
5 p.m.–2 a.m. (Mon–Thurs),
5 p.m.–3 a.m. (Fri–Sat)

SIMON: This is one of the most difficult bars to get into, so to do so you'll have to be staying at the Gramercy Park Hotel (although that's still no guarantee), or know someone. However, once there, it is something special. The music is eclectic: old and new, remixes and originals. You will want to dance but it's too crowded. Jason Statham and Luke Wilson were there the night I went. There is the feel of a secret club as everyone is friendly and smiles at you. Even the supermodels are happy to chat for a sentence or two. I'm guessing they must think you are pretty cool just to have gotten into the famous **Rose Bar**.

ROSE BAR
Bar
Gramercy Park Hotel
2 Lexington Avenue
(1 212) 920 3300
gramercyparkhotel.com
Noon–4 a.m. (Mon–Sat);
reservations required
from 9 p.m.

GRAMERCY, FLATIRON & UNION SQUARE

FLATIRON LOUNGE
Bar
37 West 19th Street
(1 212) 727 7741
flatironlounge.com
5 p.m.–2 a.m. (Sun–Wed),
5 p.m.–4 a.m. (Thurs–Sat)

**GALLERY AT THE
GERSWHIN**
DJ bar
7 East 12th Street
(1 212) 447 5700
6 p.m.–midnight

**LIVING ROOM AT THE
W HOTEL**
Lounge bar
201 Park Avenue South
(1 212) 353 8345
7 a.m.–midnight

PETE'S TAVERN
Pub
129 East 18th Street
(1 212) 473 7676
Noon–2 a.m.

230 FIFTH
Cocktail bar
230 Fifth Avenue
(1 212) 725 4300
230-fifth.com
4 p.m.–4 a.m.

LUXURY HOTELS

ACE
20 West 29th Street
(between Broadway and
Fifth Avenue)
(1 212) 679 2222
acehotel.com/newyork
Rating: 4★
Rooms: 258
Hotel rates: $269–599

One of the cheapest four-star hotels in Manhattan, the **Ace** is designer heaven. It is hardly boutique at 258 rooms, but it is a fascinating reinvention of a historic building and hotel (The Breslin) by local artists and designers. The smallest sleeping abodes, the Bunk-Bed Rooms, are just that: two vertically stacked metal beds you would expect to see in a school camp. Whether such sleeping arrangements constitutes good value is up to you, but the design is spunky and the bathroom prison-bold. The penitentiary vibe is reinforced by the cell-like door to the corridor. Cheap Rooms have a bed, which is nice, but the space is at way too much of a premium (an outrageously meagre 13 square metres). Even the second-largest room is just 16 square metres, which is fine for a large dog, but that's about it. Not that the scarcity of space bothered the critics, all of whom raved about the Ace as one of the hotels of the year. Maybe they just gathered in The Breslin Bar & Grill (run by The Spotted Pig's April Bloomfield and Ken Friedman), one of *New York* magazine's hot spots.

ADAM: Regarded as one of the 'cool' places to stay, we found it very overrated. The foyer, while having character, is usually full of people who have purchased a coffee at the in-house Stumptown Coffee Roasters and are using the hotel's free Wi-Fi. This adds a vibe, but also is annoying, particularly when the DJ starts up early in the evening. The rooms are noisy. The staff range from friendly to super arrogant and just 'too cool for school'. We also found the rooms overpriced for what we got.

However, Stumptown is one of the better coffee experiences in New York and the staff there were great.

The highlight of the **Carlton** is its three-storey lobby: it is a masterpiece, the sort of wow number a set designer with a hefty budget on a 1940s Hollywood film might have conjured. If you are not staying here, take a look anyway. It was recently renovated to great effect by David Rockwell, who spent $60 million redoing the whole building. The guestrooms are large.

CARLTON

88 Madison Avenue
(between East 28th and
29th Streets)
(1 212) 532 4100
carltonhotelny.com
Rating: 4★
Rooms: 293
Suites: 23
Hotel rates: $459–519

GRAMERCY PARK HOTEL

2 Lexington Avenue
(at East 21st Street)
(1 212) 920 3300
gramercyparkhotel.com
Rating: 4★+
Rooms: 140
Suites: 45
Hotel rates: $565–725

The star of the district is clearly the **Gramercy Park Hotel**, one of the most iconic boutique hotels in Manhattan. Opened by hotelier Ian Schrager and painter-filmmaker Julian Schnabel, it is so over the top it is hard to know how to describe it: some ascribe to it a 'Kasbah look', others 'chic bohemian' and 'madly eclectic', yet more a 'total mess'. It just depends on what gets one through the night, and given the rages celebrated in the hotel's Rose Bar and Jade Bar that probably isn't sleep. Most critics make much of the blend of genuine antiques and modern pieces, a Venetian chandelier contrasting with artwork by Schnabel or a Warhol with louvered wooden blinds. Some of the public rooms look as if a Gulliverian child has scrawled on them with a giant Texta or the largest piece of chalk ever invented. The bedrooms are more discreet, but you have to love red (curtains, doors, rugs, chairs) and green or blue (the rest). The smallest are way too small for the price (20 square metres) but have a bath and a shower, as every half-decent hotel should. The floors are red oak, which look spectacular, but there's a good argument never to stay in hotels with wooden floors for obvious reasons. The restaurant, Maialino, is a trattoria run by Danny Meyer of Eleven Madison Park and Union Square Café fame, while the aforementioned bars (where you must reserve a spot by 9 p.m., even if a guest) are two of the grooviest in New York. The outside terrace at night is an enchanting magic kingdom. As for the famed Gramercy Park across the road, like many parks in London it is gated. Residents of the hotel, though, are temporarily granted a key.

SIMON: The wonderful thing about this hotel is that you are inside a creation by one of the great artists of our time, Julian Schnabel. Primarily a painter, he also directed the films *Basquiat* and *The Diving Bell and the Butterfly*.

This hotel was for a time the coolest place in New York. The rooftop restaurant is so filled with plants that you feel outdoors. The mirrors and lighting are all original designer pieces, the artwork museum quality. The rooms and corridors are unbelievably dark and a bright phone is handy to use as a torch. The location is perfect and a room with a view to Gramercy Park is magic.

Due to New York's famous rent-control laws, the hotel was required to renovate the existing tenants' rooms as well. You may be lucky enough to meet these tenants in the lift. They are older folk who seem quite bemused by the new, odd people they come across in the corridors. I found them delightful and friendly, the opposite of the hotel's clientele who are in the uniform of modern cool: black top, blue jeans and black Prada shoes.

The staff, as in most boutique hotels, are pretty hopeless, with the emphasis on pretty. Forget this place if you need a proper concierge. My last stay included two security staff entering my room at 3 a.m. through a connecting door to the next room, walkie-talkies blaring. I thought it was a raid.

ADAM: One of the Ian Schrager 'empire' hotels. We were given the 'rock star suite', which was great, and had the advantage of the equivalent of two bedrooms. The suite was well fitted, spacious and remarkably quiet—possibly one of the quietest in New York. The hotel restaurant-café, Maialino, produced great coffee, good food and excellent service. The rooftop terrace and the Rose Bar and Jade Bar are great places to relax and have a drink, but it is annoying that they are often booked out for private functions so they cannot be used by hotel guests.

. . . .

After a complete and rather chic refit, **The Marcel at Gramercy** reopened in 2008. The lobby is a mod stunner, with a shiny and curving black leather couch, gloriously spotted cushions and a swirling wall mural. There is a great view of the Empire State Building out one side, so you can relive *An Affair to Remember* for a few happy moments. In the guestrooms, the beds have brightly coloured leather headboards (in a yellow/lime green), the walls are textured fabric and the curtains a lush velvet. The inevitable zebra prints can be found on the throw cushions. All rooms have baths and rain shower heads. The Hg2 guide loves The Marcel in part because it is close to that 'bastion of burger goodness Shake Shack', but you will easily find a thousand more convincing reasons to stay.

THE MARCEL AT GRAMERCY

201 East 24th Street
(at Third Avenue)
(1 212) 696 3800
themarcelatgramercy.com
Rating: 4★
Rooms: 135
Hotel rates: $359–409

. . . .

Occupying the 1911 Beaux Arts Guardian Life building, and renovated by David Rockwell (who recently did the nearby Carlton), **W New York—Union Square** is one of three W hotels in Manhattan. The designer wing of Starwood Hotels, all the Ws are luxuriously elegant. They vary more than brand hotels usually do, and the Union Square goes for the calmness of beige and chocolate in its guestrooms. If you can get past the silly names (Spectacular, Mega, Fantastic, Extreme Wow), you will find a room and a size that suits. But it is certainly not cheap.

**W NEW YORK—
UNION SQUARE**
201 Park Avenue
(at East 17th Street)
(1 212) 253 9119
whotels.com
Rating: 4★
Rooms: 257
Suites: 13
Hotel rates: $589–909

OTHER HOTELS

Though expensive for a three-star hotel, **The Inn at Irving Place** is very highly regarded. It is gloriously done up in mid nineteenth-century style, and it feels like an inn rather than a hotel—or even someone's private brownstone. The entrance parlour is something out of Edith Wharton or Henry James.

INN AT IRVING PLACE
56 Irving Place (between East 17th and 18th Streets)
(1 212) 533 4600
innatirving.com
Rating: 3★+
Rooms: 12
Hotel rates: $415–545

An impressive 1906 building (in Midtown, it could easily be mistaken for a gentleman's club), **Park South** is an extremely comfortable hotel that, depending on the season, can offer great value for money (in May it is a steal). The guestrooms are colourful and a reasonable size, very comfortable and homely. They have high ceilings, cove mouldings and cherry-wood headboards. There is a well-stocked library and a gym, and continental breakfast is included. The casual restaurant, Black Duck, offers Pan-Atlantic bistro cuisine.

PARK SOUTH HOTEL
122 East 28th Street
(between Park Avenue South and Lexington Avenue)
(1 212) 448 1024
parksouthhotel.com
Rating: 3★
Rooms: 140
Hotel rates: $265–335

FOIE GRAS SANDWICH

I'm not going down the ethical brainwash road. Anyone who sends death threats is definitely not going to change my mind or, I hope, those of the chefs in New York who have access to some of the best foie gras in the world. This recipe is dedicated to those of you who enjoy the luxury of being able to head up to Zabar's on Broadway (quite a long way up Broadway) to get a lobe of duck foie gras, a loaf of brioche and some apple slaw.

1 lobe of duck foie gras (8 slices)

8 2cm-thick slices of medium-size brioche, toasted, buttered and hot

4 tablespoons of quince jelly/jam

1 cup white cabbage, thinly sliced

1 cup of Granny Smith apple, julienned

1 small white onion, very thinly sliced

2 tablespoons of mayonnaise

sea salt

baby English watercress

Preheat a heavy, flat barbecue grill or fry pan. Keep the slices of foie gras in the fridge until the minute you are ready to cook them.

Have the brioche hot and ready. Spread a generous layer of quince jelly on each slice.

Combine the cabbage, apple and onion with the mayonnaise and season well. Add a generous spoonful to each slice of brioche.

Season the slices of foie gras and add them to the hot pan or grill. Do not add any oil to the pan and make sure the extraction fan is on.

Fry for 30 seconds. Turn over, making sure a golden crust has formed on the exterior of the slice, and cook for another 30 seconds. Control the heat if you feel the slices are starting to overcook. Don't be concerned that you will lose approximately one-third of the slices' original volume after completing the cooking process.

Place a slice on top of each brioche. Add a few sprigs of baby English watercress (refreshed in iced water). Season and serve immediately with a great glass of sauternes or Arkenstone Sauvignon Blanc from the Napa Valley, 2007—I was served this exceptional wine at The French Laundry in the Napa—or a glass of very cold rosé champagne.

Serves 4

MIDTOWN
WEST

FINE DINING

Charlie Palmer's **Aureole** is as revered a restaurant as one can find in Manhattan. It used to be located on the Upper East Side, but now it resides in Adam Tihany's dramatic Bank of America Tower near Bryant Park. The restaurant is as striking as the building that houses it. Aureole doesn't offer à la carte, but you can choose an $85 three-course prix fixe, beginning with, say, a Diver Scallop Sandwich with Seared Foie Gras, Sugar Snap Peas, Passion Fruit and Chives. The mains—Guinea Hen, Lamb Rib-eye, Alasakan Halibut—are all testament to Palmer's passion for farm produce over 'factory' and using French cooking techniques to produce intense, clean American flavours. The wine list is as excellent as you would expect. Palmer has thirteen restaurants across America and is almost an institution.

AUREOLE
Contemporary American
Chef: Christopher Lee
Bank of America Tower
135 West 42nd Street
(between Broadway and
Sixth Avenue)
(1 212) 319 1660
charliepalmer.com
Michelin: ★
Zagat: 26/30
Menu: $34 (lunch)/
$49 (Sunday in Bar)/
$85/$108 (dinner;
5 courses)/$135
(chef's tasting)

GORDON RAMSAY AT THE LONDON

Contemporary
Chef: Gordon Ramsay
The London NYC
151 West 54th Street
(between Seventh and
Sixth Avenues)
(1 212) 468 8888
gordonramsay.com/
gratthelondon
Michelin: ★★
Zagat: 23/30
Menu: $110/$150
(menu prestige; 7 courses)

British super chef Gordon Ramsay continues to wow critics and diners at The London NYC hotel. The food is what one expects: clean and precise, a brilliant fusion of British and European food. Ramsay is at his best when inspired by the south of France. After all, he was mentored by Joël Robuchon and Roger Vergé. But his food is much lighter. People still don't realize how much he has done for the industry and how he brought luxury ingredients to the everyday table. (See also Maze by Gordon Ramsay at The London.)

SHANNON: The hype surrounding Gordon Ramsay opening a fine-dining restaurant in New York was huge. It was portrayed as Gordon's big move into a forbidden city, where the precious and tender line of what constitutes fine food, held together by a few special mortals, was about to be challenged. In fact, that was all a load of bullshit and what really went on was Gordon and his father-in-law, Chris Hutchinson, made a very shrewd decision: when offered the site, they took over the food and beverage service for the whole hotel.

To reach Gordon Ramsay at The London, you walk through the bar to the right and pass Maze on the left—which I find a little odd as people stare at you as if they think you are better than them. You then find yourself in a very large rectangular room with no windows apart from a very odd one through which you can see some bins silhouetted against the light. The tables are well spaced and all have the accoutrements that you'd expect of a Gordon Ramsay establishment.

The food was fine and very enjoyable. The three-course prix fixe menu for $110 was very good value. It was a meal that took me back to the great Michelin food of the 1990s. However, it was still not as good as the first time I ate Gordon's food at Aubergine in London in the middle of that decade. Where had the Mediterranean touch that made the food really tell a story gone? At the time, I think Gordon was cooking the best food on the planet, up there with Alain Ducasse for me. But, as usual, by the time a chef has made it, the food though still great has lost that little touch. That's how I would describe this meal.

It started with a lovely little scallop *amuse bouche*, then moved on to a pressed Hudson Valley Foie Gras Terrine with Sour Cherries and Toasted Brioche. Really great stuff.

I chose a couple of good bottles from the wine list. The sommelier was a really nice guy, which sometimes didn't come across. I found all the staff were really lovely, friendly people; the service was up there with Per Se.

I should have ordered a sauternes with the terrine, but as usual was too busy lecturing my boys, Josh and Ryan, who were with me. Their dishes looked great and, as young, starving chefs, they cleaned them up. My main course was also really smart: a Roast Pigeon with Celeriac and Buttered Cabbage and a very light Truffle Jus. For dessert, I had a Caramelized Banana Cream with Coconut Mousse (foam) and Pineapple Granita, which once again was very nice. Really good two-star Michelin food.

Would I go back? Yes, sure. The service was excellent and the room was atmospheric. It wasn't a mind-blowing location, but a lot of money had been spent on this place for all the right reasons.

People have written that Ramsay was aiming for three stars at this establishment and that he failed when he received only two. Give me a break: in his first year of opening in a foreign land, he gets to two stars and the place is full on a freezing Wednesday night in January? What knob would think that is a failure?

From a chef's perspective, when we were invited into the kitchen I found some of the senior chefs had a few egos directed up their own rectums, which disappointed me. As Gordon Ramsay is such a nice, down-to-earth guy, I felt it was sad that these guys looked a little bitter. Hey, I have just spent a thousand bucks in your restaurant and you are the ones that invited me into your kitchen, so at least smile. If that had not happened, I probably would have come away with a happier memory.

LE BERNARDIN

Seafood
Chef: Eric Ripert
155 West 51st Street
(between Seventh and
Sixth Avenues)
(1 212) 554 1515
le-bernardin.com
Michelin: ★★★
Zagat: 29/30
Menu: $70 (lunch)/
$112 (dinner; 4 courses)/
$138 (tasting menu;
6 courses)

The story of **Le Bernardin** is often told. It began in Paris in 1972, with a restaurant started by the brother and sister team of Gilbert and Maguy Le Coze. Then, in 1986, they rather surprisingly moved to New York to tremendous acclaim; but the happiness was short-lived, with Gilbert dying eight years later. For a time it looked as though Le Bernardin might close, but Maguy decided to keep going, promoting Gilbert's sous chef, Eric Ripert. At first, Ripert recreated the dishes of his former patron, but, with Maguy's encouragement, he gradually began reinventing the classics and creating new dishes to suit his palate. Today, the restaurant is regarded as one of the best two or three restaurants in New York.

SHANNON: I had never eaten at this revered establishment before, but had heard plenty of great things. The chef's name is Eric Ripert and this guy is an unsung hero internationally. He is well known for his philanthropic work in the city and also for mentoring young chefs. Unfortunately, the night I dined he was in Paris with his mate, Tony Bourdin.

After Gilbert Le Coze passed away in 1994, many people felt this would mean the death of the restaurant. But Maguy formed one of the great partnerships in American restaurant history with Eric, and thanks to this I was treated to one of the best seafood meals I have ever had. Not only that, it restored my faith in the Michelin guide. My only gripe is that the girl who opened the front door for me greeted me with one of the most miserable welcomes I have ever received. She looked down, made no eye contact, and

just gave a robotic welcome that was hollow and snobby. That all changed when the maître d' welcomed me inside with 'It is such a pleasure to have you here'.

I waited at the bar while my mate Adam was his customary thirty minutes late. I've gotten used to this and enjoy the serenity of knowing I have private time at the bar scoping the scene.

The menu works simply: four courses for $112, with ample choices for all courses and supplements thrown in for caviar. There are four meat choices for the mains and a pleasing selection of vegetarian options that read really well.

We stared at the Salmon Caviar, which was plated beautifully in a boat-shaped plate. The thinly pounded Smoked Salmon Carpaccio was cut to mirror the shape of the plate, with the cantered caviar reflecting the shape of the salmon—just so simple and beautiful. I wish all the chefs out there trying to inflate their reputations by reinventing ice cream could have tasted what I was tasting.

Next, I had the Alaskan King Crab, Stuffed Zucchini Flower with Peekytoe and a 'Fine Herbs-Lemon' Mousseline Sauce—a kind of hollandaise with chives and a little whipped cream. Adam had a great dish of White Salmon with a prawn sauce that bore a resemblance to XO sauce, but was much lighter and smoother in texture. It was seriously delightful. We matched this with a glass of Meursault.

Next came our main courses. I had the Striped Bass with Corn 'Cannelloni', consisting of corn purée wrapped in a layer of leek and rolled. The Bass had been very lightly baked, then served at the table with a light Périgord sauce, which was a meaty jus. The dish was perfect apart from one fault: I couldn't finish it. Blame it on eating for five days straight.

Adam's Barely Cooked Organic Salmon with Kolhrabi, Baby Leeks and Horseradish Scented Broth looked great. The Salmon was cooked on just one side. The only thing I picked up on was the Salmon looked unusual on the cooked side—nearly white—where the residual heat from the cooking had made the fish bleed its protein.

Dessert once again was a highlight, with a beautifully presented Pistachio Mousse with Caramelized White Chocolate, Lemon and Bing Cherry. It came with small cubes of pistachio frangipani. Perfect. Dessert was matched with a glass of 1998 Chateau La Rame sauternes. In fact, wines by the glass were a real highlight here.

I had a few issues when booking Le Bernardin, particularly with its policy of two sittings. I had to eat at 6 p.m. and hand the table back by 8.30 p.m. In fact, this worked out okay and enabled us to go for a drink afterwards and walk off the meal. So, I have come to accept this as a part of New York dining, whether we like it or not.

The biggest issue I now have to deal with is deciding which of the two great restaurants in New York is my favourite: Le Bernardin or Corton?

SCOTT: The story of Le Bernardin is so fascinating, so much a triumph over personal tragedy, that to eat at this restaurant is to enter culinary history. The emotional experience is only intensified by the iconic painting near the front door of Maguy and Gilbert Le Coze setting out to sea from Brittany in a small rowboat, a metaphor for their voyage across the oceans to New York. If that weren't enough, Mme Le Coze later came out during my meal and almost eerily wandered around her grand dining room, without stopping or speaking, alone but still victorious.

Unlike Shannon and Adam who went for dinner, I preceded them by a month and went to lunch. At Le Bernardin, that means a three-course prix fixe for an eminently reasonable $70.

The choice was astonishing, even if Le Bernardin divides the menu, rather pretentiously I think, into Simply Raw, Barely Touched and Lightly Cooked. Surely the dividing line between the second and third categories must be at times diaphanously thin.

As I sat, a waiter brought a large serve of a salmon roulade for me to pick at. It was pleasant, but unrefined and heavy. An *amuse bouche* should be lighter and more thrilling on the palate.

My appetizer was called Kumamoto: Progressive Tasting of Kumamoto Oysters 'en gelée', from Light and Refreshing to Complex and Spicy. The toppings included the inevitable yuzu. (Is there a restaurant in New York that doesn't use it by the crate-load?) Sadly, the menu description far outweighed the taste of what was on the plate.

The variations between toppings were too subtle and uninteresting, hardly the zingy journey from Refreshing to Spicy that was promised. The real problem, though, is that Kumamoto oysters are dreary and near the bottom of any bivalve-lover's wish list.

The entrée was a tricky choice because there were ten fish dishes and one lobster dish to choose from in the Lightly Cooked section alone. I went for what sounded the most interesting sauce. Sadly I have forgotten what it was and the menu changed just days later, removing the description from the website I had relied on to revive my memory. Anyway, it came with Codfish, which is hardly the king of fish. The dish was clever and perfectly cooked, but why a fish as mundane as Cod is on a three-star menu is a mystery. Still, I chose it.

The dessert, from pastry chef Michael Laiskonis, was brilliant: Pear: Cinnamon Caramel Parfait with Liquid Pear, Smoked Sea Salt and Fromage Blanc Sorbet. The little teardrops of liquid pear were divine, molecular gastronomy producing a stunning visual creation with almost unbelievable intensity of flavour. The sorbet was perfect, the caramel parfait making one dream of another serve. This was a great dessert and worthy of any three-star restaurant.

But, at least for me, Le Bernardin falls a star short of its Michelin rating. One dish (the dessert) was perfect; another (the Cod) was extremely good; the third (oysters) a sad misjudgement. There are also the issues of its barn-like size and the hurried way guests are catered for. Some tables had three sittings during lunch, and as the restaurant must seat at least 120 that means up to 300 were pushed through. It was way too bustling, hurried and noisy for a restaurant of its reputation. Then again, compared to Jean Georges, it was an oasis of calm.

However, there is no doubt Eric Ripert is one of the finest chefs in New York. After all, I have only ever had one better fine-dining experience in all my fifteen or so visits to New York and that was at SHO Shaun Hergatt.

MATT: Le Bernardin is fantastic. The dining room is as beautiful as any you could find in the world. The food is great. Very classic. Great service. The sommeliers come out with their big tasting pendants slung around their necks.

ADAM: A most memorable dinner. The service was exceptional and the seafood was amazingly prepared.

MAREA

Seafood
Chef: Michael White
240 Central Park South
(between Columbus Circle
and Seventh Avenue)
(1 212) 582 5100
marea-nyc.com
Michelin: ★★
Zagat: 27/30
Menu: $42 (lunch;
2 savoury courses)
À la carte: $65–100

Along with Le Bernardin, the premier fish restaurant in Midtown is **Marea** (sister restaurant of Alto and Convivio). The raw bar is simply astonishing, from oysters (Dennis, Tomahawk, Glidden Point, etc.) to sliced Pacific Jack Mackerel, and Duck Prosciutto and Rhubarb. The caviar is from China and California. But the real test is the secondi di pesce: Seared Black Bass, perhaps, with Walnut Agrodolce (sweet and sour sauce), Charred Cauliflower, Pickled Grapes and Treviso. This dazzlingly modern cooking comes in equally spectacular surroundings: backlit walls, golden polished wood, bright-red lampshades. Marea recently won the James Beard Best New Restaurant Award.

NEIL: Marea is another good Italian for lunch. Great quality food and the crudo (especially the Alaskan Spot Prawn) and pastas are particularly good. The sea urchin spaghetti and the penne with spicy sausage are standouts. We drank some smart wines by the glass here. It is a good lunch place if caught shopping Midtown.

MASA

Japanese
Chef: Masa Takayama
Time Warner Center
10 Columbus Circle
(1 212) 823 9800
masanyc.com
Michelin: ★★★
Zagat: 27/30
Menu: $400 (minimum)

Masa is the most famous Japanese restaurant in New York and the most expensive: at least $400 per person for the omakase (the only option). Some of the dégustation will be sushi (diced Fatty Toro and caviar), but the majority are dishes marrying Japanese techniques with worldwide ingredients, such as foie gras cooked in a shabu-shabu pot, or Fugu served on a bed of shiso blossoms and covered in flakes of gold. There are just twenty-six seats, so start planning. (A cheaper option is Bar Masa.)

SHANNON: Masa and Bar Masa are two of the greatest Japanese restaurants of their time. Nobu is good and reliable, but really there are a thousand just as good in Tokyo and another thousand that are even better. Masa is in a different league, but I have to say it was one of those experiences I wanted to hate because the price really pissed me off. Neil Perry had warned me that the set menu was $300 plus supplements, and the restaurant was in a shopping centre, near Per Se. It also had two Michelin stars at the time I dined there. Why didn't it have three if it was charging those prices? I felt I had to eat there just to justify the next time I was in a negative mood, so I could bitch about the time I ate at Masa.

My favourite flavour profile is umami and this is what the whole flavour profile of each dish on their menu works up to. Think miso, oyster sauce and mushrooms, and the balance of slight acid with sweetness. That was what I tasted for at least an hour after leaving this place. I was also blown away by the fit-out and how the use of materials made the small but contritely spacious space what I, as restaurateur, aim to do in designing a new place, but can never find the restraint or confidence to do: 'Simplicity devoid of unnecessary elements, and the honest presentation of materials'.

The blend of seafood I had that night was mind-blowing. Snow crab and lobster were ever so slightly grilled with warm foie gras—delicate and amazing. The Wagyu tartare-like texture with some sort of herb-flavoured blossoms scattered over it served with delicate ponzu-like cold broth was amazing. I sat at the bar and very much enjoyed the interaction with, I think, the chef himself, Masa Takayama, but the interaction was never more than what it took to describe the food and the body language and smiles of 'I'm glad you are having a great time'.

I was told by several people that Takayama is famed for his White Truffle Tempura, which he serves from late October to December. I was also told that the amazing seafood I tried could have been ordered and flown in from anywhere in the world, as Takayama has a network of suppliers who will organize overnight delivery. If the Aussie dollar stays above US$0.85, then go; if it drops below that, try Bar Masa, because I do not want to be responsible for any disappointments. Japanese food is the hardest of any cuisine to recommend to someone.

....

THE MODERN

Contemporary
Chef: Gabriel Kreuther
Museum of Modern Art
9 West 53rd Street (between
Sixth and Fifth Avenues)
(1 212) 333 1220
themodernnyc.com
Michelin: ★
Zagat: 26/30
Menu: $48/$58 (lunch;
3/4 courses)/$88 (dinner)

Another of Danny Meyer's ever-expanding restaurant group, **The Modern** is stunningly located inside the Museum of Modern Art. With its floor-to-ceiling glass overlooking the central Abby Aldrich Rockefeller Sculpture Garden, it is as pleasant a place to eat as one can find in New York. In warm weather, you take your drinks and so on outside to some sofas and cement coffee tables. Alsatian chef Gabriel Kreuther comes via Jean Georges and Atelier at the Central Park Ritz-Carlton. It is light, modern food, elegantly plated, revealing perhaps more of his time in Switzerland at the two-star L'Ermitage de Bernard Ravet than his Alsatian heritage.

SCOTT: The entrance on 53rd Street is very modern, a curved white hallway that leads like a *2001: A Space Odyssey* tunnel to the reception desk and the bubbling Bar Room. It is separated by a frosted glass wall from The Modern and is dark compared to the main restaurant's sunlit magnificence (at least at lunch).

There was on offer à la carte and a prix-fixe menu, with two courses and dessert for $48, with an extra savoury course for $58. The staff were among the best I have encountered, charming and efficient with none of the snobbery that can so annoy in France, nor the forced overfriendliness often found in the United States.

The *amuse bouche* was a Cauliflower Panna Cotta with a Grapefruit Vinaigrette, Grapes and Flowers (miniature violets?). It tasted fine, but was way too sweet and dessert-like to begin a meal. The first course was Soft Polenta with Wild Ramp Froth and Mousseron Mushrooms (plus the same flowers). It was superb, a classic savoury dish that was as texturally sublime as its taste. The wine I selected was a dull Alicante rosé from the Barossa. Yet again, few decent American wines were available by the glass.

The next course was Soft Shell Crab with Baby Spinach, Hazelnuts and Passion Fruit. It didn't work at all. The batter was too thick on the crab, killing much of its flavour. A Japanese tempura would have been far better. The roasted nuts were okay but didn't marry with the crab in any noticeable way and the passion fruit sauce (it may have just been juice) was simply horrible with everything on the plate. Some things go together (lamb and riberries, chicken and tarragon), but crab and passion fruit don't.

A charming waitress, beaming with pride, asked how I liked the crab. I gave an honest response. She was surprised but polite, even genuinely interested. As I waited for the next course, I noticed almost everyone was having the crab. No one seemed to dislike it as I did.

The Organic Chicken En Cocotte with Sherry Vinegar, Spring Garlic and Fiddlehead Ferns was beautiful. The chicken was flawlessly cooked and full of pure flavour. The buttery tagliatteli served on the same plate with it was a tad rich, but overall it was a wonderful dish.

I generally don't order dessert (except when helping Shannon write books), but it came with the menu. I asked the waitress to choose and she selected the Baba Grand Marnier with Roasted Mango, Vanilla Ice Cream and Lime Sabayon. The baba was okay, the mango and ice cream very good, and the lime sabayon beyond divine. And around the edge of the plate was sugared crystallized lime peel: fabulous.

The waitress then appeared with a selection of chocolates from the chocolate trolley, saying this made up for her not selecting the other dessert, the Milk Chocolate and Hazelnut Dacquoise with Raspberry Sorbet. The best of the chocolates, all extremely good, was broken pecan nuts covered in chocolate and gold dust. The double espresso was perfect, proving you can get great coffee in New York.

When the bill came, they charged me for three courses not four, because I had not liked the crab. Michelin gives this one star and the food deserves it. The location, setting and staff deserve more.

....

Oceana, which recently moved from 55 East 54th Street, offers a choice of seafood dinner experiences. First up is the Café & Raw Bar with its 50-foot bar, where, apart from oysters, clams and the like, there are Shiitake and Seafood Spring Rolls, an Alaskan Wild Choho Salmon Burger and Beer-Battered Fish and Chips. There are more than twenty outstanding wines by the glass and a range of beers. If you prefer to sit in the formal dining area (it is like being onboard a passenger liner, with the dramatically curved wood ceiling), then the menu is a roll call of America's finest fish: Wild Alaskan King Salmon, Crispy Wild Striped Bass, Tapioca Crusted Halibut and so on. There is 28-Day Dry-Aged Prime steaks and Roasted Natural Amish Chicken for anyone not interested in seafood or crustaceans. The wine list has more than 500 labels.

OCEANA
Seafood
Chef: Ben Pollinger
120 West 49th Street
(between Seventh and Sixth Avenues)
(1 212) 759 5941
oceanarestaurant.com
Michelin: ★
Zagat: 23/30
À la carte: $53–89

....

PER SE

Contemporary
Chef: Thomas Keller
Time Warner Center
10 Columbus Circle
(1 212) 823 9335
perseny.com
Michelin: ★★★
Zagat: 28/30
Menu: $175/$275
(including taxes and tip)

Per Se is almost universally agreed to be the finest restaurant in New York. Owner-chef Thomas Keller is an icon of American cuisine, the founder of The French Laundry in California's Yountville and now this East Coast extravaganza. Its interior may be austere (even bland), but his food is not. This is a big-night-out experience, worth the difficulties of getting a table.

SHANNON: Who would have imagined that Thomas Keller would open a restaurant in a shopping centre, let alone that Michelin would award three stars to a restaurant located in such a place? The wildcard here is that this is not just any shopping centre, it's the Time Warner Center. Ted Turner is reported to have personally worked on getting Keller to New York ever since the concept of the development was conceived.

You enter the shopping centre and proceed up a couple of flights of escalators. I love to roam through the bookshop and be inspired by some of the books they have on food and other chefs before heading up to the second-floor entrance, where a bucketload of money has been spent on detail. The bar/lounge area is spacious and opulent without being over the top and has very dim, atmospheric lighting. The main dining room is small and on two levels, with the lower tier close to the windows overlooking Central Park. The raised level also has an outlook onto the park, but comes with a lot more movement and a bit more noise. I'm personally not fussed where I sit at great restaurants.

The food is classical down to plates and cloches, but I get the feeling when eating this style that great food is timeless. There were three set menus to choose from, with a couple of choices of extras such as Maine lobster, when in season. The wine matching was modern with sakes and spirits being put forward, which I really like. Something about Per Se just makes me feel like I'm in New York.

A Cornet of Smoked Salmon Mousse and Salmon Eggs was a great little canapé presented very classically in a little stand. Next was some Hudson Valley Foie Gras with Cherries, a great example of the foie gras being produced in the United States.

The Novia Scotia lobster, poached in butter, was the perfect portion size. 'Oysters and Pearls' is a must-try, consisting of poached Island Creek oysters, soft, exploding balls of tapioca, a very light sabayon and amazing Sterling White Sturgeon caviar. The dish was delicate and very complex.

Another standout was the Wagyu beef, which I'm proud to say is Blackmore's Wagyu from Victoria. Beautifully presented with a very small bouquet of onions and root vegetables, the beef itself was either short rib or strip loin that had been slow-cooked, then finished in a pan. The desserts were technically amazing.

Having now been here for dinner twice, I really think lunch is the best way to go. At night, I didn't give the desserts the attention and respect they deserved, as I was starting to feel the effects of long travel and too much food.

The kitchen is amazing, all 300 square metres of it. It has its own video link to The French Laundry, where daily meetings take place to decide on new dishes and any issues that may have arisen from the day before are discussed. The pastry kitchen is huge, with all one could want to produce great dishes from great ingredients. It's immaculate, with white tiles and clean cooking lines and thirty or so chefs plus stagières (chefs or aspiring chefs who work for free to learn as much as they can in as short as possible a time, anywhere from one day to six months). Ask for a kitchen tour and see why you pay the money you do for such a unique experience.

I take my hat off to Thomas Keller and his team. They are keeping the New York fine-dining scene alive along with the likes of another half-a-dozen leading chefs. Keller has placed the focus right back on this town in the past five years because of his attention to detail. Not all of you will love it, but I hope you respect it.

NEIL: Per Se is the must-do fine diner in New York; this is a deserved three-star restaurant. Thomas Keller has this place humming. It has a stellar wine list and fabulous set menus. You can enjoy the daily menu or a vegetarian one, and, let me tell you, this isn't just vegetarian, but some of the best food you can eat. The menu can include 'Oysters and Pearls', the classic Keller dish that everyone needs to have at least once in their life; a foie gras course that will leave you thinking that perhaps this is also a benchmark; amazing chicken with four stories; and Elysian Fields lamb, usually slow-cooked. This, of course, is merely a selection of the many courses you will receive, and you will finish with great desserts. I love the warm professional service and the eye for detail that leads me to believe that this is the best service on the planet.

BRYAN: Per Se and The French Laundry are probably two of the most sought-after dining experiences in America. I was lucky enough to dine at Per Se in 2009. It had all of the hallmarks of a great dining experience: amazing food, superb service and an elegant dining room. It is a brilliant restaurant where everything is in absolute harmony, confident in and of itself.

The food was exemplary, starting with English Pea Soup and the signature 'Oysters and Pearls', then Snake River Farm's 'Callotte de Boeuf Grillé' and finishing with the playful 'Coffee and Doughnuts'. The punctuation and definition of flavour was outstanding. The wine was matched expertly and really complemented the food. It is always great to see these two elements designed in such harmony with one another.

The service was friendly, knowledgeable and very professional, without being intrusive in any way. All in all, this is an amazing dining experience and one that shouldn't be missed when visiting New York.

MATT: What can you say? Cutting edge. I had a plate of gnocchi covered in white truffle. It has the most pristine kitchen you will ever see in your life. They all wear gloves!

SHARLEE: I can't be sure if I was more impressed by the seven different salts that were offered on the table or that the servers had memorized the flavours of the twenty-four different chocolates offered at the end of the meal. Per Se is the ultimate dining experience. As soon as you enter through that blue door, the intention is for you to feel absolutely comfortable in the surroundings. Mix that with divine food, stunning views of Central Park and faultless service, and you will enjoy one of the most memorable dining experiences ever. Make sure you have the 'Oysters and Pearls'.

ADAM: An amazing experience. Its accolades are justified, the service faultless. Difficult to select one course that was a highlight.

ANNA: For a very special birthday party, we went to Per Se. Our New York friends were very impressed that we procured a table, but our secret was that we had a great contact in Melbourne (SB), who arranged it. A very beautifully organized restaurant, lovely attention and refined interesting food.

SCOTT: Per Se was to be the big experience of my recent trip to New York. Rarely have I looked forward to a restaurant with such pleasurable anticipation.

After a brisk walk through a storm-lashed Manhattan to stimulate the appetite, I arrived at the glitzy and overcrowded Time Warner Center. Per Se shares Level 4 with Masa, Bar Masa and a branch of A Voce.

At the door, I was met by an elegant hostess who informed me there was no reservation for me, Shannon Bennett, Vue de monde or any other name I could think of. I had a print-out of the confirmation back in my hotel room, but had failed to bring it as no restaurant in the past week had asked to see one.

For the next thirty minutes, I debated as best I could my right to enter, but it got me nowhere. The hostess looked at me with increasing disinterest. The only kindly soul was the maître d', Gregory Tomichich, who seemed genuinely upset by the situation. He brought me a superb glass of champagne (I couldn't catch the marque) and some *amuses bouche*: a warm cheese puff with molten cheese inside (delicious but still not as good as the ones at Benoit) and a miniature cornet with a ball of raw salmon (sorry, Shannon, I thought it was dull).

Tomichich was trying to fit me in somewhere, booking or no booking, but wasn't having much luck. He suggested I have the full menu in the Bar, but it would have meant sitting in an armchair leaning over a coffee table.

By now the rest of the staff were doing their best to convince me it was all my fault. How could their perfect system have made a mistake? It never had done so in the past. I must be confused. Did I book for May or was it June? Perhaps I was just a fool who had wandered in deluded, or, worse, knew he didn't have a booking and was trying to bluff his way in. I have never been made to feel worse in a restaurant anywhere in the world. So, I left.

To cheer myself up, I decided on a hamburger at The West Branch (since closed). It was, of course, full. Next door, the Fatty Crab was also packed. So, rather than face a third restaurant rejection that evening, I went to my hotel room and ate a tin of salted mixed nuts.

I emailed Per Se, but the person who had taken and confirmed the booking was 'Out of the Office'. Clearly it wasn't my day. But then it was never my day because Per Se chose not to contact me as the staff had repeatedly promised.

I finally rang them three days later. The booking person freely admitted her mistake, but made no effort to soothe the troubled waters, such as offering a meal (or part thereof) at Per Se's expense. Losing me as a client was clearly of no concern. I decided Per Se was a place I never wanted to try and revisit.

SEÄSONAL RESTAURANT & WEINBAR

Austrian
Chefs: Wolfgang Ban,
Eduard Frauneder
132 West 58th Street
(between Seventh and
Sixth Avenues)
(1 212) 957 5550
seasonalnyc.com
Michelin: ★
Zagat: 25/30
Menu: $27 (lunch)/
$64 (5 courses)
À la carte: $45–69

Perhaps the greatest surprise of the New York culinary scene is the number of high-end Austrian restaurants and the high regard in which they are held: Blaue Gans, Café Sabarsky, Wallsé, Thomas Biel and **Seäsonal**. Chefs Wolfgang Ban and Eduard Frauneder, both from the Vienna Culinary Institute, are producing light and flavoursome modern cooking with their clever revisions of traditional dishes. The dishes include, thank heaven, a Wiener Schnitzel (veal not pork), served with potato, cucumber and lingonberry. New York chefs certainly have a thing for pairing schnitzel with lingonberry (see Wallsé), and it does grow in Austria, but in Vienna a far more common accompaniment is potato salad and pumpkin-seed oil. However, traditions should never stand still, and Seäsonal is into new fusions. The Zweiebelrostraten uses Wagyu beef, and the Tafelspitz is served with spinach and rösti rather than cabbage. The wine list is predominantly Austrian, which should please everyone. For a red, try the Pichler-Krutzler Blaufränkisch Weinberg.

RESTAURANTS, STEAKHOUSES, BISTROS, CAFÉS

BAR MASA

Japanese
Chef: Masa Takayama
Time Warner Center
10 Columbus Circle
(1 212) 823 9800
masanyc.com
Zagat: 27/30
Menu: $49–156

A cheaper, but still expensive at times, adjunct to Masa.

SHANNON: The sushi and sashimi here are great. Not cheap, but really fresh and classical. Just remember that this is in a shopping mall. The booths seat six people really well. On the occasion I dined here for lunch, I was in the company of Neil Perry, his assistant Sarah and some of his crew from Rockpool. When chefs eat out for a quick lunch, it always ends up being a food experience.

This is the first sushi bar I have been to where we were waiting for the doors to open. So were several other people. It was a strange group-like experience. Well worth it, though.

The several types of Tuna belly were perfect. Braised mushrooms in a ponzu broth were incredible, as was the scallops sashimi. This is not a place you go for a big night out—or maybe it is for some—for me it's just a great place to eat whenever I am in the area. It is good with a group, but it hasn't the same sort of feeling for a single diner. You simply don't get the same buzz as you would being in a bustling street-level Japanese sushi bar, which one expects when eating out in the big smoke of Manhattan. I like it, but don't plan to eat here if you are staying down on the Lower East Side or somewhere similarly distant.

COMPILATIONS OF RECIPES BY VARIOUS MASTER CHEFS

The date is of the first American edition. Only one book per author/editor.

1. *New American Chefs and their Recipes* (Lou Seibert Pappas, 1984)

2. *Cooking with the New American Chefs* (Ellen Brown, 1985)

3. *Home Food: 44 Great American Chefs Cook 160 Recipes on Their Night Off* (Debbie Shore, Catherine Townsend and Laurie Roberge, 1995)

4. *The Chefs of the Times: More than 200 Recipes and Reflections from Some of America's Most Creative Chefs Based on the Popular Column in The New York Times* (Michalene Busico, 2001)

5. *Cooking from the Heart: 100 Great American Chefs Share Recipes They Cherish* (Michael J Rosen and Richard Russo, 2003)

6. *The 150 Best American Recipes: Indispensable Dishes from Legendary Chefs and Undiscovered Cooks* (Fran McCullough, Molly Stevens and Rick Bayless, 2006)

BENOIT

French
60 West 55th Street
(between Sixth and
Fifth Avenues)
(1 646) 943 7373
benoitny.com
Zagat: 20/30
Menu: $19/25 (lunch; 2/3
courses)/$36 (dinner)
À la carte: $38–66

The most starred chef in the world, Alain Ducasse, has two restaurants in New York: Adour Alain Ducasse in The St. Regis and **Benoit**, a bistro on 55th Street. It is an offshoot of his Benoit in Paris, founded in 1912 and one of the City of Light's most treasured restaurants. The New York café's design—with its moulded wooden walls, inset with framed caricatures of Anglo-Celtics, large expanses of mirror and simple tables set with white linen and a metal runner down the centre of each that also acts as a clamp—is stunning. An added bonus is the huge bowl of white hydrangeas resplendent atop a high pillar. It feels more Parisian than most Parisian bistros. The menu is extensive, with a daily special (such as Braised Lamb Shoulder with a Confit of Apricots) and, at lunch, a two- or three-course prix fixe.

SCOTT: This is a great French bistro by any standards. Almost instantly a waiter arrived with a basket of fine bread (baguette and warm toasted pain de campagne) and four of the most divine cheese puffs I have ever tasted. They alone are worth the price of the meal.

I started with the Half Avocado with Baby Shrimp, Grapefruit and a Cocktail Sauce, which came sitting atop a large stainless steel bowl filled with finely crushed ice. The prawns were large and delicious, the cocktail sauce refreshingly sharp and tangy, while the avocado, cut into neat cubes, was the best I had ever eaten. (This has since been surpassed by an avocado salad in one of Shannon's Café Vue lunchboxes.)

Other prix-fixe appetizers were a Soup of the Day (carrot or cold tomato) and a Goat Cheese and Spinach Quiche.

The three mains on offer included Artisanal Pasta with Mussels, Red Pepper, Zucchini and Fresh Herbs (served in a Le Creuset saucepan) and Hacis Parmentier (beef and vegetable shepherd's pie). I went instead with the Puff Pastry Crusted Salmon with Julienned Vegetables and a Shallot-Tarragon Sauce. It was like a Fish Wellington, with everything but the buttery tarragon sauce inside the puff-pastry wrapping. The pastry was to die for (literally), due to the staggering amount of high-quality butter some genius had managed to add to the mix. Also divine were the julienned carrots and leeks, and the feather-light Salmon. This is one of the greatest fish dishes I have ever eaten, and probably the richest. (A bit scary, really, as three-star Daniel beckoned a few hours later.)

The desserts included a range of fine cakes and pastries (individual chocolate cake, raspberry tart, vanilla macarons, lemon tart), all presented under separate glass cubes on a rotating trolley. The staff (all French-speaking) were charming and efficient, and, like all good New York waiters, obsessed with sweeping away crumbs from the tablecloth.

There were twenty odd wines by the glass (I had a delicious Viognier from the Languedoc) and a short but fascinating wine list of bottles. Everything was of excellent quality and well priced.

The prix fixe is the most astonishing value for Michelin-quality food (Benoit doesn't have a star but should). Forget Paris; come here instead.

....

Owned by Mario Batali and Joe Bastianich, **Esca** is one of New York's premier seafood restaurants, obsessed with serving fish within hours of capture. Dave Pasternack's food is simply prepared (Spigola comes with wild mushrooms and braised young leeks) and fairly priced (oysters are $3 each, a main of Zupa de pesce $29).

ESCA
Seafood
Chef: Dave Pasternack
402 West 43rd Street
(at Ninth Avenue)
(1 212) 564 7272
esca-nyc.com
Zagat: 25/30
Menu: $75 (5 courses)
À la carte: $53–80

NEIL: Another Italian place well worth a visit is Mario Batali's Esca. It is over on the West Side, and is a truly fantastic seafood restaurant. The crudo is wonderful, the Razor Clam Crèche is not to be missed, and I do think they do the best lobster pasta I have ever had. Spaghetti with Tomato, Chili and Mint is to die for. The roasted fish is amazing too and the contorni (side dishes) are well-roasted and -braised vegetables that could make a great lunch in their own right. As with all of Mario's restaurants, the wine list is a trip through Italy from bargains to all the heavy hitters.

ADRIAN: Another one of über-chef Mario Batali restaurants. It's modern seafood, of which Manhattan has the pick, with a strong Italian bent. I recommend lunch; it's hard to get into for dinner, though a smart suit and an Aussie accent is worth a try.

Located in the aptly named Hells Kitchen area, I walked into this place with a considerable hangover; a few hours here and I was cured. This place has sharp, modern, interesting and tasty food. I loved the crudo selection: fourteen different fish and seafood offered raw with a hint of something (for example, Red Sea Bream with Liguria Oil; Diver Scallops with Tangerine Pressed Oil) at $18 each or $30 for a tasting of six.

I ate with three friends. My mate Todd, a builder, had never eaten so well in his life. He is a steak-sandwich and meat-pie lover, so this place did well to convert him.

The service? Where do I start? Our waiter, Robert, was fantastic. One of the best and I have seen some good ones. Friendly, professional and extremely well informed, a joy to have floating around the table. He earned his tip and we tipped well. He nearly out-did the chefs, and they did an excellent job.

ADAM: Great pasta with sea urchin and crab.

MA PÊCHE
Vietnamese
Chef: David Chang
Chambers
15 West 56th Street
(between Sixth and
Fifth Avenues)
(1 212) 757 5878
momofuku.com
Zagat: 22/30
Menu: $85 ('Beef 7 Ways';
pre-order)
À la carte: $40–60

The latest venture of David Chang, **Ma Pêche** opened in the basement of the Chambers hotel in June 2010. With communal tables and no tablecloths or cutlery (wooden chopsticks are all that's on offer), Ma Pêche is what critics love to call 'stripped-down dining'. Chang being Chang, there is a lot of sticky pork on the menu in some way or other (Spring Rolls, Ribs with Lemongrass and Caramel, Spicy Pork Rice Noodles with Sawleaf Herb). There are no reservations but you can reserve online 'Beef 7 Ways' (tongue salad, artisanal meat wrapped in lettuce, beef shank, etc.). If you can work out that apparent contradiction in the reservation system, you are an honorary New Yorker. Try the Moroccan shiraz from Alain Graillot.

Gordon Ramsay's second restaurant at The London NYC is another in his chain of Maze restaurants. The chain has had some setbacks (Prague's has closed), but in London Maze holds its one star and Ramsay hopes for the same accolade here. It is incredible he can offer Aged 10 oz. Rib Eye as part of a two-course lunch menu for just $26.

MAZE BY GORDON RAMSAY AT THE LONDON

French
Chef: Gordon Ramsay
The London NYC
151 West 54th Street
(between Sixth and
Seventh Avenues)
(1 212) 468 8889
gordonramsay.com/
mazeatthelondonnyc
Zagat: 22/30
Menu: $26/$35 (lunch;
2/3 courses)/$70 (dinner;
7 courses)
À la carte: $40–60

SHANNON: Maze is a bar and eatery that has a nice ambient touch to its fit-out that I like. The food here is simple, French in style with a few American touches, such as maple syrup in a lobster bisque. It is also very well priced.

....

Milos, Estiatorio specializes in the freshest seafood, cooked simply in the Greek manner. This is not a cheap restaurant: it uses only organic ingredients and sources the best-quality ingredients (seafood, honey, yoghurt), no matter the price. That is perhaps why an appetizer of Eggplant and Saganaki costs $28.75. Most mains are in the mid to high $40s (Prime Black Angus Fillet, Colorado Lamb Chops). The highlight of the menu is arguably Lavraki and Petropsara Soup at a staggering $120 for two. Still, Zagat rates it one of the best restaurants in New York, a view not shared by Michelin, which does not list it at all. You will have to check it out for yourself. It is a bland, white-walled taverna-style space, with a fresh-fish display in the corner.

MILOS, ESTIATORIO

Greek
125 West 55th Street
(between Seventh and
Sixth Avenues)
(1 212) 245 7400
milos.ca
Zagat: 27/30
À la carte: $45–105

....

SHANNON'S FAVOURITE NEW YORK TREATS

WINE STORES

APPELLATION WINE & SPIRITS
156 Tenth Avenue (between West 19th and 20th Streets)
(1 212) 741 9474
appellationnyc.com

ASTOR WINES & SPIRITS
399 Lafayette Street
(near East 4th Street)
(1 212) 674 7500
astorwines.com

BEST CELLARS
1291 Lexington Avenue (between East 86th Street and 87th Streets)
(1 212) 426 4200
bestcellars.com

DONNA DA VINE
355 Atlantic Avenue
(between Hoyt and Bond Streets)
(1 718) 643 2250
donnadavine.com

Small, quirky shop with unusual wines that was featured in *O*, the Oprah magazine.

SCOTT: I went with Susi and didn't recognize a single bottle of wine, from America or anywhere else. Most had such out-there hippie labels I feared the wine itself. Ever brave, Susi bought six bottles while I was muttering in the corner.

Back at Susi's Brooklyn condominium, we opened each bottle over the next two days and all were brilliant. Especially fine were the Match Book 2007 Dunnigan Hills Tempranillo (which outshone Viña Cubillo's 2003 Rioja Crianza), the Thelma 2006 Ktima Pavlidis (a stunning Greek wine) and a seductive Cabernet blend from Revelry Vitners in Washington State. So, never judge a wine by its label—or a wine shop by a cursory glance at what's on the racks. I stand corrected.

THE GREENE GRAPE WINE STORE MANHATTAN
55 Liberty Street (between Broadway and Nassau Street)
(1 212) 406 9463
greenegrape.com

THE GREENE GRAPE WINE STORE BROOKLYN
765 Fulton Street (between South Portland Avenue and South Oxford Street)
(1 718) 797 9463
greenegrape.com

ITALIAN WINE MERCHANTS
108 East 16th Street (between Union Square East and Irving Place)
(1 212) 473 2323
italianwinemerchants.com

MORRELL

One Rockefeller Plaza
(1 212) 688 9370
morrellwine.com

PARK AVENUE LIQUOR SHOP

292 Madison Avenue (between
East 40th and 41st Streets)
(1 212) 685 2442
parkaveliquor.com

SHERRY-LEHMANN WINE & SPIRITS

505 Park Avenue (at East 59th Street)
(1 212) 838 7500
sherry-lehmann.com

The most famous of the all the great
Manhattan wine merchants. Its
range of quality wine is phenomenal,
as one would expect. What one
mightn't expect is how friendly and
helpful all the staff are, no matter
how little or how much you want
to spend. A great wine store.

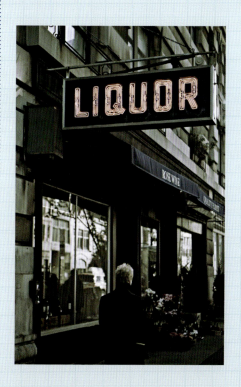

NOBU FIFTY SEVEN

Japanese
Chef: Nobu Matsuhia
40 West 57th Street
(between Sixth and
Fifth Avenues)
(1 212) 757 3000
noburestaurants.com
Zagat: 26/30
À la carte: $51–78

Midtown West outlet of TriBeCa's (and the world's) Nobu.

SHANNON: This place pumps. Literally. I estimated at least 300 seats and they were all full! Walking upstairs into a big space that has been given the Nobu treatment with mood lighting and stylish fixtures sometimes throw me a little. I actually think the best fit-out of any Nobu is in Melbourne. Its use of wood and lighting in a difficult space is first-class, and I'm sure the fit-out bill was too!

The one thing I do like about Nobu Fifty Seven is that there are vantage points from which the kitchen is in full view. All the action and the number of chefs on show is incredible.

The food, as at all Nobus, is consistent and very good. I had the more expensive Bento lunchbox and from memory it was only $39 plus tip. It was great value, served very quickly and made me feel as though I had eaten wisely and healthily. It is a good spot to eat at while in the area.

I know some Melbournian readers will hate Nobu. Well, I'm not one of them. I think that a town like New York has great qualities that influence all the big cities of the world. My five-year-old Phoenix thanks America for McDonald's for the toys she gets there, and her Dad thanks New York for bringing Japanese to the world and providing the springboard for a lot of great Japanese chefs to beat the bar that was raised by this very well-planned restaurant chain.

The Russian Tea Room is one of the most famous restaurants in New York, and where Michael (Dustin Hoffman) has lunch with his agent (Sydney Pollack) in *Tootsie*. Opened by members of the Russian Imperial Ballet in 1927, it was closed in 2002 after being sold, but reopened four years later in all its glitzy splendour. The food is classical Imperial Russian, including Chicken Kiev, brilliantly paired with an Almond Saffron Plov and an Apricot Cumin Chutney, or Bœuf à la Stroganoff with Homemade Buckwheat Noodles, Porcini Cream and Red-Wine Reduction, Topped with Foie Gras. There is an excellent caviar menu.

THE RUSSIAN TEA ROOM
Russian
Chef: Mark Taxiera
150 West 57th Street
(between Seventh and Sixth Avenues)
(1 212) 581 7100
russiantearoomnyc.com
Zagat: 19/30
Menu: $35 (express lunch; 3 courses)
À la carte: $56–94

PATRICIA: I once asked Melbourne chef Greg Malouf for his favourite restaurants in New York and I remember him telling me that he loved The Russian Tea Room and Per Se. I'd already been to Per Se and so I was determined to visit The Russian Tea Room on my next trip to the Big Apple. That was in 2009 and on this first visit I took along my friend Joel Reed, who had known the place in the late 1950s when it was a hub for the theatre crowd. He told me that back then it was neither downmarket nor too élitist; you could get Russian blini for $2 or $3 per serve and ordinary New Yorkers could rub shoulders with 'Ivy Leaguers' such as Jackie Kennedy and Peter Lawford.

Over and above such colourful history is the magnificence of its décor. I had the feeling that I'd gleaned something of the grandeur and sophistication of Czarist Russia, even though renovations were completed only a few years prior; the décor is so incredibly opulent that it borders on kitsch.

It had such a wonderfully convivial atmosphere that I went again in 2010. This time I was on my own and, like most New York restaurants, The Russian Tea Room has a bar catering for single diners or those who prefer light meals. I really enjoyed just sitting at the bar, sipping champagne and sampling their selection of caviar. It's not a huge bar, so it doesn't ever seem to get too crowded and raucous, and you can strike up a friendly conversation with just about anybody.

The Russian Tea Room first opened its doors in 1927, but, despite renovations, changes of ownership, and the evitable change in clientele that comes with a hike in prices, Carnegie Hall and the Lincoln Center will always be nearby, and only a few doors away the Directors' Guild of America. So, don't be at all surprised if—as in its heyday—you happen to spot a celebrity or two while waiting for your blini and caviar.

SCOTT: I was in New York the day The Russian Tea Room closed its doors in 2002, seemingly forever. The line of people wanting to make one a final pilgrimage stretched for a block. The pall of sadness hanging over the city had to be experienced to be believed. Restaurants really do matter.

....

XIE XIE

Asian
Chef: Angelo Sosa
645A Ninth Avenue
(between West 45th and
46th Streets)
(1 212) 265 2975
xiexieproject.com
À la carte: $11–30

A new venture from Angelo Sosa and partners Emilio Barletta and Giuseppe Marcia, Xie Xie ('shay shay') is a casual restaurant (sandwiches, salads, ice creams) delighting in the colours and flavours of Asia.

ANTOINETTE: It's hard not to love anything Angelo Sosa does. What other young chef could put his mind to doing Asian-inspired sandwiches out of a tiny white box of a restaurant with mod, purple furniture and a funky, futuristic æsthetic, and follow through with such passion? Sosa took his Jean-Georges Vongerichten training in spice and Asian techniques, combined it with what he was exposed to on his own travels, and brought those flavour profiles into very approachable, and highly addictive, sandwiches that everyone can enjoy. I actually find myself making excuses for a trip up to the Theater District just to have one. And tongue-in-cheek additions like canned champagne, juice boxes of wine and a '1000 Year Old' Ice Cream Sandwich are the finishing touches to this cheeky out-of-the-box experience.

....

BARS

||||||||||||||||||||||||||||||||||||||||||||||||||||||||||||||||||||||||||||||||||||||||||||||||||||||||||||||||||||||||||||||||||||

THERAPY

Bar
348 West 52nd Street
(1 212) 397 1700
therapy-nyc.com
5 p.m.–2 a.m. (Sun–Wed),
5 p.m.–4 a.m. (Thurs–Sat)

UNDERBAR

Bar
201 Park Avenue South
(1 212) 358 1560
mocbars.com
4 p.m.–2 a.m.

....

LUXURY HOTELS

The **Algonquin Hotel** has one of the most iconic reputations of any hotel in New York, due to its fabled Round Table and the literary wits, including Dorothy Parker, who eviscerated friends and foes while dining and drinking there. And there's the rub: the Algonquin is most famous as a hotel for those who gathered there but didn't actually stay. Not that it isn't a charming boutique hotel to reside in, with unusually quiet and calm rooms off hushed corridors, and famous *New Yorker* artwork and cartoons framed on the walls. And then there is the lobby's Lounge, the place to have a drink or two before seeing a Broadway play a few steps away. (You might also try the Blue Bar.) For diners there are two choices: The Round Table Room (formerly the Rose Room) with its famous table, and the wood-panelled Oak Room Supper Club, where some amazing musician will play or sing for you, sometimes before they become famous (Harry Connick Jr, Diana Krall) or after (Bobby Short).

ALGONQUIN HOTEL
59 West 44th Street
(between Sixth and
Fifth Avenues)
(1 212) 840 6800
algonquinhotel.com
Rating: 5★
Rooms: 150
Suites: 24
Hotel rates: $450–550

SCOTT: I have stayed here at least ten times. It was a ritual: Cannes in May for the film festival, a drive through France to Paris, a few days on the Left Bank and then a flight to New York before heading back to Oz. The New York trips were always brief (there was work waiting at home) and run like a military operation, mostly involving clothes-shopping at Saks and book-buying at Scribners and Doubleday (both sadly no more). The Algonquin was the perfectly placed hotel, but, more important, felt like home. There is such a sense of personal ease and security there it felt an insult to lock your door.

The rooms used to be a bit dowdy and small unless you had a corner one (where once I saw Edward de Bono through an open door sitting in an armchair), and the air conditioners were as noisy as only Americans can make them. But there was such calm and reassurance about the place that the dowdiness equalled charm. And, of course, there was always the Lobby, where one tends to live. The pre-show cocktails (and gratis snacks) are a ritual no one should miss. If you want a slightly more substantial meal in a hurry, the Lobby has an interesting short menu.

The Blue Bar is an equally fun choice, despite its being tiny and always packed. One day while ordering a gin and tonic I turned to find out who was bumping solidly into me and it was Norman Mailer.

The Algonquin is probably most famous for its Round Table, now sitting in the main restaurant, with all the literary connotations that follow. And it is fun to imagine all the banter that went on there. (Someone: 'President Coolidge has just died.' Dorothy Parker: 'How can they tell?') But the literary life continues there, and William Styron was a regular guest when I stayed here. So, where else would one want to read *Sophie's Choice* on the day it was released but in the lobby or the quiet of one's Algonquin room, as I did?

Change inevitably came to the Gonq (as some cheekily call it), when its Japanese owners restored it perfectly but lost some of the atmosphere. The renovations have continued and the rooms are now refreshed, but the design is bland. But the Alqonquin was never about its rooms; it is about the ambience, the Lobby, the Round Table and the Oak Room, and the musical stars plying their trade there.

A recent visit revived all the great feelings of the past. I took my mother Gillian there, to show her where I had been staying all these years. We had a lovely drink in the Lobby and became so comfortable and at ease that we abandoned plans for a big night out and decided to eat in the Rose Room. The cooking (including Chilean Sea Bass) was better than in any of the more-fancied restaurants we visited on that trip.

There is no doubt: the Algonquin is still one of the great hotels of the world.

....

SCOTT'S FIVE FAVOURITE NEW YORK HOTELS

1. The Carlyle
   (Upper East Side)

2. Algonquin Hotel
   (Midtown West)

3. The Cooper Square Hotel
   (East Village)

4. The Wall Street Inn
   (Financial District)

5. Helmsley Park Lane
   (Midtown West)

One of the best newer hotels in New York, the **Chambers** sits on an uninspiring bit of 56th Street just off Fifth Avenue. Inside, it is a different story, a revelatory cavern of Manhattan cool. The lobby has a dramatic double-sided fireplace below a mezzanine floor seemingly suspended in mid-air. The corridors to the guestrooms are outrageously over the top (raspberry-vine wallpaper), but the seventy-seven rooms are coolly restrained. They are large (starting at 28 square metres) with a lot of polished wood, and simple but elegant modern furniture. The dearer rooms have baths. There are more than 500 original paintings throughout the hotel. In the basement is David Chang's newest restaurant, Ma Pêche.

CHAMBERS

15 West 56th Street
(between Sixth and
Fifth Avenues)
(1 212) 974 5656
chambershotel.com
Rating: 4★+
Rooms: 72
Suites: 5
Hotel rates: $495–725

HELMSLEY PARK LANE

36 Central Park South
(between Sixth and
Fifth Avenues)
(1 212) 371 4000
helmsleyparklane.com
Rating: 4★
Rooms: 583
Hotel rates: $391–620

Though mentioned rarely in guidebooks, this a great hotel. The 46-storey tower sits on Central Park South with the best views of Central Park in all Manhattan. Its only rival is the Jumeirah Essex along the same street to the west, The Plaza not being tall enough or as well positioned to offer such spectacular views. Inside it is like a time capsule, some of the light fittings and wallpapers looking as if they have been there half a century (or, if new, brilliantly chosen). This is a New York hotel as they used to be, with a European elegance and more personal space than you ever dreamed possible.

SCOTT: My Park View King room on the thirty-first floor had a view that took the breath away. The room was huge (larger than many suites), with a bed seemingly designed for six. I have never felt so alone at night.

The furniture was wonderfully from times past, the carpet, furnishings and especially the cut-glass light fittings evoking the 1950s and '60s. The wallpaper in the rooms was a comforting rose colour, whereas in the corridors it was a 1950s horror so striking it is almost acceptable today. Though the hotel is constantly being refurbished, they have managed to make it feel as if it hasn't been touched.

Unlike, say, the Waldorf=Astoria, the minibar was well stocked, and reasonably priced for New York. But the real bonus was a fridge in the bathroom for your own use. Brilliant. The bath was large and the plug worked, the bedroom divinely spacious, the two chairs and sofa extremely relaxing.

Breakfast is served in The Park Room, which is also the main restaurant. It has an impressively high arched ceiling, with magnificently tacky chandeliers. The view out of the massive windows onto Central Park and The Pond is fabulous. It is hard to imagine a nicer place to sit for a meal.

Though a large hotel (583 rooms), you hardly notice anyone there and even the lobby feels oddly deserted. Given the location, the views, the space, the furnishings, the quiet and the price (if you book well ahead, you will get an excellent deal; I paid just $320), this is one of the great New York hotels. But save your pennies and stay for a longer time. One night was not enough.

....

Another Morgans hotel, the **Hudson** invites you through a small front door into a Philippe Starck 'decompression chamber' to begin the transformation from the buzz of New York outside to the calm chic of the interior. Decompression chambers might also spring to mind if you opt for the cheaper rooms at a staggeringly small 13.38 square metres at so elevated a price. They are pretty, no doubt, with polished wood and glistening white beds and back curtains, but ...

HUDSON HOTEL
356 West 58th Street
(at Ninth Avenue)
(1 212) 554 6000
hudsonhotel.com
Rating: 4★
Rooms: 831
Hotel rates: $449–649

SHANNON: Wow, this hotel has the most unassuming entrance of any hotel in America. I travelled up an escalator into another world, where artificial light has been mastered to make you feel like one man is your god, and that man is Philippe Starke. I will not be able to describe the geography of this place and its spaces in words. You will either hate it and think I'm a tasteless egocentric who should just stop writing, or you will agree with me that this is a bold, well-thought-out insight into the now and the future.

The rooms are very small and in many ways not the main event. The spaces within the hotel are what you really own when you stay here. Hudson Kitchen is a great breakfast space, with good use of wood and a nice courtyard. The kitchen itself is big and open, and adds to the electric atmosphere. It is a good one to work in as well: I cooked here for a Wolf Blass promotional lunch a few years back and it really is the drawcard to the room. There is certainly no hiding if you're a chef here.

The bar is well worth a drink, but avoid Friday nights, as there is one thing that everyone reading this agrees on: you don't buy my books to line up in queue for a drink. You are better than that!

THE IROQUOIS NEW YORK

49 West 44th Street
(between Sixth and
Fifth Avenues)
(1 212) 840 3080
iroquoisny.com
Rating: 4★
Rooms: 114
Hotel rates: $409–489

On the same section of West 44th Street as the Algonquin and the Royalton, The Iroquois New York is a small and stylish hotel. The Deluxe rooms are only marginally dearer than the Classic and Superior, and make for a spacious and restful home away from home.

PATRICIA: I stayed at The Iroquois in 2008 on the recommendation of a New York businessman who said it was one of the city's best-kept secrets. I took that recommendation with a grain of salt, knowing that The Iroquois—like other hotels I've stayed at on West 44th Street—is in the very heart of the Big Apple and not more than five minutes' walk to most of New York's popular landmarks.

When I got there, though, I was indeed surprised by the low-key elegance of both the façade and the interior. It's a small boutique hotel that I feel is dead set on retaining something of the charm of Old New York. I can well remember the noise level dropping dramatically and feeling as though the place was wrapped in a tranquil air as soon as I walked through its doors.

But don't think for a second that The Iroquois is just a grand old dame that has aged gracefully with the years. I actually believe it's the refurbished gem of that whole area and brimming with charisma. I was further surprised to discover it was once home to James Dean, which made me wonder if, perhaps, The Iroquois was to actors of the 1950s what The Algonquin—with its famous Round Table meetings—was to the literary set of the 1920s. It's a strong possibility, because I was told that in 1950 the front of the hotel served as the only logical place from which to start a public protest over two Hollywood screenwriters who were wrongly imprisoned on suspicion of being communists.

History aside, the room and service exceeded my expectations. I took a single room and it had all the amenities I could ask for, including a walk-in wardrobe. It was a classical style of room with a spacious bathroom and a bed so comfortable that on some nights I actually looked forward to going to bed, rather than going out on the town. I also used the concierge service a great deal, and they were very friendly and always helpful at recommending restaurants and making bookings for me. Any request was met within a minute.

I wouldn't hesitate recommending The Iroquois to anyone, though that means I don't get to keep New York's best-kept secret all to myself.

For foodies, rather than hotel aficionados, **Essex House** is famous mostly for being the first attempt of brilliant French restaurateur Alain Ducasse to take on New York. His attempt at a three-star restaurant there failed to dazzle in the way he hoped and he is now running a one-star at The St. Regis. The Essex itself was later sold to the Jumeirah Group and, after a $90 million refurbishment that highlighted the buildings Art Déco treasures, it is once again a key player on Central Park South (along with The Plaza and Helmsley Park Lane). The rooms are supremely elegant and those facing the park have glorious views. South Gate, the dazzling restaurant (all gold and mirrors, beautifully done), specializes in modern organic American cooking under chef Kerry Heffernan.

JUMEIRAH ESSEX HOUSE

160 Central Park South (between Seventh and Sixth Avenues)
(1 212) 247 0300
jumeirahessexhouse.com
Rating: 5★+
Rooms: 428
Suites: 81
Hotel rates: $599–929

Although five blocks from Central Park, **Le Parker Meridien** still has stunning views of Manhattan's greatest treasure. This very tall tower is a stark five-star hotel with austere rooms and a lobby that feels like one of those enclosed laneways unique to New York. (You can enter from 56th or 57th, depending on your whim.) But people who stay here love it and the website scores kudos for its irreverent Gallic humour: 'Comfy Beds? Better than sleeping with the fishes ... Humungous TVs? Stole 'em from Times Square.'

LE PARKER MERIDIEN

119 West 56th Street (between Seventh and Sixth Avenues)
(1 212) 245 5000
parkermeridien.com
Rating: 5★
Rooms: 510
Suites: 221
Hotel rates: $519–679

GILLIAN: My husband David and I stayed here when he was launching a CD at the Blue Note nightclub. We loved the hotel, with its amazing views of Central Park, the spaciousness and quality of the room, and the quietly efficient service.

THE LONDON NYC

151 West 54th Street
(between Seventh and
Sixth Avenues)
(1 212) 307 5000
thelondonnyc.com
Rating: 5★
Rooms: 549
Suites: 13
Hotel rates: $599–769

This 'all-suite' hotel has standard rooms of a gracious 33 to 47 square metres. Some are open plan, others have French doors. The rooms are very modern, but may seem a tad bare to some. It is the antithesis of the traditional New York approach of stuffing guestrooms with 'antique' furniture. Expect a *Vogue* shoot—and not just in either of Gordon Ramsay's restaurants downstairs.

THE PLAZA

Fifth Avenue (at Central
Park South)
(1 212) 759 3000
theplaza.com
Rating: 5★+
Rooms: 800
Hotel rates: $965–1015

The Plaza is the most famous hotel in New York, the dream holiday destination of so many characters in Hollywood films. Donald Trump enthusiastically spruiked it in recent times, but the hotel became a little shabby and fell off the fantasy-retreat radar. That changed when the Israel-based El-Ad Development Group took over and spent $450 million on a controversial renovation. However, all the rumours about a supposed lack of taste destroying this landmark hotel missed the mark, the hotel now living up to nearly everyone's dreams. It may be a little tacky and way over the top (24-carat gold faucets, for one), but the new Plaza is absolutely in the spirit of the old—just a much better version of it. The Louis XV–styled guestrooms are stunning and huge, the public rooms are some of the finest in the world (The Champagne Bar, The Palm Court). There is simply nothing like The Plaza.

ROYALTON

44 West 45th Street
(between Sixth and
Fifth Avenues)
(1 212) 869 4400
royaltonhotel.com
Rating: 3★
Rooms: 168
Hotel rates: $459–659

The **Royalton**, founded by Ian Schrager in 1988, was reopened in 2007 after a massive redesign by Roman and Williams for the new owners, the Morgans Hotel Group. All are agreed it is a stunning achievement, from a lobby that seems to utilize every known shade of brown, juxtaposing (to quote the hotel) 'an icy cast-glass vestibule and brutalist steel and brass furnishings with soft suede upholstery, thick leather walls and hide-covered chairs'. But you hardly need convincing, as the hotel already had you (to misquote *Jerry Maguire*) at the bold red front door. The guestrooms are starker, utilizing slate greys, white and black.

PATRICIA: I tend to book into a different hotel every time I go to New York so that I don't feel like I'm visiting the same sights or doing the same things (which is something that's pretty hard to do in New York anyway). On my last trip there in 2010, I stayed at the Royalton, which is on 44th Street opposite two of New York's landmark hotels, **The Iroquois** and the **Algonquin**.

The funny thing is that I'd noticed the hotel a number of times on previous trips but this time around it wasn't my choice. It was actually chosen for me by *hotwire.com*, which I was really nervous about. Yet it turned out to be one of my best stays in New York at the most incredible rate. For the rate I was paying, I was surprised that my room, although small, was nowhere near as cramped or claustrophobic as I thought it would be, and I was consistently impressed by the friendliness of the staff and the general good service.

But I think the best value I got from the Royalton was the fantastic location. Like The Iroquois and Algonquin hotels, it's in easy walking distance to the theatre district, Saks and other luxury shopping outlets on Fifth Avenue, Grand Central Station, the Rockefeller Center and so many other well-known attractions.

Another feature that's really nice about the Royalton and shouldn't be passed over is its lounge bar downstairs, Bar 44. When I was there, this was a happening place almost every night, but it was also great to just walk in and relax there after a day's shopping or a night at the theatre. I think the bar is actually a hang-out for a lot of New Yorkers to meet after work and take a load off.

ELOISE AT THE PLAZA

A lot of people have dreamed of living at The Plaza, and actress, musician and author Kay Thompson did. Remembered by most film lovers for her role as magazine editor Maggie Prescott in *Funny Face* (1957), Thompson was also the grandmother of Liza Minnelli, who used to visit Thompson at The Plaza with mum Judy Garland and dad Vincente Minnelli. The antics Liza got up to there became the basis (in part) of the four legendary *Eloise* children's books written by Thompson and illustrated by Hilary Knight. Though the divinely irrepressible Eloise visited Paris and Moscow, it is her time living in The Plaza on the 'tippy-top floor' that seems to delight most readers.

PORK PANCAKES WITH APPLE SAUCE

This is my version of something I once found very hard to comprehend. Let's call the recipe more of an inspiration than an attempt to make sense of serving food such as bacon, pancakes and maple syrup together. This is a nice little appetizer or stand-up canapé. The dish also goes well with grilled slices of fresh foie gras.

180 ml buttermilk

1 egg

165 g plain flour

1 tablespoon of caster sugar

1½ teaspoons of baking powder

1 pinch of sea salt

75 g cultured butter, melted

4½ cm-thick slices of pork terrine, each cut into sixths

1 cup of apple purée (made from Granny Smith apples)

4 pinches of either Vue de monde 8 spice or 5 spice powder

Using a whisk, combine the buttermilk, egg, flour, sugar, baking powder and salt until a smooth batter is formed. Whisk in 25 g of the melted butter.

Preheat a heavy cast-iron pan over a very gentle heat and add some of the butter. Place soup spoons full of mix into the pan to form mini pancakes. The size of the pan will determine how many can be made at one time, but do not attempt too many at once—this will end in disaster. Keep them at least 5 cm apart.

Once the pancakes are formed (1 minute), add a slice of the terrine to the middle of each pancake. Cook for a further minute, then flip over and cook a further 30 seconds.

Keep the pancakes warm in a very low oven until all the batter has been used.

Serve with a pinch of spice to the side and a dollop of apple purée.

Serves 4

MIDTOWN EAST & MURRAY HILL

FINE DINING

After his tenure at Essex House came to an end in 2007, French master chef (and holder of nineteen Michelin stars) Alain Ducasse started again the following year at The St. Regis. His new restaurant is **Adour Alain Ducasse** and it has so far garnered just one star. Following the pioneering example of Alain Senderens in Paris, Adour is a wine-focused restaurant with an emphasis on pairing wine with food. Executive chef Joel Dennis' food is contemporary French, simplified and pure, using the best ingredients from across America (Colorado lamb, Maine lobster). That simplicity can be seen in an appetizer of Black Truffle Salad with Parmesan, White Mushrooms and Country Bread or an entrée of Sautéed Diver Scallops with Endive (Cooked and Raw) and a Brown Butter Scallop Jus. The dining surroundings are sumptuously magnificent, the wine list magisterial. You can even have your own personal wine vault there with your name engraved on the small metal door. How New York.

ADOUR ALAIN DUCASSE

French
Chefs: Alain Ducasse,
Joel Dennis
The St. Regis
2 East 55th Street
(at Fifth Avenue)
(1 212) 710 2277
adour-stregis.com
Michelin: ★
Zagat: 26/30
Menu: $110 (5 courses)
À la carte: $75–115

ALTO

Italian
Chef: Michael White
11 East 53rd Street
(between Fifth and
Madison Avenues)
(1 212) 308 1099
altorestaurant.com
Michelin: ★★
Zagat: 26/30
Menu: $84 (4 courses)/
$130 (7 courses)
À la carte: $62–75

Unlike most Italian restaurants in New York, **Alto** is famous for specializing in cuisine from the Alto Adige region of Italy near the Austrian border. The food is exquisitely plated, modern but not molecular. The Seared Duck Breast comes with Tuscan Lentils, Duck Cotechino and Huckleberry Jus, an Egg and Nettle Ravioli with Crisp Sweetbreads and Black Trumpet Mushrooms. Unlike almost every other restaurant in New York, Alto allows you to bring one bottle of wine to a late-night booking (after 9 p.m.) at no charge. This is a brilliant idea, especially for wine-loving tourists who find a great wine in a bottle shop and wish to drink it somewhere good. Alto also has a stunning wine list of its own, a deserved Grand Award Winner from *Wine Spectator*.

SCOTT: Whenever one makes a trip to a food destination like New York or Paris, one has to do the research and then hope that the chosen restaurants deserve your precious time. Always there are some that get away; no time, bad fortune, clashing schedules. For months afterwards they haunt you with the thought, 'That could have been the one'. Looking at the photos of Michael White's dishes on the Alto website, I can't help but feel I would love his food. Along with Corton and Bouley, Alto is for me the great missed regret of a recent trip to New York. Still, it is something to look forward to. And I want to be there with Shannon and watch him go crazy with the wine list.

CONVIVIO

Italian
45 Tudor City Place
(between East 42nd and
43rd Streets)
(1 212) 599 5045
convivionyc.com
Michelin: ★
Zagat: 26/30
Menu: $62 (4 courses)
À la carte: $64–80

Owned by the same people as Alto, **Convivio** specializes in the rustic food of southern Italy. Think Culingiones (Sicilian ricotta ravioli, morel mushrooms, fava beans), Fusili (Neapolitan pork shoulder ragu, caciocavallo fonduta) and Malloreddud (Sardinian saffron gnocchetti, sea urchin). It is a simple but convivial space, with dramatic white walls and bright-red curved banquettes. The wine list dazzles with Italian joys, from Falanghinas and Fiano de Avellinos to Nero d'Avolas, Aglianco del Vultures and a staggering array of Taurausis. Pure heaven.

The Four Seasons opened on 29 July 1959 in the dazzling Seagram Building, designed by Mies van der Rohe, on the corner of 52nd Street and Park Avenue. Since then, it has been the iconic New York fine-dining restaurant, the epitome of power dining in status-hungry Manhattan. There are two restaurant spaces, the Bar & Grill and the Pool Room. Most prefer the former for lunch and the latter for dinner. If you are into celebrity spotting, it is the Bar & Grill's lunch that is the eye-opener. So are the restaurant spaces, designed by Philip Johnson and van der Rohe, with a Picasso tapestry in the corridor, seats modelled on Mies' Brno chair and Johnson's famous banquettes. It is hard to imagine a visit to New York without a visit to this extraordinary space, a paradise for the senses in so many ways. And new chef Fabio Trabocchi is credited with once again having The Four Seasons back near the top of the culinary tree.

THE FOUR SEASONS
American
Chef: Fabio Trabocchi
Seagram Building
92 East 52nd Street
(between Park and
Lexington Avenues)
(1 212) 754 9494
fourseasonsrestaurant.com
Zagat: 26/30
Menu: $25 (Bar & Grill
lunch)/$45 (Pool Room
lunch)
À la carte: $65–95

SCOTT: At lunch, everybody who is anybody wants to be in the Bar & Grill, with its black leather banquettes and chairs, and wooden tables. There is a square bar with twenty-eight seats, and a balcony with five tables, but the best spots are the 'five main crescent-shaped banquettes' to quote the charming and recipe-studded *The Four Seasons: A History of America's Premier Restaurant*, written by owners John Mariani and Alex Von Bidder in 1994. In truth, only three are crescent-shaped and the others rectangular. No matter, because that is where you want to sit. But you can't, because they are always taken by regulars with billions in their personal or corporate bank accounts.

The Grill (as most call it) is the most prestigious lunch rendezvous in Manhattan and has been since 1959. The food is better in many other fine-dining establishments, but The Bar Room (as others call it) reeks of wealth and power. It is also one of the most beautiful architectural spaces in the world, with its walnut panelling, 6-metre-high ceiling and a spectacular Richard Lippold sculpture of bronze rods dangling ethereally over the bar.

For dinner, people shun the Bar & Grill (though it is always full) for The Pool Room. There is a square, white marble, raised pool in the centre with four large plants (changed seasonally) at its corners, light shimmering not just on the water's surface but around the room and on the stunning aluminium-beaded drapes by Marie Nichols, which waft gently in the warm air currents and provide endless fascination if conversation should flag mid-dinner. Forget Disneyland, this is the true Magic Kingdom.

As soon as you walk in, you know the night will be special, as it was on a visit with my mother, Gillian. We had booked a month in advance by email and were given a perfect table between the pool and the window. The service is that typically New York blend of casual and imperious, Gillian made to feel like a most-welcome first-timer at the start, but as the evening progressed a treasured regular. The only other place to have made such a fuss of her was Harry's Bar on Via Veneto in Rome, where she could have been Sophia Loren the way the mature and elegant staff tended her every need. Not all restaurants, thank heavens, employ only the young and spunky.

Sitting in this space is a treasured experience and the food doesn't really matter. There are attempts every now and then to improve the style of cooking and make it more of the moment, but most people there probably want shrimp cocktails and Long Island duck. We went during the time of Christian Albin, who passed away at just sixty-one in 2009 after nearly twenty years at the helm.

Today, the menu follows in the agreed Four Seasons style, with the Maryland Crab Cakes and Dover Sole with Lemon-Caper Sauce pretty much as they always have been. The lavender sauce on the rabbit loin with baby carrots and turnips is about as radical as it gets, and that's a very traditional recipe. But who minds that a filet of bison comes with foie gras and a black Périgord truffle? No one, surely.

In that sense, The Four Seasons parallels the legendary La Tour d'Argent in Paris, which has been serving *Quenelles de brochet 'André' Terrail'* (Pike Dumplings) and *Caneton Tour d'Argent* in essentially the same manner for more than decades—if not centuries!

Certainly there was nothing to fault in the Roasted Spice Duck that Gillian and I shared. It was cooked through according to the traditional American style, but was still sufficiently moist and flavoursome. Michelin thinks the food is on a par with a 'fancy wedding banquet', but Zagat gives it 26/30, the fourth-highest rating. So, it is clearly a different restaurant to different people depending on their expectations and desires.

As a special night out, though, it is probably unequalled in New York. It is the most stunning space imaginable, in the most beautiful modern building in Manhattan, and perhaps the world, with some of the greatest artworks ever conceived hanging on the walls.

....

The glitziest restaurant in New York (it is wow times ten), with a bar that legendarily attracts many of New York's most beautiful, **Gilt** is dazzling in almost every way. Situated in The New York Palace, the main dining room, with its intricate wood panelling and high ceiling, at first reminds one of grand European eating spaces, such as the famed Operkällaren in Stockholm. But the food is quintessentially American. Like most top Manhattan restaurants, it follows—or is based in—French concepts and techniques, but there is something about American plating—the colourfulness, the gaiety, the slight sense of recklessness—that sets it apart, and Gilt more so than others. It is cheeky, in a word. If the look of the food doesn't make you feel better about life (especially David Carmichael's desserts), or at least more frivolous, then you are beyond salvation.

GILT
Contemporary
Chef: Justin Bogle
The New York Palace
455 Madison Avenue
(between East 50th and
51st Streets)
(1 212) 891 8100
giltnewyork.com
Michelin: ★★
Zagat: 24/30
Menu: $89/$110 (5 courses)

....

L'ATELIER DE JOËL ROBUCHON

Contemporary
Chef: Xavier Boyer
Four Seasons New York
57 East 57th Street
(between Madison and
Park Avenues)
(1 212) 829 3844
fourseasons.com/newyork
Michelin: ★
Zagat: 27/30
Menu: $45/$60/$80 (2/3/4
courses)/$90 (tasting
menu; 8 courses)

Joël Robuchon's **L'Atelier** empire spans the globe and, while his New York outpost is far from his most acclaimed (the one in Paris has two stars and is threatening for a third), it remains a most desired spot for sophisticated New Yorkers. The drill is the same—tapas-style French-Asian dishes, brilliantly cooked—but you don't have to sit at the bar if you don't want to (though Americans usually do). The L'Atelier classics—such as *Pommes purée truffée* (truffled mashed potato), *Caille farcie de foie gras et caramelisée* (free-range quail stuffed with foie gras), *Langoustine dans une papillote croustillante au basilic* (crispy langoustine paillote, basil pesto)—are always available.

SHANNON: This was the first time that I dined at a one-Michelin star restaurant and wasn't 'happy' with alcohol by the time I left. In fact, it was the first time I did not have one drink during a fantastic two-hour lunch, made even more unbelievable by the fact I was with Luke Mangan! (For those of you foodies who don't know Luke, Google him. He no longer calls himself a chef but a restaurateur.)

To get to the restaurant, walk through the foyer of the Four Seasons to the back of the hotel, then up a few stairs into the very small dining room. The setting here is magic. The fit-out is so Four Seasons, and I think it's perfect for the marriage of this great hotel with one of the greatest living chefs.

We sat at the bar after realizing we had not made a booking, which was my fault. The staff were very nice and, because Luke had been recognized by one of the chefs, we were offered the tasting menu, which is normally only served at dinner.

After accepting the offer, we were taken on a great journey of the simple, extravagant and creative. My favourite ideas were the beer-battered lobster pieces with a black-pepper salt and a red fruity sauce laced with ponzu and shaved black winter truffle. The chef at the time was a young French-trained Japanese guy who has since been replaced by the equally talented Xavier Boyer.

Desserts were great, with an assiette of chocolate, dark and white, hot and cold, all served in a coupe glass. It was entertaining from a chef's perspective because of the warm chocolate mousse (which is easy to make; see recipe on p. 52), but it came with chocolate sorbet, warm cookie mix and a white emulsified snow, all of which I loved.

The food was great and simple overall, with some sort of skilled technique gently pushing the ingredients to a boundary beyond which no highly talented cook dares go.

If a lot of the recipes or dishes were placed before a less talented head chef, he or she would add another element or two to completely stuff the dish up and make it look like it was meant to be served in a hotel dining room run by a training college.

Eating at L'Atelier de Joël Robuchon in New York is very different from eating at the establishment of the same name in Paris. I recommend going for the classics in Paris, such as the *Pommes purée truffée*, which is half butter and a whole truffle blended into the creamiest mashed potatoes you have ever tasted, or the Scottish hand-dived scallops with cabbage and ginger sauce. There is something that makes these dishes taste better in that city. Maybe it's the lighting or the ghosts of old sous chefs still yelling in the ears of young, terrified commis in the days of Jamin, Robuchon's three-star restaurant that most gastronomes say was the last old-world restaurant to survive and where the best meals in the world were served. Robuchon retired his three stars the day he turned fifty, vowing not to end up like Alan Chapel, who died of a heart attack at the stove at the age of fifty-two.

....

Rouge Tomate is at the forefront of combining environmentally friendly, health-enriching cuisine with a luxury dining experience. Although it originated in Belgium, the emphasis of these two principles makes Rouge Tomate quintessentially at home in New York—and maybe that's because New York is a town where all things are possible and outsiders can excel at such imaginative offerings.

ROUGE TOMATE
Contemporary
Chef: Jeremy Bearman
10 East 60th Street
(between Fifth and
Madison Avenues)
(1 646) 237 8977
rougetomatenyc.com
Michelin: ★
Zagat: 23/30
Menu: $29 (lunch)/
$49 (pre-theatre)
À la carte: $47–58

PATRICIA: I went to Rouge Tomate with Australian friends who were in New York at the same time as me, and it was quite a memorable experience for all of us. On the previous evening, the restaurant had hosted an after-party for the premiere of the film *It's Complicated*, and the buzz was still lingering when we got there.

But that didn't faze the staff one bit: the service was absolutely exemplary. We were given a warm welcome at the door and the maître d' ensured we were promptly seated at our table. She then introduced us to the sommelier and our waiter for the evening.

There were three of us and we had duck, Black Cod and Trout, which were simply prepared and with flavours that were distinct and fresh. The sommelier took an interest in what we were eating and suggested a couple of wines to match. Knowing we were from Australia, she even engaged us in light conversation about our own wines.

The restaurant is spread over two levels—the upper level for intimate dining, the lower for small parties or groups—with a kitchen on both levels. The tables are generously spaced, the lighting is subdued and the noise is surprisingly moderate considering how large the restaurant is.

Rouge Tomate puts a lot of effort into making you feel comfortable and at ease no matter what is happening around you, and it is obvious that the staff are passionate about what they do. We were well looked after and made to feel as important as the Hollywood A-listers who had dined there the night before.

....

RESTAURANTS, STEAKHOUSES, BISTROS, CAFÉS

AQUAVIT
Scandinavian
Chef: Marcus Jernmark
65 East 55th Street
(between Madison and
Park Avenues)
(1 212) 307 7311
aquavit.org
Zagat: 25/30
Menu: $35/$42 (lunch; 3/4
courses)/$78 (dinner)/$105
(chef's tasting; 7 courses)

The finest Scandinavian restaurant in New York is **Aquavit**, a Midtown gem filled with blonde wood and Arne Jacobson egg swivel chairs. There is an elegant main dining room, and also a bistro. The latter has lighter and smaller snacks, so those interested in grand, modern Scandinavian cuisine should head straight to the dining room. Executive chef Marcus Jernmark offers dishes that range from the traditional (Herring Degustation) to the modern (Bone Marrow Crusted Maine Lobster with Breakfast Radish, Celery and Grapefruit). Some plates exquisitely combine the past and future, such as Hay-Smoked Sweetbreads with Parsnip Purée, Fava Beans, Grilled Bread and Apple Cider. The wine list excels in lighter-style whites from Germany, Austria and Spain, along with a good range of American wines and, as one would hope, many delicious aquavits.

....

There are several fine French bistros and brasseries in New York, but this is a stunning architectural space in one of the landmark Manhattan buildings (the Seagram). Opened in 1959, Brasserie has obviously seen some changes, including a major fit-out that sees the world's first slope-backed dining cubicles. In lime green! But if the décor doesn't convince you, the food will, ranging from Maine Mussels with Frites to Wild Steel Head Salmon with Beluga Lentils and Ramps or Lobster Risotto with Green Asparagus and Fava Beans. It is great fun.

BRASSERIE

Bistro
Chef: Luc Dimnet
Seagram Building
100 East 53rd Street
(between Park and
Lexington Avenues)
(1 212) 751 4840
patinagroup.com
Zagat: 20/30
Menu: $35 (lunch)
À la carte: $45–56

For more than a decade, **Le Cirque** was Manhattan's premier restaurant. Some would argue better food could be found elsewhere, but Le Cirque had the A-list cachet that La Côte Basque had when Truman Capote wrote his *Answered Prayers*. Le Cirque's owner, Sirio Maccioni, had a prominence not even Jean-Georges Vongerichten, Mario Batali or Daniel Boulud have today. (Boulud is the most famous of the former Le Cirque chefs.) Maccioni was the grand star, the master of ceremonies, the man you had to know to get a suitably positioned table. During Boulud's tenure (1986–92), the food was acclaimed by all and sundry, and the wine list certainly made you feel special (and a little poorer). Even though it still made Gayot's 'Top 40 Restaurants in the United States' in 2008, Le Cirque is no longer on people's lips as it used to be. The partial fall from prominence is sad, a bit like what happened with La Tour d'Argent in Paris, because there is history here, stunning surroundings and interesting food from Australian Craig Hopson, a mix of the modern (Wild Burgundy Escargot, Gruyère Gnocchi, Pickled Fiddlehead Ferns and Bottarga) and classic (Dover Sole Meunière). Of course, to see Maccioni still wander around the tables greeting friends and guests is to witness restaurateur royalty. His sons, Mario, Marco and Mauro, run Osteria del Circo at 120 West 55th Street, where Sirio's wife Egidana is the supervising chef. Few families have left such a mark (and still do!) on Manhattan dining.

LE CIRQUE

Contemporary
Chef: Craig Hopson
One Beacon Court
151 East 58th Street
(between Lexington and
Third Avenues)
(1 212) 644 0202
lecirque.com
Zagat: 24/30
Menu: $28 (lunch)/
$38 (dinner)/$88
(seasonal; 4 courses)/
$110 (tasting; 7 courses)

MORTON'S: THE STEAKHOUSE

Steakhouse
551 Fifth Avenue (enter on
East 45th Street, between
Fifth and Madison Avenues)
(1 212) 972 3315
mortons.com
Zagat: 24/30
À la carte: $57–93

There are nearly eighty **Morton's** steakhouses across America, with the New York outpost on Fifth Avenue. Here you can learn the difference between Kansas City Bone-In, New York Strip, Tenderloin and Rib-eye because you get to sample each before you order. And you know you'll get a decent bottle of wine when the website names its five sommeliers, but not its chefs!

PATRICIA: Morton's in New York is not the type of restaurant I would normally frequent. I went there at the suggestion of Joel Reed, a native New Yorker who directed a couple of cult films back in the late 1970s.

The *Michelin Guide: New York City Restaurants* writes, 'Morton's offers a similar experience no matter which location you visit', and judging by our experience I feel that comment is very true. The atmosphere of the place, though sophisticated, is not as innovative as I expected. Its retro style, which includes mahogany wood panelling and chandeliers, is typical of most steakhouses and felt, well, dated compared to the rest of New York. And, as you would expect, the steaks are a size up from being generous—it's a place for people who love to eat meat.

I can't say Morton's is my preferred style of restaurant when in New York, but I'm sure for many it represents an authentic American dining experience. So, on that score, as a tourist it's worthwhile going at least once because you'll be guaranteed an event unto itself. And Morton's has an extensive range of Napa Valley wines and a good selection of French wines that are reasonably priced.

Naya is a modern Lebanese-Mediterranean mezze and grill. Chef Rafic Nehme began cooking when just twelve years old at a local restaurant in Beirut. He later ran, for twenty-five years, Iyem Zaman in Mount Lebanon, before moving to New York and Naya.

NAYA MEZZE & GRILL
Lebanese
Chef: Rafic Nehme
1057 Second Avenue
(between East 55th and
56th streets)
(1 212) 319 7777
nayarestaurants.com
Zagat: 23/30
À la carte: $34–59

PATRICIA: Whenever I travel, I am always on the look-out for great Lebanese restaurants, and I must confess I was quite apprehensive the first time I went to Naya. Prior to arriving in New York, I'd spent two weeks in London, where I had tried five different Lebanese restaurants and each one was more disappointing than the last. Naya, on the other hand, I could not fault.

As soon as I was seated, out came pickled olives, labnee, Lebanese bread and zaatar already mixed in an olive oil that was the most delicious I'd had in a long while. I ordered Hommus and Baba Ghannouj, both of which were fresh, a Tabboulé salad that was amazingly crisp, and Fried Kibbé that was cooked to perfection. All of their desserts are built on traditional Lebanese sweets and I fell quickly under their spell. I had Khecef: apricots, raisins, pear and orange steeped in syrup and topped with an assortment of nuts. It sounds simple but it was to die for.

I was also quite surprised by the look and feel of the place. Naya has none of the Middle Eastern trappings you would expect in a Lebanese eatery, but felt instead like a restaurant that could have featured in *Sex and the City*. Its décor is ultra-modern—glossy, slim-line and angular—with the dining area divided in two. The front section is a long, narrow runway with white leather-padded booths on either side to seat two people, maybe four. This leads to a large, white-panelled back room that obviously caters for larger groups.

The staff are friendly, very accommodating and aim to please. I was after a Chateau Musar, but they had none by the glass and so they offered another Lebanese wine from the same Bekaa Valley and it was just as good. Because I'd complimented them on having such beautiful zaatar, not only did the staff inform me that it was brought in especially from Jordan, when I was leaving they presented me with a little decorative bag of it to take home.

Naya is the best Lebanese restaurant I've found anywhere in the world so far—apart from Abla's, of course, my mother's restaurant in Melbourne.

Once you overcome the sense of awe at this magnificent mosaic edifice on the lower level of Grand Central Station, stand in a queue for what may feel like half a lifetime and then walk through the contented din of diners perched at the long bar or around the myriad red-and-white-ginghamed tables, you must begin the gargantuan task of reading the menu. It is probably easiest and safest to head for the seasonal specials, like Herring in mid June. Not that the specials list is much shorter. There are up to thirty oysters on offer every day and a similar number of fresh fish dishes on the 'Today's Catch' list.

OYSTER BAR RESTAURANT

Seafood
Grand Central Terminal
Lower Concourse
89 East 42nd Street
(at Park Avenue)
(1 212) 490 6650
oysterbarny.com
Zagat: 22/30
À la carte: $34–75

SHANNON: Will you experience in this restaurant what I think is the best space, design and atmosphere to make you feel you are finally in New York? Eat here on your first day; it stamps your arrival.

The arched, catacomb-style ceilings are really well lit. Opened in the 1930s, the place still has the feel of that era. The space is divided into sections, with the main restaurant to the left: I recommend you eat here on the first visit. Lobster salads go out by the hundreds, served simply but generously. They are worth the $35 price tag. Everything else on the menu is also very well priced.

In the middle, there is a holding bar where a lone barman serves from a large beer and wine list. There are some simple dishes served here.

To the right is a large cafeteria-style space broken into island sections with one attendant per island. We sat down to be served by a charming lady from Dublin who had been working the same island for more than thirty years. She was so cool. She reminded me of Betty White from *The Golden Girls*.

The menu arrives on a huge A3 sheet that includes a list of at least twenty different types of American oysters that changes daily. Then there is a cold salad section with more than twenty choices and the same again for the hot section. Try to avoid the fried food; it doesn't really represent what is great here, which are the oysters and the salads. Wash the oysters down with a locally brewed Turbo Dog, a pilsner-style beer.

The guy next to Adam was a classic; he was at least ninety years of age and could barely reach the top of the table. The waitress knew him by name. I quietly asked how long he had been coming to the Oyster Bar and she couldn't recall, but she thought long before she started working there. He ordered the Mussel Chowder every day with the complimentary kish bread and crackers. I just love that! It was all around me, so many stories and such familiarity. I nearly felt guilty being here, as though I was interrupting a part of human nature taking its daily course. I was in the backbone of New York society.

Come here for lunch. There is no need to book apart from a Friday.

ADAM: A New York institution, this should be on everybody's list of places to visit. Don't expect fabulous food (not to mention the odd bad oyster), but the environment is worth having lunch.

SCOTT: From the late 1970s, on my annual trip to New York after the Cannes Film Festival, I would always lunch at the Grand Central Oyster Bar Restaurant the day after I arrived.

After the inevitably long wait, I would be escorted to a small table and start munching on a bowl of biscuit puffs. I had no idea what they were called, but they were salty and moreish. I would then study the long list of Californian Chardonnays (I drank that dreaded grape back then), selecting a whole bottle of whatever masterpiece I had been reading about in *Wine Spectator*: Stony Hill, for example. It was nearly as good as a Montrachet.

The only trick was almost every wine I ordered would no longer be available. Sometimes, so many requests were turned down in a row I would give up and say, 'Just bring the best bottle you have'. I would always leave drunk, as one did back then.

As for the food, obviously one started with a selection of oysters, then perhaps some stewed or pan-roasted Sherrystone Clams, and then whatever fresh fish on the long 'Today's Catch' list sounded the most exciting. As I ate and drank, I would study the dust jackets of whatever books I had bought that morning at Scribners. I have rarely been so happy.

Over the decades, the food continued to taste exactly the same, just as most of the wines I ordered proved to be unavailable. But who cared? The buzz of the place was amazing. Apparently, a whisper spoken in one corner travels perfectly to the other corners.

Then I noticed standards beginning to drop. Others did too. The appetizers tended to be a little overcooked and bland. The sparkle and the fun were gone. I begged off for a couple of years and then stopped going to Cannes every year, or foolishly travelled straight back to Australia.

Then, in 2004, I went to New York with my mother and took her to the Oyster Bar. It was a mistake. It hadn't picked up and the visit made us feel like tourists. Nothing we ate was memorable.

In May 2010, I stood outside debating whether to brave it again, but I didn't want to put at risk twenty-odd years of wonderful memories. But I suspect I was wrong to be fearful. Every review I have read since says the place is coming back to its best, an iconic restaurant gloriously resurgent. And then a month later Shannon went and thought it was great.

Next time I'm in Manhattan, I am going to go again. And to celebrate, I'll even order a bottle of bloody Chardonnay.

SUSHIANN

Japanese
38 East 51st Street
(between Madison and
Park Avenues)
(1 212) 755 1780
sushiann.com
Zagat: 25/30
À la carte: $35–73

A traditional sushi restaurant with a right-angled bar around the main cooking and preparation area (hard to get a seat), along with simple wooden tables and chairs.

SCOTT: It's a tribute to SushiAnn that it so quickly made me forget a not-so-great arrival in New York (my travelling companion from Istanbul cancelled at the last moment and the Waldorf=Astoria had failed to put its best foot forward when I was checking in). It was close to full when I entered and it was immediately obvious that everyone in there was very happy. That in itself was a relief, given my disconsolate frame of mind.

I sat at a table rather than the sushi bar, which is, as is always the case in New York, the desired spot, despite your not being able to talk to friends without cricking your neck.

The menu is essentially appetizers and sushi. This is not a Japanese restaurant but a sushi house. The appetizers ranged from Miso Soup (with tofu or clams) and Unagi Yaki (broiled eel with sweet savoury sauce) to the more exotic Tarabagani (Alaskan king crab legs served grilled, sashimi or with vinegar dressing). I chose grilled and it turned out to be part of one leg, which, despite having a lovely wood-smoked tang, was rather dull and a bit dry. Repeated eatings of Alaskan king crab in New York have always been disappointing. It never tastes remotely as good as Kamchatka crab does in Moscow. Is Kamchatka simply superior to Alaskan crab, or are Russians better at cooking crab than the best chefs in New York?

Fortunately, the Chef's Sushi Special Deluxe (at just $28) was superb. There were ten pieces of perfect sushi, ranging from Fluke, Bluefin Fatty Tuna, Mackerel, Japanese Yellowtail, Bonito, Salmon and Unagi to Salmon Roe and Sea Urchin. The Fluke, a wild Flounder from the North Atlantic Ocean, was the standout, but all were delicious. The sushi is cut more finely than in Australia, where it is a bit chunky and crude, and the use of wasabi was more precise. All the fish dissolved in the mouth. The rice was excellent, slightly warm, light and almost unnoticeable.

You can pay $400 at Masa or $130 at Sushi of Gari, but SushiAnn is unbelievably good value without any pretension. Even the desserts—a *mille feuille* (sort of), made with red-bean pancakes—demonstrate this place is worth a visit.

The wine list is small with sadly no American wines by the glass; a New Zealand Macia Sauvignon Blanc was, of course, just fine. The sake list is more extensive and appealing.

I loved the place. I arrived a sooky man but left a happy one. Restaurants can do that for you.

....

If you study the miles of column inches written about which is the greatest sushi restaurant in New York, it seems to largely come down to four: Masa (Midtown West), Sasabune and Sushi of Gari (both Upper East Side), and **Sushi Yasuda** (Midtown East). Masa is by far the dearest ($400 odd), but many guides, such as Zagat, think Sushi Yasuda and Sasabune have the edge.

So, if you want to try the best sushi New York has to offer, without crippling the bank balance, go to Sushi Yasuda, which offers a sushi or sashimi $22.50 dinner prix fixe.

Inside it is pared-down Scandinavian, with owner-chef Naomichi Yasuda dismissing all unnecessary ornamentation, in his food, his outfit (no name is sewn on his pristine white uniform) and restaurant. He is fanatical about obtaining the freshest of Japanese fish and perfecting his rice, which is a mix of short and medium grains, with Japanese red and white vinegars. The cooking water is purified with Japanese charcoal. This is a man who takes his sushi seriously.

SUSHI YASUDA

Japanese
Chef: Naomichi Yasuda
204 East 43rd Street
(between Third and
Second Avenues)
(1 212) 972 1001
sushiyasuda.com
Zagat: 28/30
Menu: $22.50 (sushi or
sashimi prix fixe)
À la carte: $33–60

SHANNON: If you have trouble finding this place, just remember that an image of a fossilized-looking fish is illuminated on the front door. Walk in and you see the spitting image of the guy on *Iron Chef*. Light-coloured bamboo panelling adorns the ceiling, walls and floors. It was packed when we arrived, and we had the honour of sitting next to Lucy Liu.

The menu was expansive and with a good array of sakes. We chose big mugs of green tea and iced water. The waitress was very nice and, ignoring the menu, we asked for her to choose some sashimi, sushi and a couple of salads for us.

The sushi was small but good. The Blue Fin Tuna was soft in texture and not the best I've tried. And I was not exactly sure why Tasmanian Salmon was served to us when some of the best farms in the world were less than four hours' drive away. I would rather have seen Australian Southern Blue Fin Tuna on the menu, which is the only species of its type in the world that is not endangered, and with revenue from the sales being poured into farming and breeding cycles to save the future of the species.

Overall, it was a good lunch, but once again the new school of New Yorkers need to take a Valium, because if Lucy Liu is seen in a restaurant that doesn't mean it's worth travelling across town for—especially at $100 per person for lunch, including tip but no alcohol!

ADAM: Enjoyable sushi and sashimi.

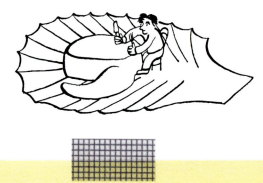

IN MEMORY

VONG
Fusion
Formerly at 200 East 54th Street (at Third Avenue)

Vong is no longer open, but I thought it would be good to mention that I ate there in 2008 and that I see this establishment in the evolution of Spice Market. The chocolate fondant with coconut sorbet was very good and a version of this is available at Spice Market. The style of food was what we used to call fusion, a cross between Asian and European. Jean-Georges Vongerichten was the architect of this restaurant, which later became a chain with outlets in Hong Kong and London. Though I found the food really good here, the place did lack atmosphere due to very few customers. However, the scallops with ginger and spring onion, plus the use of some interesting spices with the chicken, made for a good decision when I took my chefs there for dinner one cold January night after a long day in the kitchen.

Shannon

BARS

||||||||||||||||||||||||||||||||||||||||||||||||||||||||||||||||||||||||||||||||||||||||||||||||||||||||||||||||||||||

The very place where the Bloody Mary (or Red Snapper) first landed in New York, after originating, as legend has it, in the tongue-twistingly named Harry's New York Bar in Paris. If that drink's not your thing, order some other sophisticated nip and bask in the glory of the Maxfield Parrish mural behind the bar.

KING COLE BAR
Hotel bar
The St. Regis
2 East 55th Street
(at Fifth Avenue)
(1 212) 753 4500
stregis.com/newyork
11.30 a.m.–1 a.m. (Mon–
Thurs), 11.30 a.m.–2 a.m.
(Sat), noon–midnight (Sun)

BILL'S GAY NINETIES
Bar
57 East 54th Street
(1 212) 355 0243
11 a.m.–1.30 a.m. (Mon–Sat)

BOOKMARKS ROOFTOP LOUNGE & TERRACE
Bar
299 Madison Avenue
(1 212) 204 5498
hospitalityholdings.com
4 p.m.–12.30 a.m. (Mon–Fri),
5 p.m.–1 a.m. (Sat)

CAMPBELL APARTMENT
Bar
299 Madison Avenue
(1 212) 204 5498
hospitalityholdings.com
4 p.m.–12.30 a.m. (Mon–Fri),
5 p.m.–1 a.m. (Sat)

MONKEY BAR
Bar
The New York Palace
60 East 54th Street (between
Madison and Park Avenues)
(1 212) 486 2408
monkeybarnewyork.com
11.30 a.m.–midnight (Mon–Fri),
5 p.m.–midnight (Sat)

MORRELL WINE BAR & CAFÉ
Bar
299 Madison Avenue
(1 212) 204 5498
hospitalityholdings.com
4 p.m.–12.30 a.m. (Mon–Fri),
5 p.m.–1 a.m. (Sat)

SAKAGURA
Bar
211 East 43rd Street
(1 212) 953 7253
sakagura.com
11.30 a.m.–2.30 p.m. &
6 p.m.–11 p.m. (Mon–Thurs),
11.30 a.m.–2.30 p.m. & 6 p.m.–
1.45 a.m. (Fri), 6 p.m.– 1.45 a.m.
(Sat), 6 p.m.–10.45 p.m. (Sun)

SUBWAY INN
Bar
299 Madison Avenue
(1 212) 204 5498
hospitalityholdings.com
4 p.m.–12.30 a.m. (Mon–Fri),
5 p.m.–1 a.m. (Sat)

LUXURY HOTELS

THE BENJAMIN

125 East 50th Street
(at Lexington Avenue)
(1 212) 715 2500
thebenjamin.com
Rating: 4★
Rooms: 112
Suites: 79
Hotel rates: $429–449

By New York standards, **The Benjamin** is reasonably priced, a one-bedroom suite at a huge 51 square metres having a rack rate of $509. This in a classic 1927 building, restored to its original grandeur and beautifully located in Midtown East, just near the other grand dames of the Waldorf=Astoria, Intercontinental New York Barclay, the Marriott and The New York Palace. It even has a Sleep Concierge, who will set up your sleeping arrangements (a huge range of pillows and aromatherapy products) as you want before you arrive. After a long flight, not to have to waste time on such matters is a gift from hotel heaven. The Benjamin takes its responsibilities seriously in other ways, too, being one of only five properties in all the United States with a Five-Globe ECOTEL environmental rating.

FOUR SEASONS NEW YORK

57 East 57th Street
(between Madison and
Park Avenues)
(1 212) 758 5700
fourseasons.com
Rating: 5★+
Rooms: 305
Suites: 63
Hotel rates: $1050–1550

The Four Seasons hotels are all so obviously top of the range, be they in New York, Istanbul or Bora Bora, that there is little more to be said. As a chain, it has a brand that is instantly recognizable and much appreciated by those used to its charms. The **Four Seasons New York** is no exception, an IM Pei classic from 1993, with fifty-two floors of 1920s high style reworked to suit post-modern tastes. The guestrooms are said to be the largest in New York (starting at a massive 62 square metres), and they are striking in every way: from the drop-dead views out the large windows, the grand piano that may be in your room, the exquisite marble baths, the quality of all the fittings, the pared-down but still elegant furnishings. The design is hardly cutting edge, but there are few more luxurious hotels on the island of Manhattan and not many finer restaurants than the in-house L'Atelier de Joël Robuchon.

This elegantly restored neo-Federal hotel from 1926 is definitely old-style New York, from the stunning Tiffany roof in the lobby to the understated American furniture in the quiet and calm guestrooms.

INTERCONTINENTAL NEW YORK BARCLAY

111 East 48th Street
(between Park and
Lexington Avenues)
(1 212) 755 5900
intercontinentalnybarclay.com
Rating: 4★
Rooms: 685
Hotel rates: $450–531

SCOTT: One year on my annual trip to New York, I discovered to my horror that the Algonquin hotel was full. I decided to stretch the budget and go for **The Intercontinental**, as it was then called. It was my first grand Manhattan hotel (the Algonquin was a fusty but divine boutique back then), and on arriving in the magnificent lobby I felt a little out of my league. But the staff were charming and the room so large, beautifully furnished and enveloping that I almost instantly felt as if I was returning to an old home. I loved my stay here, not only for all that the hotel offers (the breakfast area off the lobby was great), but the proximity to what was then 'my' New York: the Oyster Bar at Grand Central Station, Saks Fifth Avenue, Scribners Bookstore. I have moved my allegiances since to the Upper East Side (and The Carlyle!), but I still feel so nostalgic about The Intercontinental that I took a long walk to revisit it in 2010 to see if I could still feel the magic. I did.

The **Library** is a top-end boutique hotel with five-star prices. Unlike many trendy hotels that boast a library, the Library really does have one, with 6000 volumes to peruse. Guestrooms have books as well, and this is where the Library may just get a little too cute for some: the type of books in your room depends on the floor. If you want classic literature, go for the eighth; if mathematical treatises are your thing, try the fifth. The rooms themselves are too small for the price, but the hotel makes up for it in many ways. The Reading Room on the second floor serves a complimentary breakfast, plus wine and cheese in the early evening. The Library has been a huge hit since it opened in 2000, hence the prices. For many, it is the perfect Manhattan boutique hotel.

LIBRARY HOTEL

299 Madison Avenue (enter
on East 41st Street)
(1 212) 983 4500
libraryhotel.com
Rating: 4★
Rooms: 60
Hotel rates: $429–629

MORGANS NEW YORK

237 Madison Avenue
(between East 37th and
38th Streets)
(1 212) 686 0300
morganshotel.com
Rating: 4★
Rooms: 114
Hotel rates: $439–499

This Murray Hill boutique hotel is beloved by trendy magazines due to the cool minimalist design in the guest-rooms. They have all the variations of silvery grey and the sort of white plastic furniture you find in The Standard. Not that that is necessarily a good thing. The basic rooms are a little bland, so go for the suites (same design elements but less cramped). The lobby and public rooms are anything but dull, with bold Escher-like black-and-white-tiled flooring and a Japanese screen effect on the walls of the lobby. The Asia de Cuba restaurant is even more out-there, with its yellow-lime curtains, white walls and hanging lights, and an epically long communal table covered with brightly coloured fabric. At one end is a light box 5 metres tall depicting a flowing waterfall.

THE NEW YORK PALACE

455 Madison Avenue
(between East 50th and
51st Streets)
(1 212) 888 7000
newyorkpalace.com
Rating: 5★
Rooms: 808
Suites: 86
Hotel rates: $649

You have a choice of entrances at **The New York Palace**, but head for the one on 50th Street with its courtyard and carriage gates. The U-shaped group of 1882 Villard brownstones, now conjoined, were designed by the legendary firm of McKim, Mead and White. (Scandalous, too, if you remember the girl on the velvet swing.) A huge hotel, The New York Palace still manages to feel relatively intimate once you leave its vast and imperial-like public spaces and head to the sanctity of your room. These are reassuringly spacious (starting at 34 square metres) and conservatively but still elegantly decorated. Downstairs is one of the hippest restaurants and bars in New York, Gilt. Beauty is not an entry requirement, but is preferred.

70 PARK AVENUE

70 Park Avenue (between
East 32nd and 33rd Streets)
(1 212) 973 2400
70parkave.com
Rating: 4★
Rooms: 201
Suites: 4
Hotel rates: $339–509

David Bowie's interior designer, Jeffrey Bilhuber, has gone to town on 70 Park Avenue, a luxury boutique hotel in Murray Hill. The hotel's Silverleaf Tavern reminds one of the eclecticism of the Gramercy Park Hotel. Fortunately (for some), Bilhuber's design for the 205 guestrooms is more subdued, though there are courageous flashes here and there.

Formerly the W—The Tuscany, but now owned (along with The Court at 130 East 39th Street) by St Giles Hotels, **The Tuscany** is a chic address in New York's upcoming Murray Hill district. The rooms are huge and boldly designed; you really have to love bright red. It is a short walk from the Empire State and Chrysler buildings, and a hop, step and jump from Grand Central Station. Enjoy.

ST GILES HOTEL—THE TUSCANY

120 East 39th Street
(between Park and
Lexington Avenues)
(1 212) 686 1600
stgilesnewyork.com
Rating: 4★
Rooms: 113
Suites: 7
Hotel rates: $360–439

THE ST. REGIS

2 East 55th Street (at
Fifth Avenue)
(1 212) 753 4500
stregis.com/newyork
Rating: 5★+
Rooms: 186
Suites: 70
Hotel rates: $1095–1250

Built for Colonel John Jacob Astor in 1904, **The St. Regis** is as grand as New York gets. This Beaux Arts classic is one of the world's great hotels, lavish, luxurious and, for those without concerns about credit card debt, the destination of choice. (Rooms start at more than $1000.) The smallest is 42 square metres, the tiniest bed a king, the furnishings and furniture of the highest order, the atmosphere priceless. But it is so French that when you wake up in the morning you'll think you're in Paris or Versailles. The King Cole Bar, with its Maxfield Parrish mural, has no equal in New York, while its restaurant, Adour Alain Ducasse, is a must for anyone interested in Alain Ducasse's high-end French dining with a modern American edge. The only pity is that The St. Regis sits in a bland and downmarket part of Midtown Manhattan; it deserves to be on the Upper East Side.

THE WALDORF=ASTORIA

301 Park Avenue (between
East 49th and 50th Streets)
(1 212) 355 3000
waldorfnewyork.com
Rating: 5★
Rooms: 1235
Suites: 208
Hotel rates: $499–689

Though its private underground railway platform may have been closed, **The Waldorf=Astoria** is still an undeniably great New York hotel. Originally two buildings, one built in 1893 by William Waldorf Astor and the other an Art Déco gem built in 1897 by cousin John Jacob in a feud, The Waldorf=Astoria became a single hotel in the latter year (first named with a solitary hyphen and then a double). In 1932, Conrad Hilton inscribed a photograph of the hotel with the words, 'The Greatest of Them All'. He bought the hotel seventeen years later.

The Waldorf has been referred to in so many Hollywood movies that it is impossible to count. No hotel in Manhattan has a history to equal it, which is why it remains a dream stay for thousands of people across the world. Book as long ahead as you can for the best rate. The Waldorf occupies an entire block, part of which is the even more luxurious The Towers of the Waldorf=Astoria.

SHANNON: The things I love about the Waldorf are also the things I hate about it. The grand foyer is so New York that I feel like I'm on the set of an old *Spiderman* or *Superman* film. But there are also reminders of the new America, the America that I cannot understand for all its intelligence and sophistication and world dominance.

Why the hell, for instance, would you stick a Starbucks just inside the front door of this place?

Get that out of your head and walk straight past the super-sized, over-cooked, oxidized long black with skinny whipped cream and diet hazelnut essence, and you move into rooms that are some of the biggest in Manhattan. They have an old-world charm that is neither overdone nor overpriced.

Service in the lobby bars is great: the food is good for a large hotel and the charm of one of the shrines to the modern era of hotels is here. Most rooms are devoid of good views, but so what: this hotel makes you want to explore the city. Turn left and you are minutes from Central Station. Turn right onto Madison Avenue and you have some of the smartest addresses in town. Just one block down on the opposite side, near the Ferrari showroom, is an amazing Damien Hirst installation right on the street. MoMA is a very short walk away.

The diner in the rear basement of the hotel (Bull and Bear) is a little dated, but if you are stuck and want a quick feed I can think of worse places. There is a certain old-world seediness to this place that I like.

SCOTT: The entrance from Park Avenue (you have three choices) is not as dramatic as you might expect from such a famous hotel, and the stairs inside the revolving doors are a bore if you have heavy luggage, but a charming bellboy of advancing years offered to take mine and didn't even expect a tip. In New York?

En route to the reception desk, he graciously explained aspects of the hotel without sounding at all like a tourist guide. A charming man, he sure made me feel welcome, especially with his time-honoured 'Welcome back to the Waldorf'. That's a presumption we can all live with.

At the desk, however, things spiralled downwards. The receptionist was equally charming but it was obvious the hotel didn't have the room I had booked and, with a very disappointed face, he asked if I would accept a lower-grade Deluxe Queen. He sweetened the deal by saying it was right on Park Avenue and had a spectacular view. Not so: the room was dead ordinary, in desperate need of a renovation and there was no view of Park Avenue, just a tiled roof. It also faced 49th Street, but let's not quibble.

Worse, the pushdown bathplug didn't work, so it meant waiting forty minutes for a plumber (friendly and efficient, of course) to fix it. Not exactly what you want after a flight from Australia. However, so many quality hotels don't have baths these days that one without a plug is still kind of special.

The minibar was empty and there were no bathroom slippers. This was a three-star room, not a five-star. But—and there is always a 'but'—this is a fabulous hotel. The lobby is spectacular, and would be even if the hotel didn't have this kind of history. The bars—Peacock Alley; Sir Harry's; Bull and Bear—are all classics. There is a palpable thrill in the air as you wander around, the voice of a singer at Cole Porter's grand piano in the lobby drifting ethereally through the vast and elegant spaces. Every time you walk in a Waldorf entrance you feel special, enveloped in hotel history of the best kind.

Would I stay here again? Of course, but I would insist on nothing less than a restored Deluxe King. And Shannon should relax about the Starbucks downstairs near the Park Avenue entrance. I couldn't find it on my first day there.

....

OTHER HOTEL

||||||||||||||||||||||||||||||||||||||||||||||||||||||||||||||||||||||||||||||||||||||||||||||||||||||||||||||||||||||||||||

THE VINCCI AVALON
16 East 32nd Street
(between Fifth and
Madison Avenues)
(1 212) 299 7000
theavalonny.com
Rating: 3★
Rooms: 80
Suites: 20
Hotel rates: $373–390

The Vincci Avalon is a reasonably priced hotel (especially the suites), with guestrooms that mix the traditional (dark polished wooden floors, striped wallpaper) with modern touches. The rooms are of a good size, with luxury bedding and Italian marble bathrooms. Some of the rooms feel a bit thin and elongated, but this is certainly one of the best three-star hotels in New York. It is brilliantly located in Murray Hill, a block from the Empire State Building.

....

WALDORF SALAD WITH ROAST SCALLOPS

This very popular and often badly interpreted salad was created at New York's The Waldorf=Astoria hotel in 1896, not by a chef but by the maître d'hôtel (dining room manager) Oscar Tschirky. It was an instant success.

Many associate the invention of Waldorf Salad with Auguste Escoffier, but Escoffier actually took the dish off the menu in the main dining room when he took charge of the kitchens because it had been plagiarized by many other New York hotel dining rooms by that stage.

The original version contained only apples, celery and mayonnaise. Chopped walnuts later became a 'folklore' part of the dish. Many don't realize that the walnuts were peeled before being added.

DRESSING
(this will give you more than you need)
175 ml peanut oil
175 ml hazelnut oil
75 ml De Soto sherry vinegar
juice of ½ a lemon
½ clove of garlic, crushed
sea salt and black pepper

SALAD
1 green apple, peeled
2 witlof
150 g frisée lettuce, washed
50 g walnut halves
100 ml vegetable oil
4 quail eggs
16 large scallops, cleaned
2 tablespoons of olive oil
2 tablespoons butter
juice of ½ a lemon
sea salt and black pepper

To make the dressing, whisk the peanut and hazelnut oils, vinegar, lemon juice and garlic together. Season to taste.

Slice the apple into slices 5 mm thick with a mandolin or a very sharp knife. Then cut it lengthways to make matchstick-size pieces.

Cut the bottom 1 cm off the witlof. Cut in half length-ways. Spread the leaves apart and set aside.

Place the apple in a metal mixing bowl. Add the witloff, frisée and walnuts. Dress with 4 tablespoons of the dressing. Toss together well and taste; season more if necessary.

Preheat a non-stick pan over a low heat. Add the vegetable oil. Gently break open the eggs and add to the pan. Keep the pan on a very low heat and cook for 2 minutes until the egg whites are just cooked. Remove pan from the heat and allow the eggs to sit in the warm oil for a further 1–2 minutes, then slide onto a plate. (Trim the whites neatly into circles using a small cookie cutter if you have one.)

Pat the scallops dry between paper towelling, then season with salt and black pepper.

Heat one tablespoon of olive oil in a heavy-based frying pan. Add half the scallops and cook over a medium heat for 1 minute on each side until golden brown and just cooked through. Add a knob of butter and a squeeze of lemon juice.

Remove from the pan to a warm plate and repeat with the remaining scallops.

Place the salad on the centre of each plate. Top with a fried egg in the centre and four scallops per portion around the plate. Alternatively, be creative and plate the salad using the scallop shells, as below.

Serves 4

UPTOWN

UPPER WEST SIDE ⊠ UPPER EAST
SIDE ⊠ HARLEM, MORNINGSIDE
& WASHINGTON HEIGHTS ⊠

UPPER
WEST SIDE

FINE DINING

Chef John Fraser trained at The French Laundry (Thomas Keller) in the Napa and Taillevent in Paris, before setting up house on the Upper West Side in a beautiful tree-lined street. His restaurant is very highly regarded across Manhattan, except by Michelin which, by refusing to give it a star, is seriously out of step with the critical consensus. Fraser is a three-star chef according to *The New York Times* and his restaurant rates 26/30 in Zagat. The food is exquisitely plated and light. His Maine Lobster comes, intriguingly, with Artichokes, Eggplant, Olives and Lemon Verbena, his Colorado Lamb Loin with Carrot Cake Crêpe and Fiddlehead Ferns. **Dovetail** prides itself on its extensive sherry list; the wine list isn't bad either.

DOVETAIL
Contemporary
Chef: John Fraser
103 West 77th Street
(at Columbus Avenue)
(1 212) 362 3800
dovetailnyc.com
Michelin: ★
Zagat: 26/30
Menu: $24.07/
$66 (5 courses)/
$105 (8 courses)
À la carte: $52–85

Jean-Georges Vongerichten is a phenomenon. Born in Strasbourg, France, he began his culinary career as an apprentice at the three-star Auberge de l'Ill in Illhaeusern. After working under Louis Outhier and Paul Bocuse, Vongerichten opened Le Marquis de Lafayette in Boston and his great American adventure had begun. Vong (since closed) made Vongerichten's name in New York, and today he has an empire of fifteen main restaurants in Manhattan (including JoJo, Spice Market and Perry Street), but his most famous is the eponymous **Jean Georges** (mysteriously without the hyphen) at the Trump International Hotel. (Next to it is his less-expensive bistro, Nougatine at Jean Georges.) Many chefs believe Vongerichten has done more to influence New York food than anyone else in recent history. All his restaurants appear in Top Ten lists of some kind or another. To many, he is a national living treasure.

JEAN GEORGES
Contemporary
Chef: Jean-Georges
Vongerichten
Trump International Hotel
1 Central Park West
(between Columbus Circle
and West 61st Street)
(1 212) 299 3900
jean-georges.com
Michelin: ★★★
Zagat: 28/30
Menu: $26 (lunch)/
$38 (dinner)/
$98 (3 courses)/
$148 (4 courses)/$168
(7 courses)

SHANNON: I was building this up and really looking forward to the Jean Georges that everybody in the United States raves about. Its dinner reservations are much more flexible than the likes of Le Bernardin, but how can a three-star restaurant get away with turning over so many tables? A three-star is not a place you visit to eat pre-theatre—that's what bistros are for.

Walking through the busy atmosphere of Nougatine into the serenity of the dining room had mixed emotions for me. I saw revenue. What would Donald Trump say of a three-star restaurant where you have to fight for an avenue into a memorable dining experience? The answer would be it's fine if he is operating it. But if he were not and had to part with $1000 for dinner for two, then a vocal 'No!' would probably be the answer.

What also got me was that you could tell this space was built by a developer, with just three toilets for the bistro, the bar and the fine-dining restaurant. Not good! One more gripe before the good stuff: the sommelier was a snob. He was smiling to all the big-spending tables, laughing and having a great time. If my team treated people like that, in a discriminatory way, I would sack them. Well, I wouldn't, my maître d' Bryan would! None of the food runners made eye contact and they all took themselves a little too seriously.

As for the food, it was great but not three-star. The food works this way: three courses for $98, which is basically à la carte, the menu being extensive in the choice for each course; the Jean Georges signature tasting menu is $148; and a more extensive dégustation menu is available for $168.

We were first served a small plate of three little canapés that were all nice. The outstanding flavour was a warm pumpkin soup. I realized from reading the menu, and eating the small tasters, that a fusion meal of Asian and French was coming my way.

Harry had Santa Barbara Sea Urchin on (toasted) Black Bread with Jalapeño and Yuzu. It looked good, nice and neat, and he loved the freshness. For those of you who have not eaten the sponge of the sea before, do so only when guaranteed the ultimate in timing and freshness.

A warm salad of fresh ceps (a type of mushroom) with lettuce and pieces of foie gras and a nice dressing was a good dish. The presentation was again simple and neat, but not world-class. I then ate Green Asparagus with Morels and Asparagus Jus, a kind of morel hollandaise sauce. It was a simple presentation of a great dish that I would eat anytime, but once again it was not worth three stars. Harry had the Veal Sweetbread Salad with Breakfast Radishes. The sweetbreads were golden and crispy with real sweetness and moisture on the inside, a really nice dish that was worth the exalted rating.

This was accompanied with a half bottle of an Oregon wine that was a blend of Sauvignon Blanc and Gewürztraminer. I personally dislike Sauvignon Blanc as it makes me feel like I'm drinking a 'presse' of grass clippings at grandma's house, so I was hoping the blend and familiarity of a real grape would make this wine drinkable. It didn't, and at $95 for a half bottle one has to ask why was it on the list.

Mains were served with nice little cloches of different types appropriate to the plates. I ordered Maine Lobster with Ginger Butter and Shredded Cabbage. Nice dish, but a little greasy from the butter and a really big portion size. The lobster was perfectly cooked but I passed half of it on to Harry. His Crunchy Rabbit with Citrus-Chili Paste and Soybean Purée was a boned rabbit rolled and fried in Asian bread crumbs, accompanied by a 'poured at the table' Asian broth with a pea purée that was really tasty, though once again not what I would call a Michelin three-star dish. A 2006 Burgundian Clos de Lambray Grand Cru half bottle for $150 was good value and opened with nice bouquets that didn't interrupt the lobster or rabbit.

Desserts were themed into seasonal ingredients. There were four choices: Rhubarb, Citrus, Chocolate and Garden. Each dessert was made up of four smaller desserts served on an assiette-style plate. I chose the story of Chocolate, Harry the Citrus. To be honest, the 'guru' pastry chef, Johnny Izini, has a big name and I was expecting better. They were nice but quite old-fashioned. My favourite out of the chocolate plate was the Jean Georges signature of chocolate fondant with vanilla-bean ice cream.

Petit fours were abundant, but by now I was defeated. The price of Jean Georges is cheap considering it is a three-star, and I personally enjoyed the meal. It's a nice place that I would go back to, and even better at lunch with a $43.50 *menu du jour*.

In my opinion, Michelin has got it wrong and should not be in New York. It's a different type of dining here and my mindset was wrong, influenced by expectations set by three-star restaurants in Europe. I hope this sets people's minds right before they dine at Jean Georges, realizing that part of the story of what New York is to me is Jean Georges.

FRED: Fine dining. Mary and I have our anniversary lunch here when we are in town.

BRYAN: Jean Georges is one of the institutions of New York and one, in my book, that shouldn't be bypassed. Elegant, modern and seamless, Jean Georges doesn't miss a beat. The food is brilliantly executed, the service engaging and interested, and the room comfortable. I thoroughly enjoyed that great classic, Egg Caviar (lightly scrambled egg with cream and caviar), as well as a delicious Butter Poached Maine Lobster with Ramp Ravioli and Bacon Vinaigrette. It is difficult to get in, but well worth the effort.

SCOTT: It was Saturday lunch and a 'Tastes of Spring' prix fixe was on offer, an amazing $29 for two courses ($14.50 for an additional one) in a three-star restaurant. Disappointingly, there was no à la carte, though all the dishes on offer were from the evening's main menu.

The maître d' at **A Voce** said he felt Jean Georges was the most beautiful restaurant space in New York, and one could sympathize with that view, though I think **SHO Shaun Hergatt** is far more dramatic and restful. Jean Georges' design is clean and beautiful, with white walls, pale beige banquettes and chairs, and huge windows that allow masses of light to stream in during the day and summer evenings.

But for a three-star, Jean Georges is unacceptably noisy and hectic, probably because it is just off the foyer of the huge Trump International Hotel. It actually feels like a railway café at a major provincial French railway station. Many of the guests were not dressed for the occasion: twenty-somethings in jeans and t-shirts, with backpacks thrown to the carpet, were just as numerous as the quiet and elegant elders.

After a trio of *amuses bouche*, including a delicious fluke tartare, came Sea Trout Sashimi Draped in Trout Eggs, Lemon, Dill and Horseradish. The fish was small chunks of rather ordinary raw flesh stacked up on one side of a large bowl, at the bottom of which was a lemon, dill and horseradish foam. It was so mouth-puckeringly sour it made unadulterated lemon juice seem sweet by comparison. Perhaps something had been forgotten in the foam mix; they surely couldn't intentionally send out anything as ghastly as this.

The Sea Scallops with Caramelized Cauliflower and a Caper-Raisin Emulsion ($8 supplement) was better, but seemed not to be 'scallops' but one cut into three, given the height of the scallops everyone else was offering in New York. The slivers were pan-fried to opaque near-dryness and topped with a sliced of simply roasted cauliflower. The caper-raisin emulsion tasted like the mustard you get on hot dogs from street vendors. Not good.

Sweetbreads with Lightly Pickled White Asparagus, Coriander and Orange came on a plate with an indented oblong. Two small sweetbreads sat in diagonal corners in a liquid covered with drops of orange and coriander oils. Again, the liquid was blindingly sour. The pickled asparagus was delicious, as were the sweetbreads, but one wasn't properly cleaned. The bread roll was stale and dreary.

The dessert, called Rhubarb, was a shocking pink foam (or glug, really) on top of some nondescript tart, with a Strawberry, Rhubarb, Mango and Passion Fruit Soup.

The highlights of the meal, in fact, were the Grüner Veltliner Federspiel 2008 Gritsch Mauritiushof and a Côtes Roannaise Les Originelles 2008, Domain Robert Sérol. None of the food was remotely three-star (it wasn't even vaguely one-star) and it was served at breakneck speed, with tables changing at a frenzied pace. I was there for just ninety minutes and one table had three seatings in that time.

My waiter was friendly (in an incredibly dishevelled suit) but some of the others were charmless. I had no choice but to listen to the sommelier harangue two elegantly dressed Asian women, who had had the temerity to suggest that their white wine was incorrectly spritzig. The sommelier responded by declining to taste the wine again and then giving them a condescending lecture on 'how sprightly young acid can fool some into thinking that a wine may be pétillant'. Oh, get a life.

The worldwide consensus is that Jean Georges is a great restaurant, one of New York's shinning stars, but the place I went to didn't even deserve five out of ten.

PICHOLINE

Contemporary
Chefs: Terrance Brennan,
Carmine Digiovanni
35 West 64th Street
(between Broadway and
Central Park West)
(1 212) 724 8585
picholinenyc.com
Michelin: ★★
Zagat: 27/30
Menu: $92/$145
(menu royale; 6 courses)

The cream-and-lavender décor of **Picholine** may not be to everyone's taste, but the food will be. Chef Terrance Brennan runs one of only two starred restaurants on the Upper West Side, and while Jean Georges tends to outlandish Asian experimentation, Picholine charts a steady course through what Brennan knows best. His (and chef de cuisine Carmine Digiovanni's) Provençal-style cooking is unfussy and clean, proudly seasonal and, whenever possible, organic and local. (The name gives the clue: Picholine is a small green Mediterranean olive.) So, expect appetizers such as White Gazpacho with Red Gazpacho Granité and Smoked Paprika Shrimp or Sheep's Milk Ricotta Gnocchi with Artichokes Barigoule, Bottarga and Parsley Pistou. The entrées are divided into 'Day Boats' (Casco Bay Cod, Wild Striped Bass) and 'The Land' (Heirloom Chicken Kiev, Squab). There is also a Cheese and Wine Bar offering small plates at $10 to $20.

RESTAURANTS, STEAKHOUSES, BISTROS, CAFÉS

BAR BOULUD

French
Chef: Daniel Boulud
1900 Broadway (between
63rd and 64th Streets)
(1 212) 595 0303
danielnyc.com
Zagat: 23/30
Menu: $42 (pre-theatre)
À la carte: $43–68

Bar Boulud is Daniel Boulud's casual bistro. You go here for charcuterie (from Paris' Gilles Verot) and seasonal French cooking: Potage Parmentier, Coquilles Saint-Jacques Meunière, Poulet Roti. As you would expect from anything Boulud has a hand in, the food is beautifully plated and pretty. The tunnel-like interior is tightly packed and always buzzing.

Café Luxembourg has been serving French bistro food since 1983 and has hardly put a food wrong or changed direction. It is the genuine article, and a good choice for the All Natural Steak Tartare, All Natural Roasted Chicken and (you get the point) All Natural New York Strip Steak with Frites. Wash it down with a Cornas from Domaine du Tunnel from a fascinating and wide-ranging wine list. It is a fabulous, genuinely French-feeling space that even has a zinc bar. Francophiles will feel totally at home.

CAFÉ LUXEMBOURG
French
200 West 70th Street
(between Amsterdam and West End Avenues)
(1 212) 873 7411
cafeluxembourg.com
Zagat: 20/30
À la carte: $45–58

FRED: Great after the theatre.

There are two **Carmine's** restaurants in New York (apart from other American cities), but the original is on the Upper West Side on Broadway. It's both homely and elegant, with wood panelling to halfway up the walls, inset with period photographs. The beamed ceiling is like that of a Tuscan locanda, the overall atmosphere warm and embracing. The food is traditional Italian but can get rather pricey ($42 for the Chicken Contadina, $20.50 the Tiramisu).

CARMINE'S
Italian
2450 Broadway (between West 90th and 91st Streets)
(1 212) 362 2200
carminesnyc.com
Zagat: 20/30
À la carte: $54–86

FRED: Worth a visit as they have gigantic portions of excellent old-style family Italian. Best place for a group.

Maine Crab Meat Salad, Kid Arrabbiato and Peach Pie: what more could you want? This charming neighbourhood restaurant serves classic Italian cooking in surprisingly elegant surrounds. There are many fabulous and well-priced wines.

GABRIEL'S BAR & RESTAURANT
Italian
Chef: David Lopez
11 West 60th Street
(between Columbus Avenue and Broadway)
(1 212) 956 4600
gabrielsbarandrest.com
Zagat: 22/30
À la carte: $47–80

FRED: Another option that's great after the theatre.

GOOD ENOUGH TO EAT

American
Chef: Carrie Lewin
483 Amsterdam Avenue
(between West 83rd and
84th Streets)
(1 212) 496 0163
goodenoughtoeat.com
Zagat: 20/30
À la carte: $28–48

Owner-chef Carrie Lewin was born in New York but moved with her parents to Belgium at age five (the reverse of the usual American success story). As a child, she hung around two family restaurants and later studied cooking in London. Back in Manhattan, she worked at The Russian Tea Room and then The Four Seasons under Seppi Renngli. She then decided to use her fine-dining experience to produce 'good old-fashioned American food'. Her **Good Enough to Eat** restaurant does skilful versions of American comfort food, from Turkey Hash and BBQ Chicken Sandwich to Organic Roasted Chicken. There are plenty of vegetarian and vegan dishes.

SHUN LEE WEST

Chinese
43 West 65th Street
(between Columbus Avenue
and Central Park West)
(1 212) 595 8895
shunleewest.com
Zagat: 22/30
Menu: $60–100 (banquets)
À la carte: $41–55

With its black carpet and black lacquered walls set off by bursts of gold on white, **Shun Lee West** reminds one of a Parisian nightclub from the 1960s. There is a traditional menu (Drunken Chicken, Shanghai Dumplings) along with a range of specialities (Crispy Prawns with XO Sauce, Lobster Szechuan Style). There is also an extensive array of dim sum, plus banquet menus (including Kosher) for ten people or more. RECOMMENDED: FRED

TELEPAN

American
Chef: Bill Telepan
72 West 69th Street
(between Columbus Avenue
and Central Park West)
(1 212) 580 4300
telepan-ny.com
Zagat: 26/30
Menu: $39/$55/$65
(3/4/5 courses)
À la carte: $51–72

Owner-chef Bill Telepan is a great believer in sustainable organic food, and his highly acclaimed restaurant is testimony not only to his skills as a chef but to the quality of American produce. A lot of his food is vegetarian (Beet Salad, Eggplant Parmigiano), though there is also Wild Striped Bass, Trout, chicken and pork. Americans call his approach 'Greenmarket cuisine'. Whatever the label, his charming restaurant and celebration of nature's bounty have won him many appreciative fans. The wine list is brilliant.

SHANNON'S FAVOURITE NEW YORK TREATS

THE BEST DELIS

CARNEGIE DELI

854 Seventh Avenue (between
West 54th and 55th Streets)
(1 212) 757 2245
carnegiedeli.com
Zagat: 22/30
À la carte: $25–45

Founded in 1932, and open for
breakfast and until very late (4 a.m.),
Carnegie Deli serves exactly what
you would expect: gargantuan
sandwiches (make your own for $23),
Baked Meatloaf, Sautéed Chicken
Livers, Hot Tongue Platter with Sweet-
and-Sour Gravy, Potato Pancake and
Fresh Vegetables. The Strawberry
Cheesecake is iconic—as is the
deli itself, starring in Woody Allen's
Broadway Danny Rose.

SHARLEE: The quintessential
New York deli. Go here for amusing
people-watching and 'The Woody
Allen', a sandwich with layer upon
layer of corned beef and pastrami
served with the largest pickles you
have ever seen. Take some friends
with you as you will need help to
finish the enormous slices of cakes.

DEAN & DELUCA

560 Broadway (at Prince Street)
(1 212) 430 8300
deananddeluca.com

If you want your Pigs in a Blanket to
be made with Wagyu beef, this is your
place. A proudly upmarket deli, it has
ten major outlets across Manhattan.

JANE: In 1991, I managed to wrangle
myself into acting school in New
York. It was Stella Adler's and was
quite a prestigious school to attend
in the Village. I found the classes
completely overwhelming and the
students way out of my league. It
didn't take long to discover I was
never going to be Cate Blanchett.
So, to relieve my anxiety, I used to
wag acting classes and walk down
Broadway towards SoHo and hang
in a place I felt happiest. It was **Dean
& Deluca**.

Now at the time it was the first
store of its type I had seen—a cool,
spacious, dedicated space for the
serious home chef. Sparkling tins of
herbs and spices with handwritten
labels filled the racks, and the
produce was of the highest quality.
All the staff knew what they were
talking about and the coffee was
excellent. The kitchen equipment
and utensils were the best I'd ever
seen. I spent all my savings that were
supposed to go on costumes and
scripts on cookbooks and knives, but
I still use them all today.

It feels like stores such as Dean
& Deluca are ubiquitous today,
but I love the fact I fell in love with
the original.

Nothing beats an original New York deli. I haven't visited for a few years, but I'm sure it's still worth checking out.

MATT: Dean & Deluca, you can't miss it. It's a classic. It has been there forever. Sample the wares, including some quite good books, and eat the amazing chocolates which they hand make.

KATZ'S DELICATESSEN

205 East Houston Street
(at Ludlow Street)
(1 212) 254 2246
katzdeli.com

RUSS & DAUGHTERS

179 East Houston Street
(between Allen and Orchard Streets)
(1 212) 475 4880
russanddaughters.com

Great providore with home-smoked salmon, caviar and Jewish breads (a little on the sweet side but still great stuff). If you have an apartment nearby, then this is the place to be inspired by an old-world charm of Jewish ingredients, salads, preserves and cold cuts—in fact, all you can think of to make a great lunch, dinner or hamper.

2ND AVE DELI

162 East 33rd Street (between Lexington and Third Avenues)
(1 212) 689 9000
2ndavedeli.com
Zagat: 22/30
À la carte: $21–55

This is a legendary New York deli, with everything from Franks and Knishes (potato, spinach, kasha) to 3 Decker Sandwiches (name it) and Chicken in a Pot (with noodles, carrots and matzoh balls). The menu is a time capsule of Jewish cooking throughout the ages. Where else would you see 'chicken fat' listed as an ingredient?

MATT: The 2nd Ave Deli has moved, but it was always famous for the pastramis and corned beef sandwiches. If you have one of them, you don't need to eat for three days. They are typical of a Jewish deli, with pickles on the side and half a pound of pastrami in each one.

ZABAR'S

2245 Broadway
(between West 80th and 81st Streets)
(1 212) 787 2000
zabars.com

Everything from sliced deli meats and foie gras to bottled sauces (Vodka, Filetto di Pomodoro), certified Kosher coffee, cakes, cookies and caviar. And don't forget the smoked fish or the delight of a crescent rugelach with raspberry or apricot filling. They may proudly claim 'New York is Zabar's … Zabar's is New York', but at least they are partly right. This is an iconic deli.

BARS

|||||||||||||||||||||||||||||||||||||||||||||||||||||||||||||||||||||||||||||||||||||||||||||||||||||||||||||||||||||||||||||||||||||||||||||||||||||||||||||||||||||

DING DONG LOUNGE
Bar
929 Columbus Avenue
(between 105th and 106th Streets)
(1 212) 663 2600
4 p.m.–4 a.m.

PROHIBITION
Bar
503 Columbus Avenue
(near West 84th Street)
(1 212) 579 3100
5 p.m.–3 a.m.

LUXURY HOTELS

|||||||||||||||||||||||||||||||||||||||||||||||||||||||||||||||||||||||||||||||||||||||||||||||||||||||||||||||||||||||||||||||||||||||||||||||||||||||||||||||||||||

MANDARIN ORIENTAL NEW YORK
80 Columbus Circle
(at West 60th Street)
(1 212) 805 8800
mandarinoriental.com/
newyork
Rating: 5★+
Rooms: 202
Suites: 46
Hotel rates: $955–1275

Located on top of the Time Warner Center (so you can sort of claim Per Se, A Voce and Masa as your in-house restaurants), the **Mandarin Oriental New York** is everything you'd expect from this luxury chain of supremely five-star hotels. Even if the bold colours of your room are a bit much, the view from your room will be one of the greatest offered anywhere on this planet.

SHANNON: Along with Four Seasons, the Mandarin Oriental group is now the leader in luxury-hotel chain accommodation. Their New York property in the Time Warner Center is no exception, and is probably more special than its other properties around the world because Columbus Circle has something no other has: Central Park. My 42nd-floor room was a standard one but had a great view onto the park and the magnificent skyline bordering it. The rain shower was one of the best I have had, and everything in the room was opulent. But, really, it is all about that view.

The lobby is on the thirty-fifth floor. It's a busy hotel with lots of comings and goings. Good people-watching, in fact: wealthy families with fathers busy on their mobiles and daughters the perfect clones of their mothers, plus throw in a few small packs of media execs and Asian tourists who have more money than you or I could poke a stick at, and then you begin to understand that I like this hotel, but I don't love it. It's not 'Shannon Bennett', but, hey, if I was asked to stay here because of work or a conference or I got a great price on the Internet, then why not.

The Wi-Fi is $15 a day but breakfast is really good for a hotel chain. The dining and bar area on the thirty-fifth floor is incredible, and worth coming up for a drink alone.

If you do decide to stay here, make sure you push for a corner room with a Central Park view. That will turn your stay into a memorable one.

The **Trump International Hotel** is a gigantic, 52-storey, steel-and-gold edifice overlooking Central Park and Columbus Circle. Nothing is understated, from the marble-floored lobby with its exquisite wood panelling to the loud bursts of gold here, there and everywhere. Sunglasses would be handy. The rooms start at a commanding 41 square metres and get considerably bigger from there. The décor is subdued (a lot of silvery grey) and beautifully done. The views are extraordinary, as are the marble bathrooms. This is a five-star hotel on every level, and most people come here for one of the 129 suites, which are stunning indeed. Off its busy foyer are the equally busy Jean Georges and Nougatine at Jean Georges restaurants. The Time Warner Center (with Per Se, Masa and a whole lot of shopping) is just a few minutes' walk away.

TRUMP INTERNATIONAL HOTEL & TOWER
1 Central Park West
(between Columbus Circle and West 61st Street)
(1 212) 299 1000
trumpintl.com
Rating: 5★+
Rooms: 38
Suites: 129
Hotel rates: $895–995

OTHER HOTELS

Affordable chic is how the **Hotel Belleclaire** sells itself, and rightly so. With their polished floorboards and dramatic red leather headboards, the guestrooms manage to feel as much like one's own home as a hotel room. The curved windows are what you'd expect on a Woody Allen movie set. In other words, this is pure New York. With rooms starting as low as $189, this hotel represents exceptional value, a delightful home away from home in a beautiful area of the Upper West Side. But note: thirty-nine rooms have shared bathrooms.

HOTEL BELLECLAIRE
250 West 77th Street
(at Broadway)
(1 212) 362 7700
hotelbelleclaire.com
Rating: 3★
Rooms: 189
Hotel rates: $189–349

ON THE AVE

2178 Broadway (enter on
West 77th Street)
(1 212) 362 1100
ontheave.com
Rating: 3★
Rooms: 242
Suites: 27
Hotel rates: $215–354

Urban cool is the go at **On the Ave**, a boutique hotel on the corner of 77th Street and Broadway. Lauded by trendy magazines, On the Ave has won fans for the muted glitz of the lobby (and its shining black grand piano), the calm sanctity of its grey guestrooms and the impressive sixteenth-floor terrace. The well heeled should opt for rooms on the top three floors, with their striking views of Central Park and the Hudson River. The Upper West Side is the preferred locale for those who want sophistication with a bohemian, village edge. On the Ave provides that.

SCOTT: This lively hotel has won massive publicity worldwide for its cool design and Upper West Side location. Here you feel like you are living in a vibrant city, with fruit and vegetable markets and local shops of all kinds only a few steps away—and barely a brand name in sight.

The hotel is beautifully located on 77th Street (home of the Natural History Museum), meaning a lot of rooms have street views. (The ones that look out the back are the quietest, though.)

Like many trendy boutique hotels, what makes them look smart when they open also means they can look tatty pretty quickly. The groovy carpet here stains way too easily and the varnish on the furniture has also worn off in places. The rooms have the same carpet problems, and the brilliant stainless-steel sinks and cabinets suffer the problems all stainless-steel ones have: they seem to mark when you look at them.

But what's with all the complaints? Once the eye adjusts and day dims, On the Ave becomes a stunner. This is a hotel that looks ten times more fabulous at night. It is loaded with atmosphere and buzz.

My standard room was a cocoon of quiet and comfort, aided by a brilliantly stocked minibar (though dearer than in some five-stars), and an excellent coffee machine that made perfectly decent African coffee in large pouches from Starbucks. (Obviously, Shannon could never stay here!) The large widescreen television worked perfectly, but sadly it only showed American television. Like all New York hotel televisions, it was set to the wrong screen ratio (basketballers look vertically challenged) and nowhere can you fix it. There was also the obligatory (and much appreciated) ironing board, iron and umbrella.

The staff were relaxed and friendly, which is overall the feel of the hotel. It is a great choice for the Upper West Side.

UPPER WEST SIDE

SHANNON'S NEW YORK RECIPES

SHANNON BENNETT'S APPLE PIE

I will let a little secret slip here. I have adapted this pastry recipe from one that appeared in *Australian Gourmet Traveller*. It's a real gem. Think of a very light shortbread, just like the almond shortbread biscuits mum used to make—but with an almond and fruit filling!

It got me thinking about how traditional Southern cooks place a lot of emphasis on the quality of the short crust. The French rely on a technique that doesn't overwork the gluten in the flour.

This recipe makes allowances for most people's lack of delicateness in this area and will become the recipe of choice whenever making a sweet flan or tart. Apples can be replaced by cherries or most stone fruits when in season, or even pumpkin and pecan.

The pastry base is called *sablé* in French, the direct translation meaning 'sand'. This relates to the desired texture achieved when biting into this type of pastry; it should just crumble and disappear in the mouth.

The almond frangipane may not be necessary when using different types of fillings.

FRUIT FILLING

4 Golden Delicious apples, peeled, cored and quartered

pinch of cinnamon

1 tablespoon of unsalted, cultured butter

SABLÉ PASTRY

375 g unsalted, cultured butter (soft)

zest of 3 oranges

200 g caster sugar

3 eggs

400 g plain flour

90 g almond meal

1½ teaspoons baking powder

ALMOND FRANGIPANE

250 g unsalted, cultured butter (soft)

250 g caster sugar

4 eggs

250 g almond meal

50 g plain flour

Preheat oven to 180°C. To make the fruit filling, sprinkle the apple quarters with cinnamon. Melt the butter in a hot pan and roast the apple quarters until golden. Put to the side to cool.

To make the pastry, place butter, orange zest and sugar in a Kitchen Aid or electric mixer and process until whipped to a white colour. Add eggs gradually, making sure each egg is combined before adding the next.

Add sifted flour, almond meal and baking powder. DO NOT OVERMIX. I prefer to take the dough out of the food processor at this point and add the flour by hand on a bench.

To make the filling for the pie (almond frangipane), place butter and sugar in the food processor and process until whipped to a white colour. Add eggs gradually, making sure each egg is combined before adding the next.

Add the almond meal and flour and mix until uniform. Put mixture into piping bag. Rest to the side; do not place the almond frangipane in the fridge, as it will set hard.

Press the semi-soft sablé dough into a pie mould that is 2 cm deep to make the bottom and sides of the gâteau. The bottom and sides should be approximately 5 mm thick. Use either four small moulds or one large mould.

Pipe the almond frangipane evenly into the bottom of each gâteau to form a layer approximately 1 cm thick. Press to make even.

Place the apple pieces evenly into the pie or pies, on top of the almond frangipane.

To make the pie lids, roll more of the pastry to a thickness of 3 mm to the desired circumference.

Place the lid on the top of the gâteau and press the edges of the two pieces of sablé dough together using a teaspoon.

Cook for 25 minutes at 180°C or until golden brown. Serve hot straight from the oven with fresh cream or vanilla ice cream.

Serves 4

UPPER
EAST SIDE

FINE DINING

‖‖‖

Looking like a mid-range Chinese restaurant inside, **Café Boulud** is actually a classy restaurant owned and run by Daniel Boulud. His chef, Gavin Kaysen, has won several awards as a rising new talent. The menu is divided into four areas: 'La Tradition' (Vermont Chicken Breast with Petit Peas à la Française), 'La Saison' (Crispy Duck Egg and Langoustine), 'Le Potager' (Meyer Lemon Risotto and Grilled Green Asparagus), and 'Le Voyage' (Korean Style Beef Tartare). It is open for lunch and dinner. Bar Pleidas is next door.

CAFÉ BOULUD

French
Chef: Gavin Kaysen
The Surrey
20 East 76th Street
(between Fifth and
Madison Avenues)
(1 212) 772 2600
danielnyc.com
Michelin: ★
Zagat: 27/30
Menu: $28/$35 (2/3 courses)
À la carte: $60–76

SHANNON: I was a little confused by the positioning of the café. It does not actually open for breakfast, though Boulud's menu is served in the bar/breakfast room of The Surrey hotel, which is a nice space. The mature gentleman I encountered on my way from my room to breakfast seemed to think I was a pleb. He looked me up and down and walked straight past me. I then asked for Café Boulud and he simply pointed to the door. Surely he would have known it was closed. Anyway, by the time I figured that out for myself, my interviewer from one of America's leading magazines had arrived. The man continued to ignore us both, but then, after some furious minutes, we were told to sit anywhere we wanted. As soon as the cameras and the Dictaphone came out, he changed his tune.

The menu was divided into classic American, English and French breakfast dishes. The French ones jumped out at me the most: charcuterie platters with fresh-baked baguettes, served in the surrounds of crisp white napery, with fresh fruit jams and reasonable coffee. Prices are fine, but I'd much prefer to have had a late-morning breakfast in the café proper, which opens closer to lunchtime.

....

DANIEL

French
Chef: Daniel Boulud
60 East 65th Street
(between Madison and
Park Avenues)
(1 212) 288 0033
danielnyc.com
Michelin: ★★★
Zagat: 28/30
Menu: $105/$185/$205
(dinner; 3/6/8 courses)

In the never-ending debate about which is the greatest restaurant in New York, Michelin, without directly saying so, seems to opt for **Daniel**, a view shared by many others. Certainly in New York owner-chef Daniel Boulud shares with Jean-Georges Vongerichten the most iconic status. Outside the United States, there may be even more reverence for Boulud, because he has arguably done more than anyone else to shape world cuisine. His famous layering of a scallop with slices of truffle, encased in puff pastry, is a truly iconic dish. And Daniel feels like a three-star fine-dining experience, with its luxurious ambience, magnificent vase of flowers and immaculately trained and outfitted staff.

MATT: Daniel is probably where I ate my best meal in New York. Daniel is a great guy. He did a special dégustation menu for us and then took us through the kitchen. And then he took us to a really groovy bar in Chinatown. He's a lovely man and obviously a legend. I put him up there with the best, no doubt.

SCOTT: Daniel Boulud's restaurant on the Upper East Side is a very theatrical space, where a large rectangle is broken into two areas. There is an inner section, sunk lower than the rest and surrounded by an arched colonnade, and the dress circle behind that, with two rows of tables facing inward. Maybe New Yorkers are so keen on people-watching that they find this Coliseum approach entrancing. However, the dramatic positioning of the dress-circle tables left me with the impression of looking into a bull pit of diners, as if they were contestants on some reality television show. Should I encourage them to demonstrate their feelings about the food to passing waiters?

Still, you instantly know you are in a luxury restaurant and the staff have the same opinion. They are all very good and knowledgeable, but I hate being told how everything I order is a brilliant choice. Even worse is listening to how my wine selection (a mid-range pinot noir from Oregon) is a decision of genius, given how it will accentuate the rabbit entrée and yet still match the fineness of the scallops. Please let me discover that for myself. Waiters are not there to put guests through a twelve-step Self-Esteem Elevation course.

I was at Daniel with the daughter of my mother's best friend, whom I had dated once some thirty years ago. Lisa had moved to New York soon after (I seem to have that effect on my dates) and we had only had odd moments of contact since. Seeing her again was a joy.

There is a choice of three prix-fixe menus: $105 for three courses, $185 for six and $205 for eight. We opted for the first, which was just as well as the three courses were huge.

The meal began with a trio of *amuses bouche*: little bits of lobster, a pea purée and something else I have forgotten. It was pleasant, but unmemorable. Unless an *amuse bouche* makes one sit up in sheer delight, thrilling the diner at the thought of what is to come, what is the point? In New York, the *amuses bouche* are invariably dull (except for the delicious cheese puffs at Alain Ducasse's Benoit).

Fortunately, the first appetizer was magnificent: Hazelnut Crusted Maine Sea Scallops with a Morel Fricassée, Swiss Chard, Miners Lettuce and a Green Peppercorn Sauce. The scallops were of the most astonishing quality, with a rare delicacy of texture and taste. The hazelnut topping (more a paste than a crust) worked far better than might be expected. The sauce was a foam and, though it had little taste, looked wonderful. Overall, a delightful dish: Boulud is truly the master of the scallop.

The Duo of Florida Frog Legs with Fricassée of Kamut Berries and Black Garlic and a Lollipop with Spinach, Mushrooms and Crispy Shallots was incredibly disappointing. The flavour of the first bite was exactly matched by every subsequent bite. To the taste buds, it was gluggy and near bland. The two miniscule lollipops tasted of nothing other than deep-fried, bread-crumbed white meat. A strongly deep-fried taste in a three-star restaurant?

Lisa's main, the Sesame and Bonita Flake Crusted Black Cod with Smoked Sable, Yukon Gold Potato Confit and Glazed Asparagus, was fine. It looked thoroughly modern, but tasted like a 1950s dish of smoked Cod: pleasant, reassuring and a little weird. The three fillets of Cod were tiny and flaked too easily; a bit overcooked. The taste was smoky and there wasn't a huge difference between it and the slightly more intense bits of smoked Sable (another name for Black Cod). The asparagus was great. Overall, a pleasant dish, if a little dry.

My Duo of Rabbit with Young Spring Vegetables, Braised Leg Layered Pasta and a Sage Jus was a throwback to 100-year-old traditional French cooking. Part of a loin of rabbit was stuffed with foie gras and leg meat and neatly rolled. It looked okay but again tasted bland, as if quite under-seasoned. It sat on a pretty circle of split peas, napped by a strong but very conventional sage jus. It was so old-fashioned it was staggering. And, again, there was no evolution of flavours as one ate the dish. The braised-rabbit portion of the dish was nice but the pasta shell was stodgy and quite terrible.

So far, this was food that deserved one star at best. It was certainly not as modern as critics and the photos on Daniel's website suggest. There is no real evidence of molecular gastronomy here, just heavy, rich, traditional French food. Has Daniel Boulud in these dark financial times reverted to the safety and reassurance of conventional comfort food?

Fortunately, the desserts were infinitely better. Pastry chef Dominique Ansel has a thing with chocolate and does it brilliantly well. His variation of Michel Bras' *'Coulant' aux arômes de cacao, sirop chocolat au thé d'Aubrac* was divine. Ansel calls his a Warm Guanaja Chocolate Coulant with Liquid Caramel, Fleur de Sel and Milk Sorbet. The cylinder was perfectly and crisply formed (though it had a separate top, which is a bit of a cheat), the oozing liquid supremely unctuous and totally delicious. Overall, close to perfect and what you want in a top-quality restaurant.

The Gianduja Sablé with Nyangbo Chocolate, Puffed Rice and Hazelnut Ice Cream was fine but not of the same class. The sablé was a taco-shaped tuille, the puffed rice flavourless and textually bizarre, the chocolate flavours pleasant and comforting but never exciting, the ice cream dull.

But it didn't stop there. Lisa had wondered aloud whether to have the Coconut Lemongrass Soup with Mango–Thai Basil Gelée, Poached Pineapple and Coconut Rum Sorbet, and the kindly waiter brought out a serve as a gift. This very Australian-style dish was ravishing, all the flavours blending perfectly. Together with the coulant, it was the dish of the night.

Then came a moulded white linen napkin filled with freshly baked mini Madeleines, a plate of *petit fours* (stunningly good) and a plate of miniature chocolates, also very fine.

In short, the dessert half of the menu was easily the best and what you would expect of a genuine three-star restaurant. If only the whole sweet experience had not been ruined by the waiters (and it is the management's fault) trying to speed us up and get us out of the restaurant. I had a booking for 6 p.m., and there was clearly an undeclared second sitting at 8 p.m. Two hours is much too short a time for a full fine-dining experience. If for economic reasons there must be two sittings, then make them three hours apart, not two. The constant pressure (the waiters checked several times in as many minutes if I had signed the damned bill) ruined the end of the meal.

....

Shalezeh has had a spelling change from Shalizar, but it remains the highest-regarded Persian restaurant in Manhattan. In fact, it is the only Michelin-starred Iranian restaurant in the world!

One of the great joys of travelling in the Middle East and its surrounds is seeing the subtle changes in cuisine from Lebanon to Turkey to Iran and so forth. There are enough pleasures here to last a lifetime, with the emphasis on smoky eggplant dishes, grilled skewered meats and exotic fruits and spices, deftly used. Shalezeh is no exception, with Fesenjoon (chicken stew with pomegranate and walnuts), Kubideh (marinated kebab of ground aged sirloin) and Fahludeh (citrus- and rose-flavoured sorbet). The wine list has Château Latour, Chambolle Musigny and Darioush Shiraz from the Napa, but sadly nothing from the great wine regions of Turkey and Lebanon.

SHALEZEH
Persian
1420 Third Avenue
(between East 80th and
81st Streets)
(1 212) 288 0012
shalezeh.com
Michelin: ★
Zagat: 21/30
Menu: $20 (lunch)/
$25 (dinner)
À la carte: $29–49

....

SUSHI OF GARI

Japanese
Chef: Masatoshi 'Gari'
Sugio
402 East 78th Street
(between First and
York Avenues)
(1 212) 517 5340
sushiofgari.com
Michelin: ★
Zagat: 27/30
À la carte: $33–140

One of the five or so top sushi restaurants in New York, **Sushi of Gari** has dedicated fans who swear the omakase here leaves those at Sushi Yasuda and Masa for dead. It would need to, because the restaurant is located in a dreary locale (at least at night), and the pleasant but unexceptional interior would not justify a long walk. But the sushi is cut from the freshest Japanese fish and chef Masatoshi 'Gari' Sugio loves his subtle but spicy toppings (which can get some sushi purists in a tizz). The omakase will cost around $140 per person. (There is also Gari on the Upper West Side and Sushi of Gari 46 in Midtown West.)

SUSHI SASABUNE

Sushi
401 East 73rd Street
(between First and
York Avenues)
(1 212) 249 8583
no website
Zagat: 29/30
À la carte: approx. $110

Zagat rates this as one of the two best restaurants for food in New York. Michelin doesn't even give it a star. How is that possible? One person's sushi …

RESTAURANTS, STEAKHOUSES, BISTROS, CAFÉS

CAFÉ SABARSKY

Austrian
Chef: Kurt Gutenbrunner
Neue Galerie
1048 Fifth Avenue
(at East 86th Street)
(1 212) 288 0665
wallse.com
Zagat: 23/30
À la carte: $35–49

Open for breakfast, lunch and dinner, **Café Sabarsky** is the most casual of Kurt Gutenbrunner's three Austrian restaurants. But it is no less atmospheric or addictive. Pure Vienna. (See also Wallsé and Blaue Gans.)

David Burke is an empire builder. He opened davidburke & donatella in 2003 with business partner Donatella Arpaia, but they famously split and he renamed the restaurant **davidburke townhouse**. Next came David Burke at Bloomingdale's, Burke in the Box (at Foxwoods Resort & Casino), David Burke Primehouse, David Burke Las Vegas, and Fishtail by David Burke on 62nd Street. Others may have more restaurants, but few if any have their name so often displayed. All of which could set up David Burke for some ribbing, but the fact is he can cook … and brilliantly. He trained in France under Pierre Troigros and Georges Blanc, and he won the Meilleurs Ouvriers de France Diplome d'Honneur, cooking American food!

DAVIDBURKE TOWNHOUSE

American
Chefs: David Burke,
Sylvain Delpique
133 East 61st Street
(between Park and
Lexington Avenues)
(1 212) 813 2121
davidburketownhouse.com
Zagat: 24/30
Menu: $24.07 (lunch)/
$39 (brunch)
À la carte: $56–69

SCOTT: There is a sense of fun in what David Burke does. The restaurant is a riot of uninhibited design (Donatella Arpaia had a big hand), but it works because it doesn't take itself too seriously. You may chuckle when you see all the bold colours, the unmissable floral arrangements and the serving stations to the side where waiters dramatically prepare or plate certain courses, but then you will decide davidburke townhouse is exactly where you want to be.

The wow factor is increased when they bring out a tower of sculptured butter. Brightly speckled, it sits on a small marble plank and truly dazzles—that is, until warmed by the room's ambience, it begins to droop. Few will fail to connect the look of the humbled butter with another of life's sad diminishments.

After an *amuse bouche*, I started in earnest with Sea Scallops 'Benedict' with Chorizo Oil and Lobster Foam. This is one of Burke's most famous and photographed dishes, a witty play on Eggs Benedict. The scallop was excellent, the dish clever, the need for the crispy disk of bacon dubious.

I followed with Bacon Wrapped Rabbit Loin with Wilted Spinach and Chipotle-Grapefruit Jus. This was good, old-fashioned food, French provincial but cooked with a delicate hand. Like Scott Conant at Scarpetta, you suspect David Burke could easily run a seriously starred restaurant if he wished. There is a lot of sophistication and craft in dishes that remain defiantly middle of the road. That isn't a complaint; Burke's rabbit loin left Daniel's for dead. It was full of flavour, tender and moist. The serve may have been too large, but that is hardly a fault in America.

The dessert was a Caramelized Warm Apple Tart with Cider Caramel and Dulce de Leche Ice Cream. I chose it because of the ice cream, which is a favourite of my wife's, bringing back memories of her Russian childhood. The tart was delicious.

Most people go for the Cheesecake Lollipop Tree with Raspberries and Bubblegum Whipped Cream. It comes arranged on a metal tree at least half a metre high, and looks like something out of a children's storybook, except it was the adults delighting in it with gusto.

I loved davidburke townhouse. It is by no means the best restaurant in New York, but if I lived on the Upper East Side (one can dream!) I would make it a regular.

....

FISHTAIL BY DAVID BURKE

Seafood
Chef: David Burke
135 East 62nd Street
(between Park and
Lexington Avenues)
(1 212) 754 1300
fishtaildb.com
Zagat: 23/30
Menu: $25 (Sunday lunch)/
$35 (Sunday dinner
lobster feast)/
$45 (Saturday dinner)
À la carte: $53–80

Located in an historic Upper East Side townhouse, **Fishtail** was established by David Burke as a pioneering sustainable seafood restaurant. Much of the fish is caught aboard Burke's own fishing boat, which is harboured at Brielle, New Jersey. Burke prides himself on being creative with seafood, which might be what you would call putting pineapple with the brown butter, lemon, tomato and capers napping the Dover Sole. The Tempura Black Bass comes with a Thai Peanut Chili Sauce, the Pan Roasted Diver Scallops with Sweet Pea Purée, Foie Gras Raviolini and Summer Truffle Vinaigrette. A fun place.

....

You get a lot of historic townhouses on the Upper East Side, and **JoJo** is in one of them, though its lower façade has been concreted over and the entrance feels like a beer café in Prague. It has what one may call a Gramercy Tavern–look inside, a mix of the eclectic, kitsch and elegant, from chandeliers to gold-backed chairs with bright red cushions. Some of the tiny tables are what you would expect to see in a Victorian-era hallway. The very modern and light food encompasses Sweet Pea Soup, a Goat Cheese Panna Cotta with Pickled Beets and Crystallized Ginger, and Veal with Spring Vegetables and Parmesan Jus. JoJo was the first of Jean-Georges Vongerichten's New York restaurants; it is here the legend began.

JOJO

Contemporary
Chef: Jean-Georges Vongerichten
160 East 64th Street
(between Lexington and Third Avenues)
(1 212) 223 5656
jean-georges.com
Zagat: 25/30
Menu: $26 (lunch)/
$38 (dinner)/$65 (tasting; 6 courses)
À la carte: $52–63

SHANNON: This is the original Jean Georges. The different rooms on the ground floor have a lot of noise and buzz about them. We were seated upstairs, which feels more formal. We actually had a great table next to the front left window. It was a large round one with all the classic French trimmings, including a starched white tablecloth. The place has a classic bistro feel, but you know you are in Woody Allen Land. Older men with younger women are everywhere upstairs.

It took us a while to work out why we had been seated here. The concierge at The Waldorf=Astoria had made the booking, so there you go. Only Paris Hilton and old people stay at the Waldorf!

This is a serious restaurant that I think a lot of my Vue de monde customers would love: classic ideas and recipes with great ingredients in a really classy part of New York. Make sure you walk if your hotel or apartment is anywhere in the central Manhattan area.

I had the fortunate experience of being presented with the most beautifully cooked Warm Asparagus Salad with Mesclun, Enoki Mushrooms and Avocado, served in a half-moon pastry case. It was followed by a piece of Black Cod Poached with Mussels and Tarragon—a really great dish that I believe was a one-pot meal. I wasn't expecting the food to be so good. It's a nice feeling to have your expectations exceeded.

Dessert was a pavlova. I'm pretty convinced this is Australia's heritage here—and I'm eating it in a French bistro in New York? I have never served it apart from as a *petit four* in ten years; I'm a little ashamed. This was a passion fruit pavlova presented very neatly with a beautiful crispy shell, whipped vanilla crème (crème diplomat) and fresh passion-fruit pulp. Really nice stuff!

The wine list is great and I think this being the original Jean Georges makes it worth a visit. It's also made me think very differently about pavlova.

....

L'ABSINTHE

French
Chef: Jean-Michel
Bergougnoux
227 East 67th Street
(between Third and
Second Avenues)
(1 212) 794 4950
labsinthe.com
Zagat: 22/30
À la carte: $46–71

L'Absinthe is a quintessential Parisian brasserie in the heart of Uptown Manhattan. There is no need recite the menu: you know it already. But owner-chef Jean-Michel Bergougnoux provides some subtle twists, such as serving lobster with his Pike Quenelles. His Organic Salmon is orange-glazed and the Pieds du Porc are stuffed with foie gras. There is, of course, Choucroute. The exterior and interior are stunning, just as you want faux Paris to feel.

....

LE BILBOQUET

French
25 East 63rd Street
(between Madison and
Park Avenues)
(1 212) 751 3036
Zagat: 23/30
À la carte: $35–56

Another of Manhattan's fine bistros—and some really are as good as in Paris—is **Le Bilboquet**, which has been around for more than twenty years and has a heavenly well-worn look. It's all about Moules Marinières with Frites, Steak with Sauce au Poivre, and Magret de Canard. This is genuine old-fashioned bistro cooking without any modern twists, which explains why it is usually full. On *New York* magazine's website, it rates ten out of ten. Say no more.

SCOTT: I tried to go here, but stupidly chose a Sunday when it was closed. I stood for a good five minutes in the rain—it always pours when I am in New York—staring into its inviting space. I felt like a small child outside a closed candy store or a model railway shop watching a toy train chug past. Looking at the menu only made me feel sadder: there was nothing on it I did not desperately want to eat.

....

Don't be fooled by the name, this is not a candy store in any way. It is a diner the way you always dreamed a diner should be. And given the recent closure of the Empire Diner, that makes the **Lexington Candy Shop** even more precious. Once you get in—and there will be a queue—you are embraced by something out of the 1940s. Even the appliances proudly state their date of manufacture. The Hamilton Beach milk shake mixer is from 1940, the soda fountain from eight years later. But best of all is the counter, where you can watch the frantic but happy staff prepare the retro meals, from burgers and toasted cheese sandwiches to homemade lemonade and orangeade.

LEXINGTON CANDY SHOP

American
1226 Lexington Avenue
(at East 83rd Street)
(1 212) 288 0057
lexingtoncandyshop.com
À la carte: $15–30

SCOTT: This is a genuine American diner that looks and feels retro but in fact just hasn't changed in the seven decades since it opened. If you sit at the bar you can marvel at the stainless-steel covers on the deep refrigerated vats of ice cream and milk. The lids, about four inches thick except at the edges, fold in half with a reassuring thud. They were common in the 1950s and '60s, but are hardly ever seen now.

I ordered a cheeseburger, which comes open with the lettuce, tomato and pickle on the side. The bun had been properly toasted—so rare these days in New York—and, while the pickle wasn't up to the standard of Shake Shack's, this was easily the best commercial burger I had in New York (as opposed to the more upmarket Roquefort one at The Spotted Pig). The chips looked homemade and sat happily on a side plate. With the food I had a fresh-made lemonade, which gets rave reviews on the newspaper and magazine extracts framed on the wall, but is good rather than brilliant.

The look of the place is perfect, the bustle convivial, the atmosphere great. The owner, in his heavily marked white tunic, oversees all from behind the bar, handling the malted milks and dealing with customers who want something on the menu provided everything about the dish is changed ('Now, with the salad, I want less lettuce and more tomato ...'). One request drew an exasperated 'Oh, *please*' from the bilingual and unbelievably hardworking waitress behind the bar. I would have just bonked him on the head.

This was one of the most enjoyable dining experiences I had in New York, but it was slightly ruined at the end. No sooner was the last bite of hamburger in my mouth (and my chips only half eaten), than the waitress said, 'I guess you will be wanting your bill now'. The thought hadn't entered my mind, but a marching order is a marching order, no matter how it is phrased, and I fled as quickly as I could. I didn't turn around to watch the fight for my bar stool that I could hear taking place behind me as I headed out the door.

THE LOEB BOATHOUSE CENTRAL PARK

American
Chef: Anthony E Walton
The Lake at Central Park
(East 72nd Street and
Park Drive North)
(1 212) 517 2233
thecentralparkboathouse.com
Zagat: 18/30
À la carte: $33–50

No one particularly likes the food at **The Loeb Boathouse Central Park**, but everyone adores going here. Its location on the very edge of The Lake is stunning, especially on a sunny day. Book well ahead or be prepared to wait a long time before being given a chance to sample the simple cuisine that marries American with French and Italian (Sautéed Dover Sole, Freebird Chicken Under a Brick, Jumbo Lump Crab Cake). The outside area is known as the Bar & Grill and serves even simpler fare (Shrimp Cocktail, Beef Kebab).
RECOMMENDED: FRED

MAYA NEW YORK

Mexican
Chef: Richard Sandoval
1191 First Avenue (between
East 64th and 65th Streets)
(1 212) 585 1818
modernmexican.com
Zagat: 24/30
À la carte: $38–54

Good Mexican or Tex-Mex isn't easy to find in Manhattan, but one solid choice is Maya. Owner-chef-entrepreneur Richard Sandoval's take on modern Mexican cuisine encompasses *puesadillas surtidas*, *flautas* and *tostadas*. Entrées include Tequila-Flamed Shrimp with a Black Bean–Gouda Huarache and Chipotle Sauce (*Camarones al chipotle*) and Pipian-Crusted Pork Chop with Oaxacan Beans and Cactus Salad (*Tampiqueña*).

Yet another packed French bistro, on a bustling corner as all good bistros should be. Critics don't wax ecstatic over the food, but this place has a genuine French feel, striking décor with plush banquettes and frosted glass separating the booths, and a reassuring menu filled with bistro classics. Its sister restaurant is Brasserie Ruhlmann at 45 Rockefeller Plaza (50th Street between Fifth and Sixth Avenues). Given the recent demise of La Gouloue, owned by the same people, its chef, Antoine Camu (together with his famous Cheese Soufflé), has moved to Orsay.

ORSAY

French
Chef: Antoine Camu
1057 Lexington (at East 75th Street)
(1 212) 517 6400
orsayrestaurant.com
Zagat: 18/30
Menu: $35 (lunch)
À la carte: $45–78

Arguably the best Italian restaurant on the Upper East Side is the family-owned **Spigolo**. (The proprietors are the chefs and also do front of house.) Go for the Cavatelli with Sweet Fennel Sausage Ragu, and the Braised Amish Chicken with Roasted Tomatoes, Castelvetrano Olives and Faro. This is bare-brick-and-wooden-table convivial fun.

SPIGOLO

Italian
Chefs: Scott and Heather Fratangelo
1561 Second Avenue (at East 81st Street)
(1 212) 744 1100
no website
Zagat: 25/30
Menu: $96 (6 courses with wine)
À la carte: $46–76

BARS

BEMELMANS BAR

Hotel bar
The Carlyle
35 East 76th Street
(at Madison Avenue)
(1 212) 744 1600
thecarlyle.com
Noon–11.30 p.m.

Bemelmans Bar is not only famous for being located in The Carlyle and for the number of great musicians who have performed there (there's a grand piano in the middle of the room), but also for the iconic mural that adorns the walls. It was painted by Ludwig Bemelmans, the writer and illustrator of the six *Madeline* children's books. Entitled 'Central Park', the mural is the only artwork by Bemelmans on public display.

SCOTT: The mural here is of particular fascination to me. I have always been a follower of Bemelmans' work, less for his *Madeline* books (I somehow missed them as a child) and more for his travel books, which usually involve a boat. The mural itself is dazzling in every way, and one can spend hours in this entrancing bar studying every minute part of this witty achievement. The light level is so low, however, that you need to get quite close; pick your hour and chose a different seat near the wall on each visit. But also grab a seat at the classic bar, where traditional but still marvellous cocktails are created. It is hard to think of a better bar anywhere in the world.

BAR PLEIADES

The Surrey
20 East 76th Street
(between Fifth and Madison Avenues)
(1 212) 772 2600
danielnyc.com
Noon–midnight

CLUB MACANUDO

Bar
26 East 63rd Street
(1 212) 752 8200
clubmacanudonyc.com
5 p.m.–1 a.m. (Mon–Tues),
5 p.m.–1.30 a.m. (Wed–Sat)

LUXURY HOTELS

Brilliantly situated on the East River, with panoramic views across to Roosevelt Island, Queens, trendy Williamsburg and Brooklyn, the **Bentley** offers remarkable value for so charming and stylish a hotel. And if you think the East River location is a bit out of the way, it isn't: it's actually a short and very pleasant walk to Bloomingdale's and Central Park. As soon as you enter the lobby, you'll know you've made a good choice, but the guestrooms themselves are what will thrill you. There is so much glass, the rooms so filled with light, that you will feel as if you are floating in a hot-air capsule amid the dramatic streetscapes. Michelin calls this a three-star hotel, but most other sources cite it as a four star, which makes it a steal. (It is a sister hotel of The Marcel at Gramercy.)

HOTEL BENTLEY
500 East 62nd Street
(at York Avenue)
(1 212) 644 6000
hotelbentleynewyork.com
Rating: 4★
Rooms: 161
Suites: 36
Hotel rates: $309–339

In Oliver Stone's *Wall Street*, Gordon Gekko (Michael Douglas) discusses celebrating a windfall by grabbing a suite at The Carlyle. It is what you would expect a wealthy and happy man to do, because The Carlyle is one of the great luxury hotels of Manhattan. It is far more discrete than The Plaza and individual than the Four Seasons or the Ritz-Carlton, a true aristocratic original. Its green- and gold-topped roof dominates much of Manhattan, a symbol of the greatness and privilege of the Upper East Side. The Art Déco lobby and sitting room are quietly elegant, the lifts manned by charming operators, the rooms vast and exquisitely decorated in the English style. Its Café Carlyle is the most famous nightclub in Manhattan (with Woody Allen often playing there on Mondays), while Bemelmans Bar, with its glorious mural painted by the celebrated author, is one of the world's great bars.

THE CARLYLE
35 East 76th Street
(at Madison Avenue)
(1 212) 744 1600
thecarlyle.com
Rating: 5★
Rooms: 123
Suites: 58
Hotel rates: $595–1050

SHANNON: I have always been a huge Woody Allen fan, so The Carlyle has been a long-term top-of-the-SB-desire list. The foyer is small but grand, and the staff are the best in the field. Nothing is too much trouble. This is one of the few luxury hotels still to have the classy feature of lift attendants (no need to tip them). The experience doesn't come cheap, but bargains can be organized by directly calling the hotel and negotiating the rate or an upgrade.

Built in the early 1930s, it has old-world charm and glamour, and a great bar that is always full of residents. The public parts of the hotel have been fully renovated and have a very plush feel. Almost the only thing I don't like is the artwork for sale in the foyer: I'm not at a farmers' market! And the Internet is once again $15 a day. Why?

I was upgraded to a suite. I wouldn't call it exactly that: it's a large room with a very generous walk-in wardrobe, but a very small bathroom with separate shower with an oversized showerhead. The room itself has no great view; it only looks out onto 76th Street and over to The Surrey, which actually brought back memories of my stay there and how much better the rooms were.

What made my stay at The Carlyle memorable were the professional staff, great public spaces and, in general, the people who are residents and guests. They were all very nice people. One lady pulled me up in the foyer and asked me whether I was David Campbell. She said I looked like Jimmy Barnes and that she knew Jimmy in his wild days and to say hi to him. She wouldn't take no for an answer that I wasn't his son. I will be having a word to mum and dad when I get back!

The breakfast buffet is full-on and all top-notch ingredients. It was around the $35 mark.

ADAM: The Carlyle is a New York institution. Photographs of JFK and Jackie Kennedy Onassis greet you as you walk through the side door. Although many say The Carlyle is dated, the service is excellent, the staff attentive and it does represent 'old school' New York. A number of permanent residents live in the building and often eat in the dining room, which means the staff can handle individual requirements. The 24/7 lift attendants are a really nice touch. As the rooms and apartments are individually owned, many are decorated differently. Where else can you listen to Woody Allen playing jazz and be introduced to him after his set, as I was lucky enough to be?

SCOTT: It is silly to claim The Carlyle is the finest hotel in Manhattan, but I don't believe there is a better hotel anywhere in the world. There are equals, yes, but none better. I knew it the minute I approached its towering edifice, the gleaming spire glowing against the often-dramatic New York sky.

You walk through a revolving door into an austere Art Déco lobby of muted tones and reassuring quiet. The receptionists treat you as a returning friend, even if this is your first visit. (The Waldorf=Astoria extends the same courtesy.) An elderly bellboy will then take your bags through the beautiful sitting area to the lifts, where you will be whisked up to the calm silence of your floor. Mine was on the eighth. When the door of your room opens, you know you will never want to leave.

I had a Premier Corner Room, a delightful 54 square metres exquisitely decorated with bold floral wallpaper (black and white only), an enormous and sumptuous bed, two sitting chairs, a sofa, a desk and chair, and masses of space. You would not need to hire an extra room to have a cocktail party.

It is the quality of everything that tells: the linen on the bed, the carpet, the towels and bathrobes, the glassware, the well-stocked minibar, the tier of delicious cakes brought to you as a welcoming gift (and infinitely better than the ones I had at Jean Georges). There are also free bottles of Evian, glorious orchids in the main room and bathroom, and as many morning papers as you want. I stayed two days and resented even having to leave to eat at three-star restaurants. This is a place to live permanently (and a lucky few do).

There was a minor flaw (the internal bathplug didn't work and the plumber failed to fix it fully; a foil-covered chocolate mint helped), but how could anyone ever complain? This is a palace of dreams, with the most charming staff I have ever encountered.

Which brings me to Frankie.

When I arrived at The Carlyle, I found I had nothing smaller on me than a $50 note. So I told Frankie, the elderly bellman who had brought up my two bags, that I had no change and would fix him up later. He said not to worry, that a tip wasn't necessary, that he was more than happy to be able to assist me. I insisted I would reward him, but again he said it wasn't necessary. He just wished me a lovely day and a happy stay, and left. (You have to know New York to realize how unbelievably rare Frankie's reaction was. No tip is usually grounds for murder.)

The next morning, I saw Frankie in the lobby while I was on my way to breakfast. He beamed and greeted me like an old and dear friend. He was in no way after a delayed tip. I stopped and we chatted about what a fabulous hotel The Carlyle is, how I knew this was my kind of place the moment I entered it. He was so happy I loved the place as much as he did. He was so proud to work here; you could just tell.

After breakfast, I got some change at reception and gave him $5 (my standard tip for two bags). He momentarily declined; then, when he saw I would not take 'no' as an answer, he reached out and touched my arm. 'Thank you,' he said, so sweetly—and maybe even a little sadly. I wondered how many people had promised him something, a good tip later on, and never delivered. Why else would such a minute gesture on my part bring out such genuine gratitude from this man?

I saw Frankie many times during my stay. I always stopped to talk to him, just as he always stopped to talk to me. We shook hands every time.

When I left the hotel, fortune favoured me and Frankie came to greet me and help with the bags. He thanked me for staying at The Carlyle and wished me well, with a speedy return to the hotel. He meant it. And one of the main reasons I would go back to The Carlyle would be to see Frankie again. He is a gorgeous, gentle soul.

Frankie has a special gift for helping others, for making people away from home feel at ease and safe and secure in a foreign place. Modern hotels don't have men like Frankie: they are seen as too old, reminders of a past era. The Carlyle employs people like Frankie because it is a great hotel.

The Lowell is a luxurious five-star Art Déco boutique hotel (just seventy rooms and suites). The guestrooms are large (starting at 37 square metres) and gracious. The colours are muted and restful, gaining in décor bravura in the suites, with their boldly patterned wallpaper (the Garden Suite) and terraces beyond the gleaming white French doors.

For dining, there is The Pembroke Room. If your taste tends to the classical, there is no more beautiful dining room anywhere in New York. It is open from breakfast to dinner, with a sumptuous English afternoon tea. You can also cook yourself, if you wish, as most rooms have their own kitchens.

THE LOWELL
28 East 63rd Street
(between Madison and
Park Avenues)
(1 212) 838 1400
lowellhotel.com
Rating: 5★+
Rooms: 23
Suites: 47
Hotel rates: $625–845

The Mark is pure luxury, a precious enclave for the truly wealthy in the best part of the Upper East Side. Closed in 2007 for a complete renovation under designer Jacques Grange, The Mark is subtle Art Déco perfection in a landmark 1927 building. For some, the closets will be reason enough to visit. For others it may be the recessed ceilings, the black-and-white bathrooms (all, of course, with deep soaking tubs and polished nickel fittings from Lefroy Brooks). The Mark Restaurant by Jean Georges is run, as its name implies, by Jean-Georges Vongerichten.

THE MARK HOTEL
25 East 77th Street
(between Fifth and
Madison Avenues)
(1 212) 744 4300
themarkhotel.com
Rating: 5★+
Rooms: 118
Hotel rates: $675–865

The Pierre Hotel is synonymous with New York to such an extent it has long been used as a symbol of the city in books and films. Sitting on its prime position opposite Central Park, it famously appears in Francis Ford Coppola's episode of *New York Stories* ('Life with Chloe', co-written by his then 14-year-old daughter Sofia), and is the setting for almost the entirety of the second volume (*Bad News*) of Edward St Aubyn's Patrick Melrose quartet. The Pierre is an aristocratic grand dame, aloof and supremely unto itself. It re-opened in 2009 after a much-desired $100 million refurbishment, but you almost wouldn't know. Very little has been done to modernize the interior look of The Pierre. It just feels a sprightly, polished version of its majestic former self, albeit with every modern convenience built in.

**THE PIERRE,
A TAJ HOTEL**
795 Fifth Avenue (between
East 60th and 61st Streets)
(1 212) 838 8000
tajhotels.com/pierre
Rating: 5★+
Rooms: 140
Suites: 49
Hotel rates: $636–776

HÔTEL PLAZA-ATHÉNÉE

37 East 64th Street
(between Madison and
Park Avenues)
(1 212) 734 9100
plaza-athenee.com
Rating: 5★
Rooms: 114
Suites: 35
Hotel rates: $695–895

All the great Manhattan hotels have their own personalities, but few are as striking as the **Hôtel Plaza-Athénée**. It is the most European (you can tell by the circumflex in the word Hôtel), and venturing inside is like visiting a grand Versailles residence, with boldly colourful murals at the entrance, massive flower displays, Beaux-Arts furnishings, black-and-white marble flooring and outrageous candelabras. The guestrooms are more American in style, the suites having polished floors, large silky floor rugs and dark-wood bathrooms. Classic and Superior rooms are more muted in design and are a bit small (30 to 31 square metres) for the price. This is really a place for those who care nothing for the tab.

THE SURREY

20 East 76th Street
(between Fifth and
Madison Avenues)
(1 212) 320 8027
thesurrey.com
Rating: 5★
Rooms: 190
Hotel rates: $699–824

The Surrey was built in 1926 as a residential hotel and has been home to John Fitzgerald Kennedy, Bette Davis and Claudette Colbert, among many others. Now it is one of the most sought-after hotels in New York. The white and light grey guestrooms are deceptively simple in design but elegant and comfortable, some featuring fireplaces and soaking tubs in the spacious marble bathrooms. The hotel's restaurant is Café Boulud, the bar the Coco Chanel–inspired Bar Pleiades. You can also book the private seventeenth-floor Roof Garden for the most magical dinner of your life, with food from Café Boulud (as is the room service).

SHANNON: Situated in a great little street in the Upper East Side close to Central Park, you really notice when approaching that the real feature from the outside is Café Boulud spilling out onto the street. Inside, I love the collection of modern art, particularly the super-large photographs. The décor is a modern take on Art Déco, very similar to some of the great Park Hyatt properties, but in a very subdued form that really gives this place a touch of class. It has a small, intimate hotel feel with all the comforts of any large five-star. The door staff are friendly, so make sure you have plenty of tip money. Great rooftop bar and sandwich snacks.

The standard rooms are spacious and comfy, as you would expect with any great Manhattan hotel. Views are few and far between and my room was no exception. The rooms have iPod chargers and the extra touch of a spirits bar where, with the press of a phone button, a barman will be up to mix you your drink of choice. All food is prepared by the legendary New York chef Daniel Boulud, including the room-service menu, which has some great items listed, including seasonal dishes. It is not a very big menu but a real restaurant one, where searching for something to eat is not hard. Prices are very fair. Think roast lamb rack with gnocchi and natural jus or a spring vegetable garden plate.

No bath or free Internet were the only faults I could find. They charge $15 for twenty-four hours. But the evening turn-down is accompanied by lovely chocolate-dipped madeleines and branded water.

The rooftop deck on the sixteenth floor is very special and gives glimpses of Central Park and the surrounding skylines. Decked out in wood and hedged with flowering lavender, it's small and intimate, defiantly a little secret this hotel is very proud of. I think it makes it one of the best hotels in New York.

OTHER HOTEL

This stylish but homely hotel offers excellent value. The rooms are smartly furnished, with extravagant linens (Belgian fine cotton), bed coverings and pillows (both 100 percent goose down). The bathrooms are delightfully old-fashioned, but with the latest rain shower heads. The standard doubles are huge; if you can afford one of the suites, go for it. The roof terrace is a stunner, with sweeping views across the city to The Lake in Central Park. This is a gem of a three-star hotel.

HOTEL WALES
1295 Madison Avenue
(between East 92nd and
93rd Streets)
(1 212) 876 6000
waleshotelnyc.com
Rating: 3★
Rooms: 88
Hotel rates: $305

A VOICE FROM OLD NEW YORK: LOUIS AUCHINCLOSS

SCOTT: If Henry James and Edith Wharton reigned supreme as the greatest authors to paint the canvas of nineteenth-century New York in words, in the twentieth century one man stood unchallenged: Louis Auchincloss.

Born on 27 September 1917 to a privileged family, Auchincloss served with distinction in World War II, before working as a lawyer at the prestigious Wall Street firm, Sullivan & Cromwell.

Auchincloss momentarily abandoned the law to write his first novel, *The Indifferent Children* (published in 1947 under the pseudonym Andrew Lee), based on his experiences in Panama during the war. He later returned to the law and led a contained existence preparing wills and trusts—contained, that is, except for producing a novel or collection of short stories every year, and also often a work of non-fiction.

At first, and due in part to the efforts of Gore Vidal, Auchincloss was praised mostly as a writer of short stories. But over time (and especially after his best-selling *The Rector of Justin* in 1964) his novels eclipsed even those stellar achievements, Vidal writing: 'Of all our novelists, Auchincloss is the only one who tells us how rulers behave in their banks and their boardrooms, their law offices and their clubs. [...] Not since [Theodore] Dreiser has an American writer had so much to tell us about the role of money in our lives.'

Almost all Auchincloss' novels and stories are set in New York, with digressions to Bar Harbour, Maine, and major educational institutions such as Groton and Yale. He wrote only of the people he lived among and knew well, revealing truths about the ruling classes that lesser novels and sensationalist authors have never come close to comprehending. The moral decisions his characters face are the moral decisions of our times.

There is a famous novel, *Diary of a Yuppie* (1986), where the lead character, Bob Service, lowers his moral standards page by page. It is the great moral litmus test of the past few decades: how far can you read before saying enough is enough? When the book was released, people were outraged by the end of the first few chapters. Today, most readers can get to the end without ever pondering if Bob has done anything wrong.

Equally important, Auchincloss loved New York and lived on the Upper East Side almost all his life—except for summers in Bar Harbour, of course. No one brings the city quite so much to life—and by almost never mentioning it. The characters are so much a part of New York—Auchincloss' New York—that you understand the city through the minutiæ of their daily lives and the decisions they take.

One year I was with my mother Gillian in New York and we went to a bookshop on the Upper East Side. I noticed that there were autographed copies of Auchincloss' latest collection of short stories, *Manhattan Monologues*. I had already pre-ordered a copy via *amazon.com*, but Gillian bought me an autographed one as a gift. She is like this. The shop lady said, 'Oh, Mr Auchincloss was in here just yesterday signing these books. He lives around the corner, you know'.

As we left, Gillian turned to me and said, 'You must write to him and tell him how important his books have been to you in your life'. I had never written to an author before, but this time I did.

Much to my surprise, because I had asked Mr Auchincloss not to trouble himself with a reply, he wrote the most exquisite and charming response. In a deeply moving letter, he thanked me for my kind words and said my letter had arrived on the very day he was feeling at his lowest about his worth as a writer, that he was questioning whether there was any point in writing on. My letter had re-affirmed his will to keep writing. 'It helped' is how he concluded the note. He was always the master of the last line.

Auchincloss wrote another six novels and short-story collections, forty-seven in all. His final novel, *Last of the Old Guard* (2008), may well be his greatest achievement. A posthumous memoir, *A Voice from Old New York*, has since been released.

In 2005, Auchincloss was awarded the National Medal of Arts by President Bush. He was also named a 'Living Landmark' of New York.

That, he was.

SHANNON'S NEW YORK RECIPES

CRAB COCKTAIL

I'm about to turn food history on its head and tell you the Prawn Cocktail is actually American and not English, as many have claimed. It certainly goes back further than the 1970s, having its origins at the start of the twentieth century.

Auguste Escoffier had an Oyster Cocktail on his Waldorf=Astoria menu, inspired by Creole cooking of the South. The dining room of New York's The Russian Tea Room was also famous for its Shrimp Cocktail. The original recipe dates back to the pre–World War I dish 'shrimps in tomato catsup'. I have included the original version below.

My version is with crabmeat. I love the combination of Mary Rose sauce and crab with the crunch of fresh lettuce.

The word 'cocktail' evolved during Prohibition, when hotels utilized disused champagne glasses to serve the dish in.

ORIGINAL RECIPE
Chevrettes à la Sauce Tomate

100 River Shrimp

2 Tablespoonfuls of Tomato Catsup

3 Hard-Boiled Eggs, Salt, Pepper and Cayenne to Taste.

Boil the shrimp and pick. Put them into a salad dish. Season well with black pepper and salt and a dash of Cayenne. Then add two tablespoonfuls of tomato catsup to every half pint of shrimps. Garnish with lettuce leaves and hard-boiled egg and serve.

Taken from *Picayune's Creole Cook Book* (second edition), a facsimile reprint of 1909 edition (New York: Dover Publications), p. 67.

MY RECIPE

240 g of freshly picked Blue Swimmer crabmeat

½ cup Mary Rose sauce

2 avocados, peeled and diced

1 tablespoon freshly squeezed lemon juice

1 small head of picked and washed iceberg lettuce

sea salt and black pepper

20 croutons rubbed once with a garlic clove

20 oven-roasted cherry tomatoes at room temperature (see recipe, below)

Polish 4 large cocktail glasses on a clean bench. In a bowl, break up the crabmeat and mix in a small amount of the sauce. Add the diced avocado and season with lemon juice.

Rip the lettuce leaves into 2 cm by 2 cm pieces. Mix with the crab and avocado. Season with salt and black pepper.

Divide mixture evenly between each glass. Add the croutons and tomatoes. Finish with an extra spoon of sauce over the top and serve.

If the occasion calls for it, add caviar to the top of each dish.

Serves 4

CONFIT CHERRY TOMATOES

20 cherry tomatoes

3 garlic cloves, peeled and finely sliced

fresh thyme

sea salt

extra virgin olive oil

Set a small pot of water to boil. Using a small paring knife, cut a cross at the top of each cherry tomato. When water is boiling, blanch the tomatoes in the water for 10 seconds, then remove and put straight into iced water. Remove after 5 minutes and dry on absorbent paper.

Remove the tomatoes' skins. Put the peeled tomatoes on a baking tray. Season each with 1 fine slice of garlic, a few leaves of fresh thyme and salt. Drizzle olive oil over tomatoes and leave to sit in a warm place for 3 hours, such as a cupboard above an oven.

MARY ROSE SAUCE

300 ml mayonnaise

100 ml tomato ketchup

Tabasco sauce

salt and pepper

Whisk the tomato ketchup into the mayonnaise, then whisk in Tabasco and salt and pepper to taste.

HARLEM,
MORNINGSIDE &
WASHINGTON
HEIGHTS

Jazz club serving Southern soul food on Sundays and Thursdays. RECOMMENDED: HARRY

AMERICAN LEGION, HARLEM
Southern
248 West 132nd Street
(between Eighth and
Seventh Avenues)
(1 212) 283 9701
À la carte: $20–25

Amy Ruth was a devoted member of the Jerusalem AME Church in Alabama, and a singer in the church choir. She raised many children and grandchildren, including the restaurant's owner, who opened a restaurant here in 1998. It has been packed ever since. There are a lot of folk who will tell you **Amy Ruth's** has the best and most genuine Southern cooking in all New York. The President Barack Obama is Fried, Smothered, Baked or Bar-B-Q Chicken, The Nat Robinson Bar-B-Q Spare Ribs, The Reggis Harris Southern Honey-Dipped Fried Chicken. Go on Thursday for the Melva Smith (Savoury Jerk Shrimp), Sunday for The Bert Padel (Herb-Roasted Turkey with Fruit-and-Nut Stuffing).

AMY RUTH'S
Southern
113 West 116th Street
(between Seventh and
Lenox Avenues)
(1 212) 280 8779
amyruthsharlem.com
Michelin: Bib Gourmand
Zagat: 20/30
À la carte: $21–32

Nestled under the Riverside Drive Bridge, the **Dinosaur Bar-B-Que** is grilled heaven. The menu is a roll call of Southern classics: Swag Drunken Spicy Shrimp Boil Plate (the unpeeled shrimp are 'cooked in a raging boil of beer, old bay, cayenne, herbs & spices', served cold with Habanero cocktail sauce); Fried Green Tomatoes; and Jumbo Bar-B-Que Chicken Wings (served with a Maytag cheese dressing). It's good to know that 'Only genuine houserockin', footstompin' music [is] played here'. There are no reservations.

DINOSAUR BAR-B-QUE
BBQ
700 West 125st Street
(at Twelfth Avenue)
(1 212) 694 1777
dinosaurbarbque.com
Michelin: Bib Gourmand
Zagat: 22/30
À la carte: $19–35

SERGE: Meat-eaters from around the world descend on this authentic rib joint in Harlem to pay homage and boost their cholesterol count.

Highly regarded Ethiopian restaurant in the heart of Harlem. There is beef, lamb, chicken and fish, and a long list of vegetarian dishes. The cooking is not strictly traditionalist, using unusual flavours, techniques and presentation. It is a modern, cool space, with a striking bar display.

ZOMA
Ethiopian
2084 Eighth Avenue
(at West 113th Street)
(1 212) 662 0620
zomanyc.com
Michelin: Bib Gourmand
Zagat: 25/30
À la carte: $20–30

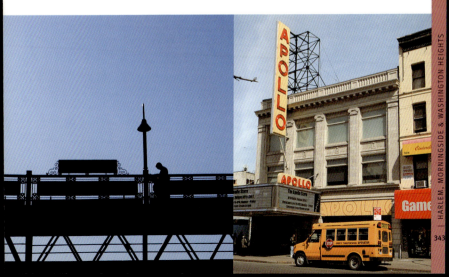

HARRY IN HARLEM

See main text for restaurant and hotel details.

My friend Danielle asked, 'Do you like jazz, Harry?' Instead of keeping my mouth shut, I told her I hated it with a passion, adding, 'You know, I think people who say they like jazz probably don't!' She went quiet, a little bored with my rant, and turned her head away. Oh damn, I realized, she's one of these jazz nuts. Danielle then looked back and patiently said, 'Look, there's this place in Harlem and it is really, really special'. It turns out Danielle has this jazz-playing family background and her father, with whom she's close, got invited on stage to perform at this 'special' jazz place, which is the American Legion, Harlem.

I wanted to go to Harlem anyway to have a glance at the Apollo Theatre (not necessarily for its jazz history), so I told Danielle I'd meet her inside American Legion.

We emerged from the subway after taking the express to Harlem, and the Apollo looked pretty impressive in all its neon-lit glory. We finally found the jazz club. Danielle pre-warned me about the person manning the door and said to make sure we signed in. There were rules.

With me was Ray, a hairdresser friend who is a bit more flamboyant than me. He started walking in, but before I could warn him he was stopped at door for not being dressed appropriately.

My mate Shannon seems to think that, as I am 'harrythehairdresser', I have a reputation for being able to get in anywhere. But this was going to be a tough gig. I convinced the gentleman at the door to let me in to talk to Danielle, who introduced me to another friend. I explained our situation and she kindly took off her shirt and offered it to me, but then began to get nervous about not being dressed appropriately herself!

I snuck the shirt out and Ray checked the label, put it on and started stroking his chest. 'It's a vintage Jenny Kee!' (I later found out the person with the shirt was a good friend of Kee's.) Ray headed to the door and the doorman looked him up and down and nodded approvingly. Yeah, now that's dressed appropriately.

Once in, I grabbed a beer in relief and realized I was hungry. The menu had dishes like fried catfish, chicken and pigs' feet, all with potato salad and collard greens. There was a nice friendly vibe about this welcoming place.

Looking at the menu, I thought of Shannon and his friend Adam, off at some fancy Michelin-starred French place. I wanted to try something a bit more authentically Harlem, and went for the pigs' feet. The others had the chicken, but wouldn't share like I did. Let's just say, only try pigs' feet if it is one of Shannon's gourmet versions.

We were persuaded to finish with very strong rum cake and then the jazz started. Yes, this place is not exactly about the food, but there is something to be said about the whole combined eating, drinking and listening to music experience. And, yes, while I mentioned I hate jazz, this was so awesome I got goose bumps listening to the guys play. I was told they sometimes played with Norah Jones. I didn't want to leave, but some of the others wanted to kick on dancing elsewhere. I got smart and went home.

Now, I'm watching the sunrise from The Standard hotel, facing the Hudson River and thinking I love New York—and that I don't mind some jazz.

GLOGG

Glogg (in Danish: Gløgg) is a hot, spiced red wine. The recipe varies from family to family and nowadays most people buy it already made. However, some people still uphold the tradition of freshly made glogg. It can be made with or without alcohol.

¼ litre of water	Add sugar, cinnamon, cloves and the peel of the orange and lemon to the water, and boil for 10 minutes.
3–4 tablespoons of sugar	
1 stick of cinnamon	
3 whole cloves	Remove the spices and peel, and add the juice of the orange and lemon. Add the raisins and almonds.
1 orange	
1 lemon	
85 g raisins	
55 g blanched and chopped almonds	Heat again until it is just about to boil. Remove the pot from the stove and pour in the wine.
1 bottle of red wine	
¼ cup of rum or port wine	Just before serving, pour in the rum or port wine.

OUTER BOROUGHS

BROOKLYN & WILLIAMSBURG
⊠ HOBOKEN [NEW JERSEY]

BROOKLYN &
WILLIAMSBURG

FINE DINING

||||||||||||||||||||||||||||||||||||||||||||||||||||||||||||||||||||||||||||||||||||||||||||||||||||||||||||||||||||||||

There seems to be a view that Brooklyn and fine dining aren't as compatible as three-star restaurants and the Upper East Side. Brooklyn is much more about cuts of meat smoked in-house, and Southern cooking, and corner cafés with toasted sandwiches and muffins. But there are exceptions to every rule, and **Dressler** is one. For owner Colin Devlin, it is a slightly upmarket version of his successful DuMont restaurant; for others, it is chef Polo Dobkin's way with modern international cuisine in a glistening, polished space that seems to promise a memorable night out. There is a range of influences, seen in the Anjou Pear, Spaetzle and Braised Red Cabbage accompanying the Long Island Duck Breast to the Creamy White Polenta and Parmesan with the Pan Roasted Hudson Valley Chicken. But you can see the Brooklyn in the St Louis–style Ribs with Bourbon Glaze and Candied Peanuts.

DRESSLER
American
Chef: Polo Dobkin
149 Broadway
(between Bedford and Driggs Avenues)
(1 718) 384 6343
dresslernyc.com
Michelin: ★
Zagat: 25/30
À la carte: $45–54

....

The most famous steakhouse in New York City, **Peter Luger** is a temple to meat. Luger's most famous dish, Porterhouse, is cut from the short loin of USDA Prime beef and then dry aged for an unknown number of days (it's a fiercely guarded secret), before being lightly grilled. It is served with your choice of accompaniment. Most people opt for the Creamed Spinach, Onion Rings and German Fried Potatoes. All are served for two. And don't forget Luger's Sizzling Bacon as an entrée (you are in Williamsburg/Brooklyn, after all). Everyone has Cheese Cake for dessert.

Peter Luger has been doing steaks for more than a hundred years and very few complain about anything other than the difficulty of getting in.

PETER LUGER STEAK HOUSE
Steakhouse
178 Broadway
(between Bedford and Driggs Avenues)
(1 718) 387 7400
peterluger.com
Michelin: ★
Zagat: 27/30
À la carte: $67–80

....

RIVER CAFÉ

Contemporary
1 Water Street
(between Old Fulton and
New Dock Streets)
(1 718) 522 5200
rivercafe.com
Michelin: ★
Zagat: 26/30
Menu: $98/$125
(6 courses)

Perhaps the most romantic New York experience is to be had at the **River Café**, which is (partly) on a houseboat moored beside the Williamsburg Bridge. The view from the Dining Room is breathtaking, right across the East River to the waterfront skyscrapers of the Lower East Side. With the lights in the Dining Room kept low, the night-time view is magical. Many restaurateurs would make much of the view and largely forget about the food, but River Café has employed and produced so many fine chefs (Larry Forgione, Charlie Palmer, David Burke) that it has almost become a cooking school as well. There is a serious restaurant, with high-end contemporary cuisine that sources and uses the finest natural ingredients. (The term 'free-range chicken' was actually coined here.) Some of the dishes may surprise; for example, the Roasted Wild Rock Lobster Tails with a Red Pepper Reduction and Celery Root Purée, or the Yellowfin Tuna with Foie Gras Stuffing, Burgundy Black Truffle Vinaigrette, Italian Bacon and Sweet Roasted Onion Froth. Other dishes are more classic. At $98 for three courses and the setting, it is a highly reasonable fine-dining experience.

SAUL

Contemporary
Chef: Saul Bolton
140 Smith Street (between
Bergen and Dean Streets)
(1 718) 935 9844
saulrestaurant.com
Michelin: ★
Zagat: 26/30
Menu: $35 (Mon–Thurs)
À la carte: $50–58

Nestled in the picturesque Boerum Hill area of Brooklyn, **Saul** is an unpretentious one-starred restaurant that fits in comfortably in an area that strives for homely rather than fine dining. Chef Saul Bolton trained under Eric Ripert at Le Bernardin, so it is no surprise he can cook or that he aims for a similar intensity and lightness. It seems a given that most American restaurants must have steak on the menus to survive, and Bolton does an Aged Rib-eye with Slow-Cooked Short Ribs, but more European is the Pan-Roasted Loin of Rabbit, and the Skate with Asparagus, Caramelized Pearl Onions, Lemon Supremes and Brown Butter.

RESTAURANTS, STEAKHOUSES, BISTROS, CAFÉS

Formerly named Pó, this is the Brooklyn offshoot of the Greenwich Village restaurant (at 31 Cornelia Street) founded in 1993 by Steve Crane and Mario Batali. Bino is still the best place for *Linguini vongole* and fresh white anchovies. RECOMMENDED: SUSI AND COREY

BINO
Italian
276 Smith Street
(between Sackett and
Degraw Streets)
(1 718) 875 1980
www.binobrooklyn.com
Menu: $62 (6 courses)
À la carte: $34–58

Here, the ice cream is made from organic grass-fed dairy and organic sugar in small batches on a Hudson Valley farm. The coffee is organic Fair Trade, the tea from small plantations in rural Asia and across the globe. There is also a wide range of pastries and breads. RECOMMENDED: SUSI AND COREY

BLUE MARBLE
Ice-cream café
420 Atlantic Avenue
(between Bond and
Nevins Streets)
(1 718) 858 0408
bluemarbleicecream.com

You come here to have mojitos with *empanadas*, *arepas*, *quesadillas* and a wide range of entrées, from hamburgers to Ropa Vieja (shredded stewed steak with olives, capers, tomato and cilantro) and Catfish Tacos.

BOGOTA LATIN BISTRO
Pan-Latin bistro and bar
141 Fifth Avenue
(at St Johns Place)
(1 718) 230 3805
bogotabistro.com
Zagat: 23/30
À la carte: $29–37

SERGE: Exceptional Colombian-Latin restaurant that's perfect for a casual drink or a raucous dinner party. Set in Brooklyn's leafy Park Slope precinct, Bogota is renowned for its Catfish Tacos, *quesadillas* and Caribbean Coconut Fried Shrimp.

Brooklyn Bridge
1883·1983
USA 20c

BROOKLYN BOWL

Bowling café
61 Wythe Avenue
(at North 11th Street)
(1 718) 963 3369
brooklynbowl.com
À la carte: $34–43

This café is, yes, in the **Brooklyn Bowl**, and is run by Eric and Bruce Bromberg's Blue Ribbon Restaurants group. Try the Egg Shooters, Fried Calamari, Rock and Roll Fries, Pork Ribs and Cajun Catfish. And if you order a Fried Chicken Dinner—you get the choice of white, dark or mixed meat—it comes with white bread, mashed potatoes, and collards with bacon and honey. Accompany it with a Bourbon Street Shake with Nutella. They will add a shot of bourbon if you ask. RECOMMENDED: SUSI AND COREY

BROOKLYN ROASTERY & COFFEE BAR

Coffee bar
160 Berry Street
(1 718) 534 5488
bluebottlecoffee.net

Run by the Blue Bottle Coffee Co., the **Brooklyn Roastery** specializes in artisanal micro-roasting. Their obsession is keeping the beans separated from the CO_2 that is released after roasting. The coffee beans are sourced from around the world, including Ethiopia, Honduras, Sumatra and New Guinea.

SERGE: A caffeine 'lab' of sorts in über-cool Williamsburg just off the East River. Get a coffee and walk to the water. You have to wait a bit, since it's a drip-brew place, but very good. It is well worth the train ride.

CHAR NO. 4

Southern
196 Smith Street (between
Baltic and Warren Streets)
(1 718) 643 2106
charno4.com
Michelin: Bib Gourmand
Zagat: 22/30
À la carte: $35–59

Smokehouse meats and smoky bourbon meet in this bar-come-restaurant. Everything is done in-house, except for the bourbon and whiskeys. There are 150 to choose from. RECOMMENDED: SUSI AND COREY

JEREMY: Southern comfort food and an extensive whiskey and bourbon list in Brooklyn's Carroll Gardens.

SCOTT: Char No. 4 is known for its stunning array of bourbons and single malts. The impressive backlit array sits behind the bar on the right as you enter from the street. It is straight on to the narrow restaurant at the back, with its American diner–type cubicles. Rather like a bourbon cellar, it is quite dark. And the menu is the sort of food you expect to go with a shot of bourbon (available in 1- and 2-ounce pours): smoked bacon, meat and more meat.

I went with friends Susi and Corey, formerly from Melbourne but now dedicated Brooklynites. For appetizers, we tried the House-Smoked Thick-Cut Bacon with Marinated Mushrooms and Thyme; Cornflake Crusted Crab Cake with Lemon Bay-Leaf Sauce; and Smoked and Fried Pork Nuggets with Char No. 4 Hot Sauce (yes, it is hot).

We then had Jambalaya with Homemade Andouille Sausage, Shrimp and Manila Clams; and House-smoked Spare Ribs with a Side of Bacon-Jalapeno Cornbread and Baked Beans. Sadly, they were out of Shrimp & Grits (beloved by Susi and Corey, who nearly cried).

The food is obviously Southern and long-cooked, which can result in sweetness and flavour (the baked beans) to mucky mush (the Jambalaya). The cornbread was delicious, the bacon yummy and the crab cake bland. In other words, a mix, but it was a great chance to try classic Southern food, which isn't as common in America as you might think. Not being a bourbon drinker, I have to trust Corey who says the food goes brilliantly with it, the smokiness of both the liquor and tucker merging beautifully.

As they were out of the Les Clos de Caveau Vacqueyras 2007, Susi and I went instead for a neighbouring '07 Cayron Gigondas. American red wines, as is so often the case, were noticeably scarce.

Shannon: "I ♡NY"

CLOVER CLUB

American
210 Smith Street (between
Butler and Baltic Streets)
(1 718) 855 7939
cloverclubny.com
À la carte: $25–42

Clover Club is a fashionable restaurant-bar with a retro vibe. The mahogany bar is impressive, as are the leather banquettes, tiled floor and pressed-tin ceiling. The simple food ranges from Devilled Eggs to Shrimp Roll Sliders and Brioche Bread Pudding. RECOMMENDED: SUSI AND COREY

. . . .

FATTY 'CUE

BBQ
91 South 6th Street
(between Berry Street and
Bedford Avenue)
(1 718) 599 3090
no website
Zagat: 23/30
À la carte: $26–40

Ribs and more ribs.

JEREMY: BBQ with Asian and Middle Eastern spices in Williamsburg.
. . . .

FETTE SAU

BBQ
354 Metropolitan Avenue
(between Roebling and
Havemeyer Streets)
(1 718) 963 3404
fettesaubbq.com
Zagat: 25/30
À la carte: $16–36

Carnivore heaven, with organic pork and beef.

JEREMY: Traditional BBQ done right in Williamsburg.
. . . .

This is a very cool Brooklyn restaurant, run by owner-chefs Frank Falcinelli and Frank Castronovo, who grew up together in Queens but moved to Brooklyn to take over what had been an Italian social club. They star on their own television show and have just released their first book, *The Frankies Spuntino Kitchen Companion & Cooking Manual*. If not for the light, modern Italian cooking, go for the romantic fairy-lit garden on balmy nights. There is also a Frankies in the Lower East Side at 17 Clinton Street. RECOMMENDED: SUSI AND COREY

FRANKIES 457 SPUNTINO
Italian
Chefs: Frank Falcinelli,
Frank Castronovo
457 Court Street
(between Luquer Street
and 4th Place)
(1 718) 403 0033
frankiesspuntino.com
Michelin: Bib Gourmand
Zagat: 24/30
À la carte: $23–36

The epitome of what is called New Brooklyn Cuisine: rustic American cooking, prepared with subtle modern techniques and presentation. RECOMMENDED: SUSI AND COREY

THE GENERAL GREENE
American
Chef: Nicholas Morgenstern
229 DeKalb Avenue
(at Clermont Avenue)
(1 718) 222 1510
thegeneralgreene.com
Zagat: 20/30
À la carte: $30–46

Founded in 1950 and world famous for its cheesecake, the restaurant cooks everything from Char-Broiled Steakburger to Grilled Salmon Club Sandwich and Shrimp Parmigiana. RECOMMENDED: SUSI AND COREY

JUNIOR'S
Diner
386 Flatbush Avenue
(at DeKalb Avenue)
(1 718) 852 5257
juniorscheesecake.com
Zagat: 17/30
À la carte: $12–30

Chef Ivan Garcia made quite a name at Barrio Chino and Mercadito, so it surprised some that he upped and crossed the East River to Williamsburg—even if that is the dream of many young Manhattanites. His 'haute tacqueria' is a striking place, with a long two-sided table and stools, and little booths. The food is beautifully presented, traditional Mexican, the cocktails brightly colourful and exotic.

MESA COYOACAN
Mexican
Chef: Ivan Garcia
372 Graham Avenue
(between Skillman Avenue
and Conselyea Street)
(1 718) 782 8171
mesacoyoacan.com
Michelin: Bib Gourmand
Zagat: 24/30
À la carte: $22–31

Milk Bar uses only organic eggs and hormone-, antibiotic- and nitrate-free meat. There is a full egg menu (such as scrambled on toasted brioche), various toasts (sourdough with strawberry butter, cinnamon and sugar), sandwiches, soups and salads. A heartier entrée is the Sheep Station Pie. The bread is made daily at the Pain d'Avignon Bakery.

MILK BAR
Café
620 Vanderbilt Avenue
(at Prospect Place)
(1 718) 230 0844
milkbarbrooklyn.com
À la carte: $7–20

SERGE: Run by Melbournian Alexander Hall (ex–Il Fornaio, one of my St Kilda favourites), Milk Bar is one of the few cafés in New York where you'll find a flat white. 'The concept is straightforward. We serve lattes in glasses, flat whites in ceramic cups and offer basic Melbourne hospitality: remember what people drink, pat the dog outside and give people a smile', reckons Hall.

The food at **Prime Meats** is influenced by German alpine cuisine, but served in the atmosphere of an early twentieth-century American inn. So expect Sürkrüt Garnie (slow-cooked pork belly, Thuringian bratwurst, calf tongue and knackwurst with homemade sauerkraut) or Beef Sauerbraten (slow-braised beef brisket in red wine, vinegar and juniper berries, with braised cabbage and pretzel dumplings). There are more traditional American offerings as well. It is owned by the Franks of Frankies 470 Spuntino fame. No reservations and cash only.

PRIME MEATS
Gastropub
465 Court Street
(at Luquer Street)
(1 718) 254 0327
frankspm.com
Michelin: Bib Gourmand
Zagat: 24/30
À la carte: $33–45

JEREMY: Excellent meat and traditional cocktails in Carroll Gardens.

One of the Best New Restaurants of 2010 according to *New York* magazine.

VINEGAR HILL HOUSE
American
72 Hudson Avenue (between Water and Front Streets)
(1 718) 522 1018
vinegarhillhouse.com
Zagat: 25/30
À la carte: $34–58

JEREMY: Seasonal, simple American food in Vinegar Hill.

BARS

||||||||||||||||||||||||||||||||||||||||||||||||||||||||||||||||||||||||||||||||||||||||||||||||||||||||||||||||||||||

THE BROOKLYN INN
Bar
148 Hoyt Street
(1 718) 522 2525
no website
4 p.m.–4 a.m. (Mon–Thurs),
3 p.m.–4 a.m. (Fri),
2 p.m.–4 a.m. (Sat–Sun)

The massive carved wooden bar came from Germany in 1870, while the eight beers on tap are from boutique breweries. There's a pool table. If you want something to eat, there is a pile of take-out menus. RECOMMENDED: SUSI AND COREY

. . . .

FLOYD
Bocce bar
131 Atlantic Avenue
(1 718) 858 5610
floydny.com
5 p.m.–4 a.m. (Mon–Thurs),
4 p.m.–4 a.m. (Fri),
10 a.m.–4 a.m. (Sat),
11 a.m.–4 a.m. (Sun)

You can bring your own food when drinking and playing bocce here, or the bartender will arrange for you to order take-out from a nearby restaurant. They're nice and helpful people in Fort Greene, Brooklyn. RECOMMENDED: SUSI AND COREY

. . . .

HOTEL

||||||||||||||||||||||||||||||||||||||||||||||||||||||||||||||||||||||||||||||||||||||||||||||||||||||||||||||||||||||

NU HOTEL
85 Smith Street (between
Atlantic Avenue and State
Street)
(1 718) 852 8585
nuhotelbrooklyn.com
Rating: 2★
Rooms: 90
Suites: 3
Hotel rates: $329–345
Internet: $296–310

The one fun boutique hotel in all Brooklyn is the **Nu Hotel**, not that you would guess it from the outside. It looks eminently avoidable, especially if you go in the entrance of the next-door apartments by mistake instead of the hotel entrance to the left. The guestrooms, beloved by *Wallpaper** kind of people, are Scandinavian stark. Grab a King room; some even have hammocks.

. . . .

SUSI (AND COREY'S) BROOKLYN

See main text for restaurant details.

FRANKIES 457 SPUNTINO

Owned by two chefs, both named Frank. 'Frankies' is the plural of Frank. If that isn't enough to charm you into going, Frankies' Extra Virgin Olive Oil, available for purchase at the restaurant, will do the trick. Even visiting Italians think this oil is good—it is, of course, from Italy. We find Frankies to be a reliable modern Italian restaurant with all the usual Brooklyn sensibilities: sustainable and local produce, artisan suppliers, eclectic décor and casual t-shirted service with no Manhattan attitude—the kind of place we take visiting Australians. It's capable of the occasional spectacular moment—an intense mushroom crostini was one, a very slowly roasted roast pork another. On the down side, the restaurant takes no bookings and no credit cards. Visit the ATM, check in and go drink at the dive bar across the street until summoned.

CHAR NO. 4

A dimly lit but friendly neighbourhood bourbon bar with a very genial owner (whose wife runs Tía Pol, the site of my favourite New York tapas), specializing in Southern-influenced smoked meats to slow the bourbon down. Corey will go to Char No. 4 at the slightest excuse for both the meat and the bourbon. It reportedly has the best pastrami in New York City, but if, like me, you have no idea what pastrami is all about, it's something that's hard to get excited about. I do get excited about the smoked and fried pork nuggets, which are exactly that: fried nuggets of gooey, bacony, porky bits, served with a hot sauce that's actually hot. At $4, I find it difficult not to order them every time. If I'm not in a meaty mood, I order the Shrimp & Grits (probably the lightest thing on the menu). The specials—whatever they've smoked out back this week—are usually worth the calories, especially if they come in sausage form. Oh, and the BLT, made with a thick slice of deep-fried pork belly rather than bacon, is a mild heart attack before noon—if you order it for brunch—mild because it's sanely sized, rather than the usual triple-bypass American size. Most men seem to like the place, so, if you go, bring a couple of them with you, then you'll get seated at a booth rather than at a teeny tiny table for two. Leave the vegans at home.

THE GENERAL GREENE

After reading all the glowing reviews when it first opened, we actually walked to Fort Greene to try The General Greene—further into Brooklyn than we'd ever ventured before. The food is described as 'new Brooklyn cuisine', which as far as I can tell is old American comfort food, given new life with farm-fresh local ingredients and more flavour, served up on small plates to be shared, tapas style, at very casual tables (perhaps too casual if there are spoilt Brooklyn brats at the next one). The matching casual lighting is provided by exposed light bulbs that I coveted while renovating my apartment. I don't like steak but I like the steak at The General Greene. It's a streak of a steak, seared, sliced and drenched in garlic and oil. Small if you like your steak cow-butt size, but still a steal at under $15. The cold-poached shrimp stood out last time I was there, not the least because I got to eat the last one as my reward for being the only woman at the table. It was also at The General Greene that I rediscovered iceberg lettuce, in wedge form, covered in a bacon, buttermilk and blue cheese dressing. It was unexpected, simple and delicious, and I had the added bonus of seeing a character in *Mad Men* order the same thing in a restaurant in 1963 (or thereabouts). Since then, we've paid attention to the vegetable plates, which are generally unusual and interesting, and nothing like vegetables you'd find in an American restaurant circa 1963.

CLOVER CLUB

A cocktail, small plate and American Apparel–clad hipster festival by night, and our favourite Brooklyn brunch spot by day (weekends only). I find the wood and leather speakeasy style and inventive cocktails more attractive and far more ironic in the morning light. Especially as they come with French-pressed Stumptown coffee and old-fashioned baked eggs with not so old-fashioned truffles and leeks. They also offer a bacon tasting, a plate of pepper, maple and duck bacon that Corey finds impossible not to order 'as an appetizer' every time we go. There are other things on the brunch menu that look interesting but I never get to them— did I mention the baked eggs with truffles and leeks?

THE BROOKLYN BOWL

A very hip bowling alley in painfully hip Williamsburg—think *Big Lebowski*, in a warehouse, with huge leather couches. It has Blue Ribbon food and the best fried chicken in Brooklyn (better than the buttermilk fried chicken at Buttermilk Channel by a long way). A heaped family-style platter of this crunchy, piping hot, excellent fried chook delivered to your lane and chased with local Sixpoint beer (available on tap) is as good as it gets in a place where grown-ups dress in matching shirts on purpose. You don't have to bowl to eat but, if you do, don't make the same mistakes we made: eat your chicken with your non-bowling hand and avoid The Brooklyn Bowl on live music nights unless you actually want to see the band, are a twenty-something hipster or want to lose your hearing.

We also like:

Bino, on Smith Street for the *Linguine vongole*, which has exactly the kind of clams that should be in a *linguine vongole*—little ones—and pancetta, which I'd no idea was required in a *linguine vongole* until I tried this version.

Blue Marble Ice Cream, on Court Street and Atlantic Avenue for their high-fat, grown-up strawberry ice cream—which, considering that all their other flavours are great and that I don't normally like strawberry ice cream, is quite something.

Junior's, for the cheesecake. It's an awful, touristy place with basic deli food, but their cheesecake is as good as they claim, as long as you stick to the plain version and avoid the ones that look like they've been topped with plastic fruit coated in shellac.

The Brooklyn Inn, for the history and beer. Popular nights find it full of the usual suspects, but go on a quiet night and you'll find yourself sitting at the bar with female truckers and a guy who's been sitting on the same barstool for thirty years, after his father warmed it for the previous thirty years. A shallower reason to go: it was used as a location in *Gossip Girl*.

Floyd, for the bocce. It's the kind of bar people sit in and read (real books), and the only bar we've ever been in with a permanent bocce game set up—inside. The more you drink, the better you get.

HOBOKEN
[NEW JERSEY]

PAULA AND PATRICK'S HOBOKEN

Hoboken is the sixth borough of New York—well, that is what the locals say! The first baseball game was held in Hoboken, but it is probably most famous for once being home to Frank Sinatra. The town is only 1 square mile and sits on the Hudson River, and was predominantly of Italian and Irish population before the real-estate boom.

ARTHUR'S TAVERN

American
237 Washington Street (at 3rd Street)
(1 201) 656 5009
arthurstavern.com
À la carte: $15–55

The best baby-back BBQ Ribs in town and huge steaks all at a reasonable price. Everything is served with pickles, coleslaw and potatoes. The restaurant has three or more sections. We suggest that you sit in the back section. The décor is basic, with traditional red-and-white tablecloths.

BAJA MEXICAN CUISINE

Mexican
104 14th Street (between Bloomfield and Washington Streets)
(1 201) 653 0610
bajamexicancuisine.com
À la carte: $20–39

Sit at the bar and devour the best Margaritas you will ever have. Make sure you choose your tequila; there are about fifty on offer.

THE DINING ROOM AT ANTHONY DAVID'S

Italian
Chef: Anthony Pino
935 Bloomfield Street (at 10th Street)
(1 201) 222 8359
anthonydavids.com
À la carte: $43–59

A romantic Italian restaurant off the main street in Hoboken, this is only a small venue and they do not take bookings on a Friday or Saturday night, so be prepared to walk to 10th and Willow for a quick vino until they get a table ready. Everything on the menu is delicious. Also, it is BYO, so make sure you bring a tasty bottle of wine. The best wine selection is at Sparrow Wine & Liquor at 126 Washington Street.

10TH AND WILLOW BAR & GRILL

American
935 Willow Avenue (between 9th and 10th Streets)
(1 201) 653 2358
10thandwillow.com
À la carte: $26–53

Sports bar and restaurant: basically a man's dream! The wings are great with three flavours: hot, barbecue and teriyaki. Make sure you taste all of them. The burgers and the steaks are also tasty. This is great for a Sunday afternoon during winter. There are fantastic happy hours, such as half-price martinis on Thursdays.

JERK CHICKEN WINGS

1 onion, minced

⅔ cup finely chopped spring onion

2 garlic cloves, crushed

½ teaspoon fresh thyme, crushed finely in a mortar and pestle

1½ teaspoons sea salt

1½ teaspoons ground allspice

¼ teaspoon freshly grated nutmeg

½ teaspoon cinnamon

1 tablespoon minced pickled jalapeño pepper

1 tablespoon oyster sauce

1 teaspoon black pepper, freshly ground

½ cup ground nut or extra virgin olive oil

16 chicken winglets (tiplets removed and the other two joints separated)

In a food processor or blender, purée the onion, spring onion, garlic, thyme, salt, all-spice, nutmeg, cinnamon, jalapeño, oyster sauce, black pepper and oil.

In a large shallow dish, arrange the wings in one layer and spoon the marinade over them, rubbing it in (wear rubber gloves). Let the wings marinate, covered and chilled, turning them once, for at least 1 hour or preferably overnight.

Preheat oven to 230°C. Arrange the wings in one layer on an oiled rack set over a foil-lined roasting pan. Spoon the marinade over them, and bake the wings in the upper third of the oven for 30–35 minutes, or until they are cooked through.

To make the wings a meal, serve with brown rice, fresh coriander, toasted flaked almonds, and a cos lettuce and avocado salad.

Serves 4

PICTURE CREDITS

© iStockphoto.com/Bill Noll; **p. 102** © iStockphoto.com/David Meaders;
p. 106 © iStockphoto.com/Lew Zimmerman; **p. 111** Scott Murray; **p. 114** left:
© Michel Stevelmans, used under license from Shutterstock.com, right: Scott
Murray; **p. 116** © iStockphoto.com/naphtalina; **p. 117** © iStockphoto.com/Jay
Lazarin; **p. 119** © Andrew McDonough, used under license from Shutterstock.com;
p. 121 right: © Volant, used under license from Shutterstock.com; **p. 124** Scott
Murray; **p. 129** Scott Murray; **p. 131** left: Scott Murray, right: Harry Azidis;
p. 132 © iStockphoto.com/Lauren Cullen; **p. 133** left: © Suzan Oschmann, used
under license from Shutterstock.com, right: © iStockphoto.com/Terraxplorer;
p. 137 © iStockphoto.com/blackwaterimages; **p. 140** Scott Murray; **p. 145** © Karen-
Louise Clemmesen, used under license from Shutterstock.com;
p. 147 © iStockphoto.com/Frank van den Bergh; **p. 149** Harry Azidis; **p. 150** Dean
Cambray; **p. 151** Tom Samek; **p. 152** background: © iStockphoto.com/Bill Noll;
p. 157 © iStockphoto.com/Roland Andrijauskas; **p. 159** Adrian Lee; **p. 161** right:
© nine7982, used under license from Shutterstock.com; **p. 164** Scott Murray;
p. 170 centre: © nine7982, used under license from Shutterstock.com, right: © fzd.
it, used under license from Shutterstock.com; **p. 174** © iStockphoto.com/Mickey
Marrero; **p. 176** Dean Cambray; **p. 178** © iStockphoto.com/rorem;
p. 179 background: Clare Marshall; **p. 180** background: © iStockphoto.com/Bill
Noll; **p. 181** left: Scott Murray, right: © iStockphoto.com/Bill Stamatis;
p. 183 © iStockphoto.com/Andrea Gingerich; **p. 188** left: © iStockphoto.com/
Nicole K Cioe, right: © Ulrich Mueller, used under license from Shutterstock.com;
p. 189 left: © iStockphoto.com/sx70, right: © iStockphoto.com/Jay Lazarin;
p. 190 left and right: © iStockphoto.com/Jay Lazarin; **p. 195** Adrian Lee; **p. 197** Dean
Cambray; **p. 198** background: © iStockphoto.com/Bill Noll; **p. 200** © iStockphoto.
com/Stephen Brake; **p. 201** left: © fzd.it, used under license from Shutterstock.com,
right: © nine7982, used under license from Shutterstock.com; **p. 203** Scott Murray;
p. 205 © Songquan Deng, used under license from Shutterstock.com;
p. 207 © iStockphoto.com/Nicole DiMella; **p. 208** Tom Samek; **p. 210** left:
© iStockphoto.com/Nicole DiMella, right: Adrian Lee; **p. 212** © iStockphoto.com/
sx70; **p. 215** iStockphoto.com/Nicole K Cioe; **p. 216** © sepavo, used under license
from Shutterstock.com; **p. 217** left: © Oxlock, used under license from
Shutterstock.com; **p. 219** © iStockphoto.com/Samuli Siltanen;
p. 222 © iStockphoto.com/Shane Stezelberger; **p. 225** Dean Cambray;
p. 226 background: © iStockphoto.com/Bill Noll; **p. 227** © iStockphoto.com/
tifonimages; **p. 229** iStockphoto.com/Jeremy Edwards; **p. 230** Scott Murray;

INDEX

THE MIEGUNYAH PRESS

This book was designed by Trisha Garner
The text was typeset by Megan Ellis
The text was set in 8 point Meta Serif and
Meta Normal with 12 points of leading
The text is printed on 128 gsm matt art

This book was edited by Eugenie Baulch

THE
MIEGUNYAH
PRESS